Hadlow

Life, Land & People in a Wealden Parish 1460 - 1600

Edited by
Joan Thirsk

i

Published by the Kent Archaeological Society, 2007
ISBN 978 0 906746 70 7

Produced by:

Heritage Marketing & Publications Ltd
Hill Farm
Castle Acre Road
Great Dunham
Kings Lynn
Norfolk
PE32 2LP
www.heritagemp.com

Heritage
Marketing & Publications Ltd

HADLOW

Life, Land & People in a Wealden Parish 1460–1600

Page iv **List of Diagrams & Maps**

v **Acknowledgements**

vi **Authors' Notes & Invitation to Readers**

Picture Credits

INTRODUCTION 1 **Subject and Authors**

CHAPTER 1 3 **The Document**
i Its origin
ii Its history

CHAPTER 2 5 **The Lords of Hadlow**
i The Clares and their successors
ii Other manorial lords

CHAPTER 3 7 **A First Look at the Hadlow Survey**
i Knights' fees
ii Tenements in general

CHAPTER 4 10 **A Walk round Hadlow Manor in 1460**

CHAPTER 5 25 **Tenants' Rents, Dues in Money and Kind & Labour Services**

CHAPTER 6 30 **Manorial Courts and their Business**

CHAPTER 7 42 **Hadlow between 1460 and 1600**

CHAPTER 8 47 **Getting a Living from the Land**

CHAPTER 9 54 **Rivers: the Medway and the Bourne**

CHAPTER 10 60 **Roads**

CHAPTER 11 64 **Commons**

CHAPTER 12 67 **The Church**

CHAPTER 13 71 **Some Families**

CHAPTER 14 97 **Topographical Problems**
i Hadlow Stair
ii Roadside Crosses
iii Law Day Place
iv North Frith Park

CHAPTER 15 107 **Hadlow in a Wealden Context**

119 **Bibliography**

122 **The Survey of Hadlow Manor, 1460, in English Translation**

190 **Appendix: The last pages of the manuscript**

200 **Index**

LIST OF DIAGRAMS &MAPS

Page 6 Map showing Listed Buildings and roadside crosses in Hadlow parish

8 Map showing Hadlow in context with other parishes

9 Map showing position of tenements in Hadlow manor and the sub-manors in Hadlow parish

10 Aerial photo-map showing Hadlow Stair and immediate tenements

11 Plan of Cowling tenement

12 Plan of Kenes tenement

14 Dumbreck's map of Poulthouse and Correnden lands in 1842

16 Plan of Brewis tenement

17 Map showing Palmers, Welshes and Wekerylds tenements

20 Plan of part of Coiffe's tenement

22 Aerial photo-map showing Stoperfield tenement, demesne land, and position of Lawday Place

24 Plan of houses in the village street

47 Chart showing distribution of farms by size in five sample parishes

52 Map showing orientation of the Herberys

52 Plan of the Herberys

54 Aerial photo-map showing aspects of the Medway

57 Map showing contours, bridges over the Medway and ancient course of the river

60 Extract from Symonson's map of 1596 showing Hadlow in context with surrounding villages

61 Aerial photo-map of Hadlow parish, looking south, showing roads and sub-manors

64 Extract from Andrews, Dury & Herbert map of 1769 showing Hadlow Common

71 Fane family tree

79/80/81 Fromond family trees

84 Bishop family tree

90/91 Bealde family trees

92 Stoperfield family tree

101 Extract from Hasted's map of 1799 showing woodland in Hadlow

104 Extract from Speed's map of 1611 showing North Frith

ACKNOWLEDGEMENTS

For help with this work, the authors acknowledge their greatest debt to the late Commander W.D.Dumbreck whose lifelong study of Hadlow's history and topography resulted in notes and transcripts of documents from many sources, and some unique maps, compiled by him, which have proved invaluable. They were deposited by his widow, Mrs Nora Dumbreck, in the Centre for Kentish Studies, Maidstone, and the authors are deeply grateful to Mr Stuart Bligh at the Centre for facilitating their use of them.

Warm thanks are also due to Mr Ian Coulson, who photographed the whole document when it came into the possession of the Centre for Kentish Studies. This enabled Dr Bridgett Jones to transcribe and translate it, and so, with her generous help, this project was able to get started.

The authors also wish to thank Mr Matthew Williams and Mr Donovan Hailstone for taking aerial photographs of Hadlow Stair, Mr Mick Rodgers at North Frith Farm for many insights into the history of North Frith Park and the local history of the iron industry, Mr Roger Stanley and the late Mr Ken Jackson for supplying many of our illustrations, Mr Bill Hughes for his original footpath map of Hadlow Parish, and Mr Ian Goodacre for his help in finding maps of Hadlow. Mrs Margaret Lawrence has shared with us her wide knowledge of the next-door parish of East Peckham. In Chapter 13 the authors gratefully acknowledge all the information given by descendants of some old Hadlow families: they furnished a great many documents and the family trees used in the account. They are Glenda Breslin and Nola Mackey on the Bealde/Bell family, John Causton and Anne Caxton on the Caxton family, and Tim Mitchell on the Stubberfield/Stoperfield family. Catharine M.F. Davies and Professor Susan Wabuda gave us valuable information about one branch of the Playne family. Ms Jane Bradshaw lent us her dissertation on 'Traditional Salmon Fishing in the Severn Estuary', with photos of weirs, fishtraps, etc., which greatly helped us to understand the same activity on the Medway.

Dr Christopher Chalklin, knowing the histories of Hadlow and Tonbridge so well, and Professors Christopher Dyer and Harold Fox, steeped in the history of the Middle Ages, all read our text and saved us from many errors.

Permission to cite documents from the family archive of the Viscount de Lisle, on loan to the Centre for Kentish Studies in Maidstone, was generously given, for which we offer warm thanks. We have endeavoured to find and get permission for all our illustrations, and hope we have not overlooked any owners of copyright.

Finally, the authors thank the Kent Archaeological Society, for accepting this history of Hadlow on their website, and especially Mr Denis Anstey and his team of helpers for all their work in putting it on the Internet. We also thank the Society for supporting this publication in book form.

Design and layout by Caroline Wetton.

AUTHORS' NOTES & INVITATION TO READERS

This book was first published on the internet as an e-book in May 2006 when the Latin text of the Hadlow Survey was published alongside the English translation. As scholars wishing to study the Latin original are few in number, they can download it from the web (www.kentarchaeology.ac). The English translation is printed here (pp.121-188)

The authors welcome any comments, corrections, additions, and discussion of their text which should be sent to:
Joan Thirsk, c/o The Library, Kent Archaeological Society, Maidstone Museum, Maidstone, Kent ME14 1LH, or by e-mail to kentarchaeology@btconnect.com.
We expect to be able to make consequent additions and emendations on the Internet.

When interpreting the diagrams of tenements and tenemental pieces, the authors emphasise that they do not depict acreages to scale, and all diagrams omit pieces of land that were detached from the main block, whose location has not been ascertained.

PICTURE CREDITS

It is a pleasure to record the courtesy of various bodies who have allowed the use of material in their care. In addition to images supplied by the authors and immediate family, all images and illustrations were supplied by, or are reproduced by, kind permission of the following: The Dumbrek Family (14, 67a), Roger Stanley (64), Donovan Hailstone (iii, contents), Kent County Council Education and Library Service (108a), Kent County Council, Centre for Kentish Archives (4, 6, 56), The National Portrait Gallery (5, 44b), Victoria and Albert Museum (53a), The Bodleian Library, University of Oxford (85 – Bod. MS 764, 141v), The British Library (13a, 15, 27, 28, 39, 40, 48b, 49, 50, 85, 87, 98, 102, 103b), The Hadlow Historical Society (14, 18b, 30, 55b, 59b, 67b, 67c, 69, 99a).
The publishers have made every attempt to trace the copyright holders of all images used in this volume. In case of omission please contact the publishers.

SUBJECT & AUTHORS

This book presents and discusses a survey of Hadlow Manor in 1460. The manor covered about 1200 acres of land, stretching from the Medway in the south, through the village centre, which lies east of Tonbridge, to its boundary in the north with North Frith Park. What was a survey? Surveys, often in the Middle Ages called custumals, terriers, or extents, began to appear in the twelfth century and gradually became more common.[1] They were drawn up on the order of a manorial lord wanting to know how his land was tenanted, and what rents and labour services were due to him. They can vary greatly in the amount of detail that they give, but at best by the sixteenth century they listed all the land belonging to the manorial estate including demesne and tenant land, the acreages and names of the fields, the current use of the land as arable, meadow, or pasture, the names of the occupiers farming the land, the total size of each farm, the tenure by which each was held, the rents and other dues paid by the farmer to his lord, and the extent of commons and woodland.

In the Hadlow case, the document is called a rental or custumal and the information is partial. It does not include the demesne, but, so far as we can judge, it includes all, or nearly all, the tenements, the names of the pieces of land into which the tenements were divided, and the acreages, the use of some of the land, the names of the farmers and farm sizes, and the rents and other dues. It is not free from mistakes, omissions, and puzzling uncertainties of meaning, but it is unusually generous in aiming to give the names of people occupying land to the north, south, east, and west sides of each piece of land. It becomes possible to map the tenements, and gain some idea of the way they were laid out. In short, we catch sight of Hadlow and its people one hundred years after the Black Death, and 25 years before the first Tudor came to the throne.

The original manuscript was in Latin and the English translation is printed at the end of the book. Chapters 1-15 analyse the information drawn from the survey, using also other surviving archives about Hadlow at the same period in the Centre for Kentish Studies in Maidstone, the British Library, and the National Archives at Kew. They attempt to draw a picture of the way the inhabitants got their living, managed their land and lives, where they lived, and how they governed themselves.

The Weald was a distinctive countryside in many ways. It had small manorial estates, not large ones covering the whole parish, as one finds in Midland England. Its landowners were more likely to be modest gentlemen, rather than grand nobility. Its residents had a tradition of dividing their land between all sons, not passing the bulk of it to the eldest. This meant that land could quickly get divided into small pieces, but as occupiers enjoyed greater freedom than elsewhere to convey those pieces to others, amalgamations of land proceeded as readily as fragmentation. While we search here for clues to life in Hadlow, we learn more about Wealden life in general. So finally, we put the history of Hadlow into a broader context, describing what is already known about the early settlement of the Weald of Kent, and what we can add from our one village survey.

The authors of this work are five women who have shared in a cooperative enterprise, exploiting their complementary expertise. Dr Bridgett Jones is the medieval scholar who transcribed the original Latin document and translated it into English. She did the same on several medieval court rolls of Hadlow manors. Without her, the rest of us could not have ventured on this work. The remaining four of us have all lived in Hadlow for many years. Anne Hughes is a history graduate, and has gathered much information about Hadlow from the many knowledgeable local people in our neighbourhood, as well as writing about the commons and the church. Caroline Wetton is an artist and designer who has made sense of the geographical information about tenements in our survey, prepared innumerable plans and maps, of which some are printed here, and has walked tirelessly over the ground to match the past evidence with the present-day remains. Alison Williams is a history graduate who taught history for many years, and has examined all the surviving wills of Hadlow people living at the time of the survey, and constructed their family stories. She has also studied the workings of Hadlow's manorial courts using the surviving court rolls, and comparing their procedures with that of manors in very different kinds of countryside elsewhere. Dr Joan Thirsk is a historian of agriculture and rural society, who has striven to drain every drop of meaning from our documents to discover how Hadlow people got their livings, and to put our account into a wider context. In the past, she has written much about regional differences, and she holds the strong belief that Wealden society had a distinctive style that we should identify.

The survey of 1460 was copied out for some reason in 1581-3, and it is this copy that has survived. To bring the survey up to date more than a century after it had been compiled, the clerk made an attempt to scribble the names of new occupants over the old. But one cannot be certain that the document was fully revised in that respect. In one hundred years, all the occupiers' names must surely have changed, but not all the land is attributed to new owners. It is, of course, perfectly possible that many pieces of land had remained with the same families, but the document leaves the impression that the clerk was far from thorough in those investigations. Nevertheless, the revision in 1581 has persuaded us to write more generally about Hadlow's history up to 1600.

Hadlow residents will be surprised to discover the names of places and people in 1460 that are still familiar today. We encounter Watership (now Waterslippe), Blackmans (now surviving in Blackmans Lane) and Napiltons (now Appletons). Some surnames have continued to the present. Honewolds was the name of one tenement in 1460 and we still have a Mr Homewood living in the parish. Messrs. Palmer and Symonds are in the survey and are known still to be familiar local surnames. The surveyor also named lanes, roads, rivers, mills, weirs and sluices, with enough accompanying information in some cases to enable us to place them on the map. Hadlow as it was in 1460 begins to take shape before our eyes.

Hadlow village and parish today

CHAPTER 1

THE DOCUMENT

ITS ORIGIN

Readers will want to know how this Hadlow survey was discovered. It turned up unexpectedly at an auction in Mere, Wiltshire, in October 2002. Its existence had been unknown to us in Hadlow, but it had evidently been seen in January, 1772 by a member of Trinity College, Cambridge, who attached a note of commentary and explanation to it, probably for the benefit of the then owner, and signed it with his initials, S.P. The auctioneer, Mr Robert Finan, told us what little he knew about its history. He had been asked to dispose of a large, mixed collection of documents in the hands of Mr Geoffrey Woodhead, a bookseller of Honiton, Devon, when Mr Woodhead retired. Mr Woodhead died in the autumn of 2003. It took Mr Finan two and a half years to sort and sell it all. He could only guess that the collection had been built up in the course of some forty years of bookselling, and he suspected that part of it had been assembled by an earlier collector in the nineteenth century.

ITS HISTORY

The note attached to the document when it came up for auction in 2002 was dated January, 1772, and had been signed by S.P. That was Samuel Peck of Trinity College, Cambridge. He described its contents, and added a postscript, dated 15 February, 1773, saying that he had passed it on to Lord Le Despencer, then lord of Hadlow manor. Judging by his note, Samuel Peck knew something more about Hadlow's manorial

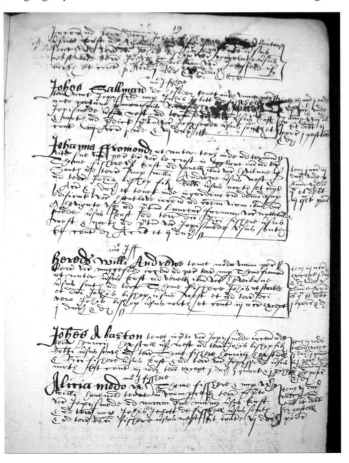

This is folio 19 of the survey and shows pieces of Jopes tenement, in the occupation of John Sallman, Joan Fromond at Water, the heirs of William Andrewe, John A Barton, and Alice, now wife of Thomas Fisher and formerly wife of William Honewold.

history than was contained in its text. It was signed by Roger Lancaster, and dated 26 September, 1583. Peck claimed to know that Lancaster had become the steward of the manor in 1581. This makes the steward sound like a new broom, entering on his responsibilities with an undertaking to clean up inefficiencies of the past. Peck guessed, without explaining why, that the date of the original survey was 20 Edward IV, i.e. 1480-81. In fact, the document gave the reign but not the exact year, and internal evidence, showing the names of the tenants, has enabled us to correct the date to around 1460 (see further below).

The librarians at Trinity College, where Peck was a Fellow and where he remained till he died in 1791, know a lot more about their former colleague. He was the son of John Peck of Market Weston in Suffolk, went to school in Bury St Edmunds, was admitted to Trinity College in 1742, graduated in 1749, and became an MA in 1750. He developed a consuming interest in law in general, and in manorial and county courts in particular. This must explain how he came to be consulted about the Hadlow survey. But he also acted as a poor man's solicitor, welcoming local people to his rooms in Trinity College on Saturdays to answer their enquiries. He took no money, but gratefully accepted any produce they brought him. At the end of the day, a servant would come with a cart from Grantchester where he lived and take it all home.

The manuscript is a beautifully written document of 116 folios bound in limp vellum. Its main content is the survey of Hadlow manor, but it ends untidily on folio 96, petering out without showing decisively that the survey is complete. It resumes on folio 99, so two pages are clearly missing. It then continues with two other incomplete documents relating to the next door parish of West Peckham: the first concerns the grant in 1387 of the Peckham Parva church, i.e. West Peckham, dated 1387, to the use of the prior and convent of Leeds; it includes a ratification of this deed by the bishop of Rochester (Hasted, in his History of Kent, summarises the transaction).[1] The second document starts on folio 101, is dated 15 June 1579, and is described as a survey of certain manors of Lord Abergavenny. It starts with the manor of Mereworth, but it is a summary, and not a full survey. On folio 109 it moves to the demesnes of West Peckham. West Peckham manor had become divided into two halves by 1365, and one half passed to the owner of Mereworth manor, hence the linking of the lordships of West Peckham manor and Mereworth. The explanation for the statement that the manors belonged to the Lord of Abergavenny lies in a legal settlement, not pursued here, when Henry, the second duke of Buckingham, died in 1483, was succeeded by the third duke, Edward, whose eldest daughter married George Neville, third baron of Abergavenny.[2] The document ends with two names of the writers, James Ron and Tomas Fet, dated 20 July 1583. Both fragments are printed here as an appendix for the sake of completeness.

1. Hasted, 1798, V, 67-8

2. For the family connection see Hasted, 1798, V, 77

This is the front cover of the survey, it shows the flamboyant signature of the steward of the manor, Roger Lancaster, and the year in which he started to copy it, 1581. The last page, folio 115, finishes with a note dated 20 July 1583, presumably when he completed it, and added another flourishing signature.

The coat of Arms of the Clares.

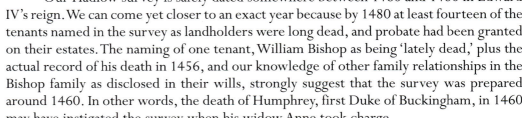

Above: Edward Stafford, the third Duke of Buckingham

CHAPTER 2

THE LORDS OF HADLOW

THE CLARES & THEIR SUCCESSORS, THE STAFFORDS, DUKES OF BUCKINGHAM

The first owners of this manor of Hadlow after the Norman Conquest were a French family that had come over to England with William the Conqueror. The same family also received the grant of Tonbridge, a strategically valuable place on the Medway, and many other estates in the vicinity. In England it took the surname of Clare after other still larger holdings (some 95 or more lordships) in Suffolk, situated around Clare, and granted to them by William I. When the male line died out in 1314, the female heirs divided the estate, and the part that included Tonbridge and Hadlow came by marriage to the Staffords, Earls of Gloucester. Humphrey Stafford, the second earl, was further promoted to be the first duke of Buckingham in 1444. Whenever the family came to Kent they dwelt, not in Hadlow, but in Tonbridge Castle.

The owner of Hadlow in 1460, therefore, was Humphrey Stafford, whose father had died in 1403 when he was only one year old. He took possession of his lands when he came of age in 1422, and was known as the Earl of Buckingham from 1438 when his mother died. He was an influential figure at court and in political life at Westminster, and was created first duke of Buckingham in 1444. He had married Anne Neville, daughter of Ralph, earl of Westmorland, some time before 1424, and she had borne him seven sons and five daughters. But Humphrey died in 1460, two years after his son and heir, another Humphrey had died in 1458. But he had left a young son and heir, and so in 1460 his grandmother, Anne, took charge of him. When he came of age in 1473, she received Hadlow manor as part of her widow's jointure. So, from 1460 until 1480 when she died, Anne, Dowager Duchess of Buckingham, was known to the inhabitants of Hadlow manor as the lady in charge of the estate. The survey plainly referred to her as the lady of the manor, and named a house of hers in Hadlow, though she may, in fact, rarely have visited it, for her favourite homes were in Writtle, Essex, and Kimbolton, in Huntingdonshire.

Our Hadlow survey is safely dated somewhere between 1460 and 1480 in Edward IV's reign. We can come yet closer to an exact year because by 1480 at least fourteen of the tenants named in the survey as landholders were long dead, and probate had been granted on their estates. The naming of one tenant, William Bishop as being 'lately dead,' plus the actual record of his death in 1456, and our knowledge of other family relationships in the Bishop family as disclosed in their wills, strongly suggest that the survey was prepared around 1460. In other words, the death of Humphrey, first Duke of Buckingham, in 1460 may have instigated the survey when his widow Anne took charge.

OTHER MANORIAL LORDS IN HADLOW

The manor of Hadlow was the largest, the most important, and the oldest in the parish. But it was not the only one. At some time in the past, fairly certainly under the rule of the Clares, grants of land in the Medway valley had been made to loyal servants who undertook to defend Tonbridge castle in time of need. These were termed knights' fees, and the grantees had turned them into manorial estates, possessing a lord's hall or dwelling house, a home farm, and other tenant farms, held by free or servile tenures. Tenants worked the land for themselves, and, if unfree, owed labour services to the lord. The inheritance custom of Kent, called gavelkind, prescribed the division of land between

5

all sons. So in the course of generations, not only did farms get subdivided, so did manors; landowners wanted to provide estates for all their sons. At the end of the Middle Ages, therefore, Hadlow parish had splintered into some eight manors, the main one under scrutiny here, plus the others called Hadlow Place, Goldhill, Crombury, Fromonds, Caustons, Peckhams, and Lonewood. Some must have consisted of no more than 200-300 acres apiece. This means that our Hadlow manor did not extend over the whole parish; its land was intermingled with the land of other lords. So our survey does not give us a sight of every occupier or all land in the parish. But it records the largest slice, amounting to some 1200 acres.

Map showing:
Listed Buildings in Hadlow parish (2006) and which sites were, or may have been, in use in 1460; position of sub-manors; approximate position of roadside crosses.

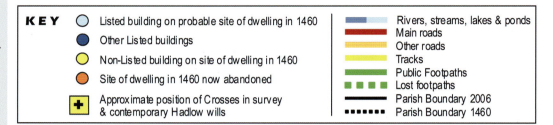

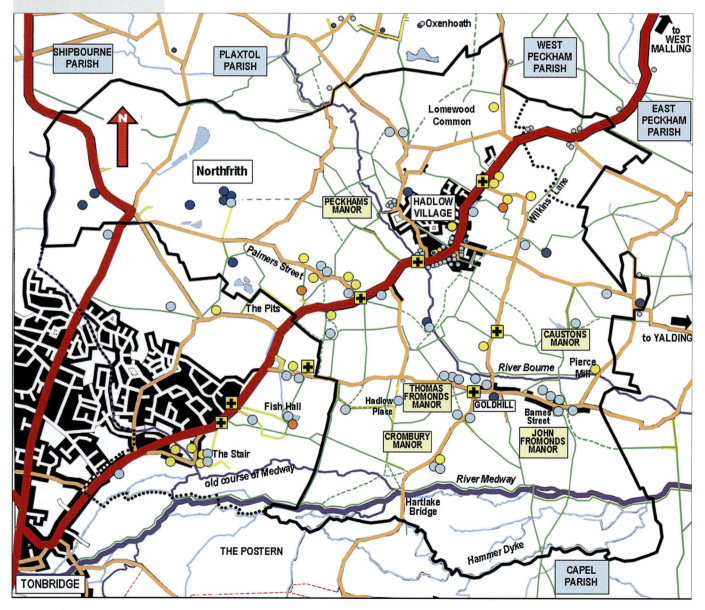

CHAPTER 3

A FIRST LOOK AT THE HADLOW SURVEY

KNIGHTS' FEES

1 See also Witney, 1976, 167-8

The first folio of the Hadlow survey starts with a listing of knights' fees, whose origins have been explained above.[1] Having been granted by the lord to followers who were near in rank to himself, they became manorial estates, and whole knights' fees had in course of time become subdivided into smaller units, thus dividing the burden of one knight's responsibilities between more people. So the list for this manor names nine people holding fractions of knight's fees, ranging from a half down to a fifth, an eighth, and a sixteenth. They cannot be added up tidily: the total amounted to one whole knight's fee and 47/6 0ths; we have to assume that the remaining fractions were accounted for by other manors belonging to the Staffords in the vicinity. The duties of a knight were described as castle guard in time of war, the payment of scutage, and suit of court every three weeks, i.e. in the Tonbridge court, not in Hadlow. John Godyng's duties, for some unexplained reason, differed from the others: he simply owed two capons or 12d. in rent at Michaelmas. Past changes in the ownership of fees were mentioned (William Watton's fee was formerly Hugh de Causton's, that is to say, of the Caxton family), and the current owners in 1460 divided themselves between well-known Hadlow gentry, like the Culpepers and Fromonds, and unknowns, like William Watton and John Godyng. Two changes were also noted in the revisions in 1581, bringing in Henry Fane and Thomas Peckham, in place of John Godyng and William Watton. One additional piece of information was the date on which John Godyng's grant was first made, in the time of Richard Clare, when Earl of Gloucester, so dating it somewhere between 1230 when he came of age and 1262 when he died.

TENEMENTS IN GENERAL

The remainder of the document lists the tenements. These were divisions of the manor land into tenements or farms, and as the survey makes clear, each had a name given to it, though that name was not permanent, and its connection with actual people, dead or living, is not usually clear. Over the years, changes in name had taken place, but even the most up-to-date ones did not usually name the current occupier, leaving the impression that changes in tenement names were a haphazard matter, without any consistency or logic, perhaps relying simply on current speech habits among the local people. As for the history of the tenements, it is not known for certain when they were originally created. Historians generally agree that original allotments represented in each district current opinion on what was sufficient land to support one family, and many of them do, indeed, cluster around the 30-35 acre size. In some other parts of the country too 30 acres or so were deemed a standard size for a family holding; in East Anglia it was only 12 or 24 acres.[2]

2. T. Williamson, Shaping Medieval Landscapes, 2003, 127-9;

Some historians believe that the first allotment of tenements was made when a lord formally took ownership of his land, but in the case of the Clare family that would take us back to some time around the Norman Conquest. Others believe that many lords favoured a reorganisation of tenancies in the twelfth century, and standard tenements were created then. In a study by Altschul of the Clare family's whole estate between 1217 and 1314, the author, without any precise reference to the Tonbridge estates, identified distinct efforts by the Clares in the second half of the thirteenth century and early fourteenth century to exploit their manors more effectively.[3] So some tenements may well have been laid out,

3. M.Altschul, A Baronial Family in Medieval England: the Clares, 1217-1314, 1965, 213.

or reshaped at that time. It is certainly reasonable to envisage a period when the Clares first took possession of their land after the Norman Conquest but did not interfere much with the occupiers already there. That might then be followed by another phase when they took stock, recognised the economic potential of their property, and started to administer it systematically. They would then have reassessed rents and obligations according to some regular set of rules and requirements. We shall return to this subject below, and hazard the suggestion that in 1460 another new broom was tidying up after many decades of neglect on the Stafford estate. But first we should analyse the layout of the tenements as shown in the survey.

The total number of named tenancies amounted to some 59-60, plus three holdings in the village centre that were not full tenements. Almost half measured (45%) between 20 and 40 acres, and a little under a quarter were between 30 and 36¼ acres; 30 acres was probably the ideal. In places the survey contains ragged notes and does not end tidily, so that the total number of tenements is inexact. What is highly significant, however, is that of all the tenements of 20-40 acres, 17 lay near the Medway or in the vicinity of the town of Tonbridge (they are listed on folios 2-45 of the survey). In other words, nearly two-thirds (63%) of what were probably the oldest holdings to be administratively designated as tenements were close to the standard 20-40 acres. Other so-called tenements were either small fragments of land (11 were under 10 acres apiece) or were larger than average; the larger ones numbered 5 tenements of between 40 and 52 acres and one outsize one, at the east end of the parish, measured 82 acres. We may picture this last one lying in a part of the parish that held no great attraction for cultivators or possibly, as will be suggested below, was regarded as being somewhat apart from the centre of village affairs since the land was intermingled with other manors.

Map showing : Hadlow in context with other parishes mentioned in the text

Each tenement comprised smaller pieces of land, some adjoining each other, some lying in the same field but not adjoining, and others separated, and often so unclearly defined that their location has not been determined. All other manors in Hadlow (some seven in all) similarly consisted of pieces that were more or less scattered in the same way, and that is made plain by the fact that sometimes adjoining parcels of land are cited in our survey as boundary pieces, which do not feature anywhere else in our survey. They must have belonged to other manors. Nevertheless, the scattered pieces of each tenement usually lay in one segment of the parish. Our maps show how the pieces of one individual tenement lay, with a few exceptions, in one general area of the parish, and the surveyor's order of working through his task was based on that knowledge.

The surveyor started down at Hadlow Stair, strongly suggesting that that is where he considered the most lively economic activity to be concentrated. We are not certain where exactly the Stair was situated (further discussion of this follows), but The Stair was the wharf and landing place on the Medway where most goods for Hadlow were loaded and unloaded. It is usual to say that the Medway was not made a navigable river until the 1740s, but that was for larger vessels of 4 tons and more. Before that the river was constantly used by small, flat-bottomed craft plying up and down on local errands carrying small goods. Hadlow people were sufficiently satisfied to make no loud complaints. It was not until the second half of the sixteenth century when commercial traffic intensified, that an agitation began to move larger vessels down the river, resulting in the early seventeenth century in a survey of all the obstructions, and endeavours to clear them.

Land in the vicinity of the river, then, was probably the scene of most farming and trading activity in 1460, and that suggestion is strengthened by the extraordinarily small size of the land parcels into which these ancient tenements on the floodplain had become divided. Pieces of a quarter of an acre and some even smaller indicate how sought after was this rich meadow land. It was liable to flooding in winter, but benefited greatly from the rich sediments that were thus deposited for they fattened cattle superbly in the summer. The family names of farmers down at the Medway and the number of individual occupiers having the same surname suggest that this was the most desirable part of the parish as far as the older families were concerned, and it was there that the competition for land was fiercest. The custom of gavelkind had resulted in people keeping such land within their own kinship circle, and dividing it into ever smaller pieces. As we walk round the whole manor, surveying all the tenements, we shall become aware of different values being set on different sectors of Hadlow land.

Map showing : the estimated position of all the tenements in Hadlow manor and the sub-manors in Hadlow parish.

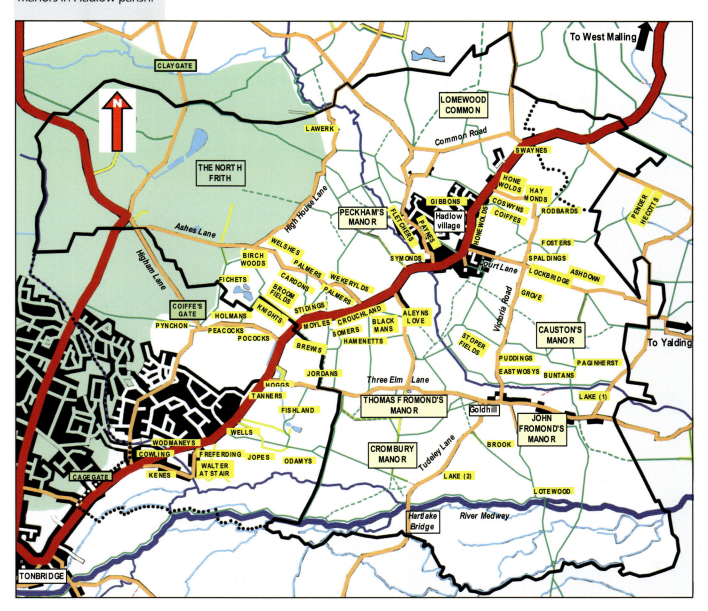

CHAPTER 4

A WALK AROUND HADLOW MANOR IN 1460

The surveyor went round the manor enumerating each tenement, usually giving it a name, identifying a main occupier (though this did not mean that the main occupier had the largest share of the land), and describing what acreage he held. Often the names of the pieces of land were given, and in most cases the neighbours to north, south, east and west. The pieces of land occupied by others (for all tenements were much subdivided) were then enumerated, the occupiers being called 'socii' or 'parcenarii' in Latin, i.e. associates or co-parceners. At the end of the account of each tenement, a total acreage for the whole was given, and dues in money and kind were stated. (The italicised words in our survey text distinguish those that were entered later, presumably in 1581, to bring the information up to date.)

COWLING

The first holding in the survey was called Cowling tenement, no explanation being given for the name Cowling. It was largely in the hands of one old family, the Bishops, and the main tenant was John Bishop, son of Robert, who had his house there. It had formerly been held by William Bishop, perhaps the grandfather or great-grandfather, but now other Bishops were occupying pieces of the tenement, namely, John, son of Richard (the cousin of John, son of Robert),

Aerial photo showing the area around Hadlow Stair which includes the tenements of Cowling, Kenes, Walter at Steyre and Freferding. Note the distinctive courses of subsidiary streams.

KEY

— Old course of Medway

— A26

- - - Hadlow Street to Tonbridge 1460

— common way to Lawrence Farman & William Honewolds' dwellings

▪ ▪ ▪ Longshots Lane

1 Mill House—John Bishop (Richard's son)

2 John Bishop (Bob's son)

3 John Bishop (Richard's son)

4 William at Hill

5 Richard Bishop (William's son) (formerly John Kenes)

6 Thomas Crudd

7 Lawrence Farman

8 Thomas Fisher (formerly William Honewold)

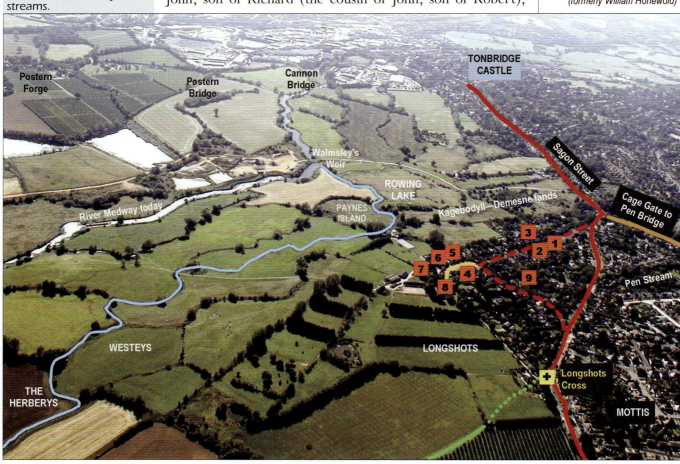

and Thomas Bishop, probably their uncle. Two other occupiers had different surnames but they could have been related to the family at some time in the past on the female side. The tenement was somewhat below the average in size, 24½ acres and 3 dayworks (henceforward the small daywork measurement will usually be omitted from this text - it was one tenth of a rod), and the land lay between what is now Higham Lane on the west and the old Hadlow Road to the south and east.

Plan of COWLING Tenement

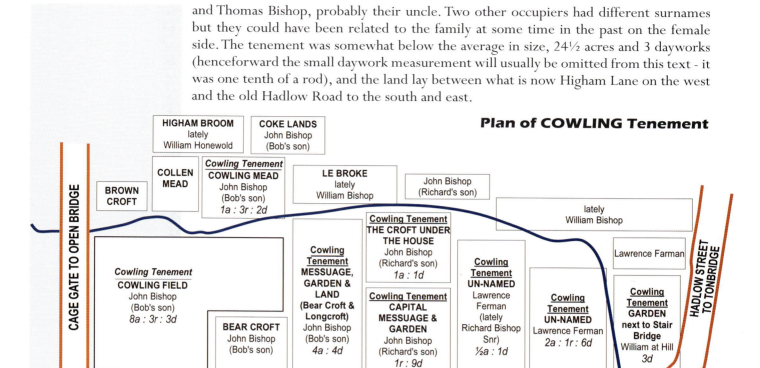

KENES The second tenement was formerly Ralph Kene's, extending to 30½ acres. His will was dated 1443, and so he was now dead and John Bishop, son of Robert, living in Cowling tenement next door was regarded as the main tenant and held the Mill House there. It lay across the road from the house in which he lived in Cowling tenement. Old William Bishop was remembered here too, having once occupied some of the land. Other tenants of Cowling tenement reappeared, including two of the Bishop family. The lady of the manor was also a tenant. Four houses were located on this holding, so although it stretched down to the Medway and part was low-lying, having the Lady's

WODMANEYS

FREFERDING

WALTER AT STEYRE

marsh, Rowying Lake, and the Mill Ditch within its compass, most of the land and certainly the houses lay above the floodplain. In the next tenement, called Wodmaneys, two more Bishops, Gervase and William, were remembered as former occupiers, and the land of Gervase still belonged in the Bishop family, having come to John Bishop, son of Robert. In other words, this one family network was still conspicuous round here, while reference to the Stair shows how near it was to the river wharf. Similarly, in the next two tenements, Freferding and Walter at Steyre, the Bishop family was successfully accumulating yet more land, all of it running towards the Medway. Indeed, Freferding land actually crossed the Medway to the other side. But the survey is, of course, referring to the old course of the Medway before the navigation that we know today was established. The old course, which was probably on average no more than ten feet wide, ran much closer to the high ground than

Plan of KENES Tenement

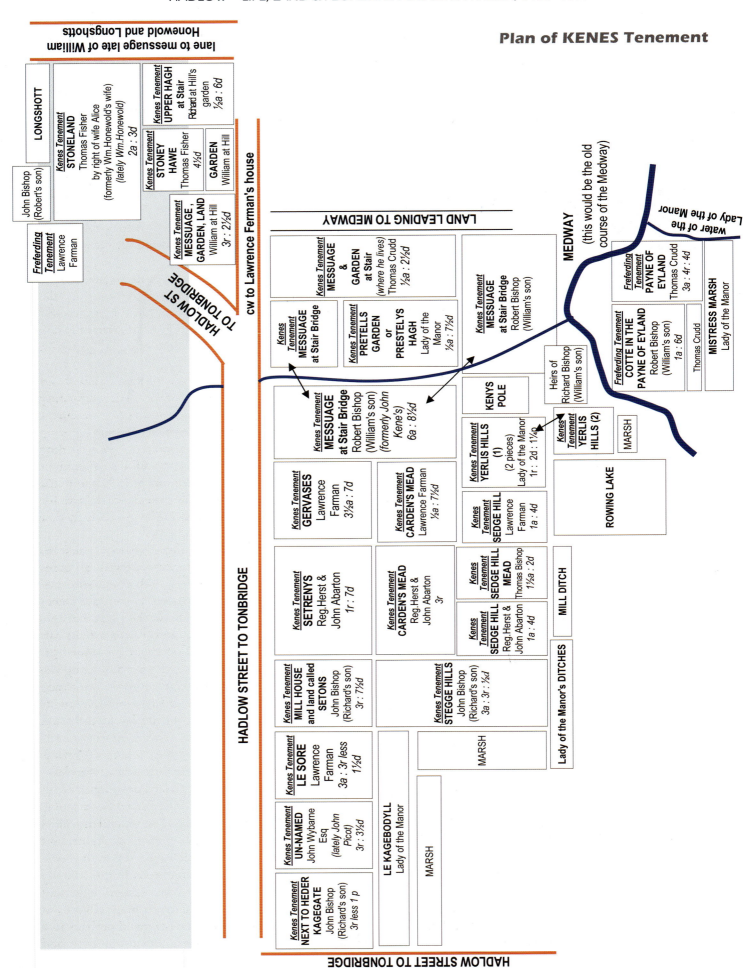

lane to messuage late of William Honewold and Longshotts

LONGSHOTT

John Bishop (Robert's son)

Kenes Tenement STONELAND
Thomas Fisher
by right of wife Alice
(formerly Wm.Honewold's wife)
(lately Wm.Honewold)
2a : 3d

Kenes Tenement UPPER HAGH at Stair
Rchad at Hill's garden
½a : 6d

Kenes Tenement STONEY HAWE
Thomas Fisher
4½d

GARDEN
William at Hill

Kenes Tenement MESSUAGE, GARDEN, LAND
William at Hill
3r : 2½d

Freferding Tenement
Lawrence Farman

cw to Lawrence Ferman's house

HADLOW ST TO TONBRIDGE

HADLOW STREET TO TONBRIDGE

LAND LEADING TO MEDWAY

Kenes Tenement MESSUAGE & GARDEN at Stair
(where he lives)
Thomas Crudd
½a : 2½d

Kenes Tenement MESSUAGE at Stair Bridge

Kenes Tenement PRETELLS GARDEN or PRESTELYS HAGH
Lady of the Manor
½a : 7½d

Kenes Tenement MESSUAGE at Stair Bridge
Robert Bishop (William's son)
½a : 7½d

Kenes Tenement MESSUAGE at Stair Bridge
Robert Bishop (William's son)
(formerly John Kene's)
6a : 8½d

Kenes Tenement GERVASES
Lawrence Farman
3½a : 7d

Kenes Tenement CARDEN'S MEAD
Lawrence Farman
½a : 7½d

KENY'S POLE

Heirs of Richard Bishop (William's son)

Kenes Tenement YERLIS HILLS (1)
(2 pieces)
Lady of the Manor
1r : 2d : 1¼d

Kenes Tenement YERLIS HILLS (2)

MARSH

MEDWAY
(this would be the old course of the Medway)

Water of the Lady of the Manor

Freferding Tenement PAYNE OF EYLAND
Thomas Crudd
3a : 4r : 4d

Freferding Tenement COTTE IN THE PAYNE OF EYLAND
Robert Bishop (William's son)
1a : 6d

Thomas Crudd

MISTRESS MARSH
Lady of the Manor

Kenes Tenement SETRENYS
Reg.Herst & John Abarton
1r : 7d

Kenes Tenement CARDEN'S MEAD
Reg.Herst & John Abarton
3r

Kenes Tenement SEDGE HILL
Lawrence Farman
1a : 4d

Kenes Tenement SEDGE HILL MEAD
Thomas Bishop.
1½a : 2d

Kenes Tenement SEDGE HILL
Reg.Herst & John Abarton
1a : 4d

ROWING LAKE

MILL DITCH

Kenes Tenement MILL HOUSE and land called SETONS
John Bishop (Richard's son)
3r : 7½d

Kenes Tenement STEGGE HILLS
John Bishop (Richard's son)
3a : 3r : ½d

Lady of the Manor's DITCHES

Kenes Tenement LE SORE
Lawrence Farman
3a : 3r less 1½d

Kenes Tenement UN-NAMED
John Wybarne Esq
(lately John Picot)
3r : 3½d

LE KAGEBODYLL
Lady of the Manor

MARSH

MARSH

Kenes Tenement NEXT TO HEDER KAGEGATE
John Bishop (Richard's son)
3r less 1 p

HADLOW STREET TO TONBRIDGE

it does today, and the Stair or riverside landing place was created on Walter at Steyre's tenement where the contours are much closer together than on any other part of the manor.

Fishing with the Lady's nets

KNETT THE HOGGS

One house on the Walter at Steyre tenement, occupied by Lawrence Farman, is now Stair Farm, and another occupied by Thomas Fisher, in right of his wife Alice, formerly Mrs William Honewold, seems to be on the site of the present Stair House. We shall recognise in due course how often women with rights to land married local menfolk and conveniently brought neighbouring fields together. The Fishers, like the Bishops, were an old Hadlow family, and this Thomas Fisher, also holding Fishland tenement, had special fishing obligations to catch fish for the lady of the manor whenever she required it, using her nets, they firmly noted.

Further along the main road to Hadlow, on Knett the Hoggs tenement, were two more Fishers, Peter and Thomas, though a Bishop, John, son of Robert, was the main tenant. Here the holding was again a standard 30 acres in size, but subdivision had produced 18 pieces of land divided between 7 people. Richard Fisher holding only one piece of 2.1 rods, shows how small some fragments could be. Some of this land was on the corner of Three Elm Lane.

As four out of these eight first tenements conformed to the 30-acre standard, we might suspect an origin more ancient than the rest, granted at a time when uniformity was expected. That notion might even draw further support from another odd statement relating to Jopes tenement. It said that joint-tenants of the manor had eleven sows grazing in North Frith throughout the year, and owed certain pigs, and money dues according to the pannage season. It sounds a generous allowance, and might well be a statement that was intended to apply to all tenements. The subsequent revisions in 1581 show that some other tenants, but not all, did indeed have grazing rights for pigs in North Frith for their obligations to pay the lord in pigs or pork were enumerated. The puzzle is further discussed below in Chapter 5.

JOPES

Looking east along the ancient course of the Medway flowing above the Herberys.

As a guide to the structure of the tenements hereabouts, we may pause to emphasise the fact that four out of the first eight tenements were exactly 30 acres

apiece, and subdivision had produced 35 separate pieces of land in the most extreme case, and twelve in the least. The surveyor continued his survey by moving along the Hadlow Road, remaining concerned with tenements that mostly lay to the south of it. This land lay on the floodplain of the Medway with names such as Warelake, Lodeweir Pool, Jopislake; in short, it was all on what we shall conclude was the most sought after cattle-fattening land, having useful access to transport on the river and Tonbridge. The tenement, called Fishland, had Thomas Fisher as its main tenant, and lay in the vicinity of the present Fish Hall. Taking all the Fisher family's land, we find them holding 68 different pieces in 1460 amounting to 111 acres. It is clear that they were a prosperous Hadlow family with a long history, and perhaps were verging on gentry. Moreover, Fishland tenement had some pieces of land called Inner and Outer Herbery and Le Arber, names hinting at land that had once made a pleasure garden. Had the house once belonged perhaps to a courtly family in contact with Tonbridge Castle? The same land was now just meadow and

FISHLAND

arable, but later documents show that Fish Hall itself remained a house with somewhat higher social standing than other tenemental messuages. Three Elm Lane was one of its boundaries, and Posterngate was mentioned, so its general location was clear.

After the first eight tenements, sizes diverged more sharply from the standard 30 acres, showing more irregularity. This fact hints at the allotment of the next farms being

Looking down Church Street towards the centre of the village. Lords Place is the large gabled building on the right.
As illustrated here the Stewards house later became the Kings Head public house, although today it is a private house once again.

made some time after the first round. Four out of fourteen were 15 acres or less, while two, nearing and reaching the present-day Ashes Lane which runs north of the Hadlow Road to North Frith Park, were larger, measuring between 39 and 41 acres. Moreover, as field names denoting land on the floodplain petered out, the tenements were less fragmented; evidently demand for this land was less pressing.

TANNERS

Tanners tenement abutted the main Hadlow Road, near Three Elm Lane, and Henry Hextall features here for the first time as a noticeable occupier from Tannerys onwards. He held pieces in Peacocks and Pococks tenements, some of which land was arable running from Higham lane towards Hadlow and reaching as far as the river Bourne; Hextall was probably more of an arable farmer than a grazier. He will become one of the more conspicuous names in our survey for he was an official of the Stafford family, and was possibly the steward. He was the leading tenant of Pococks tenement, but he dwelt in the centre of the village, in Lords Place in Church Street. (More about the Hextalls follows below).

PEACOCKS & POCOCKS

PYNCHON

Some of the land in these tenements now reached as far as the boundaries of North Frith Park (see Pynchon tenement), and it was occupied by individuals having a considerable number of pieces in other tenements as well. So the notion of 30 acres as a standard holding was being lost to sight, though the larger pieces of land around here suggest little competition for it. Thus, in Pynchon tenement, which was only 4½ acres (the surveyor showed an incorrect 3½ acre total), Richard Pynchon had 3 acres and John and Thomas Fychett had just over 1 acre. Pynchon's hardly deserved to be called a tenement, though it did have a house and garden, with some land on the highway from Coiffe's gate to Tonbridge; it looks more like a squatters holding. The next door

Dumbreck's map of Poulthouse & Correnden lands in 1842 showing pit fields, brickyard, kilnfield and furzefields

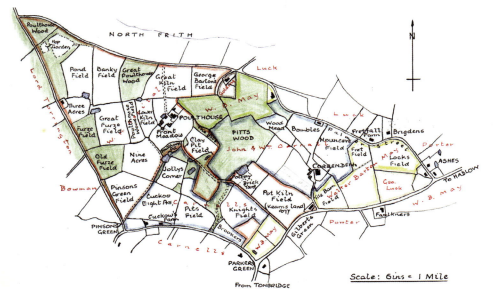

FICHET'S

An old pit in the vicinity of Knights tenement now filled with water.

HOLMANS

Brick and tile making

KNIGHTS

STIDINGS

BROOMFIELD

tenement, Fichet's, leads us to the present-day Poult House, and near the boundary of the hunting grounds of the lords of Tonbridge in North Frith Park. This tenement comprised 33½ acres. It was held by the same two Fichets, who held land in Pynchon tenement, but it was here that they had a house and garden. The only other resident hereabouts seems to have been John Crocher, and it was through his wife, Juliana, who had been married to Robert Watt, that he held the house up here where he lived, in fact, Poult House itself.

The surveyor in this area was now looking at tenements that had a far different character from those down at the Medway. It was woodland peppered with pits from which sand and brick-clay were extracted. The next tenement was Holmans, recalling a Walter Holman whose surname had not survived anywhere else on this manor. It too contained several pits, some of them lying in a line. One pit evidently yielded sand and was called Sandherst; the pits were shared between a Pynchon, the two Fychets, Henry Hextall, and the lady of the manor. All these occupiers had other land elsewhere, and must have valued the minerals on the tenement while having no desire to live on it. All the land lay near the present Pitts Wood, where the visitor can still get some impression of how the land looked then, amid pits turned into ponds, old coppicing, and sloe bushes. Later on a brick kiln was also situated here, and towards Higham Lane were furze fields, furze being valued for flash firing.

The next door tenement, Knights, was on similar terrain, although, having only 12 acres, it had little more than half the land of Holmans. It had once been occupied by a Nicholas Tanner who perhaps had followed the tanning trade and wanted to exploit the tree bark. In 1460 one occupier was John Beald, a carpenter, so he may have coppiced the timber here. But Henry Hextall was the main tenant and all around were other familiar neighbours occupying pits but not living there. Yet another rough piece of land up here was Broomfield tenement next door, comprising only 10 acres, divided between two men, John At Stable and Thomas Bishop, and owing nothing but a money rent. The condition of this neighbourhood as scrubby land is further suggested by the next door tenement, called Stidings, formerly said to have been occupied by Amicia Stidings whose surname appears nowhere else in the survey. It was less than 6½ acres and was two pieces of land sandwiched between the occupiers of Broomfield tenement. The land seems to have lain on the main Hadlow to Tonbridge road, and it is tempting to imagine it as vacant waste land on which Amicia squatted, having turned up from nowhere, and stayed till she died. Thomas Bishop already had land on one side and he was now in 1460 deemed the occupier of these two pieces as well, owing rent and relief. This was the only place in the whole survey where the rate at which relief was levied was actually stated. It was charged on tenants at all changes of occupier, whether by sale or when death brought in a new heir, and the payments feature constantly in the court rolls. Relief, explained the surveyor at this point, was a fourth part of the rent 'according to the manor's constitution'. In discussing manor court business below, we shall show how remarkably small were the sums that fell due for relief when compared with the relief levied in other parts of the kingdom. They support the notion that the Weald was a relatively poor part of the country, given a lowly valuation in the estimate of contemporaries, and not promising a high standard of living to its residents.

The surveyor now returned to the Hadlow Road and surveyed more tenements on either side. Some pieces of land lay on both sides of Brewis Lane, a footpath still known into the 1950s but since lost. It ran from the present-day Farm Shop on the Hadlow Road towards Faulkners Oast, and in the sixteenth century was known as Sherriff's Lane.

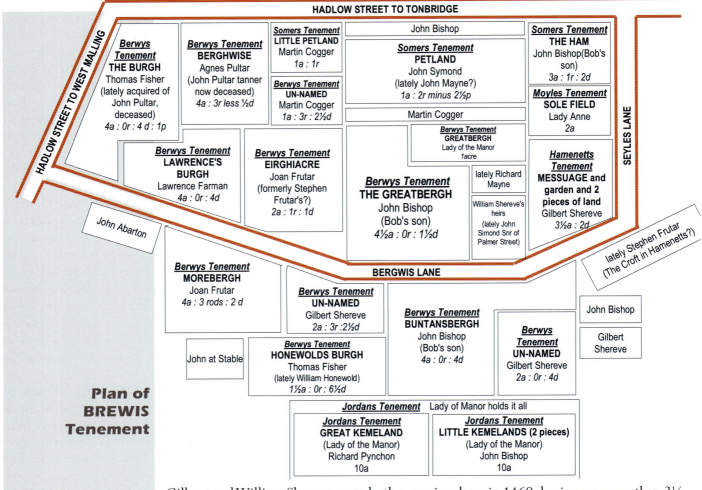

Plan of BREWIS Tenement

BREWIS

Gilbert and William Shereve were both occupiers here in 1460, having no more than 3½ acres between them in a tenement called Brewis. The element 'burgh' is noticeable in several place-names here, denoting ancient administrative terminology which is more prominent elsewhere in the Weald; it is visible here only in this one district, but that may be worth remark since, when the parish boundary between Hadlow and Tonbridge was changed in 1932, the new line was set on Brewis Lane.

John Bishop, son of Robert, was the chief occupier of Brewis in 1460, and, as we have seen, he was a notability on the manor for altogether he farmed nearly 90 acres in 11 different tenements. Indeed, he was possibly the largest of all the landholders. The Brewis tenement was largish, 39½ acres, and nine people shared in it. Moreover, dues, and labour services in ploughing, harrowing and carrying were so substantial (120 small works and 24 great works) on this tenement, and the bread and herrings given for work so precisely stated, that it is tempting to guess that it constituted a tenement newly chartered by the Stafford family in 1330 when they took possession and started to reorganise the estate to their liking. Significantly, the labour services were the same as in the case of Jordans tenement, and those were, indeed, said to have been declared in a charter made at Tonbridge Castle in 3 Edward III, sometime between January 1329 and 1330. This was not long after the Staffords had taken charge. The Clare estate, as we have seen above, had been divided between women in 1314, when the male line ended with the death of Gilbert, tenth Earl of Clare. Through marriage. the next lord of Tonbridge was Ralph, who later became the first Earl of Stafford, and died at Tonbridge. He may have been more involved in giving instructions for the managing of his estate in 1330 than the Clares had been. Miscellaneous other clues also tempt us to think that Brewis tenement lay in the more intensively cultivated arable part of the manor.

CARDONS

The surveyor was now approaching Ashes Lane, then known as Palmer Street, and was not too far from Bourne bridge and the village centre. A tenement like Cardons

**WELSH's
PALMERS**

running up to the boundary of North Frith Park with 'birch wood' place names and Welsh's tenement also having woodland names, were not greatly divided. But Palmers tenement, extending to the Hadlow Road certainly was. Its total acreage was 36 acres, but it had eight occupiers, and six houses stood here, one of which was Palmers Place, a name signifying a substantial dwelling. Henry Johnson lived in it, and occupied almost half the land, 15 acres, though he held no other land in the manor and we know nothing about him. But the subdivision of the holding and the six houses fire the imagination, since riders coming along the main road from Tonbridge must have recognised this unusually well populated corner as the point at which they had to turn left to go up to the hunting grounds at North Frith. Palmers Place lay approximately on the site of what is now the restaurant called 'The Rose Revived', and that is known to be an early sixteenth-century house; it could have been a striking building that attracted attention. Moreover, being near a cluster of other dwellings that are still there, it prompts the thought that they housed some of those who worked on the fencing and gating of the hunting park, kept watch for poachers of deer, and guarded the falcons at certain times of the year.

It is a pity that the Palmer surname has disappeared from Hadlow place-names. Welsh's tenement, the one surveyed before Palmers, had formerly belonged to a Richard Palmer, and he had also lately occupied Peckham manor (see below). The Palmer surname remained well known in Hadlow into the later twentieth century; in the 1950s a Palmer was a coal merchant; in 1975 a Mrs Palmer sold a house near the common. But the only Palmer occupying land on this manor in 1460 was Alice with only half an acre in the vicinity of the river Bourne.

WEKERLYDS

Approximate areas
covered by Palmers,
Welshes and Wekerylds
tenements

Holdings now were approaching the village centre and took unexpected shapes and sizes. Wekerylds tenement lay on both sides of the Hadlow Road, its land on the right-hand side of Ashes Lane having three houses on it. But its land was divided by the main road, for some lay along Blackmans Lane; a history of arable cultivation was possible here as labour services were due from its occupants. The next tenements were nondescript

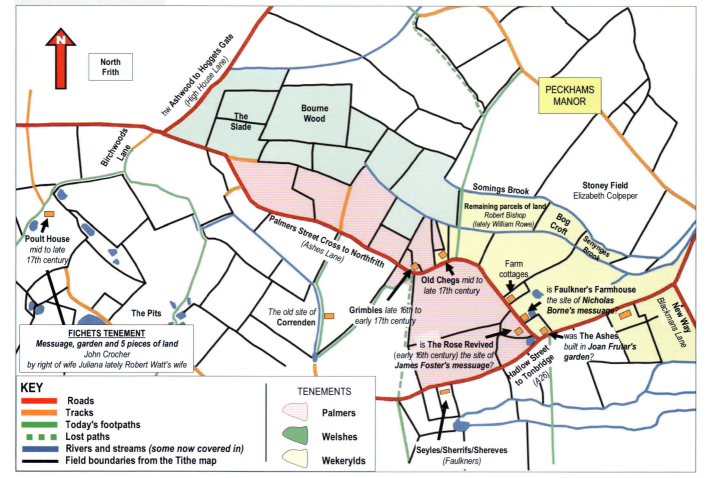

**CROUCHLANDS
ALEYNSLOVE**

Brass effigy of Elizabeth Culpeper on her tomb in West Peckham Church

holdings, smaller than the standard size but all in the Three Elm Lane, Blackmans Lane area, and all except Crouchland owing labour services. The holdings were watered by brooks or the river Bourne itself, and Aleynslove tenement seems to be the present-day Bourneside farm. In only two out of six cases was any dwelling mentioned, so we have to contemplate these farming families living in the village, but on the land of other manors. John Symonds, senior, was shown earlier to be living in a house along Palmer Street (Ashes Lane), but now the same John was named as the one occupier of a small unnamed tenement which had only two acres of land, but accommodated the maltmill on the river Bourne; Symonds, the occupier, was not necessarily the working miller. The Hadlow manor at this point was close to its northern boundary, which adjoined Peckham manor, where Lady Elizabeth Culpeper had an interest. She may, in fact, have been the lady of that manor at this time. Her tomb is in West Peckham church.

This mill was not the only one on the river Bourne at this point. We are familiar to this day with the site of one watermill here, at the bottom of the lane leading off Carpenters Lane. But our survey mentions three mills in 1460, and still in the eighteenth century documents refer to three mills, and calls them Hadlow mills. One of these must have been the cornmill, and the third was possibly a fulling mill, used for fulling cloth, because a tenterfield lay in Paynes, the next door tenement, and this was where the woven cloths when fulled were stretched out to dry. Hadlow was not a significant clothmaking village in the Weald; much more celebrated was the area around Cranbrook. But if a fulling mill did exist on the river Bourne, it suggests that Hadlow families made sufficient cloth for household use to appreciate such a labour-saving asset.

Moving into the village across the Bourne and approaching the church, one would expect to find more houses along the high street, but they were surprisingly few in number, suggesting that other manors in the parish had some houses there too. Paynes tenement, lying wholly on the north side of the village, stretched back to include the tenterfield already mentioned somewhere on the east side of Carpenters

**PAYNES
FLETCHERS**

Bourne Mill wheel in the early 20th century

GIBBONS

Lane. It had only one house standing on its 42 acres, so it was plainly not a built-up part of the village. Fletchers tenement next door was larger still, covering nearly 52 acres, and here stood the corn mill and a millpond, from which water flowed south and west to a maltmill. Fletchers, then, must be what we now know as Bourne Mill. Its leading occupier was Richard Culpeper, esquire, who lived at Oxenhoath, and also occupied the largest slice of Fletchers's land, 24½ out of its 52 acres. The whole tenement extended towards the village street, and Lady Elizabeth Culpeper, probably his mother, held a small piece of 4½ acres during her lifetime, almost certainly as part of her widow's settlement. Some of this land was meadow as one might expect so close to the Bourne; one piece was called Waterships, which we recognise nowadays as Waterslippe; and a road through it led to Lonewood, which was a considerable area to the east and north and included some common land.

The main occupier on Paynes tenement, having some 22 acres altogether, was John Newman, the village maltster, one of the few inhabitants to have a specialist occupation assigned to him. Continuing now along the north side of the village street, Gibbons tenement was a large holding of 48½ acres, with only two tenants, of whom Nicholas Stopersfield was the main one, having 33 acres and his house there. The land included a Fullersfield, reminding us again of cloth processing by the villagers. Somewhere in the vicinity was the vicarage house and rectory land, and one acre on which a barn had been built next to the vicarage. Being so near to the main street, the barn could well have looked like Old Barn, a family house which stands to this day at the corner of Court Lane.

Following on Gibbon's tenement, the surveyor then described one tenement having only one occupier (a rare example in this survey), and he was again Richard Culpeper,

Old barn in Hadlow High Street adjacent to the site of Matilda Broker's messuage, now converted to residential accommodation.

1. Hasted, 1798, V, 63-4

esquire. The Culpepers were gentry hereabouts, and we begin to realise how much land they held in Hadlow. A John Culpeper at the beginning of the fifteenth century was justice of the common pleas at Westminster and was already living at Oxenhoath. According to Hasted, it was he who gave Dukes Place to the Knights Hospitallers[1]. Some of his other land, lying in Hadlow manor, included this so-called tenement, formerly of Thomas Peckham, but it was said to be 'lying in an ancient park'. The record then particularised and stated that Richard and Joan Brewer now held the whole tenement between them, but it was 'in the new park', and it was shown in an ancient rental to have been occupied by William Gifferey and lately by Richard, son of John Palmer. The full meaning of this description is not altogether clear, but it appears to identify as a tenement what later came to be known as Peckhams Manor, though no court rolls have ever been found for it. Evidently, an ancient park had once lain here; had it, perhaps, fallen into neglect after the Black Death? Now in 1460 a new park had evidently taken its place within which a tenement had been established, though the clerk gave no acreage. We catch sight of some fundamental re-arrangement of the land here, something that was common in other parts of the country following the Black Death (see Searle on Battle Abbey estates). More changes in later centuries give us the estate known as Bourne Grange, which became part of Hadlow College in 1968.

A tiny piece of land was surveyed next, consisting of less than 4 acres of land, belonging to Richard Nepicar. It was not described as a tenement, but it had Lawday Place, a mysterious place-name discussed below, on the east, with the common of Lonewood on the west and north. Richard Nepicar, known to the locals as Richard of Loamwood (as the common was then called), lived in a house on the tenement next door, part of that

HONEWOLDS

called Honewolds, that name reminding us how long-lived is that surname in Hadlow. Nepicar, in fact, was living amid a cluster of houses in the very centre of the village; eight altogether lay on this tenement, five on the north side of the village street, and three on the south side. Most occupiers had very small pieces of land amounting to no more than 2 acres or less, enough for a garden. Plainly, their houses were relatively congested along the main village street. In the same neighbourhood, the lord also had garden land, and a field called Cotmansfield; this was the field at the junction of the village street and Court Lane. The name revived a memory of the past for the lord's home farm had once relied on serfs or cotmen to work it. These lowly servants performed the heaviest labour services on their lord's land, but nevertheless shared a field in which they cultivated food for their families. The Black Death had dealt a blow to that arrangement, for heavy mortality among the population undermined the authority of the lord, and as labourers became scarce, and wage rates rose high, manorial lords generally ceased to cultivate their own home farms. As this survey did not define the legal status of any tenants in 1460, we cannot say how many were free, how many were unfree, and whether any were called cotmen. But in the sixteenth century when tenants' status was given in some documents, none was called 'a cotman'. Our survey in 1460 shows the 'cotmansfield' belonging to the lady of the manor, and actually described as 'the lady's demesne'.

Somewhere opposite the end of Court Lane, then, we can picture village houses running eastward along what the local people then called the road to West Malling. Absolutely no mention was made in the survey of a road to Maidstone. That road did not then exist, and we find support for that unexpected fact because the road itself nowadays contains no ancient houses. Hadlow people moved between Tonbridge at one end and West Malling at the other, and seeing the width of the West Malling High Street today, we can readily imagine how Hadlow people added to the throng of people shopping in that broad street on market days.

On the south side of the main street, the surveyor now standing at its very centre, described Coiffe's tenement, formerly Richard Kempe's and before that Richard White's. He did not complete his account of its acreage; perhaps it was complicated because of the many villages houses that we suspect were there, though not belonging to Hadlow manor; he planned to finish it later and forgot. What he did mention was the path to the church, i.e. Church Street and Napiltons (the present-day Appletons). Here he named three shops, though he did not locate them exactly. Two were either on the village street or in Church Street, probably, in fact, on the corner. The man with most land here was John Newman, the maltster, already mentioned for living on Payne's tenement, but the shopkeepers were John Herberd, and John Somer. A third shop was jointly owned by John Herberd and Henry Hextall and was on the other side of Church Street, adjoining Lord's Place. Henry Hextall was shown living in Lord's Place, that is to say, the large house on the left side of Church Street that was a pub in the 1950s, known as the King's Head, and now called Church Place. If the manorial lord had been resident, he would have lived there. But Hadlow's lord had such high rank that he lived at Tonbridge Castle, and so his house was given to Hextall who was a responsible servant of the Duke of Buckingham, and may indeed have been the manorial steward. Additionally, Hextall occupied a lot of scattered land on the manor, almost as if he been picking up any land that came vacant. Assuming that the surveyor's compass points are correct, the shop of Herberd and Hextall lay to the left of Lord's Place on the site of Cobblestones, and Matilda Broker lived in the house on the other side of Cobblestones, i.e. No.1 Church Street. Behind this row of shops and dwellings lay Napiltons (= Appletons).

The surveyor now moved along the village street to Coswyn's, an average holding of 32¾ acres, lying adjacent to what is now James House and Cemetery Lane. The occupier of most land here was William Nepicar, holding 13 acres; he had the same surname as the occupier of that other house with land on the other side of the road. The highway that we now call the road to Maidstone was known as the road to West Malling, and diverging from it was one highway to Goldhill (i.e. Golden Green) and one to Yalding. Court Lane was much the most direct road to Goldhill and Yalding for people in the centre of the village. But another road led off the main road further along at a place called Dorants Cross, in the vicinity of the present James House, most likely what we now call Cemetery Lane rather than the footpath that diverges just before Cemetery Lane. William Nepicar's house lay somewhere on the right hand side of the main village street, and so did William Hogett's. But population and cultivation were thinning out along this road, so Haymonds tenement consisted of less than 5 acres with 2 occupiers, and John Pelsount, singularly, held the whole of the next tenement, Rodbards, giving him 22 acres and a house, no subdivision of his tenement having yet taken place. He had land in two other tenements but all of it lay in the vicinity, giving him a sizeable holding of some 37 acres, without close neighbours.

TONBRIDGE TO WEST MALLING

HADLOW STREET TO YALDING

UN-NAMED MESSUAGE
Matilda Broker
(formerly Gilbert Kempe
& Richard White)
acreage not shown

SHOP with small garden adjacent
John Herebarde
no size given

NAPILTON
Lord of the Manor

SHOP
John Somer
& Henry Hexstall

UN-NAMED MESSUAGE
John Somer /
John Herebarde /
Henry Hexstall
(formerly Adam Saunder)
no size given

COMMONWAY TO CHURCH

LORD'S PLACE
Henry Hexstall's messuage

Plan of part of COIFFE'S Tenement

COSWYNS

HAYMONDS RODBARDS

HECOTTS
PENDER
FOSTERS

2. It is likely that Hecotts and Pender tenements later constituted the Hadlow land named 'The Hamlet', in the nineteenth century Tithe apportionment, which lay along Stanford Lane, completely surrounded by East Peckham parish.

SPALDINGS

LOCKBRIDGE

GROVE-

We have arrived at a motley array of tenements bearing no sign of conforming to any uniform size: Hecotts amounted to little more than 3 acres, another holding of Richard Steyle's was 4½ acres, its status being left unclear; both resembled squatters' holdings.[2] Fosters tenement with 17 acres promised a better living. It is now part of Goblands farm, and lies along the parish boundary with East Peckham; hence it had a field called Boundsfield, and lay in the territory of the Fromond family. In fact, the will of Thomas Fromond of Goldhill in 1447 mentioned three pieces of land called Bounds, somewhere near here, to be sold at his death along with the tenement and adjoining garden. John Goding was the main tenant of Fosters, and his land included crofts at Bourne Stile, which can be identified in the nineteenth-century boundary perambulation as the point where the footpath leads to Peckham Bush. The same boundary perambulation claimed that the Goding family 'from time immemorial' gave cider further on at 'the cider stile' to the parties walking the bounds; but it is unlikely that 'time immemorial' reached back to 1460! (The Goding surname later became Golding, the family responsible for developing the Golding hop). The next tenement, Spaldings, was said to be 12 acres (though, correctly added, the two pieces came to 17 acres), and it had only two occupiers, of whom one was William Whettenhall, a gentleman living in East Peckham, the next door parish. Land here gave the impression of being somewhat detached from Hadlow, and not commanding much interest among the locals. Lockbridge's tenement was only 10 acres divided into 6 pieces and lay on the highway that led from Hadlow to Yalding. The surveyor was perhaps losing interest at this point; he named the tenement of Henry Ashdown on the way to Yalding but it contained only 6 acres. Grove tenement was only 9 acres divided between two people; it contained a reference to Gooseland which adjoined some land lying on the edge of Caustons manor. The land here was lying in bits and pieces of varying sizes, and was far from conveying any impression of well-established tenemental holdings. Rather it suggests an unfavoured area awaiting occupiers, available to anyone who turned up; we may wonder if perhaps it had suffered some dislocation when the Causton family departed from Hadlow, and left it untenanted?.

Having started his enquiries at Hadlow Stair, the surveyor had now described something more than a semi-circle around the northern half of the parish but had not yet taken stock of the south-eastern quarter. This was where a noticeable number of Hadlow's smaller manors lay, namely, Caustons, Fromonds, Crombury, and Goldhill, four of the seven which we assume to have been created by the Clares as a result of their granting knights' fees to loyal senior servants. Their close grouping at this end of the parish, and the fact that the surveyor left this area till last suggests that it was regarded by contemporaries as somewhat apart from the core of the manor. Its location, in fact, would be consonant with the notion that when the Clares installed themselves in Tonbridge and a castle was built there, they sought to keep the land nearest to the castle for themselves, and chose for their knightly grantees land that was still attractively near the Medway, but more distant from Tonbridge and as yet undeveloped (a similar speculation is made by Searle with reference to Battle Abbey estates). This is guesswork, but it is a credible formulation of likely settlement history, for the rivers Teise, Medway and Beult run together at this south-eastern end of the parish, joining up in Yalding parish next door. The terrain here is likely to have been more open, accessible, and ripe for development by others when the first knights' fees were granted at an early date than more wooded areas in other parts of Hadlow parish.

It may also be significant that some of the wording of the survey in the next pages hints vaguely at ancient allotments of land in this neighbourhood, possibly going back earlier than those around Hadlow Stair. In tracing the earliest settlement of the Weald, Kenneth Witney focused attention on this meeting point of the three rivers, the Medway, Teise, and Beult as an obvious first entry point into the forest of the Weald for those moving south off the downland. From Gibbons tenement onwards, some pieces of land are referred to in ferlings, which was an ancient unit of land, representing a quarter

3. Muhlfeld, 1974, xv

of a yoke (some 10-13 acres). The same measure features in Fosters, Lockbridge and Stoperfield tenements. The larger unit, the yoke, is nowhere mentioned in our survey as a basic unit of family land (though, in noticeable contrast, the survey of Wye manor on the downlands, owned by Battle Abbey, Sussex, and also having a survey of the mid-fifteenth century, uses the yoke as the standard measure).[3] The ferling, being a quarter of a yoke, is an equally ancient term, but survives in use only in this sector of the manor, and it is tempting to think that there is some significance in that fact.

STOPERFIELD

The account of Stoperfield tenement, (35½ acres), which uses the term ferling, is unusual in another respect. It was formerly a tenement of Hugh de Causton, and was an amalgam of pieces of land formerly (and presumably after Hugh de Causton's departure) occupied by five different people. It made up 15 acres plus a house and included half a ferling held by one of the five former occupiers through 'a charter of the lord Earl of Stafford as is shown in an old rental'. More pieces made up the whole of Stoperfield tenement, but it finished by adding up the money due from all the tenants as noted 'through an old charter in an old rental, as they say'. Such words seemed to imply some disbelief on the part of the surveyor, because no documentary proof was being offered.

PUDDINGS

Some land here was in the vicinity of Causton manor, and indeed, the next tenement, called Puddings, was also said to have belonged formerly to Hugh de Causton, so we may be observing here the break up of Hugh de Causton's estates, including the manor that took his name. As the date of the departure of Hugh de Causton from Hadlow is a mystery not so far solved (more on the history of the Caustons follows in Chapter 15), it is possible that, in the background of the tenemental structures described here, lies some rearrangement well before 1460 not only of tenements but of manors also. This is at variance with the manorial conventions we expect and find in other parts of the country. But a somewhat unceremonious procedure for creating and maintaining manors in other parishes of the Weald is further discussed below, and it alerts us to be watchful for a similar attitude in Hadlow; it may be that the stricter administrative formalities of the sixteenth century, which are so noticeable in other parts of the country had not yet penetrated the Weald; in accord with this guesswork runs the assumption that the whole region was economically backward.

Stoperfields tenement also attracts notice for another reason. Some of its land lay along the road from Goldhill to West Malling, that is, Victoria Road, and two occupiers held pieces of Park Field, amounting to nearly nine acres. To the north of Park Field lay

Map showing: position of Stoperfield tenement and the demesne land and other points of interest including the approximate position of Lawday Place.

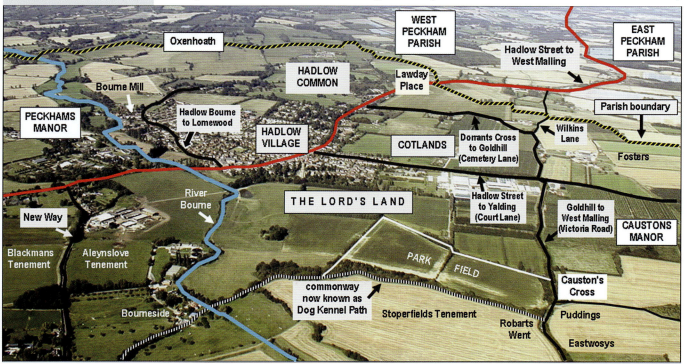

'the Lord's meadow and land'. An acre of land called Park Croft also lay in that tenement and Nicholas Stoperfield also held a piece in Courtmead by the river Bourne on the western boundary of the demesne lands. On the southern boundary of the tenement, land held by William Martyn, although not in our survey, was termed 'demesne land'. Are these the vestiges of an old hunting park? The land to the north of Stoperfield tenement later became the ornamental parkland of the old Court Lodge and subsequent Hadlow Castle. Are we witnessing here the beginning of the change from an old hunting park to the formation of more structured leisure grounds? It can be no more than a guess.

BROOKE

The last pages of the survey moved around to the Medway, and Brooke tenement. Brooke tenement encompassed much land that was surrounded by water, and is likely to have been flooded in winter. Anote Island was here, Jordanslake was prominent, and several sluices and weirs featured. Perysbrook and Perystown were place names, and it is fairly certain that Perystown was on the site of Barnes Street. Brook tenement, moreover, was the largest of all tenements in the survey, extending over 82 acres. It was divided into 37 pieces among ten people, and emphasised the importance of the Fromond family in these parts. John Fromond of Goldhill held one-sixteenth of a knight's fee and occupied 13 pieces of land, Lady Margaret Fromond held one sixth of a knight's fee and three pieces of land, and Gilbert Fromond held two pieces. (For more on the Fromonds, see Chapter 13) Some land was described as meadow and the place name, The Hills, suggests that some was lifted out of the floodplain, but the absence of any dwellings was significant.

LAKE

4. In the Court Rolls of the Manor of Thomas Fromonds of Hadlow, 1433 (CKS U55 M360) the words 'de Kympynhale' are added after Thomas Fromond at Waters name. Does this imply a connection between the two?

Lake tenement next door (of 44 acres) lay next to Hartlake bridge going east and was previously held by William at Grove. John Fromond of Kempinghale[4] held 15 acres including his dwelling house 'Clobcroft', which was probably on the present site of Hartlake Farmhouse and another house called Thomas at Grove. A third messuage was owned by Richard Knight. There was a common here called Jourdans.

JORDANS

LAWERK

The last two tenements named in the survey were both in the hands of the lady of the manor. Had her senior officials perhaps noticed the omission and drawn attention to them? Jordans consisted of two pieces of land, each of 10 acres, lying on the north side of Three Elm Lane and south of Brewis tenement. They were summarily described, with reference to a charter of 1329/30. The very last tenement was called Lawerk or Larke at Larkhale, located in the most northerly part of the manor at Stallions Green, and that too was plainly an afterthought, being far from where the surveyor had ended his enquiries in 1460. Thomas Fader occupied land by copy of a court roll of 1466/7, thus dating the entry well after the main survey had been completed. The survey petered out here, and indeed one page seems to be missing.

The surveyor had more or less returned to his starting point, and neatly it was John Bishop, who had featured so prominently at the beginning of the survey, who was here at the end, occupying one of the two pieces of Jordans tenement. We can imagine the surveyor inscribing that last note and laying his survey aside with a groan, wondering what other holdings he had overlooked.

PUZZLES IN THE SURVEY

DEMESNE LAND

5. Harvey, 1984, 18

With regard to the content of the survey, the reader is left at the end with certain puzzles that need to be discussed. The document is described as a rental or customary of all lands and tenements within the demesne of Hadlow, giving information about each tenant of the demesne. The word 'demesne', as used here, referred to the whole estate of the lord, as originally granted to him. He subsequently let many parcels to tenants, but kept sufficient for a home farm for himself. According to later usage, the word 'demesne' came to mean that portion of the land which the lord reserved for his own use, which constituted his home farm. Custumals like this one started by recording the land of tenants only, but by the end of the twelfth century, they had begun to add an account of the manorial demesne. In the Hadlow case, however, this did not happen.[5] The survey enumerated tenant land, and referred to the boundaries of the demesne land, but it did not describe or measure the pieces of demesne, or explain how they were being used by the lord, or tenanted by others, except in one or two exceptional instances.

We expect most, though not all, of the lord's demesne to have lain immediately around the manor house. So in Hadlow, we expect it around the present Hadlow Castle which now stands on the old manor house site. But all that land is omitted, apart from one piece called Cotmansfield, lying centrally on the corner of High Street and Church Street, and, significantly, near the lord's garden. It is probably explained by its special history. Cotmen were the poorest class on the manor, doing heavy labour sevices, and it may well be that this field had once been allocated to them for their families' use. When labour services ceased to be demanded, it would no longer have been so designated, and so perhaps the land was reclaimed by the lord; it is something that could well have happened some time after the Black Death. The suggestion is highly speculative, of course; it can only be judged to have any validity if similar circumstances are discovered elsewhere.

HOUSES IN THE VILLAGE STREET

Another puzzle concerns the comparatively few houses described in the main street. Those mentioned are six houses on the south side, three on the north, and one without a location. Again, we have to resort to guesswork, and suggest that more houses were, in fact, sited along the village street, but they belonged to some of the other seven manors in the parish of which we have no record.

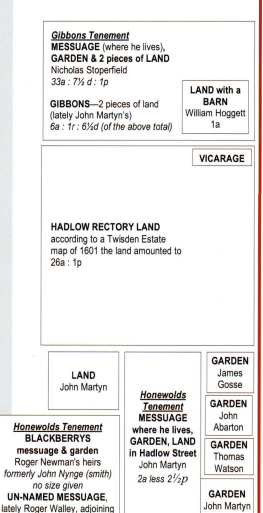
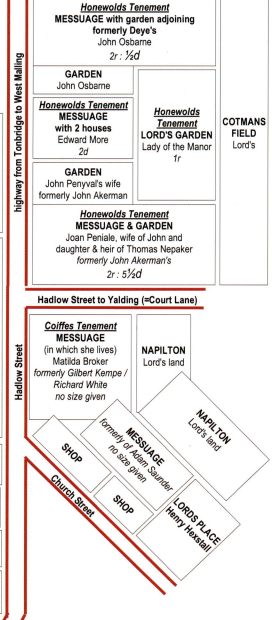

CHAPTER 5

TENANTS' RENTS, DUES & LABOUR SERVICES

In return for their land in Hadlow manor, tenants owed to their lord rent, labour services and other dues in money and kind. These were stated in the survey tenement by tenement, along with the acreages of land that they occupied. We have to imagine that the clerks held some kind of record at their elbow, and the tenants had some idea of what they owed. Supposedly, the clerk expressed his view, and tenants were asked to agree. Usually the phraseology of the document does not suggest any debate or argument about what was owed. But the occupiers of Tannerys tenement disputed the value of their labour services, and again towards the end tenants of Stoperfields named a document supporting their rights which they evidently could not produce. The clerk noted the facts 'as they say', perhaps in this case believing in the existence of a charter and an old rental, and left it at that.

Usually in a survey we look for some uniformity in the obligations and rights of tenants, but we have to bear in mind the possibility that in 1460 the lord of the manor was clarifying matters that had been long neglected. We know how lords drastically tightened up their affairs administratively and financially in the course of the sixteenth century; gradually all the lax landowners followed the example of those who had started an efficiency drive. But around 1460 these moves were only just beginning. Moreover, it is possible that tenants already held by tenures that differed between themselves. Conditions in the mid-fifteenth century, when land was relatively plentiful and occupiers were not eager to take it, were very different from those that had obtained in the twelfth and thirteenth centuries when population was rising fast, demand for land was intense, and it was in short supply; in other places we have clear evidence of young men at that time marrying old widows, in order to secure access to the women's land. So lords had had to agree different terms with their tenants in two very different economic periods. We cannot expect our survey to show uniformity throughout.

Certainly, that is the case here. All tenements owed a certain money rent four times a year and 'an aid at St Andrew's Feast', that is on November 30. These were stated in the summing up at the end of each listing of tenemental land. The aid is discussed below; we deal here with the rents per acre. The rent on Cowling tenement was said to be 3½d. 'and less' per acre, 'in all $^7/_8$ of a penny' (the meaning of those last two qualifications, is not clear, and more such obscure phrases are found later in the document that are not discussed here). The 1460 survey usually stated the rent per acre but did nothing to add up what each tenant actually owed. In 1581 the clerk did in places add the total rent due from individual tenants and it often coincided roughly with the rent per acre as stated in 1460. (The 1581 interpolations are printed in our text in italics.)

On the first tenement, namely Cowling, John Bishop's rent, unusually, was said to be 4s.4d. per annum, but his acreage was not added up. The list of pieces showed him holding 16 acres 3 rods 6 dayworks. This should have brought his rent to 4s.11d. p.a., but the surveyor reckoned the rent at 4s.4d. When the later surveyor made his calculations in 1581, he was more accurate. On John Bishop's land he picked on one piece measuring 14 and a half acres and 9 dayworks and at 3½d. the rent should be 4s.3½d; he calculated the rent for this to be 4s.2½d. p.a. The next tenant was Thomas Bishop: he had two pieces of land and the rent for one of them was stated in 1581, and that too was correct at 3½d. an acre. No rent was calculated in 1460 for the third tenant, Lawrence Ferman, but it was correctly calculated in 1581.

A closer scrutiny of the money rents would give many more insights into the reasoning behind the clerks' calculations and their accuracy, but here we draw attention only to the different valuations of the land. Starting with 3½d. per acre on Cowling tenement, the valuation changed immediately on the next tenement (Kenes) to 4d. per acre, 6d. on Woodmanyes, and 3d. on Walter at Stair and Bowlere and Wells tenements. These were all holdings in the Medway area of the manor. Fishland paid no rent, presumably because it had an unusual obligation in supplying the lord of the manor with fish whenever it was asked for. Odamys paid only 2d., whereas Knet Le Hoggs paid 5½d., Tannerys 5¾d., and Peacocks and Pococks 4d. an acre. Moving up towards North Frith, the rent per acre was significantly lower on four tenements, including those with pits, ranging from 1¾d., through 1¼d. to 1d. per acre, but returning to 4¾d. on Broomfield. Moving nearer the village centre, rents varied between 3½d. for Stidings, 4d. for Palmers, 4⅝d. for Berwys, 6¼d. for Somers and Hamenett, and 8¼d. for Moyles. The range of rents then remained at the lower end of this scale as one moved westward, but turning southward toward the Medway again, it fell to 2½d.

Rent was significantly lower on the tenements with pits

on Lockbridge tenement. On Ashdowne tenement, having only one occupier, we can work out from the rent a valuation of 1¾d. per acre. Yet Stoperfields tenement, next in line, paid 5¼d. an acre, and the tenants there held through an old charter of the Earl of Stafford, 'as is shown in an old rental' says the document in one place; in another place, more sceptically, it says 'as they say'. Land on Puddings tenement was valued even higher at 7d. an acre, whereas the very large Brooke tenement with over eighty acres was valued at only 1¼d. an acre, almost the lowest valuation of all. On the last two tenements of Lake and Lotewood the land was reckoned at 4d. and 2d. an acre respectively. In short, Hadlow land varied in its desirability, and rents ranged between 1d. and 8¼d. per acre. As suggested earlier, part of the explanation must lie with the quality and use of the soils, and part with the economic circumstances reigning when the rents were settled; we can carry the discussion no further.

Two other money payments were required from all tenants, namely 'aid' and 'relief'. The aid was due on St Andrews day, and on most tenements it amounted to 21d., presumably per tenant, except in a number of cases where it was half that, 10½d. In other cases it was an inexplicable variant: 33d. on Cowling (a slip of the pen perhaps?), 16d. on Woodmaneys, 6d. on Odamys, and a little less than 21d. on Tannerys. In some cases the aid went unmentioned, as on five tenements where the clerk was recording the land that had few occupiers towards North Frith where several pits lay. The aid resumed on Stidings tenement but cost only 6d., was back to 21d. on Berwys tenement, but was irregular on Cardon tenement (again in the North Frith area), only 14d. on Welshs tenement though (in 1581?) 21d. was overwritten. The standard charge of 21d. was set down on the next six out of seven tenements (omitting any reference to the aid on Crochland tenement, but the sums quoted now became increasingly erratic. They were 21d. or thereabouts in 6 cases, exactly half that (10½d) in 8 cases, between 2d. and 6d. in 3 cases, and 14d. to 16d. in 3 cases.

Relief was another money due from each tenement whenever it changed hands, and it involved yet more laborious counting. It appeared at the end of each tenemental account, and for Cowling it was one and five eighths of a farthing for three acres. The total in that case came to 13½d. Every tenement thereafter produced a varying valuation; in the first fifty pages of the survey, the charge varied from a ½d. per acre to one 1¼d. for 10 acres to 1d. or a 1½d. for 4 acres; Fishland tenement inexplicably owed no relief.

We next analyse labour services. In the past they had been significant in distinguishing free land from servile. Freeholders usually performed no services, whereas unfree tenants did. In this survey the clerks did not identify tenures, so the irregular allocation of labour services may be our only clue to tenurial differences. But we cannot treat them as a reliable guide. By 1460 on many manors elsewhere labour services had been commuted for a money payment, the old system having gradually collapsed after the Black Death. No sign of commutation shows in this survey, and, indeed, where labour services were deemed to be due, they were very precisely counted. But commutation could have happened silently, so that the tenements owing money rents without labour services may not, without further information, be assumed to be free land. All we can do is to recognise that in 1460 certain tenants still recognised their obligations to work on their lord's land, even though the work may not, in practice, have been called for regularly (in which case, of course, one might explain a difference in rent). We may well notice and ponder the irregular distribution of services: for example, the tenements along Palmer Street which had pits but almost no houses, and where, admittedly, some unusual duties in maintaining the hunting park may have fallen on occupiers, owed no labour services, whereas land elsewhere that is likely to have been fair arable land did owe them. But further comparisons carry us into speculations leading nowhere for we lack any secure factual foundation. Nor are the tenants' statements free of all ambiguities. All we can safely infer is that tenants were stating things as accurately as they knew, and counting the occurrence of labour services, we find them acknowledged on 39 tenements, boonwork only on 8, and no labour services at all on 17 tenements, somewhat under a third of them all. Among tenements owing labour services, one common standard was the ploughing of one acre of

Knocking down acorns to feed pigs

land in winter and one acre in Lent plus harrowing, valued at 12d. For this tenants received four loaves worth 2d. per acre and 8 herrings worth one penny, the food costs being taken into account. In some nonconforming cases the obligation was halved to the ploughing and harrowing of a half acre in winter and Lent, worth 6d., while on Tannerys tenement a quirky measure of work was required of one acre one rod, and the tenants in any case disputed their obligations with the surveyor.

Each tenement owed a certain number of small works, valued at a halfpenny, and great works valued at twopence, the usual scale being either 80 or 120 small works and 16 or 24 great works. Odd proportions may have been due to a mis-hearing or mis-transcribing by the clerk; in one case only (Walter at Stair) was a total acreage prescribed, the tenants having to plough 10 acres in winter and 10 in Lent, and in another ambiguous statement, occurring in several places, 2 acres' work were said to be worth 12d., and in one case (Fletchers) 7d. It may be that each individual tenant took responsibility for some portion of his tenement's total labour services, and as these were valued in money, and, indeed, in some years in the fifteenth century, may have been discharged in money he could reckon up how many acres of work he owed. Another slightly later document tells us that tenants had responsibility for collecting rents for their lord, so we can guess at much haggling between them each year to ensure the performance of all work due.

Along with the small and great works usually went 3 boonworks with 2 men in autumn valued at 6d. The nature of boonwork was not explained, any more than was the difference between small and great works. Small works, however, evidently included threshing, for on Kenes tenement it was said that if tenants threshed, they got two and a half bushels of hard corn and 6 bushels of oats for each small work. It is likely that this one statement, seemingly relating only to Kenes tenement, applied to all other tenements. It suggests that the manorial demesne allowed a significant amount of grain to threshers.

Carrying services were expected from most but not all tenements, and they were worth 4d. except in two cases where their value was only 3d. They were valued at more than other services, presumably because they could involve some long distances. One tenement owed only half a service, and another only a quarter service, valued at 2d. and 1d., while the disagreement that was rife on Tannerys tenement, surfaced again in 'seven parts of a carrying service' being due, valued at 3½d.

The enumeration of all these labour services leaves us totally puzzled about their practical significance in 1460. Were they regularly demanded? Were they occasionally asked for, so requiring the steward to keep a record? The fact that the steward in 1581 insisted yet again on copying out the record of 1460 begs still more questions. Medieval historians usually assume by the fifteenth century that the demand for labour services had all but ended; it only survived in unusual circumstances. Prof. Bruce Campbell has suggested that only 8 per cent of lords' farm produce was secured in the late Middle Ages through obligatory labour services.[1] Kent is certainly not a county in which one would expect them to have survived so late. A further search in other parishes of the Weald is needed.

Heriot and relief were additional obligations, subject to the concession that those owing carrying services did not give up a horse or mare as heriot; (it could have prevented them from carrying out their obligation!). The form of these words, used on Kenes tenement at the first point in the survey where labour services were mentioned, probably was again intended to apply to all tenants. Dues in kind were modest, and concerned only iron, hens, pigs, and pork, and were erratically distributed. Two tenements owed iron or plough shares, while Stoperfields, having four tenants all told, had one tenant named

Killing and cutting-up the pork.

1.   Campbell, 2000, 2-3

John Newman (he was the maltster) who was obliged to make the ironwork for one plough at his own cost, using the lord's iron; he also had the obligation to enclose the lord's Morton close, its meaning unexplained. This maltster did not owe any hens to the lord, but Nicholas Stoperfield, the main tenant in the same tenement, did owe 3 hens each year along with two other tenants elsewhere who also owed hens: John Symond of Palmer Street, holding 'one geldland in a maltmill' (sic), near Lady Elizabeth Culpeper's land towards Oxenhoath, owed two hens on Symonds tenement; so did Fosters tenement, where the chief tenant was unnamed, but the obligation showed 'in an old rental'. Surveys of manors in other parts of the country often asked for far more hens than this, from many or even all tenants.

As for dues in pork or pigs, we have already cited the words appearing under Jopes tenement describing the right of 'all tenants of the manor who are called joint tenants' to keep eleven sows in North Frith all the year round, except in the prohibited month. For this they owed 15 pigs for every two sows at the feast of St Martin (November 11). The statement is not entirely clear, however, for it then gave a different calculation that they ought to render 5 pigs for every sow at the same feast or at least their value, varying according to the plenty or scarcity of pannage each year. Two shillings per pig was due in plentiful years, 18d. in scarce years, and 12d. if there was no pannage. In winter they were entitled to receive from the lord one quarter of barley for each sow in return for a yearly payment for each pig and 12d. for each sow 'of their quarter rent'. We have to assume that they all knew exactly what that meant, even if we do not.

Pigs or pork were owing from six other tenements (Holmans, Welshes, Somers, Hamenetts, Blackmans and Lake, and after some contorted calculations the sums turn out to be approximately right for the acreages involved. The manipulation of the figures is worth attention. Holmans tenants owed half a sow and two and a half pigs in 1460 but in the revised figures for 1581 they owed three quarters of a pig and one and one eighth legs of pork. In that same year, the land and pork dues of individual tenants were then separately itemized: the main tenant's dues were in all cases not mentioned (perhaps he paid none), while those of the others were an intricate subdivision of pigs and legs of pork, all different. (The lady of the manor, for example, owed 1 pig, 1 leg of pork and 4 parts of half a leg.) At the end a total was stated for the whole tenement (still in 1581) of

20 acres 3 dayworks, owing 1 pig for 7 acres 1 daywork and more for half a daywork. This represented a total, more or less, of 3 pigs, while the total dues of individuals' pigs and pork joints added up to two and a quarter pigs, plus three and a half legs (guessing that 10 parts made a leg), to make up the missing three quarters of a pig. On Welshe's tenement, occupiers owed 5 pigs for one sow in 1460, and in 1581 5 pigs (7½ pigs were written alongside) for 8 acres. The holding was just over 41 acres, so it owed 5 pigs, and the dues individually itemised in 1581 added up to $4^1/_8$ pigs and 1¾ legs.

On Somers and Hamenetts tenements, the pig dues went unmentioned in 1460 but were given in 1581. On Somers the total due was 5 pigs but the dues from two tenants including the lady of the manor added up only to 3¾ pigs and ¾ legs. So the clerk submissively calculated the land being paid for per pig, and moved on; was the lady of the manor's due perhaps deficient, and in this way he avoided saying so? On Hamenetts, the five tenants owed 5 pigs and what they paid amounted to 4¾ pigs and 2 legs.

Blackmans was a relatively tidy tenement of 25 acres, owing one pig for every 5 acres. Five tenants shared payment, making a total of 4½ pigs and 1½ legs altogether. Many tenements following this one omitted all references to pigs until one at the end, Lake(2), owed them, and a general statement was made in 1460, showing a total obligation of 20 pigs, or 1 pig for every 2 acres 8½ dayworks. This was distributed in 1581 between 8 tenants, excluding as usual the main tenant, and amounted to 11 pigs and 5¼ legs of pork.

The enumeration of pig payments supports the many general statements by historians about the high importance of pigs in the Weald.[2] Pigs are not conspicuous as bequests in wills, and we lack probate inventories to shed light on their numbers. Nor does one expect to catch sight of them around the farmyard, since they were better off in the woodland. But significant single instances are documented below (in Chapter 8) of pigs wandering into people's living rooms and being carried upstairs into bedrooms during storms to save them from drowning. We should not underrate the role of pork and bacon in Hadlow people's food.

This survey of 1460 appears to open up a long view on Hadlow's tenurial history in the past. Otherwise, we have no way of explaining the extraordinarily complicated system of dues in money and kind that had evolved by 1460. Presumably, it had started long ago with a simple system of obligations, imposing the same dues on every family occupying a like holding. Over many generations they all had had to be subdivided, to fit in with the gavelkind system of inheritance whereby single holdings were regularly divided between all boys in the family, and if not boys, then girls. The complexities now sometimes required $^7/_8$ of a penny to be paid for land when no such coin existed; assuming the whole of a leg of pork to consist of ten parts, do we also have to picture a tenant carving eight parts out of ten from a leg of pork to carry in payment to the lady of the manor? Or was the lady content to keep a record of under-payments and over-payments from one year to another? The situation is not unlike that at which we have arrived in the twenty-first century with regard to income tax laws and social security benefits. The system then and now cried and cries out for simplification. No sixteenth-century text has yet been found expressing the need for such a solution. Yet in practice that is what must have happened. The administration of manors underwent much scrutiny in the sixteenth century, involving lawsuits at Westminster between lords and tenants. A Hadlow rental of 1587 arrives at money sums without any reference to pigs, or legs of pork, plough irons or hens. We have to guess that a red-letter day arrived when every obligation was turned into a money sum.

2.   See, for example, Peter Brandon, 2003

CHAPTER 6 MANORIAL COURTS & THEIR BUSINESS

The Hadlow manor survey offers a picture of an estate divided between the lord, who still held some land in demesne, and the tenants. The tenants made their living from over a thousand acres of its farmland, by this time divided into many separate holdings. For this they paid rent to the lord and acknowledged labour services, although, by the date of the survey, they may not have performed all or any of them. To keep such an estate running smoothly, settle disputes between neighbours, and see that the lord received his due, required a permanent administrative framework. By this time the manor court had evolved to provide just such a structure and manorial authority was exercised at its regular meetings. Some manors in other parts of the country have surviving court records covering whole centuries. In Hadlow we are not so lucky, and can only capture the flavour of its routine business by examining the record of a few years in the court rolls. Some further fragments of court rolls have survived for three of Hadlow's sub-manors, but they relate to other periods.

For the most part manor court rolls from different parts of the country, and the courts they describe, follow a standard pattern. This is especially true by the late fifteenth century by which time several guides had been written, by professional lawyers and by estate managers. It is only on closer examination that local variations show up. In earlier times and in some areas the manor court took two forms; a *court baron* and a *customary court* for free and customary tenants respectively, but in practice by the end of the fifteenth century the two courts had become one, the court baron.

The court baron dealt with the normal business of the manor, including the regulation of agricultural affairs. Principally it defined the relationship between the lord and his tenants but it also intervened to regulate the relationships between tenants and, to a limited extent, allowed villagers to have their say. One of its main functions was to register change in occupation of land, due to death or sale, and to exact payment of a *relief* for free land, or a *fine* for customary land. Either amounted to a tax on the change, sometimes a sum the equivalent of half a year's rent. In the event of death, a *heriot*, traditionally the deceased's best beast, might be claimed by the lord. In most parts of the

View of Church Street taken in 1901 by local photographer Freda Barton. Lord's Place is where Henry Hexstall, the Duchess of Buckingham's Steward, was residing at the time of the survey. It is likely that it was also the venue for Hadlow manor court

1. Furley, 1874, II (i), 756

country this was considered to be one of the signs that the land was not free, but in Kent heriots were sometimes paid on free land as well.[1] The court also ensured that all new tenants surrendered their land to the lord, to have it granted to the new occupiers. This transaction was important to the lord symbolically as well as financially as it confirmed that all land was his, to be re-granted by him under certain terms and conditions.

All those who owed *suit of court* could be *amerced* for not attending. As the court was supposed to meet every three weeks, and as some men owned land in more than one manor, the duty must have been very inconvenient, especially as it would often have involved riding or walking several miles. This is borne out by the number of excuses (*essoina*) for absence offered at the beginning of a court and the *fines* for non-attendance which were paid in advance for the whole of the following year.

In areas where common fields were the norm it must be assumed that the court played a key role in the organisation of agriculture, although there is little evidence of this in the rolls themselves. In Hadlow and Hadlow/Lomewood manors, where there were no common fields, this function of the court was probably of little importance. A lesser function of the court was to deal with disputes about trespass and debts up to the value of 40s. The court also elected manor officials such as the reeve or the beadle, normally once a year at Michaelmas.

2. Du Boulay, 1966, 305

The king might also grant the lord of the manor the right to hold a *court leet*. The court leet was usually granted 'with view of frankpledge', at which all men aged twelve and above were obliged to appear and pledge to keep the king's peace. Unlike the more frequent court baron it was usually held only twice a year, at Hokeday and Martinmas, in the autumn and spring. The court leet with *view of frankpledge* exercised many of the functions of the sheriff's twice yearly hundred courts or *tourns* and, according to Du Boulay, often had the same venue.[2] It was valued by landowners as a source of income but also as a means of keeping law and order, dealing with such matters as assaults, obstruction of waterways and highways and control of various trades, especially the brewing of ale and baking of bread. These were matters the king might have reserved for his own courts but chose to leave in the hands of the lord of the manor.

3. Du Boulay, 1966, 303

4. Du Boulay, 1966, 303-304

5. Selden Society, 1891, 70. The Society printed extracts from several manuals which were reprinted in book form in 1967

In theory the lord's steward presided at the courts although on larger estates the understeward or the bailiff must often have stood in for him. The bailiff certainly substituted for the steward on the Kentish manors of the Archbishop of Canterbury at the end of the thirteenth century, where the bailiff swore an oath on taking office, 'loyally to hold the leets and courts in my bailiwick at the due times and usual places and make them profitable to the lord according to right and reason and the custom of the manor'.[3] It is heartening to read that Archbishop Kilwardby also issued a set of instructions to his stewards and bailiffs, 'for we desire and order you who are judges to hold simple courts and instruct those who do not know how to plead in the telling of the truth', nor were his judges to take any present from either party or organise unjust exactions, even for the benefit of the archbishop's finances.[4] One of the manuals has a similar passage.[5]

THE DOCUMENTS

So far we have found only two short sequences of manor court rolls for Hadlow, one between 18 October 1478 and 19 February 1482/3, the other between 7 October 1512 and 28 July 1513. The manor court roll dated 1512/13 is in Staffordshire Record Office, and is part of a large roll of miscellaneous documents relating to the Stafford family possessions in the south-east. It is one of a series of documents written in a clear, legible script, obviously that of a well-educated professional.

The earlier manuscript is by far the longer and far the more interesting because it is nearer in time to the survey, but there is some question of whether it refers to Hadlow manor or to Lomewood manor. One possible explanation is that Lomewood was a small manor or sub-manor which held its own court baron but joined with Hadlow manor for the more formal view of frankpledge. Similar arrangements certainly pertained with Kirtlington and its smaller sister manor, Northbrook, in Oxfordshire, and in the vast manor of Wakefield which was divided into graveships. The word 'Lomewood' only appears in conjunction with the view, the courts baron being introduced simply with the formula, 'Hadlow, court held there,' and the date. Analysis of the various land transactions recorded by these courts shows that a great many of the people involved are familiar from the survey of Hadlow manor and so are the names of tenements and land holdings when they occur. Even if the rolls are those of a separate Lomewood manor, as Hadlow manor had the same lord/lady, the Duke or dowager Duchess of Buckingham, and presumably the same bailiff or steward presiding, its proceedings are of obvious relevance.

The record of one court held for another manor, Hadlow Place, on 30 March 1518, is of some, mainly negative, interest as is a much earlier view of frankpledge (1305) for 'Hadlow Vill'. Records also survive of manor courts held in the manor of Fromonds, 1339-1438, and again from 1596, for the manor of Caustons, 1598-1698, and the manor of Crombury, 1596-1641.

The Hadlow manor court roll of 1512/13 began with the recording of two courts with views of frankpledge held between 10 October 1512 and 9 April the following year. These accounts were followed, on a new membrane, by the record of five 'courts' 'held there', between 7 October 1512 and 11 June 1513, and one 'court of Swan' 'held there', 28 July 1513.

Of the two courts with views of frankpledge, held six months apart, one was closely preceded and the other closely followed by an ordinary court session. Unlike in some other areas the view of frankpledge in Hadlow did not cover the business of the normal manor court but was held separately. After stating the date of the court and the common fine, the two views have the phrase 'Thomas Chaplam tithingman there came with his suit and presented that'. The court's business followed. At the end of the October session arrangements were made for the election of a new tithingman and constable by the Jurats. These were not listed by name. The document concluded with the total sum of the common fine and of the amercements collected. The intervals between ordinary courts varied between five weeks and ten weeks but were always longer than the traditional three weeks. They were introduced with the words 'The Homage presents' and ended with the total of sums collected in reliefs, fines and amercements. In this document Hadlow is the only place mentioned for holding the court.

The Hadlow/Lomewood court rolls were arranged differently. The series began with an account of a view of frankpledge for Hadlow/Lomewood on 6 October 1478. The views appear to have dealt with matters from three different locations, each with its own aletaster, namely Hadlow Street, Goldhill and Stair. Then five courts were held between 4 November 1478 and 22 April 1479, all introduced by the formula 'Hadlow-court held there the -- day of --', no other place being mentioned. The pattern continued; a view of frankpledge held at intervals of roughly six months, interspersed with between three and five courts (baron), held roughly four weeks apart. The format of the courts did not change except that in the views of frankpledge held in May and October 1481 there was no separate aletaster for Goldhill and in April 1482 Goldhill and Stair were taken together. At the end of each court baron a total was given of all the money collected in fines, amercements and relief. The largest amounts for the courts were in October-November because they included fines (2d. or 4d. a head) for those who wanted to be excused attendance for the following year. On those occasions the total could be as much as 8s. The value of a heriot also increased the total. In between, the average collected was 12d. though once it was nothing.

Each of the Hadlow/Lomewood views of frankpledge began with the name of the tithingman, a restatement of the common fine (10s.), and a list of excuses for absence, with the 'fines', usually 2d.- 4d., which bought the right not to attend for the following year. There followed a list of those amerced for non-attendance without an excuse, usually 2d.- 4d. per 'default'. At the end of each court was a list of the names of the Grand

Inquisition later called the Grand Jury, and a total of all the money collected in fines, amercements or relief. The sums were more substantial than from the ordinary courts, on one occasion yielding 70s. 3d. though more usually about 20s.

A new roll was begun in October each year and at the end of the old roll a summary was given of all the fines collected for the year, broken down into categories. For example:

Full total of 2 views and 9 aforesaid courts is 64s. 4d. and ½ farthing

Of this total	20s.	is from the common fine
	6s.	is for remittance of suit of court
8d. ½ farthing		reliefs
	12s.	heriots
	26s 8d	from other perquisites

As in the later Hadlow manor rolls, a new Constable and Tithingman were elected each autumn.

THE COURTS

Both the Hadlow and Hadlow/Lomewood courts baron and views of frankpledge conformed to the general pattern for manor courts discussed above, and the following comments are based on the two series. The survey of 1460 recorded 105 individual names and of these no less than 35 reappeared in the court rolls, although some of these may be family members with the same name as a forebear. If family names instead of individuals are counted, the proportion rises to 28 out of a possible 74.[6] As one might expect there were more people from the survey in the Hadlow/Lomewood rolls which date from 1478, eighteen years later, than in the Hadlow rolls which did not begin until 1512. More names from the survey appeared in the transactions of the court baron than in the view of frankpledge, again unsurprising when it is remembered that one of the main functions of the court baron was registering the change of land ownership and those in the survey were all land owners. Very few of the names which appeared in these transactions were not in the survey and most of the land names were also familiar from it.

6. Individual names in italics mean that they are names which also appear in the survey; if only the surname is in italics, only the family name, not the individual, appears in the survey.

THE COURTS BARON

During the four years covered by the Hadlow/Lomewood rolls 33 changes in land occupation were recorded. The term normally used was that A '*alienated*' the land to B. On seven occasions B was said to have '*purchased*' the land from A. The money levied on these transactions was always referred to as a 'relief', not a 'fine'. Several times fidelity was sworn to the lord for pieces of land held by '*feoffment*' of a third party. In the Hadlow manor rolls of 1512-13 there were six land transfers and here '*feoffment to use*' was the norm. Joint ownership of land seemed to have been common and the majority of the changes resulted in more rather than fewer individuals sharing the holding. On only five occasions was the land transferred as a result of a death and on three of these the lord c l a i m e d a heriot. When John and Richard, the sons of *Thomas Fisher*, inherited Agnes Stabbykobit's lands they had to hand over 'one bullock four years in age, price 12s.'. The *Hale* brothers, inheriting land from their father, *Robert Hale*, had to give the lord, 'one bullock, price 4s.', and *John Fitchet*'s son, Richard, paid one cow, valued at 6s. 8d. If in each case these animals were the tenants' best beast it confirms the importance of cattle to the farmers of Hadlow.

Compared with the value of a heriot, reliefs, claimed by the lord when land changed hands, were very small. They were consistently said to be 'a fourth part of the rent,' ranging from half a farthing to 7d. However, occasionally 'no relief' was recorded 'because according to the custom of the manor coteland does not pay relief'. Once there was no relief 'because the lands are held in fee farm' and once 'because the lands are held by Petyseramuth'. There was no record of an entry fine as opposed to a relief. Disputes about trespass and debt made up the rest of the business of the court.

In a typical entry for a Hadlow/Lomewood court held 4 November 1478, those fined for 'remittance of their suit this year', included *Elizabeth Colepeper*, *William Wotton*, *John Bishop*, *John Fromond of Goldhill*, Richard *Fromond*, *Peter Fisher*, *Martin Coggar* and the *heirs of Richard Bishop*, *Richard Styles*, and Margaret *Burgeys*. The court also dealt with the admission of two new tenants, *John Somer* and Richard Aysschedown to lands alienated to them by Thomas *Stopperfield* and Thomas and *Nicholas Bourne*, for which they swore fidelity and paid 4d. and 1 farthing relief. Thomas Tewssnoth, William *Godyng*, *James Grosse* and *John Croucher* were involved in pleas of debt and *John Symonds* was elected reeve.

The one account of a court held for Hadlow Place manor, on 30 March 1518, followed a very similar formula. It began with a list of 'Jurors, homagium'. It is noticeable that not one of these twelve nor any of the fourteen others appearing at the court, were mentioned in the survey of Hadlow manor. This document too includes a heriot, 'of one brown ox'. More importantly, a day was appointed for *all* tenants to appear to prepare 'a new rental' for the lord. The document followed and was presumably the reason why this one court record was preserved.

COURTS WITH A VIEW OF FRANKPLEDGE

The courts with view of frankpledge provide a glimpse of village life. Numerous individuals with the same names as those from the survey were recorded going about their lives, remarkable when it is remembered that we are looking at documents dating from between eighteen and fifty years later. Unfortunately the time lag does make it difficult to deduce much from the number of people who appeared in the court rolls but did not appear in the survey. It would have been useful to form an idea of the proportion of landless people in the manor. Many of those with trades regulated by the views or punished for minor crimes may not have owned land but it is often difficult to be sure if new names represent those without land or simply newcomers to the manor since 1460.

While it is of great interest to follow the land transactions of individuals from the survey nothing compares with learning more personal details. *Thomas Bishop*, of that seemingly respectable family, was twice in trouble, once when he attacked John Galton, 'with a *biniculus* called A styk and thrashed him contrary to the lord king's peace', and again when he, 'offered insult to Nicholas *Taylor* with a round staff". The first time *Thomas Fisher* and Richard Kebyll stood surety for him, the second time (only a year later) the court sentenced him to pay 2d. Standing surety was rather more than standing bail. It meant Thomas and Richard were friends or relatives who were prepared to stake their reputation on his good behaviour and support the truth of his statements. What of Isabelle *Somer*, regularly amerced for brewing ale 'against the assize'? Was she wife, sister, daughter or merely cousin of *John Somer* the shopkeeper of Church Street? Was Richard Miller who scandalised the community by maintaining a 'disorderly house' with his own wife as the centrepiece, related to anyone we know from the survey?

The way the court was organised seems to have remained consistent over the years. The earliest record of a view 'de hundr' de Littlefeld de villa de Hadlo' was dated the Wednesday next after 'Hokeday' in the year 1305. It began by giving the communal fine of 10s. (which was to remain the same at least until 1512) and went on to list those making excuse for absence. It then named Nicholas *Fromond* 'borsholder' or tithingman of Hadlow, 'who with the whole borgh (or tithing) presents that...'. Here followed a list of six offences against the peace, in two of which blood was drawn, indicating a more violent society than appeared in the court records of 150 years later when one or two assaults per court were the norm. The court then named four aletasters, including a Nicholas *Fromond*, who between them presented twenty-eight people for brewing 'against the assize', one of them being William *Fromond*.

This pattern had not varied very much by the time of the first of the Hadlow/ Lomewood views, on 6 October 1478. The court began with the name of the tithingman 'there as sworn' who came with his tithing and presented that 'they give the lord 10s. as common fine as from ancient times'. Next, 26 people who had 'made default of their attendance at this view' were listed and their amercement of 2d. each recorded.

A butcher's shop

The next section, where various trades were regulated, took up a large part of the court's business. John Walter, butcher, was amerced 2d. for selling his meat at 'excessive profit', a charge to be repeated at each of the following nine views, including two in 1512 and 1513. He was joined later by John, then Richard, Wyks, and in the 1500s by three others including a Richard *Newman*. Not all butchers were dishonest, however, as at least one, *John Fisher,* appeared in the roll for other reasons but was never charged as a butcher. The butchers were followed by a single tanner, John *Farman,* seemingly amerced for operating outside the borough. Described as a 'red tanner', presumably handling red leather, that is leather from cattle and horses, he was amerced each session. In 1512 his successor, Thomas *Farman,* 'a common tanner of white tawed leather', that is soft pliant leather from sheep, was also amerced 2d.

The number of millers amerced for taking 'excessive toll' during the five-year period covered by the rolls would seem to bear out Chaucer's cynical attitude. No less than 11 names appeared, most of them again and again. The amount of the amercement varied from 2d. to 6d. but one miller, Thomas Dunbar, surely not a local man, always seemed to attract the higher penalty. Were his tolls even more 'excessive' than those of the other millers or was it an example of national prejudice?

Hadlow does not appear to have had any mechanism for the regulation of the sale of bread. No mention was made of anyone being presented for breaking the assize, although there were several instances in local wills of money being left for the distribution of bread to the poor at the will maker's funeral and 'month's mind'. We must assume that Hadlow had no professional baker. Perhaps the community was too scattered and housewives found it more practical to bake their own bread.

The ale wife. A misericord carving from a church.

The regulation of brewing, however, was a serious matter reported at the end of the court proceedings. Each area, Hadlow Street, Gold Hill and Stair, had its own ale taster and no less than 41 of those 'licensed to brew' were amerced over the four year period. This was brewing on a very small scale. Ale without hops did not keep well and had to be made in small quantities for speedy use. However, the amercements, always 2d. or 4d., were the same as those imposed on butchers and millers, which implies that the ale sold was of similar value. Forty-one brewers must represent a fair amount of ale and these were only those caught 'breaking the assize' or selling before their ale had been tested. The vast majority of the brewers were female, as was usual at the time. One, Isabelle *Somer*, was amerced in every one of the views held between October 1478 and October 1481. What was wrong with her ale? How did she keep any customers? Or perhaps it was so good that they were prepared to put up with short measure, one of the commonest offences. It is tempting to see the amercements as merely a type of value added tax or licence fee taken by the lord though not every brewer was amerced at each view.

These entries show that there were other means than farming or fishing for making some part of a living in Hadlow. As well as the regulated trades, other occupations were mentioned in the rolls. There were two carpenters, Henry Pottekyn and William Norton, John *Newman* a 'poulter' (not to be confused with John *Newman*, labourer), William Shaw, 'a dyer of old cloth', three clerks, Ralph Houghton, Thomas Aland, and Thomas Down, and one Richard Shoemaker, as well as labourers and serving men. Probably most of these men owned land but such occupations help explain how some of the holdings could be so small.

The next section of the court dealt with general offences. They could be described as of two types, civil and criminal, all fairly petty. Of the 'civil' offences, 30 out of 35 in the earlier rolls (1478-1482) and 6 out of 12 in the later rolls (1512-13) were about damage to the 'highway'. A typical entry reads 'that the highway is out of repair and of uneven surface towards Richard Carter's land from Sagon Cross as far as Rysebreyge Lane, thus causing great danger to the countryside because the same Richard's ditches have not been cleaned; now he is amerced 6d. as above'. This complaint of ditches not being cleaned was repeated on 27 of the 30 occasions when the highways were declared in a bad state of repair. Often the amercement was followed by the threat of a much heavier 'penalty', if the ditch was not cleaned before the next view. Even the Lady of the manor herself was not exempt. In April 1480 it was reported, 'that the highway is much out of repair at Castle Field because the ditches of the most honourable lady the Duchess of Buckingham have not been cleaned; now she is amerced as above and she is presented to amend same before the next court under penalty of 40d'. She was amerced again the next year, once in respect of the highway at Castle Field but also at Hvet Gate. The following year the highway was still very dangerous at Castle Field 'for want of cleaning of the ditches' but now it was the 'farmer of the aforesaid field' (unnamed) who was amerced 4d. and threatened with a penalty of 3s.4d. if he had not cleaned them by the next court. This was about the time that the duchess died.

As well as problems with ditches Thomas Tewesnoth was accused of breaking up and digging sand from the highway at Berghwys and John *Fruter* for causing damage with his untrimmed oak trees. There were four occasions when bridges were said to be broken and individuals were amerced, and a further two, at the bridge at Solomons and later at Goldhill bridge, when the damage was said to be 'by neglect of the whole tithing'. On three occasions common waterways were stopped up and in 1512 Henry Fane enclosed part of Common Lane between Goldhill and Jordans Lake for which he was amerced 10d.

Sixteen cases of assault were recorded during the six views of frankpledge held between October 1478 and May 1482, and one in the two courts held in October 1512 and April 1513. Usually this was described as 'offering insult' 'contrary to the lord king's peace'. If it was done with 'the fist' the crime attracted the comparatively light amercement of 2d. Attacks with some type of weapon were sometimes amerced more severely, especially when the offender 'drew blood'. The weapon was always described. *Thomas Fisher* for instance was attacked with 'a staff called werehokys', *Thomas Bishop* 'thrashed' John Galton 'with a biniculus called a stick' and later 'offered insult' to Nicholas *Taylor* with a 'round staff', while Simon Everard, one of the millers, used a 'certain ryfyle' (presumably only as a threat as he was amerced the usual 2d.). An attack by Richard Kebbyll with a 'knife called a hanggar' resulted in the comparatively heavy amercement of 12d. More serious still was the attack by the carpenter Henry Pottekyn who hit John Welde on the head with a 'hegebyll, entering his brain from which blood flowed'. He fled the manor and the officers of the court were unable to apprehend him. Sometimes we can see the follow up of an attack. In the view held in April 1470 *James Grosse* was amerced 2d. for offering insult to Isabel *Newman*, but then *John Newman*, labourer, was amerced 4d. for offering insult 'with a staff' to *James Grosse*.

Clearing a watercourse

Theft was much less common than assault and taken far more seriously, judging by the amercements. There were only three cases. Alice *Symonds* broke into Thomas Tewsnorth's close, 'forcibly with a staff and knife' and stole a lamb worth 3d. and drove away a bullock. For this she was amerced 40d. as was Thomas *Symonds* for attacking the same Thomas Tewsnorth and stealing 4d. A poor labourer, William Ayshdownn, was amerced 6s.8d. for stealing half a measure of wheat, value 8d., from *Nicholas Bourn's* barn.

Only one case did not fit either category. In the view of April 1513 the tithingman presented that 'William Bugge harbours a suspected concubine and insulted Richard Miller's wife in that Richard's house and had carnal knowledge of her contrary to the king's peace'. He was amerced 12d. That the story was more complicated than appeared at first is shown by the next entry. Richard Miller was amerced 8d. because 'he keeps a reputed disorderly house and knowing that the said William cohabits with the said Richard's wife....he permitted and assisted William and concealed his deeds'.

Each of the Hadlow/Lomewood courts ended with a list of the 'Grand Inquisition', usually twelve men, while the later Hadlow courts recorded 'the Jurats'. Nearly all of the members of the inquiry that drew up the survey were also members of the Grand Inquisition at one time or another. At the October view each year officers were elected for the next twelve months, as tithingman, constable, and ale tasters. These, with two 'afferatores' or assessors who assessed the amercements, were the court officials in Hadlow, presided over by the Lord's chosen bailiff.

COMPARISON WITH OTHER MANORS

How do the procedures and contents of Hadlow's courts compare with those in other areas and with the 'ideals' presented in the manuals? The manuals, although written and later printed at intervals over several hundred years, are in general agreement over the proper conduct of the manorial courts. Samples of court rolls have been examined, coming from four different areas and ranging in date from the earliest, beginning in 1348, to the latest which ends in 1650. The samples are:

Wakefield, Yorkshire, 1348-50
Walsham le Willows, Suffolk, 1351-99
Kirtlington, Oxfordshire, 1500-1650
Tottenham, Middlesex, 1510-1531

In 1348 Wakefield was part of the dower lands of Joan de Bar, the Countess Warenne. Since the Conquest it had been part of a well-organised estate belonging to an aristocratic family of similar status to the Clares. Centred on the small town of Wakefield it consisted of two large blocks of land divided into eleven graveships, each under a grave or reeve. It included upland areas with scattered communities. The courts for the manor were held in three different locations where each graveship had its own representative. Next in date are the rolls from Walsham le Willows, a vill in the fenland, ten miles north-east of Bury St.Edmunds. The vill had a population estimated at between 1300 and 1500, but no great house or resident great family. Walsham manor was the larger of the two manors of the vill, containing approximately six hundred acres. There is an almost continuous series of rolls covering the period 1351-99. Kirtlington, one of two manors in a parish of about 3,582 acres in Oxfordshire, and its smaller sister manor, Northbrook, both owed suit to Kirtlington court. They were both part of one, typically Midland, field system which contained at least 700 acres of common land. Again there was no great house or resident aristocratic family. The rolls show the development of the court between 1500 and 1650. Tottenham was already, in 1510, showing characteristics of a more urban manor. Although it still contained some common land much enclosure had already taken place. Merchants from nearby London were buying land and the views held there show much greater evidence of 'strangers' passing through the manor. It had been granted by Henry VIII to Sir William Compton. Situated in a low-lying area close to marshes, Tottenham shared Hadlow's preoccupation with scouring ditches. The section of rolls examined here ends in 1531.

7. Selden Society, 1891, 68

Hadlow conformed quite strictly to the 'official' pattern for holding its courts. One manual states explicitly ' that the court of the view of frankpledge should be holden but twice a year' and that 'all male laymen of the age of twelve years or above should be in a frankpledge or, which is the same, in a *tithing*'.[7] Hadlow's views were held twice a year at six monthly intervals and we have a reference to two new members of the King's assize, Thomas Bacon and John Hogyn, 'aged twelve years and more,' being sworn in. In between the views, courts baron, called simply 'courts', were held at intervals of roughly four weeks rather than the three weeks recommended by the manuals. In Hadlow a strict distinction was made between the two types of court and the business conducted in them. This was not true in Kirtlington, where normally only two courts were held each year, one at Michaelmas, with a view of frankpledge with the proceedings of the court baron at the end, and one at Easter which was a court baron only. In Walsham the lord did not have the authority to hold a court leet with view of frankpledge but did deal with assizes of bread and ale and poaching offences in his court baron. These were only held about twice a year. Wakefield's court baron was extremely active, obviously the arena for the settlement of all manner of local disputes and covering many of the functions of the *turn* or view in other manors. Here too the *turn* or view often included business more properly covered by the court baron. In Tottenham the pattern was nearer to Hadlow with two regular views held each year, interspersed with courts baron, though there were fewer than in Hadlow and they were sometimes merely tacked on at the end of the record of the view.

The court officials were much the same in each manor. The court rolls of Hadlow never mentioned the name of a presiding steward, unlike those of Walsham le Willows where the current steward's name was recorded and where he seems to have held the courts with the aid of a recording clerk. At Kirtlington and Wakefield too the steward appears to have been the judge of the court. The steward of the vast Clare estates would probably have been far too important to preside at a small court like Hadlow. However, one of the sample letters quoted in a manual was from the Clare family steward to all the bailiffs throughout the honour of Clare; 'we command you that each of you do cause

8. Maitland, 1888, 70

his court to be summonsed for the day named below to meet us'.[8] This would imply that at least from time to time the steward would be present to check the way the court was run, and indeed on at least one occasion in Hadlow the bailiff retained custody of a stray

9. 23 March 1479

animal on the express order of the steward.[9] Normally it was the bailiff who was the lord's representative and who presided over the court. Even in the other manors the bailiff (or sergeant/grave in Wakefield) had an important function, as the local man, in the choosing of juries and carrying out the orders of the court.

At Hadlow each view ended with a list of the twelve members of the Grand Inquisition, later called the Grand Jury, and the ale tasters and assessors were also named. At the view held in the autumn a constable and tithingman were elected and sworn in to serve for the year. Much less regularly the intermediate 'courts' recorded the election of reeves and beadles. All the other manors named assessors and ale tasters. Tottenham, mentioned a constable, but only once. Kirtlington courts changed over the period covered by the rolls. In 1470 there were ale tasters but no constable, later the ale tasters' job was done by the tithingmen and the constable became the most prominent manorial official. The courts baron of both Walsham and Kirtlington noted the election of lesser manorial officers such as haywards, woodwards, foresters, pinders, herds, and surveyors of the common fields, in addition to the reeve and beadle, reflecting the importance the courts had in these areas for the organisation of common agricultural matters. In Hadlow only reeves and beadles were elected. The general impression is that the Hadlow courts, were both more regular and more formal, making a clear cut division between the functions of the court baron and the court with view of frankpledge, a situation which was only approached by Tottenham among the other manors considered.

The number of Jurors and their social mix make another point of comparison.

10. Grant, Internet pages

11. Griffiths, 270

12. Winchester, 2000, 42

13. Lock, 2002, 8

It has been argued[10] that the jury was selected from the 'chief tenants of the manor'. This was certainly true in Kirtlington according to Matthew Griffiths's account of the proceedings of the manor court there. In a detailed analysis, he considered that 'juries were dominated by the larger farmers and the middle-ranking copyholders of the parish', although, 'occasionally lesser men were jurors or tithingmen' and it was from this lower class that officials such as haywards were chosen.[11] In 1528 all twelve of the jurors were fairly substantial men and the constable, who was to serve for fourteen years, was deemed a 'gentleman' in the lay subsidy of 1523. Selected by the steward or bailiff, most Kirtlington juries numbered between fifteen and twenty for a court with view and twelve for a simple court baron. We have no detailed examination of the Wakefield jurors but Angus Winchester has commented of the area in general that 'decision making at the manor courts was firmly in the hands of the more substantial members of the community'.[12] He shows that over a six year period the jurors were drawn from a small pool in each community, one serving in each court and a quarter serving in more than half the courts. The juries could consist of up to twenty-four men. In Walsham the jury 'ill defined and subject to variation' numbered between ten and eighteen.[13] In Hadlow, during the period of the rolls, the jury for the view varied only between eleven and thirteen men. The 'homagium', or jury for the court baron was never specified by name or even number. The Grand Jury certainly contained the names of some substantial farmers, such as *John Bishop* and *Thomas* and *Peter Fisher*, but it also contained John *Newman,* whether the 'maltster' or 'labourer' is unspecified; John *Newman*, labourer, certainly served as an ale taster. Constables and assessors came from much the same group. Many of the jurors do not appear in the survey but this could be accounted for by the passage of time rather than the fact that they had no land.

The relative importance of the two types of court differed from area to area. Walsham only had a court baron which carried out some of the functions of the court with view, including the assizes of bread and ale. In Wakefield the regulation of trade was confined to the twice yearly '*turn*', often recorded on the back of the record of the court baron held the same day. It was that court, held frequently at three different locations in the huge manor, which was of greater importance to its inhabitants, including many of the functions elsewhere covered by the view. Tottenham had the traditional mix of functions

Some manor courts passed by-laws on agriculture

spread between the two courts while Hadlow seems to show, from its way of recording the proceedings, that the court baron was of less importance.

The sums levied by the courts baron varied very little in regard to amercements for absence, failure to pursue or defend a suit, or permission to settle a dispute. They were nearly always between 2d. and 4d. By far the most numerous cases pursued were cases of debt, followed by trespass. In Kirtlington and Wakefield some details of the actual disputes were given, the sum of the debt, how it was incurred, how damage was done during trespass and its extent. In Hadlow only the amercement due to the court was noted. Hadlow was also unusual in that pleas of trespass were few. In other manors, particularly Walsham, trespass, often on the lord's property, was common and sometimes amerced more heavily if damage was done. A difference between the functions of the court baron in Hadlow and in Kirtlington, was that in the latter the court was used to pass detailed by-laws. For example, in Kirtlington it was specified that no more than 40 sheep should be put in the West Field and no more than one cow per cottager on the common. Angus Winchester also talks of this important function of the court in the border country but the Wakefield rolls show no evidence of it. No regulations of this kind were made by the court in Hadlow, neither did the manor court there seem to interfere in the upkeep of tenants' houses as was the case in both Walsham and Tottenham. In Wakefield regularly, and Walsham occasionally, there were also fines for marriage, and, once, for the birth of an illegitimate child. The impression is that Hadlow inhabitants were less at risk from interference by the manor court in their personal lives.

When it came to reliefs or entry fines paid on inheritance or sale or transfer of property they were also at a great advantage over the inhabitants of the other manors. The standard relief seems to have been a quarter of a year's rent rather than half a year or even a year's rent paid for entry fines in other areas. During the years recorded this was as little as half a farthing and only twice more than 5d., once 7d. and once 2s.4d. The first of these was on inheritance so presumably represented relief on the whole of a man's holding, the second involved a joint venture by four substantial landholders taking over a whole tenement. It was only when a heriot was claimed, in one case a bullock worth 12s., that the incoming tenant had to pay a relief even approaching the value of the entry fines paid in the other manors. In Walsham they ranged from 6d. to 26s.8d., usually between 1s. and 2s. In Tottenham they were between 11d. and £6.13s.4d., usually over 5s., and often over £1. On the few occasions when a relief rather than a fine was paid in other manors it too was quite light. One of the reasons the reliefs in Hadlow were so small may be that most land was freehold and land holdings were comparatively small. As Witney has argued, where land was less burdened with services due to the lord a much smaller sized plot could support a family.[14]

14. Witney, 2000, lxxi-lxxii

Apart from the private examination of women landowners to make sure their consent to a transaction was genuine, there is no evidence in any of the manors of interference in the free transfer of land, provided the relief or fine was paid and the lord's authority acknowledged. However, the earlier rolls from Wakefield and Walsham reflect a society more closely regulated by its courts, while Kirtlington used its courts to organise its agricultural community.

Walsham had no court leet but in the other manors the court leet with view of frankpledge was the main instrument the lord had for controlling social behaviour. One of the main functions of the court was to regulate trade. In Kirtlington, Matthew Griffiths is of the opinion that, 'in 1470 it was the ale tasters who regulated the assizes of bread and ale and other local trades'.[15] It may well have been the same in Hadlow, they certainly seem to have been fairly important officials whose duties were supervised by the grand jury who had to swear that they had been carried out efficiently. In Tottenham too ale tasters were regularly elected. In Walsham, this function of the court was carried out by the ordinary court baron. The main difference between Hadlow and the other manors was

15. Griffiths, 277

Stocks were purchased in Tottenham but not mentioned in Hadlow

that whereas brewers, millers, butchers and leather workers were all amerced for various misdemeanours, there was no assize of bread. In comparison with Kirtlington, Hadlow's brewers seem to have offended regularly rather than just occasionally. The amercements charged in the manors were similar, 2d. or 4d. with an occasional 6d.

942.05

HAD

BENCHMARK

BUSINESS TRAINING

PERSONNEL DIRECTOR:

Like Tottenham, a large part of the business of the court in Hadlow was the maintenance of local facilities, mainly the highways. In both Tottenham and Hadlow the state of the ditches was a major cause of concern and numerous inhabitants of both manors were amerced, initially moderately but for a repeated failure to comply, quite severely, in theory if not in practice. Encroachment on or damage to the highway was also punished as was the blocking or diversion of water courses, and the failure to maintain bridges.

Another aspect of the court's work was the prosecution of minor crimes of a criminal rather than civil type. In other areas of the country one of the main phrases appearing in the rolls was to do with the 'hue and cry' raised when a crime had been committed and a criminal had to be apprehended. The manual specified 'he who levies the hue wrongfully shall be amerced, also he against whom it is levied rightfully'.[16] If the hue was raised unnecessarily all involved were amerced, if justly the offender. Strangely, of the five manors it was only in Wakefield that the phrase was used. Otherwise the types of crime were very similar. Assault was common, probably more so in Tottenham than in Hadlow or Kirtlington. Stealing was not very common and heavily amerced, though again there were more instances in Tottenham. Each community also seemed to have had an occasional case of someone 'keeping a disorderly house' or 'harbouring suspicious strangers', but Hadlow had no cases of scolds or 'barrators', nor of amercements for playing at dice, cards, football, or for neglect of archery.

In the three later series of court rolls the full range of society appeared before the courts, not just the court baron to register their land transactions but also before the views, to be amerced for various offences both civil and criminal. In Kirtlington the Prior of Bicester was amerced for default of suit and members of the Arden family, lords of the manor, were several times presented for breaches of custom or by-law. In Tottenham the Prioress of Clerkenwell, Sir Robert Southwell and Sir Thomas Lovell were all amerced on several occasions for failure to scour their ditches. In Hadlow *Thomas Bishop*, a substantial landowner, was twice amerced for assault and no less a person than the lady of the manor, the dowager Duchess of Buckingham was amerced twice for allowing her ditches to overflow. The earlier courts at Walsham and Wakefield do not show such independence. It would appear, however, that by the late fifteenth century the manor court represented not only the lord's will but also that of the local community, and in some areas had an authority over and above that of the lord himself. Of the five manors studied the inhabitants of the manor of Hadlow appear to have been the most fortunate. Although in comparison with the other manors the courts were both more regular and more formal, they impinged less on everyday life, and in general the fines they imposed were lighter.

16. Maitland, 1888, 83

CHAPTER 3

HADLOW BETWEEN 1460 & 1600

Historians regard the fourteenth and fifteenth centuries as a long bleak period of famines, plagues, war, declining population, and economic stagnation. But it is an ill wind that blows nobody any good, and in hard times some people spot new opportunities where others see nothing but misfortune, and profit from them. Today we see farmers in the midst of a similar bleak phase of fortune, and watch some of them adopting alternative strategies and making a success of them. So we can reasonably guess that the same mixed picture obtained in 1460. Moreover, having the benefit of hindsight, we know that the next century developed into an era of remarkable enterprise and economic progress, so that we should expect some faint signs of economic revival to show as early as 1460.

Our survey first points us back to a distant past when a farmholding of 30-36 acres was deemed a standard sufficiency for a family. But then it shows clearly how subdivided the holdings had become through the practice of gavelkind and the free market in land. Yet some of our small peasants were plainly building up larger than average holdings, by taking up pieces of their neighbours' land as they fell vacant, acquiring other more scattered pieces, and sometimes marrying a woman holding Hadlow manor land that was then added to their own.

Thus the low state of economic life immediately after the Black Death gradually improved, and hard days gave way to hopes of a better future. In that spirit, Christopher Dyer has recently depicted a fifteenth-century scene that modifies the bleak accounts of the pessimists, preferring to view it as a transitional phase that was already showing signs of fresh enterprise.[1] In that same spirit, we can interpret the scene in Hadlow in 1460 where some families like the Bishops had become conspicuously acquisitive towards land down at the Medway. Even the compiling of a survey by the lord can be interpreted as a sign of the landowner taking stock of his/her estate with fresh interest.

So when in 1581 the steward copied out the Hadlow survey of 1460 afresh, we should judge that as another moment of stocktaking undertaken in an increasingly optimistic mood; moreover, it matches similar activity in Wrotham, a next door parish, where the steward at much the same time was rescuing from obscurity records of former surveys and scrutinizing them anew. Our Hadlow steward, for his part, endeavoured to bring the old survey up to date by scribbling in the margin the names of tenants who had followed those of 1460 and those in current occupation. Unfortunately for us, he does not seem to have done a very thorough job. In the interval of some 120 years, some three generations had come and gone. All the tenants must have changed, yet he only scribbled changes in some cases and not in others. We cannot therefore judge accurately the new pattern of landholding that had resulted. We would have expected a trend towards larger holdings and fewer tenants to have continued, since that is what was happening in other parts of the country in the course of the sixteenth century. Farming became prosperous again, food prices rose substantially, many landowners returned to the direct farming of their home farms, while a class of substantial yeomen farmers also emerged. But all these events lay silently in the background; what our survey emphasises is changes in the identity of some of the influential landowning and farming families. We can also make use of other Hadlow records to fill in a picture of other economic developments that gave a new look to the Elizabethan age.

In 1581 somewhat less than half of the old families were still prominent, including the Bishops and the Fishers, both of whom had taken up yet more land on the manor. Some seventeen family surnames had survived from 1460, compared with 21 that were new, though the designation 'new' may include women of old families whose surnames had changed through marriage. Also others will have belonged to old families who had

1. Dyer, 2005

long held land in Hadlow but it belonged to the sub-manors. We notice some surnames that had changed their spoken form and spelling: Broke looks like the old Broker, Farman became Ferman, and Steyle became Style (and we still have a house in the parish called Style Place). Henry Hextall who had held so many scattered pieces of land in the manor in 1460, and probably held some administrative role in the service of the Duke of Buckingham, had evidently left no descendants, for his lands were dispersed among five people, four of whom came from old families, the Somers, Fishers, Crudds, and Bishops. The Hextall name had entirely disappeared from Hadlow, though it would be long remembered in neighbouring East Peckham because William Hextall had built and lived in Hextall Place.

A noticeable feature of the survey of 1460 was the absence of any attempt to identify the tenures by which the land was held. In most surveys that were being undertaken by 1581 this was deemed crucial information, but no attempt was made in this revision to add anything on that score. We do have a rental of Hadlow manor in 1587 that differentiates them, though without inspiring much confidence in its completeness. It named but did not identify a first group of tenants (probably free tenants), a second group as tenants at will, and a third as tenants for years. The occasion for the rental was the conveyance of the manor to Sir George Carey, (the Queen's cousin), and the incoming lord seized the opportunity to come to a new agreement about rents with David Willard who was expanding his activities in shipping iron from Tonbridge and Hadlow.[2]

The new settlement by which Sir George Carey raised the rent paid by David Willard draws attention to a highly important aspect of the economic changes taking

place in and around Hadlow; the farming is more fully dealt with in the next chapter. The production of iron affected Tonbridge and South Frith more than Hadlow, but the finding of a heavy, carefully shaped, iron bowl buried in North Frith park yields fairly conclusive evidence that some forging of iron was carried on there. Certainly, the burning of the wood for charcoal took place in the Frith, for Hadlow streams and the river Medway through Hadlow lay conveniently near to carry it all to the furnaces and forges in Tonbridge; and David Willard's diversion of one stream at Fishall to suit himself is documented below.

The speed with which the timber in North Frith was being destroyed resulted in the lease of woodland for 40 years in North and South Frith being cut short, as those renting it declined to pay any further rent.[3] It is difficult fully to comprehend all the many other consequences that surrounded this dramatic change in the landscape. The woodlands were ancient, and enormous human effort was required to cut down oak trees that could have been as much as five hundred years old. Mick Rodgers, farming at North Frith (and still repairing the paling round the park!), uses power tools, but he marvels to think of the human strength and time needed to cut down so much timber. The men will all have come from Hadlow and Tonbridge, perhaps from Shipbourne too, and so a pressing demand for workmen must have wrought a major change in the expectations of Hadlow menfolk. They may also have reflected sadly on the loss of the hunting that followed, for they had had many a good night's sport poaching deer in North Frith in the 1530s (see Chapter 15).

The iron industry had received its first strong stimulus to enterprise in this neighbourhood from the Sydneys of Penshurst. To begin with, the effects were felt in the vicinity of Robertsbridge and Lamberhurst. Only subsequently did they spread to Tonbridge and South Frith, and it was then that greedy eyes fastened on the timber in North Frith as well. Thus with remarkable speed its woodland was stripped, with little

2. CKS, U38 / M1

A curious 'bowl' of iron found in North Frith. Opinions differ as to its use; one suggestion is that it may be the rear portion of a siege cannon.

3. Thirsk, 2000, 87

43

subsequent success in coppicing or fresh planting. Those involved did not altogether neglect the need to conserve the woodland. The documents suggest that leases to the iron founders insisted on their reinstating the woodlands. But the ironmasters failed to do so, and this accusation was specifically directed at Willard in 1586. It may not have been entirely his fault. A different lawsuit against the Bishop family described

Old trackway through the woods at North Frith. Old woodland on the left, coppiced woodland to the right

a tumult when Tonbridge men violently resisted the planting of fresh coppice after the land had been cropped with wheat. One can imagine a fierce argument raging between those wanting bread rather than fuel for iron casting. The result was that new farms were laid out across a great swathe of former hunting parkland, and the memory lives on in such names as Trench Farm and Little Trench Farm.[4]

4. NA, E178 / 1093; Stac. 2 / 5; Chalklin, 2004, 103, 109, 112-3

Some of the Hadlow people that saw the process at closest quarters were Thomas Somer, Thomas Barton, Wyatt and Michael Playne, Alexander and Lawrence Salmon, Henry Stubberfield, William Weller, Walter Trice and more (all from Hadlow). They were summoned by a Commission, issuing from the Court of Exchequer, to assemble at the Lodge in South Frith by 9am on December 10, 1570, and conduct an enquiry. Their task was to determine the present, reduced value of South Frith, Postern, Cage, and North Frith Parks, and so it was that they testified to the fact that the woods were now 'well nigh spent'.[5]

5. NA, E178 / 1093

We have already seen how the Staffords, Dukes of Buckingham, were the ruling family in Hadlow in 1460 and for twenty years after, when Anne, the Dowager Duchess was in charge. For all we know to the contrary, the administration of the estate in her time ran smoothly. But a stormy period in the life of the last duke ended in an accusation of treason against him, his execution, and the forfeiture to the Crown of the entire estate in 1521. We can only guess at the disruption this caused to administrative routines on Hadlow manor. What is clear is that it brought a crowd of speculative courtiers and local gentry onto the scene, at a time when economic life in general was reviving, and the dissolution of the monasteries in the next decade would bring another large quantity of land onto the market. That further stimulated the expectations and schemes of acquisitive gentlemen, while wealth in lay hands was also increasing. The ambitions of Henry VIII at the same time created a demand for more ample state revenues that could only be met by picking the pockets of his subjects. They faced a demand for higher taxation, which turned the first half of the sixteenth century into what W. G. Hoskins has called The Age of Plunder.

Edward Stafford, the last Duke of Buckingham, who was beheaded by Henry VIII

Along with a changing economic ethos, social and spiritual aspects of Hadlow life were also much altered during the sixteenth century. Historians working in other parts of the country have noted a significant increase in the numbers of people claiming the title of gentleman, and acquiring manorial, or near-manorial estates. This obliged some of them to build entirely new houses, and to settle in hamlets rather than villages. We have noted already in 1460 the Culpepers and Fromonds as gentry families owning sub-manors here. But the Culpepers did not live in Hadlow, and although the Fromonds did, they were modest parish gentry who do not appear to have taken part in public affairs, and they had virtually gone from Hadlow before the end of the sixteenth century. (See Chapter 13 for more on the Fromond family.) The most prominent Hadlow gentry from 1533 until 1551 were the Fanes. We can be sure that Sir Ralph Fane, until his execution in 1552, brought the flavour and the latest news of London life to Hadlow, since he was closely involved at court as a Gentleman Pensioner; and he almost certainly entertained some high-ranking visitors at Hadlow Place. Then the Fanes were followed by the Rivers at Fishall from the 1560s onwards, and they formed a longer-lasting bond with Hadlow, though without leaving any great memorial by building a substantial house. (See Chapter 13 for more on both these families.)

Both the Fanes and the Rivers families, however, almost certainly made a significant contribution to the spiritual life of Hadlow in this century of religious reformation. Both were devout Protestants, though they have left no strong memory of this loyalty in our documents, and we only find the evidence by digging deep. Protestant sympathies in the Weald are a long story starting with the Lollards at least from the fifteenth century. Most evidence then focuses on Cranbrook and Tenterden rather than on Tonbridge, though heretics were found in West Malling, Brenchley, and Yalding, and one man, called Richard Herberd of Hadlow, was under suspicion for keeping heretical books in 1431.[6] A clue to some of the same sympathies is found in the different styles of early wills of the Bealde family, not always in what they did or said, but rather in their silences. A traditional Catholic preamble to a will contained bequests for masses for the soul or for lights and images, while a Protestant will omitted such things; and some, of course, showed mixed sympathies. Richard Bealde in 1456 was a conformist Catholic, leaving his soul to God, the blessed Virgin Mary and all the saints. He left money for 300 masses to be celebrated at Aylesford for his soul and the souls of all his benefactors. In 1491, his son, Lawrence Bealde, on the other hand, left his soul simply to God Almighty, and in giving money for works of mercy, he defined them as being for 'foul ways and poor maidens' marriages'. His spare text almost certainly would have been read by his contemporaries who knew him as a judicious statement that avoided charges of heresy.

Reading more wills between 1500 and 1560 for four parishes in and round Tonbridge, Alison Williams concluded that while the Tonbridge area was more strongly Protestant than the country as a whole, the Hadlow wills were the most conservative in her sample in the early years.[7] But the coming of two new resident gentry families to Hadlow from 1533 onwards changed the situation. Everything suggests that both the Fanes and the Rivers families played an influential role through their support for Protestantism. Ralph Fane left no clear statement of his religious sympathies, but as he was closely connected with Protector Somerset's circle, his Protestant convictions can be assumed, and were in accord with those of his wife. Her fervent Protestantism is on record in Foxe's *Acts and Monuments* where she was described as 'a special nurse, and a great supporter' of imprisoned Protestants', that is to say, those who were persecuted in Mary's reign. She corresponded with them, exchanged books and spiritual advice, and may have disseminated their prison writings.[8] In Hadlow, she was the mistress at Hadlow Place from 1533 until some time around 1558. She had no children, so she removed to London, where she died in 1568, and was buried in St Andrew's church, Holborn.

The Rivers family were also dedicated to the reformed faith, choosing a simple, even austere style of life, judging, at least, by their wills that prescribe the form of their funerals. Lady Joan Rivers, in particular, attracts attention as a devoted mother, commanding the respect and loyalty of her children (see more in Chapter 13). In short, these two gentry families seem to have offered strong leadership in the Protestant cause.

It is difficult to generalize about how things stood in Hadlow in 1600 compared with 1460. Much had changed in religious, economic, and social life. Almost certainly people wondered what could possibly lie ahead for so much of the future seemed uncertain. The Queen was an old lady, unpredictable, lively and sick by turns, and the succession was unsettled. A run of bad harvests between 1594 and 1597 had produced alarming food shortages throughout the kingdom, a national index of mortality rates showing deaths rising by 52% in 1597. Indeed, the whole of western Europe had suffered. Tonbridge now nurtured an iron industry, which had caused so many furnaces and forges to be set up in

6. Thomson, 1965, 173-190. See also Chapter 12 below.

7. Williams, 1985, Chapter 5

8. Oxford DNB, 2005 , under Elizabeth, Lady Fane

the parish by 1550 that the woodlands of North Frith had been devastated, and efforts at reinstating them was being contested. Iron had turned David Willard into a rich man before he died, (probably) in 1587, and his sons were continuing in the same business. In South Frith its vanished woods were already being replaced by farmland, clearing a site for the building in 1611 of a splendid Jacobean house at Somerhill by the Earl of Clanricarde, based on a plan of Palladio.[9]

The Protestant reformation in Tonbridge and Hadlow seemed to be secure, but no one could be sure. The Gunpowder plot at the beginning of the next reign would show how much rumbling opposition simmered under the surface, and in the 1620s the Whetenhall family in East Peckham, Hadlow's next door parish, would startle their neighbours by renouncing their devotion to Calvinism and turning to Roman Catholicism.[10] The brightest outlook at this time, perhaps, lay in farming, which was prospering as more people demanded more food. Fortunately, that was the calling which gave the majority of Hadlow people their livelihood. We turn to their routines of life in the next chapter.

9. Chalklin, 2004, 95-115; Newman, 1969, 515

10. Lawrence, 2004, 26-29; Petrie, 2004, 151-152

CHAPTER 8

GETTING A LIVING FROM THE LAND

Almost everyone in 1460 lived off the land, but we cannot say anything reliable about the size of their holdings. We can add up the scattered pieces occupied by each individual, but that does not give us a reliable measure of any man's total farmholding since every single one of them could have held pieces of other manors in Hadlow, not to mention land in neighbouring parishes. All we know is that the original tenements had been laid out on the assumption that about 30-36 acres could sustain a family. One of the largest tenants here in 1460 occupied over 80 acres on this manor alone, whereas Robert Hall held 3 acres, and Richard At Hill just over an acre. Inequalities of wealth in the fifteenth century were substantial, and that is corroborated by a wider-ranging study of Wealden holdings by Michael Zell in which he presented a table grouping by size the holdings in five sample Wealden parishes (see diagram below).[1] It shows the large number of farms having 10-29 acres, a lesser group with under 10 acres, and two much smaller groups with 30-59 acres, and 60 acres and more. This analysis makes it certain that some people had to do extra work apart from farming, like carting, carrying, shopkeeping, and fishing to make a living. No one needed to earn a lot of cash, however, since, among those living modestly, the need for money was small - to pay dues to their lord (some of which were anyway paid in work or kind) and to the church for the peace of their souls. They needed to buy pots and pans for the kitchen, farm tools, and salt, but most of their needs for food were met by producing it on their own land and by exchanges with their neighbours.

So how did Hadlow people use their natural resources? We cannot rely on any document of the time to answer that question directly, but we can look for indirect clues. Hadlow's heavy clay soils were not easy to cultivate, and it was not until the twelfth century that population in the Weald began to increase noticeably and people sought more permanent homes there, rather than simply exploiting the forest's resources seasonally for grazing. It is true that Hadlow lies on the rim of the Weald, so that the movement of more people settling permanently in the Weald began somewhat earlier there than in the parishes deeper into the woodland. Also the presence of Tonbridge Castle only four miles away meant that kings and courtiers arrived from time to time for the hunting and made heavy demands on the locals for attendance and sophisticated services. North Frith and South Frith were attractive hunting country, and some Hadlow people were needed to attend to the deer, nurture falcons, keep up gates and fences. The total population

1. Zell, 1994, 93

Distribution of farms by size in five sample parishes

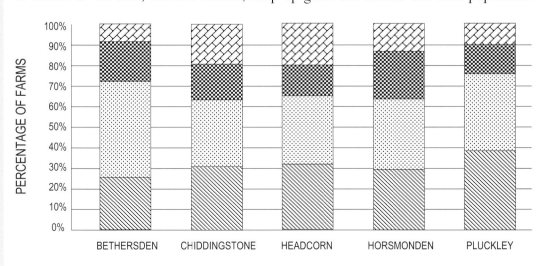

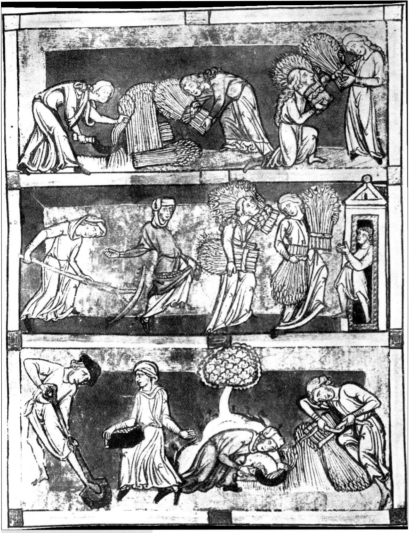

Gathering in the harvest.

2. Dyer & Palliser, 2005, 521,lxxii

3. BL, Add. MS 34218, ff.37-57

Selling eels

at Domesday was modest, and interest in attracting settled tenants, to lay out farms, and improve cultivation did not begin to hold a firm place in the administrative schemes of landowners until the twelfth and thirteenth centuries.

After that, we can only guess how the population grew, for we have no figures. Our only firm figure for Hadlow's total population shows 110 communicants in 1608 (compared with 110 at Shipbourne, and 80 at Mereworth), suggesting about 150-165 people in the parish in 1608.[2] Around 1460 and, indeed throughout the sixteenth and early seventeenth centuries, our researches have shown that people in the Weald were generally poorer than those living in other parts of Kent. They lived simple lives, building their houses out of local timber, clay and wattle, and relying for food on what they could produce for themselves. When they made wills, the most valued personal possessions left to their children were their animals, notably cattle. At the same time, our survey shows that considerable labour services were nominally required of servile tenants for working the arable land and harvesting the cereal crop. So arable farming was expected to afford self-sufficiency in food.

Reading between the lines of our survey, we have seen the small sizes of pieces of tenemental land on the floodplain of the Medway, and so have guessed at some pressure of demand for land at that point, and registered the importance of the river to Hadlow's inhabitants. They fattened their cattle there and ate the beef. They also had fish for food from the river. The value of the eels is confirmed in a statement by Yalding people, living in the neighbouring parish in 1600, when the Sewer Commissioners tried to clear a deeper passage down the river to Maidstone and sought to remove the weirs.[3] The locals stoutly defended their weirs, for, they said, they greatly increased the quantity of fish caught by angle and net, and their value was estimated at some 200 marks p.a. In spawning time, the locals had been known to catch two bushels of eels in a night. Since two days a week in the fifteenth century were obligatory days of abstinence from meat (increased to three days a week in 1563), people ate a lot of fish, and still more during the whole of Lent. So having the river Medway running through Hadlow was a precious asset. Our survey has shown us how the mistress of Hadlow manor required the family occupying Fishland tenement (and, incidentally, having the surname Fisher), to supply her with fish whenever she asked. Another insight is afforded in a later document of 1627 when another attempt was made by the Sewer Commissioners to clear the river from Penshurst to Maidstone, and the locals protested at new restrictions which seemed to them to prevent them fishing from their boats and taking their friends on board with them. The Commissioners allayed such anxieties by saying that they did not intend to be 'so strict'. But the alarm of the local people also conjures up a lively picture of old routines when friends joined together to fish for eels from boats belonging to the men who occupied land along the river.

Additional details about the condition of the river in 1627-1629 make it clear that occupiers of land on the banks had been accustomed for centuries past to do what they liked with their own stretch of water. Intelligent self-interest and common sense obliged them to clear away trees and shrubs from the banks and pull out fallen logs, but individuals had freely constructed bays to make use of the flowing water for washing and watering animals as well as other jobs, and had erected weirs to catch goodly quantities of fish for themselves and for sale. This free-for-all world worked amicably until new commercial pressures arose between the 1540s and 1570s and iron forging developed in the Tonbridge area. Local resources of timber in North Frith and the Hurst lay ready to hand to fuel the iron furnaces, and a change of life style threatened the local people as woodland was cut down on a massive scale to provide charcoal.

Sowing seed

The stimulus to the iron industry filtered into Kent from the Sussex Weald, urged on by the Sydney family among others when they installed themselves at Penshurst. Industrial activity then spread to Tonbridge, and David Willard, some time in the 1550s or 1560s, set up an iron forge in the vicinity of Fishall, stopped up a stream leading into the Medway, and diverted it to enable him to send iron by boat from a different spot, down to Fishall and so to the Medway. We have already described the destruction of timber in North Frith that followed.[4]

4. Thirsk, 2000, 87;
   CKS, MS S/MN A21, pp 47-48

Returning to the years around 1460, however, these pressures were as yet unknown. Other resources of value to Hadlow people that they drew from the river were water birds, ducks, geese, and swans, and wild birds that arrived seasonally. All these supplied eggs and meat for family food, feathers that filled mattresses and pillows, and quills for pens; quills from swans were deemed the best writing implements of all. So when strangers arrived in the 1620s to clear obstacles from the river, and roamed freely up and down the towpaths, they helped themselves to some of these natural assets, and we hear the people at Yalding complaining bitterly of their losses. Hadlow people will have had the same experience; having been accustomed in the past to enjoy a quieter life among friendly, less grasping neighbours, commercial intrusions introduced them to a very different world.

Our attention so far has been focused on the Medway, silently omitting the river Bourne. It was another valuable waterway, entering the parish at its northern end and joining the Medway in the south-east corner. It was a source of valuable soil nutrients for it watered lands that are named as meadows in the tenements lying across its course. It also served another vital purpose in supplying water to mills that were situated towards the central part of the parish.

The congestion of small pieces of land down at the Medway has already suggested that Hadlow people at this period met each other more often in the vicinity of Hadlow Stair and along the Medway than in the village centre. But the low-lying land on the wide floodplain and the interlacing of many meandering streams left them few dry sites on which to place their houses. Some of their dwellings, therefore, plus the obligation on all to attend services at church, and the need for social diversion brought them to the village centre.

The need to mill cereals for making bread also regularly brought Hadlow people this way. The river Bourne, flowing across the main road between Tonbridge and West

Malling, provided water power for the mills that are mentioned in the survey. Fletchers tenement accommodated the corn mill and a mill pond. The malt mill, says our survey, was also 'lately situated there' on Symonds tenement, but seemingly had been moved. Instead, another maltmill was mentioned, standing to the south and west of the corn mill. Located somewhere on the river Bourne but before the river crossed the main road, its site has been lost. As for the one-time malt mill, we may wonder if it had been turned into a fulling mill, since the tenterground for drying cloth that had been fulled stood so near. It is a distinct possibility.

Hadlow people, then, had their essential corn and malt mills sited near the centre of the village. Walking along Carpenters Lane and down the narrow lane to Bourne Mill, we can see how high the banks and houses stand above the road level and appreciate how many generations of people trudged down those roads cutting their course deeper into the muddy clay. But we have to ponder also the relatively long walk that was involved for those with houses down near the Stair. Admittedly, they were not likely to be growing much cereal down there. But if any was growing nearby, it may be that people had a concession to use the cornmill in Tonbridge; after all, Tonbridge belonged to the same lord. Also we have to ponder the mystery surrounding John Bishop who lived in 'The Mill House at the Stair', suggesting a mill that we have not identified. Where the survey returns to the Medway at the south-eastern end of the parish, it describes William at Lake's smallish tenement of 17 acres, and mentions also a highway from Perys mill (i.e. Pierce mill) to Saffrayns Plain. That mill probably served the sub-manors of Caustons and John Fromonds (Barnes Street) in Hadlow parish.

The next major natural resource of Hadlow was the land. The survey did not regularly distinguish the use to which the fields were put, but it did often differentiate land, meadow, and pasture. From this, it is fair to guess that what was called 'land' was the ploughland, growing cereals for bread and some pulses. In the Weald as a whole in the sixteenth century, we find some Wealden farmers with no more than 5-8 acres under the plough; that gives a reasonable measure of arable for a family holding in Hadlow in 1460.

Ploughmen using oxen. Taken from the Luttrel Psalter of 1335-40 Oxen, and certainly not horses, were needed on Hadlow's clay.

5. Thirsk, 2000, 90

Some of the cereal was probably wheat, though not grown in any large quantity. The soil was certainly better suited to wheat than barley, but much land in the Weald at this date was generally cropped with oats; indeed, one man with land in West Peckham, the next parish north of Hadlow, asserted that he grew nothing but oats, and in the next century the Weald was known for growing oats for seed to sell to other regions. So oats may well have played rather more than a subsidiary role in Hadlow people's diet in 1460. It was certainly also used in brewing beer, either mixed with barley or not.[5]

Economic conditions in 1460, however, did not yet exert any pressure on Hadlow people to grow a great surplus of grain. Mortality at the time of the Black Death in 1348 had dealt a heavy blow, and about half the population had died. The kingdom as a whole showed no sign as yet of numbers rising again and stimulating energetic agricultural improvement. But in an earlier period before the plague, in the twelfth and thirteenth centuries, strong efforts had had to be made to improve arable soils. A growing population had pressed hard on food supplies, and among the fertilisers that greatly enriched arable land then was marl - a compost of chalky, mineral substances - that lay underground in many parishes on the fringe of the Weald including Hadlow. The effort devoted then to getting marl is reflected in the many accidents recorded in the Plea Rolls between 1241 and 1255 reporting the deaths of adults and children who fell into marlpits or were crushed by falling earth when marl was being dug out.[6] The farmer at North Frith some five years ago found some splendid blue/yellow marl when plunging his spade into a pit that he had always suspected was a marl pit; and one of Commander Dumbreck's historic maps now deposited in CKS shows a marlpit field next to Sole Street, i.e. Three Elm Lane. Our survey also shows in Knet the Hogg's tenement some land actually called marlpit, and in Somers tenement lay a Pit Lane, though that may have led to claypits rather than marlpits.

At all events, the past digging of marl was evident in the landscape in 1460, and the memory of it all was revived among Hadlow people when they began to take a fresh interest in agricultural improvement and the digging of marl around 1600. A fine account of various kinds and colours of marl and how to use it was published in 1625 by Gervase Markham, a writer on farming who had some kind of friendly connection with the Rivers family of Chafford and Hadlow, and dedicated his work to Sir George Rivers. In the public interest, Markham decided to publish the manuscript, though he had not written it; the land responded 'miraculously' to marl, he said. It is tempting to think that it had been written by one of the Rivers family, who were gentleman farmers here; at all events, it showed much practical knowledge, and experience of the way marl improved land, and it could easily have derived in part from farming in Hadlow.[7] It is not at all fanciful to imagine Gervase Markham riding through Hadlow or hunting in North Frith. As for the Rivers family they are commemorated in Hadlow church by one monument on the south wall of the chancel, remembering Sir John Rivers who died in 1584 and his wife Joan, who died in 1618.

Fifteenth-century documents about Hadlow give almost no information about the keeping of livestock, and for lack of any probate inventories little more is found in the sixteenth century. Wills show that a common bequest consisted of a team of four or six oxen, the size of the team underlining the heaviness of the arable land. Cattle were more important than sheep, and cows came before bullocks, since cows were essential for household milk as well as for breeding.[8] However, a clue to the potential for fattening bullocks in Hadlow is conveyed in a document of 1541 describing the condition of North Frith Park. Henry VIII was temporarily owner of Penshurst and was contemplating enlarging the Great Park there by buying more land. For some unexplained reason, his survey of Penshurst included Hadlow manor and North Frith, and it tells us that North Frith park was divided into three walks in the charge of three keepers, who in addition to receiving wages of 40s. each p.a. had the right to feed in the first walk 20 bullocks, 10 cows and 2 horses, in the second walk 24 bullocks, 6 cows and 2 horses, and in the third walk 8 cows.[9]

The large size of the first two herds, belonging to two men only, gives some idea of the grazing potential in the parish, for these men who grazed such large numbers on the less than ideal herbage of the wooded Frith must have expected to fatten them in summer on the meadows along the Bourne or the Medway. The numerous small parcels into which the meadows on the Medway had become divided by 1460 have already alerted us to the value of grazing in that area. Men in the Frith with 20 and 24 bullocks apiece fit comfortably into an image of lush river meadows, and if those by the Medway were the ones selected, then perhaps Ashes Lane was the drove road, leading across the main road to Tonbridge to two paths (FPs MT141 and MT142) that led south to the Medway. One of these joins up with Blackmans Lane, and Blackmans lane in 1460 was called New Lane. The name may, in fact, have been tolerably old already, but it could have historic significance as a route that became much more frequented when the woodland of the Frith was opened up by commercial felling for timber, and glades were created where young cattle could graze before being sent down to fatten by the Medway.[10]

6. Furley, 1871, II, i, 41-43, 44, 46-47, 49-51

7. Markham, 1625

8. Williams, 1985, 7-10

9. CKS, MS U1475 / E12

10. Witney, 1991, 20-39

Another source of food to Hadlow people came from their gardens which are named in almost all cases in the survey as adjoining their houses. Here they grew herbs and greenstuff for their daily food. They did not yet have fine lettuces, cabbages, turnips, and carrots, for improvements to those basic vegetables did not begin until the later sixteenth century. But they ate many more of the varied green leafy plants and roots that we now ignore; they ate a primitive cabbage that they called colewort, picking off the leaves individually, and many differently flavoured roots, including the roots of parsley. Their many plants taken from the fields and hedgerows as well as their gardens gave varied flavours to their pottage, which was their main daily dinner. It combined greenstuff with cereals, peas, beans, and a little bacon or other meat.

A herbery is named in the survey, which we have already mentioned when walking round the manor in Chapter 4. It is an old word for a fine garden, and could have contained treasured herbs for medicine and kitchen use. The actual names in the document appear as 'Herberys', 'Outer Herberys', and 'Inner Herberys', lying somewhere in the vicinity of Fishall and Hadlow Place. It arouses our curiosity in the former occupier who had made it, making us wonder whether it had perhaps been cultivated by a gentlewoman attached to the courtly circle that frequented Tonbridge Castle. No orchards are mentioned anywhere in the survey, though in the next century contemporary comments about plentiful fruit trees growing in the hedgerows of Kent make it clear that the climate had made a congenial home for wild fruit trees. So we cannot know how much hedgerow fruit grew in Hadlow, but because of the many gardens around the Hadlow houses, we may wonder what Hadlow contributed already to the later reputation of Kent as the garden of England.

The northern boundary of Hadlow manor was aligned with the hunting grounds of North Frith park, and several tenements cite the park pale as one boundary. We can be sure that the land on both sides of the boundary was shrubby woodland. Deer will have tried to jump over the palings, wild birds flown in and

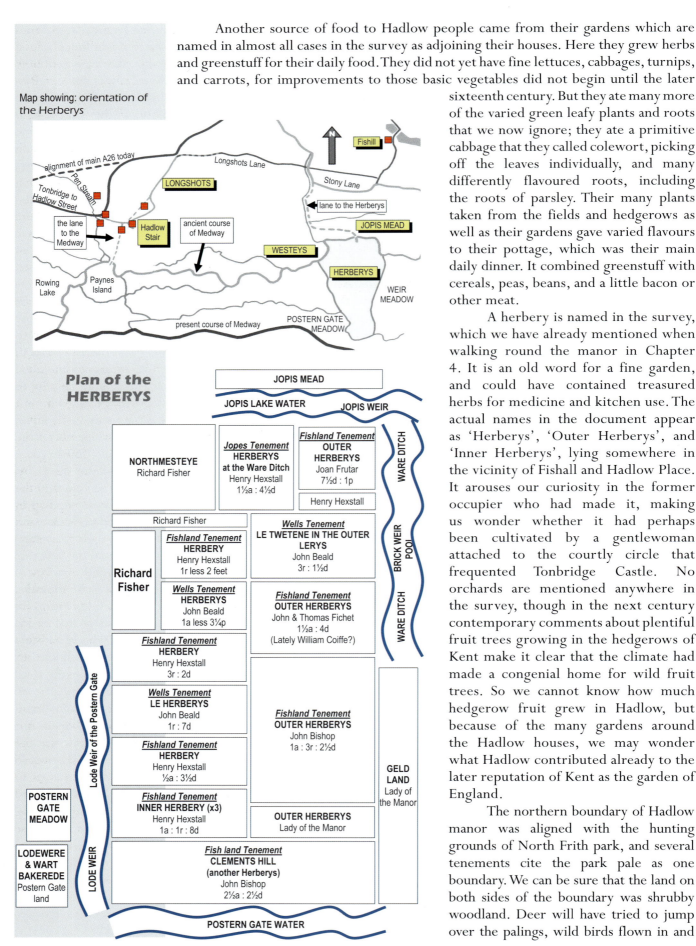

Map showing: orientation of the Herberys

Plan of the HERBERYS

Picking fruit

11. Foard and others, 2005, 15

12. Furley, 1871, II, i, 49

The lane to the Herberys. One of the 'lost' ways to the Medway meadows, which were of importance to the working man at the time of the survey

out, plants and trees bearing berries and nuts spilt out through the fences. At all times it must have been a happy hunting ground for kindling, and in autumn was much valued for fattening pigs on the acorns, beech nuts, chestnuts, and berries in the park. But how many Hadlow people were allowed to drive their pigs into North Frith is unclear. Pigs were precious animals to all peasant families, and we can reasonably guess that they were numerous in the parish. (A significant study of a parallel economy in the Rockingham Forest, Northamptonshire, has recently commented on the advantages such people had in the numbers of cattle and pigs that they could feed in their woodlands when compared with common field countryside.[11]) Pigs in Wealden villages were also sometimes visible around the farmyard; they are depicted in a graphic account by Yalding people in 1600 when floodwater from the rivers encircled their houses (we saw it happen all over again in the year 2000), and they said they were driven to carrying their pigs into their bedchambers to save them from drowning. A picture of pigs roaming through the downstairs rooms is also conjured up in a case (*circa* 1241-55, in Londingden, its whereabouts unknown), of a small boy sitting at home near a fire over which an earthen pot of boiling water was hanging, when a pig brushed past, overturned it, and scalded him to death.[12]

Official recognition by the lord of the pigs kept in Hadlow is best shown in our survey when it names, in the revision of 1581, the annual dues owing from some tenements, consisting of pigs or joints of pork. We normally interpret that obligation to mean that tenants were thereby paying their Hadlow lord, who was also lord of North Frith park, for the right to drive their pigs up there in the autumn to fatten on the nuts. But not all tenements paid this due. The 1460 text of the survey, describing only Jopes tenement, makes what may then have been intended as a general observation about joint tenants having the right to graze eleven sows in North Frith throughout the year. But it occurs only once, leaving its full implications unclear. If, indeed, all joint tenants on the manor had equal rights, then that allowed something over 100 tenants in 1460 to graze 11 sows apiece in North Frith. Not all of them will have availed themselves of this right, of course, but we can reasonably contemplate about a thousand pigs in the woods in the autumn, knowing also that it was not at all unusual elsewhere for owners to keep pigs in woods all the year round and take food to them in hard weather. The deep lanes that lead up to the further woodland in The Hurst in West Peckham certainly suggest that many animals once trudged that way.

In other parts of the country we are accustomed to find a considerable quantity of commons where all farmers had the right to graze cattle and sheep, abiding by the rules of the manor court. Our survey names several small pieces of common, but only one larger piece at Lonewood. It is likely that commons did not have the same significance for our tenants in the Weald as in common-field country, for all could lease land very freely in small pieces and large, and Hadlow had plenteous grazing. The problem is further discussed in Chapter 11.

We construct from all this a picture of the way Hadlow farmers got their living from the varied resources of their land. We do not expect to find rich people, and we know that the natural resources were not evenly distributed among them. But they were varied enough to provide a sufficiency, and they doubtless yielded something more to the most resourceful and energetic inhabitants, whose drive and enterprise is suggested by the large holdings that some of them accumulated in the manor.

CHAPTER 9

RIVERS: THE MEDWAY & THE BOURNE

It is usually said that the river Medway was not navigable from Maidstone to Tonbridge until after 1740 when the Medway Navigation Company was set up. But we can be sure that Hadlow people in 1460 found it navigable for their own purposes. How then did they use it? When more ambitious schemes to make it 'navigable' for larger vessels emerged in the early seventeenth century, reports were assembled about the river's condition which give us some answers to this question. Thus we can begin to build up a picture of the scene in 1460.

Nowadays we are accustomed to seeing a river consisting of one main current with firm banks defining its course. In the fifteenth century, however, the Medway looked very different. Doubtless in some places it did have a recognisable main course,

A flat-bottomed river boat probably similar to those being used in 1460.

Aspects of the river Medway, looking south.

especially where the river valley narrowed or the water was channelled for strategic purposes at Tonbridge or Maidstone. But in Hadlow the floodplain was, and still is, wide and a multitude of subsidiary streams wound their way alongside. Farmers having land hereabouts naturally altered the course of the streams to suit themselves and where our survey touches on the Medway we are aware that the sluices and weirs controlling the watercourses are an important and integral part of daily lives. Indeed Thomas Fromond of Goldhill in his will of 1447 bequeathed to his son John 'all rents, weirs, waters and fisheries in Hadlow'.

When the local parish representatives were asked to survey the river and make a list of obstructions and alterations in 1627-9 they could not always decide which was the main course of the Medway and which was a subsidiary stream. We can almost see them scratching their heads, arguing with each other and then, in the end, shrugging

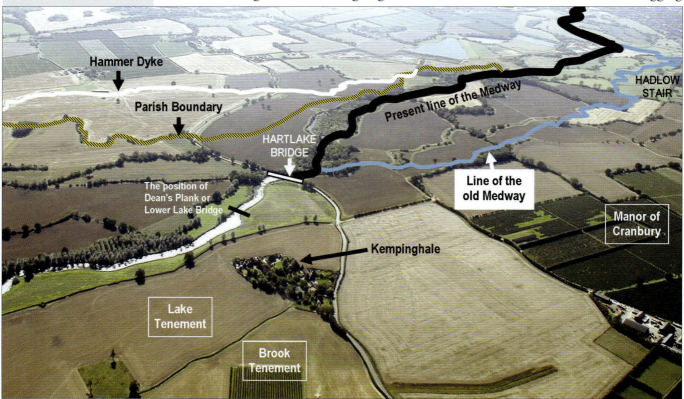

Hammer Dyke

Parish Boundary

HARTLAKE BRIDGE

Present line of the Medway

HADLOW STAIR

Line of the old Medway

The position of Dean's Plank or Lower Lake Bridge

Kempinghale

Manor of Cranbury

Lake Tenement

Brook Tenement

their shoulders hopelessly when they failed to reach agreement. They left the Sewer Commissioners to decide, who, being local gentlemen and landowners, were in no better position than the villagers to give a definitive answer.

Nevertheless, the jurors put a lot of work into their report, and although it was drawn up more than a hundred years after our survey of 1460 (though only forty years after the survey was rewritten and revised in 1581), it gives us a rough idea of how Hadlow people had made their way across the river at many different points. Their report is not entirely crystal clear to us who look on a very different scene, so this interpretation contains quite a few question marks about its meaning. But one can appreciate all the work that went into it, including the endeavour to state at each point along the river who were the landowners and who were the occupiers.

The ancient course of the Medway near the Stair in 2006 gives a clear indication of how it would have looked in 1460

Some farmers had land on both sides of the water, so there was a need to drive cattle across or take hay to their animals, possibly using a cart. Inevitably there would have been a need for heavier wagons carrying corn, wood and stone to cross the river, and equally travellers on foot or horse had somehow to cross the river at a convenient point. But now in 1627 the Sewer Commissioners were intent on stopping the locals from using any sizeable boats, because they were conferring monopoly rights on one individual to carry all heavy goods on the Medway in the future. In return he undertook to clear a passage for boats of 4 tons burden which included a need for sufficient headroom to pass under all bridges.

In their report the jurors listed the crossings that already existed. Any low-slung and rickety bridges, not designed to let a boat of 4 tons pass, would have to be rebuilt. Starting at Penshurst, the jurors moved through Tonbridge, which had five bridges across the Medway, and arrived in Hadlow parish. The ancient course of the river passed under what is now Little Bridge in Tonbridge High Street (presently called the Botany Stream). At Strawberry Vale lay 'a main carrying bridge called **Wichenden Bridge**', a 'horse bridge' (probably no more than 3 feet wide) was identified where today's Morley Road crosses the stream into Vale Road; Postern Bridge is then described as a 'carrying bridge'. David Willard, who had occupied the forge at Postern some 50 to 60 years previously, was blamed for having turned the course of the Medway 'for his own use for the passage of his iron by boats from thence down to Fishall'; with the passage of years it is difficult now to see how this was achieved but his activities were worthy of being mentioned twice by the jurors.

The ancient course of the river turned along what today forms the main stream (which runs below the castle walls and under the Big Bridge) near the site of the now defunct Child's Lock. Within a short distance the jurors found that the river 'divide[d] itself into two heads at a place called Walmsleys Wear', one arm 'running

Hartlake Bridge in the late 1800s, its appearance was probably little changed from the time of the survey.

with his compass northwards and the other shooting forward'. The northerly stream led through 'an ancient Wear called Cranborrow's Wear' which had paid 'certain Sticks of Eels unto the Castle of Tonbridge'. The jurors were naturally doubtful as to the main stream and left it to the Commissioners! (See *Topographical Problems*, Chapter 14, where Hadlow Stair is discussed.) Next came a 'carrying bridge' and a 'footbridge' before 'one main carrying bridge called **Hartlake Bridge**' was reached. The first carrying bridge was where the track from Fishall land to Somerhill crossed the river. The crossing was noted as being out of repair in 1800 and 'destroyed' by 1824. The footbridge lay at Porter's Lock where a 'lost' footpath once crossed the river. Hartlake Bridge was known to exist in 1460 as in 1451 John Tatlyngbery (who lived at Barnes Place) left money in his will for the repair of the road and bridge at Hartlake, as did Henry Fane in 1533.

Kelchers Lane, Golden Green, now a farm track used as a footpath (MT156)

At Hartlake the jurors were again confronted with a river which 'divideth itself into several branches'. Here they were more decisive and agreed that a 'horse bridge called **Dean's plank**' crossed the main stream. A bridge existed at this point until the mid- twentieth century called Lower Lake Bridge which gave access to a dairy farm south of the river. A past occupant of adjacent Hartlake Farmhouse recalls seeing the more recent iron bridge being taken downstream on a barge – where did it end up? Although the jurors seemed more convinced as to the course of the main stream, they continued to describe it as attended by subsidiary streams and 'islands', although these are little more than ditches today. Between Dean's Plank and Ford Green Bridge lay another footbridge and a carrying bridge. The carrying bridge would have lain at what is now East Lock. Here the lane now called Kelchers crossed the river on its route from Goldhill (Golden Green) to Moat Farm and Five Oak Green, using midstream Weir Island as a stepping stone – the perfect place for a navigational lock. Definitive footpaths MT156/160/159 now mark this route. It is sometimes difficult to correlate stretches of water in our survey with that of the Commissioners' Report but Mrs White's Weir (1627) and Fromond's sluice (1460) are, no doubt, one and the same and Weir Island provides the clue. The 'footbridge called **Ffoard**' is where 'Watery Lane' (FP.MT158) from Barnes Street crosses at Ford Green Bridge also known as Booth Bridge.

Waines Hopes Bridge is likely to have been where the boundary between Hadlow and East Peckham parishes crosses the river at Oak Weir Lock. The crossing is described as a 'main carrying bridge' which indicates a public highway. Although a public crossing no longer exists at this point, the existence of the boundary, lock and an island ('**Lord's Island**' is mentioned in the text) appears relevant; a track is indicated on Twysden's Estate map of 1632 giving access from what is now Three Elm Lane to the river. The next bridge is **Keysers** and recalls the Cayser family which was prominent in East Peckham. This is well documented as being below Stilstead House, Little Mill, and still exists as footpath MR555 which eventually leads across the meadows to Whetsted. Two footbridges come next, one called **Duck's Bridge**, sometimes called Duke's Bridge (after the Duke of Westmorland). The river Bourne, which runs through Hadlow village falls into the Medway on the north side of the mid-stream island to the west of the bridge. Footpath MR545 from Snoll Hatch, East Peckham crosses here. Our reporters now arrived at an arm drawn from the river, they said, to serve

An engraving of Branbridge from 1793. ('Medway Bridges', Kent County Library, 1978)

Branbridge Mill and 'one main wear built upon the old river there penned up to turn the water course unto the said mill'. Beyond that point came an ancient stone bridge with two arches called **Slades Bridge**, also known as Branbridges, over which ran the Kings Highway - today it is the old B2015 which ran from Pembury to Wateringbury. At the confluence of the Medway and the Teise the river was crossed via ancient *Twyford Bridge* at Yalding.

Along the way the jurors described innumerable logs in the river, willows

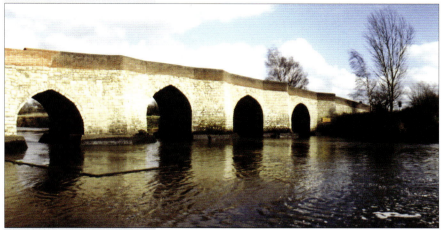

growing on the banks and earth fallen in. At various places the water was unusually shallow and it was there that farmers led their cattle across and carried hay in dry seasons. The jurors made a general reference to these at the end but did not identify them individually. It is clear that they knew many different kinds of crossings, bearing different weights, and we can readily understand the seriousness of their statement at one point that these were not being reported as annoyances or impediments; they were passages

Ancient Twyford Bridge at the confluence of the Medway and the Teise

and churchways that were essential in the workaday routines of the inhabitants. The jurors did not know who had originally constructed them ; they were the work of long dead forebears working their land to their best advantage. But, plainly, people were constantly changing the landscape or allowing it to change in small ways. David Willard's cut for carrying his iron gave a vivid picture of the way another piece of the Hadlow scene was changed. Taking a wider view on the outside world, the locals, in their Report claimed to have knowledge of a time when a clear passage existed on the river as far as Maidstone, but it had decayed through neglect. This was surely an accurate memory from Yalding onwards, but whether from Tonbridge to Yalding, we cannot be sure.

The report on the Medway showed the whole river liable to yearly changes, though

Map showing: contours in relation to the Medway in Hadlow parish; bridges on the river, and its ancient course.

KEY

▬▬▬	Roads
▬▬▬	Tracks
▪ ▪ ▪ ▪	Lost tracks
▪ ▪ ▪ ▪	Footpaths
● ● ● ●	Lost footpaths
▬▬▬	Rivers & streams
▬ ▬ ▬	Parish boundary (pre 1900)
⬭ 20m	Contours

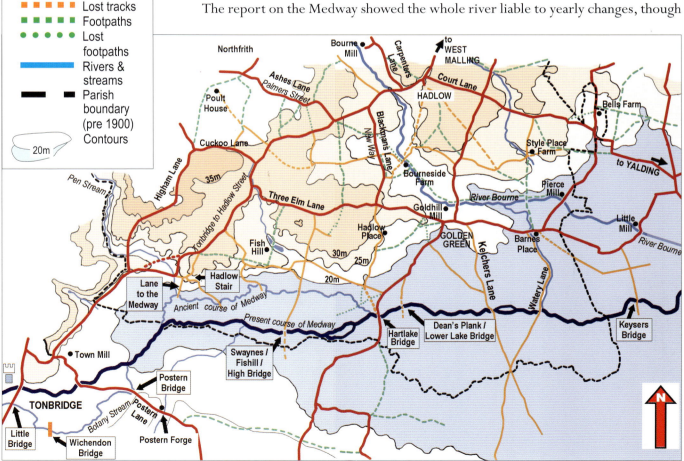

in 1460 they were still relatively small. It was lined with alders, willows, and tree stubs and required constant vigilance, which it did not get. Earth fell into the river and created shelves that settled firmly. These were probably some of the shallows that were used as crossing points in drier seasons. Even so, things were satisfactory enough not to arouse any movement for change, and we should not underrate the importance of the river, as it was to Hadlow people. Their farming depended on it as winter floods brought fertility to the grazing land, and so did their access to places west and east. Not least, it was important for its access to fresh food — fish, especially eels. Hadlow Stair was the major point of access for goods to and from Tonbridge, while our survey makes so many references to the roads to Yalding that we must assume that Hadlow people absolutely relied on getting there if they wanted to go eastwards towards Maidstone and so to the Thames estuary. The survey nowhere mentioned any road to Maidstone for the present one did not then exist. It was a totally different scene from today. Yalding is now a picturesque backwater on a commuter rat-run whereas Maidstone has retained its commercial importance and is easily accessible to all, thanks to the turnpike revolution.

THE RIVER BOURNE

It seems hard to imagine that today's river Bourne once provided the power for twelve known mills, four of which lay in the parish of Hadlow although only two lay in our manor at the time of the survey. The river rises above Ightham and drove 4 mills between Borough Green and Plaxtol. Roughway paper mill was situated at Dunk's Green, and Hamptons (formerly Puttenden) mill also manufactured paper during its working life. Oxenhoath mill just outside our parish is claimed to date from 1259 and was a fulling mill which later converted to grind corn; it was part of the Culpepers' Oxenhoath Estate. The river runs under a bridge in High House Lane which our survey alluded to as 'the highway at Ashwood' (in 1557 — it was the 'high road from (West) Peckham to Tonbridge'). The river crossed water meadows at Larkhale before an arm was diverted to feed the mill pond at Hadlow.

Bourne Mill is situated off Carpenters Lane and in common with other surviving mills its wheel has gone, but the present building and its surroundings give us a good idea of what the scene would have been like in 1460. Documents in the possession of the current owners refer to it as Hadlow Mills, with the description of 'three mills under one roof' until the mid nineteenth century, when it was rebuilt.

Bourne Mill

The Sedgebrook

Our survey tells us that the Mill Bourne (4½ acres in Fletchers tenement) was held by Lady Elizabeth Culpeper and an adjacent twenty-four acres were held by Richard Culpeper esquire (died 1484). The Culpepers lived at Oxenhoath which, in its present form, is a substantial, mainly Georgian house in an elevated position overlooking Hadlow village.

As today, the main road between Hadlow and Tonbridge crossed the Bourne at land known as Sedgebrookgate. Our survey tells us that John Symonds of Palmers Street held 2 acres here, and a half acre containing the Malt Mill, of which no trace remains. Sedge Brook, also known as Somings Brook, skirted land in Welshes tenement, on Palmers Street and formed the westerly boundary of Peckhams Manor. It now feeds into the Bourne just below the bridge. Although a bridge at this point was not noted in our survey, James Grosse, who held 13 acres in the manor,

Hadlow's High Street stream, now culverted except for a short stretch at James House (formerly Durrants)

left money in his will of 1493 for the repair of the cross at Hadlow Bridge. In 1800 landowners below the bridge were ordered to remove stubs and other obstructions which stopped the flow of the Bourne. Judging by the Commissioners' report on the Medway it was a situation which was probably little changed from the time of our survey.

The river flowed on marking the boundary between Aleynslove tenement and the manorial demesne lands which were not included in our survey. At Bourneside Farm the river was crossed by Skeffe's Lane (now known as Dog Kennel Path) linking Victoria Road with Blackman's Lane. In 1656 it had a bridge called Deering Bridge, but this ancient crossing was lost in the 1970s when the footpath was diverted to a point further along the Bourne. Before reaching Rotford bridge the river turned the mill at Goldhill, part of Thomas Fromond's Manor, while the road was described as 'the highway from Goldhill to West Malling' (i.e. Victoria Road). Moving east, Hadlow Manor lands at Buntanhall lay to the north of the river, adjacent to Caustons Manor. Perys Mill (today's Pierce Mill) would have served Barnes Street and possibly Causton's manor; 18 acres of Lake tenement (1) lay close to the mill and at the furthest point east of our parish. Leaving our parish boundary with East Peckham the river reaches Little Mill where a mill house can still be seen. A short way across flood meadows the outfall into the River Medway is reached at Ducks Bridge.

No doubt fish weirs were constructed in the river Bourne as in the Medway. It may also have been navigable by small craft in its lower stretches and perhaps, in the upper reaches at Basted, there may have been a forge where the narrow valley above the mill was dammed at some time in the past to make two large ponds. In Hadlow village the river is still regarded as liable to flood. It is an old story as the Court Rolls show, for a stream that is now culverted used to pass down the High Street from Cemetery Lane (Durrants Cross) and caused many problems to local residents. More recently still, in living memory, this same stream flowing from the hills above the village, joined with the flood waters of the Bourne to put the centre of the village under water, probably not for the last time!

Looking west along the river to Bourneside Farm

CHAPTER 10

ROADS

We know from flint implements dredged from the Medway and Roman remains along the valley of the river Bourne that, from the earliest times, the local Wealden landscape was attractive to hunters and settlers alike. When people began to open up the area by seeking pasturage for their pigs among the trees, our road network finally began to take shape and ancient trackways into the Weald have become part of the familiar infrastructure we use today by foot, horse and car.

Hadlow today lies on a main arterial road which crosses Kent from the Medway Gap at Rochester to Tonbridge and the A21 in the south-west; it experiences over 4 million traffic movements through the village every year. In 1460 the road connected the administrative and market town of Tonbridge to the west with the market town of West Malling to the east and these towns were possibly as far as most of the residents ever travelled. The importance of getting a living in the parish (see Chapter 8) and therefore getting about the lanes and fields was probably all that concerned the majority. Every resident needed access to the fields, the mill, the church, the forge, the common, the woods, the river and meadows, so a network of roads, lanes and commonways grew up in the parish.

The main grid of roads and tracks can still be identified, but some have simply lost their meaning in the intervening years as patterns of agriculture have changed. There is no longer the need for the many to reach fish weirs along the Medway and larger feeder streams, or commonways for cattle to reach the enriched water-meadows. Tracks once used to reach further destinations are no more than footpaths for leisure purposes, and routes which had a meaning and a purpose are often now cut short at adjoining parish boundaries.

Almost without exception the roads would have been poor by modern standards, the ubiquitous Wealden clay being responsible. Anyone who has walked the local footpaths after rain will appreciate the difficulties experienced by fifteenth-century travellers and farm workers.

Extract from Symonson's map of 1596.
Northfrith park is impaled; crossings of the Medway are shown at Tonbridge, Brandbridge, Twyford and Teston (on the coach road from Wrotham).
Mereworth church is shown without a steeple, so it represents the old church before Mereworth Castle was built.

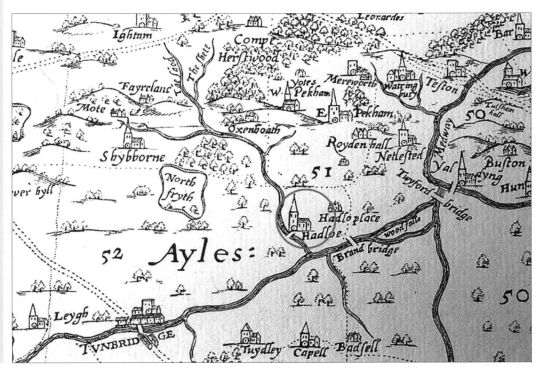

14th CENTURY ROADS IN KENT

Symonson's map presents us with a global picture of Kent in 1596. To the west of Hadlow lay the highway from London to the port of Rye, crossing the Medway at Tonbridge. To the north lay the road from Sevenoaks to Rochester, roughly following today's A25, which joined the Pilgrims Way near Trottiscliffe and crossed the London to Hythe road near Addington. A looping, more southerly, road from West Kingsdown to Lenham via Coxheath, passed, until the early years of the twentieth century, across the woodland and heath between Hadlow and West Malling (turnpiked in 1828), which now forms part of the new parish of Kings Hill and is lost forever amongst the new houses and high tech buildings on the old airfield. It crossed the Medway at the medieval Teston bridge.

The map shows the crossing of the river Bourne at Hadlow, and the nearest easterly 'highway' crossings of the Medway to our parish at Branbridges (Hale Street), which was originally a ford, and the medieval Twyford bridge at Yalding.

MAIN HIGHWAYS IN THE SURVEY

Hadlow in 1460 would certainly have benefited from travellers, traders and pedlars moving between the two market towns, on a road that we still enjoy today. Although there would have been considerable wear and tear on this main thoroughfare, its importance probably meant that more attention was paid to the condition of its surface than other manor ways and money left in contemporary wills for the repair of this and other main highways pays testament to this. The fact that indulgences from the church were granted for such piety was another encouragement.

The road to Tonbridge can be plotted through the manor by the description of the tenements. It follows the present day course, except for some modern straightening out here and there, especially at Hadlow Stair where a once important landing place is now a residential backwater.

The road to West Malling has suffered a fate similar to other main roads with turnpiking and modern straightening masking the original route. One other complication lies in the fact that Mereworth village was displaced by the building of Mereworth Castle and the old road system was disrupted.

The other important highway was that to Yalding. It was from this point that it was still possible to reach Maidstone by water. We can say with some degree of certainty that the route left the village via Court Lane, but after this point there are various possibilities. Apart from the way we might travel there today, i.e. via Snoll Hatch, Branbridges and

Aerial view of Hadlow parish, looking south, showing roads and sub-manors

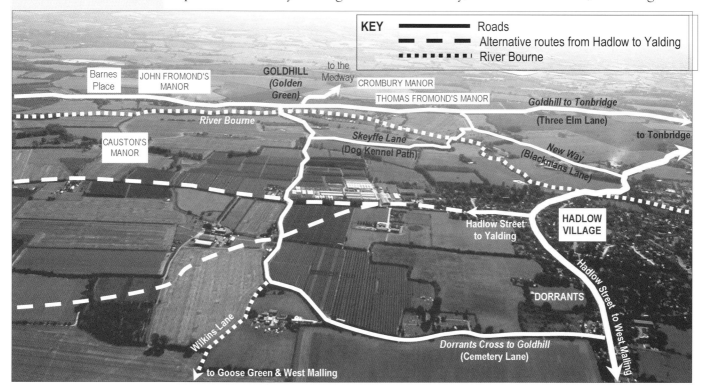

Laddingford, it was also possible to travel via Goblands, Peckham Bush, Nettlestead Green and Twyford Bridge, or via Bell's Farm, Addlestead, Nettlestead Green and Twyford. These last two routes lie on paths and tracks, some of which are either now lost or are no more than badly maintained footpaths. No doubt, the route one chose depended upon the weather and the state of the rivers, streams and ditches that one had to cross and whether it was by foot, horse or cart.

THE MANOR NETWORK

We only gain information about the 'highways', 'lanes' and 'commonways' because they are mentioned as bounds to the holdings and although today's road and footpath network in the parish seems complete many paths have been lost or diverted within living memory so that it is likely that even more will have been lost in the intervening centuries. This would explain why we cannot always be sure as to the exact position of holdings. Survey descriptions of the various ways appear to be interchangeable, i.e. one tenant may describe the route as a commonway whereas the next may call it a highway. On later estate maps 'landways' and 'footways' are sometimes shown running parallel to each other (like roads and pavements today) which may furnish the explanation.

Old farm track across the fields at East Peckham (FP. MR534) which may have formed one of the ways from Hadlow to Twyford Bridge at Yalding. It could almost be 1460!

1. CKS, TR1335,3, Dumbreck maps

The road from *Goldhill to Tonbridge* (Three Elm Lane) forms the main east/west route across the southern half of the parish (and manor). This route continued westwards via the *highway from Bredett Common (or Broads Plain) to Coiffe's gate* (Cuckoo Lane). In this case, 'gate' may indicate one of the ways into North Frith park as William Coiffe held North Frith meadow there. Turning south-west from the gate ran *Coiffe's gate to Pen Bridge (or Tonbridge)* (Higham Lane). Access to the pits in Holman's and Knight's tenements was off Cuckoo Lane.

Palmer's Street Cross to Northfrith described the present-day Ashes Lane from its junction with the Hadlow to Tonbridge road to the pale of Northfrith park (at Pittswood). *Ashwood to Hoggett's gate* (High House Lane) ran along the park pale up to and beyond Stallion's Green. *Birchwoods Lane* followed the public footpath west from Pittswood to the Poult House and from thence to the junction of Higham Lane and Cuckoo Lane. It also defined the edge of the park.[1]

From Three Elm Lane ran the access routes south to the Medway and the alluvial-rich flood meadows. Thomas Fromond's Manor, later Godings (Hadlow Place) lay south of this highway, as did Crombury Manor and Barnes Place so this was an important route. Victoria Road, Cemetery Lane and footpaths MT128 and MR561 (*Wilkins Lane*) were described as the highway from *Goldhill* (Golden Green) *to West Malling*. It joined the highway from *Hadlow Street to West Malling* at Goose Green. Crossing the main road, it is still possible to continue to West Peckham village green via a public footpath, no doubt an access route to the Medway which was also used by residents of that village and parish.

Barnes Place

Nearly every highway, lane or commonway in the survey was named, although the ambiguous 'a certain lane' was occasionally used. Routes were generally known by their destination, e.g. 'highway from Hadlow Bourne to Little Loamwood', or had dedicated names, e.g. 'Skeyffe Lane', related to the land owner, e.g. 'Peter Fisher's lane', or were field names, e.g. 'lane leading to Stony Field'. Interestingly Skeyffe Lane (aka Piper's Lane, Park Lane and Robarts Went), now a footpath, still has a local name – Dog Kennel Path, and local oral tradition claims it as a Roman road; in places it is still possible to distinguish its original twelve foot width and drainage ditches.

As well as money to mend the roads, some people left an amount in their wills for other repairs. It is clear that the causeways at Sedgebrook Gate (Hadlow College entrance) and Three Elm Lane (at the junction with the main road), suffered from water erosion, and bridges across the river Bourne at Hadlow and Golden Green (*Rotford Bridge* in Victoria Road) also received bequests.

The commonway, between Thomas Salman's house (Bournside) and the highway from West Malling to Goldhill (Victoria Road), known today as Dog Kennel Path. To the left lay the Lady's demesne land and Park Field, to the right Stoperfield's tenement.

In 1456 Richard Bealde left money to 'make a footpath' between Longshots Cross and Monk Style (Monks Field lay at the junction of Blackmans Lane and the main road).

The Court Rolls give us further clues as to the difficulties encountered by travellers and locals alike. In 1479 the court was told that 'Thomas Tewsnorth has broken the land in the King's Highway over against **Berhwys** and there dug and removed gravel to the hurt of the neighbourhood'. In 1481 the 'King's highway' was damaged in Palmer Street, Wells Street, Wyatt's Gate and Castle Field. In the same year the pond at Goldhill was 'weakened to the hurt of the neighbourhood'; no doubt it flooded the road. Two hundred years later the causeways at Sedgebrook gate and Three Elm Lane were still causing trouble!

We do not know whether Thomas Tewsnorth's 'hurt' endangered anyone's life but the story of a Leighton Buzzard glover's fate illustrates the dangers which could befall a traveller. While returning home from Aylesbury market just before Christmas 1499, the man fell into a pit in the middle of the highway. The pit, which measured eight by ten feet on the surface and eight feet deep, had been dug during the day by the servants of an Aylesbury miller to obtain 'ramming clay' for the repair of his mill. Having filled with rain water the hole looked indistinguishable from the rest of the highway in the dusk and the poor glover drowned.[2]

In 1555 the first steps were made towards the formalisation of road repairs. An Act was passed which provided for two parishioners to be elected as Highway Surveyors, or Waywardens, to inspect roads, water-courses, bridges and pavements within their parish and report on their condition thrice yearly. Unfortunately it was up to the lord of the manor (whose own ditches were often neglected) and the local justices to do repairs; and as it only applied to highways, commonways and lanes, no doubt, remained as bad as before, as they were the responsibility of the landowner. Under the Act the better off landowners were required to supply labourers, horses or oxen and tools to do the work. The Act remained in place for nearly three hundred years

2. Addison, 1980, p.85

3. Addison, 1980, p.87

Looking east along 'Stony Lane' (currently a farm track and footpaths MU16 & 17 and MT153) which lies south of Fishall and Hadlow Place. The route lies along the high ground above the Medway, which lies to the right of the picture, and runs roughly parallel to Three Elm Lane between the A26 and Hartlake Bridge.

CHAPTER 11

COMMONS

Our assumptions about the use and conventions associated with common grazing lands are based on clear evidence drawn from areas of England which had common fields, notably in Midland England. The court rolls of manors in those areas stipulate regulations, and show officials insisting that they be observed. The common was usually one or more substantial pieces of land lying towards the outskirts of the parish representing poor land that had not invited early cultivation. It yielded rough grazing, shrubs, underwood, trees and often some minerals like sand, gravel and stone.

Kent, however, was not a county of common fields, yet historians have found some evidence of commons (Blackheath is often cited), along with restrictions on the numbers of animals that could be pastured on them (i.e. stinted), and disputes about the unlawful use of commons by outsiders. They imply that the same conventions ruled commons in Kent as in common field country. But evidence from the Weald suggests rather that conventions ruling elsewhere were only creeping into Kent, probably under the influence of trained lawyers who often became stewards of manors, and were schooled to favour uniformity. Dr Chalklin, writing specifically on Kent, recognised that the Weald had many small heaths rather than large commons, and Helen Muhlfield, publishing a survey of Wye manor on downland, 1452-4, showed no reference there to any common at all.[1] Michael Zell, also concentrating on the Weald, emphasised how different was its agrarian regime from common field England, and made no reference to any commons.[2] E.C.K. Gonner also pointed out a difference in Kent because the Weald was heavily wooded and land was taken into use only as the woods were cleared and the land was enclosed.[3]

Commons did not, of course, pertain to manors but to parishes, and as Hadlow had several manors, we have to assume that tenants' use of commons was somehow agreed between all manors in the parish. All this prepares us for problems in interpreting the

1. Chalklin, 1965, 19-21; Muhlfeld, 1933

2. Zell, 1994, 109-110

3. Gonner, 1912, 238-240

Extract from Andrews, Dury & Herbert map showing the position and extent of Hadlow Common in 1769

Hadlow survey. A statement by William Lambarde in 1570 that 'it was tried by verdict that no man ought to have common in lands of gavelkind' is probably relevant here since pieces of land scattered among the lands of other tenants were likely to be held in gavelkind along with that of their neighbours. Five commons, excluding Lonewood, two of which were called small, are mentioned in the survey (Broads Plain, Tothe Hill, Fish hill, Slethe and Jordans) as adjoining eight tenements Fishland, Knights, Pococks, Tanners, Hoggs, Welshes, Birchwoods, Brooke and Lake; no acreages were stated. Were they lands held in gavelkind, and, if so, did it mean that local people gave the word 'common' a special meaning in these cases? We know well that customs and conventions governing enclosure differed between regions: we find, for example, in a lawsuit relating to Prestbury in Gloucestershire a statement that for the last forty years they had allowed enclosure 'by custom and tolerance'.[4] Was it perhaps usual in the Weald to take a casual attitude towards the appropriation of small pieces of so-called commons by neighbours, without raising a great outcry about their robbing the whole community of its common rights? In any case, Lambarde also alerts us to a changing scene in his day. Having said that land in gavelkind could not be held in common, he added that, nevertheless, 'the contrary is well known at this day, and that in many places'.[5]

Efforts have been made to locate the various small commons mentioned in the survey. Broads Plain Common, also known as Brodetisphayne and Bredett, mentioned

4. NA, C3 / 227 / 58

5. Lambarde, 1970, 511

Old barn, now demolished, which stood adjacent to the 'little common of Fish Hill'

in the descriptions of Hoggs, Knights and Pococks tenements, is on the junction of Cuckoo Lane and the A26. There is now a grain-drying business on the Tonbridge side with a small industrial estate, converted from former chicken sheds, on the Hadlow side. The 'small common called the Slethe' in Welshes tenement is at the junction of High House Lane and Ashes Lane. A smallholding with a few sheep is close by. To the Hill Common in Hoggs tenement was in the area now known as Hogswell, at the junction of the A26 and Three Elm Lane. A petrol station was built here in 1995. David Gurney researched the area for several years for his book 'A Small Kentish Hamlet through Four Centuries', but found no reference to a common.

Two other commons are now part of open farmland. They are Jordans, on land to the east of Hartlake Bridge, and 'a little common' in Fishland tenement, which is to the south of Fish Hall. This latter area may only be reached by farm tracks and has a certain timeless atmostphere, perhaps an echo of earlier times.

The 1587 Rental for the Manors of Hadlow and Tonbridge also suggests a compliant attitude by the manorial lord towards the enclosure of commons, so long as rent was paid. It includes examples of individuals occupying pieces of the common and pieces of waste for which they paid the a lord a capon, a hen, or 2d. Pawley Paler and Thomas Lamparde both had a cottage and croft taken out of the common at Cage Green, and paid the lord 10s. in one case and 4 hens or 2s. in the other. Henry Fane held a piece of Jourdans Common – this was in Brooke tenement. Others holding pieces of common where the location was not identified were George Colleyne, John Marten, Nicholas Miller and Widow Philpott.[6] The lord's evident acceptance of enclosures of commons is in accord with Elton's statement in his *Tenures of Kent* that the lord could enclose lands in gavelkind at his discretion.[7]

One large common in the parish was Loamwood (or Lonewood, later Hadlow Common), although it was not actually in the manor. Its size suggests that it must have played an important part in agricultural life. The name Lomewood appears in a perambulation of the Lowy of Tonbridge in 1259.[8] It is mentioned several times in the survey as many pieces of tenemental land adjoined it. The area it covered in the fifteenth and sixteenth centuries is not known. It is shown on old maps but no two depict the same

6. CKS, U38 M1

7. Elton, 1867, cited in Gonner, 1966, 240

8. Dumbreck, 1959, 138-47

boundaries and some give an indication of a general area, rather than an exact location. The 1769 map by Andrews, Dury and Herbert gives the clearest picture: a narrow strip bordered on the northern part of Carpenters Lane, the northern boundary followed the footpath at the side of Steers Place cottages, then ran in a north-easterly direction close to the Oxenhoath estate to the present Matthews Lane, turned south along Matthews Lane and returned to the southern boundary along the main Hadlow road. The western boundary from the Hadlow Road towards Carpenters Lane is suggested by a track on the same map leaving the main road at right angles, then veering left to Steers Place through the present Hayward Farm. Three tracks are shown crossing the common, but Common Road is of more recent construction. Present-day footpaths MT122 and MT123 and part of MT124 cross the former common.

The few surviving court rolls for Hadlow manors make no mention of the commons and so give no information on its management. An indication of local custom may be deduced from the common called the Hurst a few miles away where 'the woods on the same belongeth to the lord of this manor, the pawnage (pannage) and harbegg (herbage) to the tenants'. A few odd pages at the end of the Hadlow survey referring to the manors of Mereworth and West Peckham include mention of 'The common called Little Lomewood containing 30 acres and lying in Hadlowe the which the tenaunts saith that they have h(e)ard it shuld belonge to the Lord of this manor'. Several pieces of land in West Peckham are described as adjoining Little Lomewood or Lomewood, so it may well have separated Hadlow from West Peckham and/or Mereworth. No further reference has been found suggesting any dispute about ownership, although in the eighteenth century the manor of Lomewood alias Caysers/Kaysers was included with rentals for Wateringbury, East Peckham and Nettlestead

The 1769 map shows three ponds on Lomewood Common, a few scattered trees and three houses on the edge, indicating that encroachments on the common had begun. The symbols used by the mapmaker were the same as those used to denote East Malling Heath and Cocks Heath; they would suggest scrubland. The soil is largely clay, particularly at the eastern end where brickmaking businesses are recorded as operating in the eighteenth, nineteenth and early twentieth centuries. By 1835-1848 many small and some larger enclosures dotted the common, although they still left substantial open land as confirmed by an 1835 survey of Hadlow Parish that listed 109 acres of unenclosed land there. A map dated 1858 showed that this had dwindled to 19 acres.

Today the only memory of Lomewood Common is a signpost to The Common, the comparatively new road called Common Road, and the cricket ground on former common land. Some bungalows built in the 1950s off the main Hadlow Road on land that became part of the Oxenhoath estate bear the name of Lonewood Way. Perhaps closer in spirit is the sight of horses grazing in a field off Carpenters Lane, formerly part of the common.

CHAPTER 12

THE CHURCH

St.Mary's Church drawn in 1839

The earliest reference to a church in Hadlow is in the 'Textus Roffensis' c.975 – the Rochester Register – which records a contribution to Rochester Cathedral. The church is also mentioned in the Domesday Book entry for Hadlow. It stands close to the site of the former manor house, called Court Lodge (later replaced by Hadlow Castle). The present-day Church Place, known in 1460 as Lords Place and later as the Kings Head public house, stands on the northern side.

It is probable that the first church was a simple wooden building, rebuilt in stone in 1019 when the den was granted to Eddeva, the queen of Edward the Confessor. The lower part of the tower dates to this time, with long and short quoin stones visible in the outside north-east corner. The church was rebuilt and extended in the twelfth century, probably by Lord of the Manor, Richard de Clare, before he granted it to the Knights Hospitallers of St John of Jerusalem in 1166. The Knights had a preceptory in nearby West Peckham, surviving today as Dukes Place.

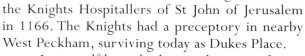

Late twelfth- early thirteenth-century lancet windows may be seen in the north and south walls, and a thirteenth-century south door was blocked up in 1853 but the archway remains. Above the present west doorway are traces of an earlier arch to a doorway. Stonework would also indicate that there was a small Saxon window just underneath the clock. It is thought that the upper part of the tower was added in the fifteenth century, together with a small spire. Windows would seem to have been inserted in the tower at various times, but there is one very small window high up on the east face of the tower which would appear to have been part of the original tower. Recent (August, 2005) work on the south wall has revealed rough stone work with dressed stones at the end of a wall underneath the Roman cement.

Above: Traces of an earlier archway above the west door

Upper right: The thirteenth-century south door

Lower right: Crusader's cross carved in the Saxon doorway

The interior of St Mary's has been altered many times over the centuries: the chancel was rebuilt in 1847, and the north aisle added in 1853. The late twelfth- early thirteenth-century chancel arch has survived. During alterations in 1936 the Saxon doorway at the west end of the church was exposed, and small crosses carved in the stonework were discovered. These are attributed to Nicholas de Hadloe and his son of Hadlow Place on their return from the Third Crusade (1189). The only monument to survive is that to Sir John Rivers and his wife Joan of Fishall, c.1619, Sir John dying in 1583 and Lady Joan in 1619 (see Chapter 13, on the *Rivers* family). None of the stained glass is older than Victorian.

The church played an important part in the life and well-being of the community. Dates of wills, etc., were normally identified by Saints' Days or other church festivals. Payments promised in wills were often made on church premises, as in the case of William Palle (Pawley is a surname in 1460) in 1465 who requested that an annuity be paid to his wife on the Wednesday after each Easter in Hadlow Church. Later, in 1543, Margaret Grenetre (the surname first appearing in 1581-3) left £7 to her son Thomas on the condition that

'the legacy (to) be paid on day of St Michael the Archangel next ensuing
the date of making hereof within the parish church of Hadlow between
the howers of 9 and 12 of the clock in the forenoon of the same day.'

Clergy and staff involved with the church were often left money in the wills of local people. The Sacrist, Thomas Gosse, was left money in several wills (1443-7), also his successor John Knyght (1471-76). Parish clerks named were Richard Blakehouse (1471), John Bembuin (1509), John Bedyndennn (1512), John Mardebery (1529) and Robert Buttlar (1530). None of the Vicars who served during the time of the survey had local family names. They were John Plumpton (1460), David Howell (1465), David Hewe (1475), Thomas Benson (1496), Ralph Houghton (buried in the belfry) (1504), John Turner (1513), Ralph Colcoff (buried in the chancel) (1514), Thomas Awland (1517), John Crosse (renounced Papal authority) (1528), Henry Medow (1536), John Betson (1540), William Pattenson (1545), John Best (1546), John Meer (1554), Thomas Snowe (1555), Thomas Wyxe (1556), Thomas Snowe (1560), William Stace (1572), William Leder (1587), John Starkey (1595).

Church Communion

Bequests for repairs or specific items for the church give an indication of its interior. There would seem to have been two statues of the Virgin Mary, as some bequests for wax candles were for the altar of Our Lady, while others specified the 'image of Our Lady in the chancel' and 'Our Lady in the bodie of Hadlow church'. Reginald Hadecher in 1516 instructed his executors 'to cause the image of Our Lady in the chancel of Hadlow church to be well and sufficiently painted'. Other bequests included velvet and a silver cope for the image of the Virgin Mary. Also mentioned were images of John the Baptist, St Katherine (among the most popular saints in the fifteenth century), St Sight (St Zita, patroness of maidservants at the same time) and the Trinity. Sir Ralph Colcoff, Vicar from 1514 to 1517, left a 'best coverlet to be laid before the altar' plus 8d. 'to the altar that I used to synge within church of Hadlow'. Henry Fane left two chalices to the value of £4 in 1533 and was of sufficient status to have had his own chaplain, Sir James Baynes, to whom he left four marks.

Many planned for their legacy to continue into future years, such as William Palle leaving a cow in 1465, the profits to be used for the maintenance of a lamp in the chancel. In 1514 John Walter instructed his wife to maintain a wax taper twice a year before the Trinity and the image of Our Lady in the chancel, while in the same year John Brooke asked his wife to give 1lb. of wax a year to keep tapers burning before Our Lady. The sons of John Somer (a shopkeeper in 1460) were to find 'for their lives and the longest liver of either' wax tapers before the image of Our Lady in the chancel and before St Katherine twice a year.

The priest administered to the dying and often acted as a scribe and draughtsman of parishioners' wills, or acted as witness. This could well have meant that he was in a position to suggest legacies. John a Barton evidently had a poor opinion of priests as in 1530 he left messuages to his son Thomas 'if he finds an honest priest to say masses'. Burial instructions were frequently included in wills – Vicar Ralph Houghton requested burial in the belfry (1513), William King 'to be chested and buried in Hadlow Churchyard beside his first wife' (1576), while John Byshop asked that he be buried in St Olaves, Southwark, or Hadlow depending on where he died (1516).

Several people left bequests to other churches, mainly to those in neighbouring villages. Richard Bealde in 1456 left 40s. each to Tonbridge, Tudeley and East Peckham (John Beald is in our survey, but not Richard). Thomas Lakk in 1527 left instructions for a gilded tabernacle to be made for the image of Our Lady on the Cross at Larkfelde (Larkfield), together with a cote cloth of velvet. (The Lack surname first appears in 1581-3.) Vicar Ralph Colcoff left 20s. to St Giles, Newcastle under Lyme – perhaps an earlier parish – in addition to 6s.8d. and his best coverlet for Hadlow church..

1.   Clark, 1977, 58

The changes in Hadlow brought about by the Reformation can be traced through wills. If treated with caution the religious preambles to the wills provide a rough guide to changes in religious feeling. Peter Clark in a detailed study of religious trends during the period has divided these preambles into three categories: conservative, reformist and 'committed Protestant'.[1] The traditional, conservative, dedication was 'I leave my soul to Almighty God, the Blessed Virgin Mary and all the saints in Heaven'. This phrase, with slight variations, was used in Hadlow wills up to the 1490's when the simpler 'I leave my soul to Almighty God' became increasingly common. Clark defines such wills as reformist as they 'omit all mention of intermediaries with the deity'. This is slightly misleading as often the 'Almighty God' is followed by 'etc.' and the wills sometimes go on to leave money for masses and/or lights before images, showing that the will maker was more conservative than first appears. However, there is little evidence of massive enthusiasm for the cults of the saints shown in the west country parish of Morebath.[2] Out of fifty-two wills written between 1500 and 1530 only fourteen contained bequests for lights or images. Many more wills contained specific requests for masses. In 1447 Thomas Fromond left 25s. for the Carmelite brothers of Aylesford to say 300 masses for his soul. He also arranged for a tenement to be sold and the money to be used to celebrate masses for the souls of his father and mother. Richard Bealde left 3s.4d. to the altar of Hadlow church for masses in 1456, plus 16s.8d. to the Carmelite Friars for masses for his soul, those of relatives and all deceased faithful. In 1461 Dionysia Ippenbury left 3d. for masses each year for twelve years, with land to be sold for masses in both Hadlow and East Peckham. Sir Raff Houghton, vicar of Hadlow in 1513, particularly asked for 'the trental of St. Gregory' to be sung for his soul.

2.   Duffy, 2001

The last specific bequest for masses for the soul came in John Born's will of 1543 and soon after, in 1547, came the first 'committed Protestant' will, that of Richard Harmon, a tanner, who left his soul to 'Almighty God, my Maker and Redeemer, desiring Him through the merit of Christ's Passion that I may be the child of Salvation'. After 1543 there were only five wills which mentioned the Blessed Virgin Mary, all the rest would be termed 'reformist' or 'Protestant' and bequests to the church, even for the obligatory 'forgotten tithes', always specified in earlier years, dried up completely. In 1559 an injunction instructed the clergy to discourage parishioners from religious provisions other than bequests to the poor. There had been some earlier provision for the poor; for example, Dionysia Ippenbury left land to her husband in 1461 on condition that he distributed 6s.8d. a year for twelve years to the poor of Hadlow at Quadragesima in bread, and James Gosse in 1493 left the profits of a field at Newy, called the Reade, for the benefit of the poor people of Hadlow. These bequests to the poor, including gifts of wheat, cash or clothing, increased from the 1540s and many, like John Holybone, left bequests for 'foul ways' (road repairs) and 'poor mades marriages' (dowries to help poor girls to marry).

The house of Dionisia Ippenberry, who died in 1461. The house which stood in 'Hadlow Street' was demolished in 1965

The wills show no evidence of resistance to the extreme reforms of Edward's reign. The preambles were solidly reformist (5) or Protestant (5). There were a few bequests to the poor and one to Goldhill Bridge but it has to be said that the sums did not equal the sums formerly given for masses and lights. The people of Hadlow were taking the opportunity to save their money. What is very striking is that during Mary's reign there was no attempt to revive the old ways. Even the three wills which contain dedications to the Virgin Mary and the saints left nothing to the church. Of the other fourteen wills written during Mary's reign, seven were reformist but seven were clearly Protestant. After the revival of the Heresy Acts in 1554, to advertise religious commitment in this way showed courage and possibly local protection and sympathy. John Barton (1554), John Wellar (1556) and Nicholas and Richard Somer (1557) were all prepared to use the formula 'I leave my soul to Almighty God my Saviour and Redeemer, whom I desire for the merit of Christ's Passion that I may be the child of Salvation'.

There is some evidence that the Hadlow/Tonbridge area was one particularly susceptible to Protestant ideas. Its position on one of the main routes between London and the Continent, and on the fringe of the Wealden cloth industry, had undoubtedly brought contact with Lollard influence. Lollardy had at least one supporter in Hadlow, for Richard Hebard of Hadlow was brought to trial with Thomas Hellis of Brenchley in 1431. (A John Hebard was a shopkeeper in Church Street in 1460.) Richard Hebard owned English books containing heresy and had spoken out against the veneration of images. Both had to do penance in their parish churches, in Rochester cathedral, and also in Tonbridge and in Malling, suggesting they had been active in a wide area. Christopher Payn of Tonbridge admitted in 1496 that he had held meetings in his house and that he had been a Lollard for five or six years. On the whole the wills support the idea that Hadlow was, like the South East in general and the Weald in particular, ahead of the rest of England in its conversion to Protestantism.

The registers of St Mary's Church began in 1558. From these it can be seen that some of the families mentioned in the Survey were still in Hadlow at the end of the sixteenth century. Among the names are Barton, Bishop, Fisher, Gooding, Honewold (Homewood), Johnson, Newman, Reeve, Simond, Somer and Stubbersfield, with Bourne, Burton, Colyn, Crud, Fane, Pawley, Salmon, Trice and Wells from those who took over tenements c.1581-3. No entries appear for Fromund, Nepaker or Pynchon, who were among the names of men who gave information at the original enquiry. Some may well have descendants in the village today, although family trees have not been checked.

The survey has entries referring to crosses at various places. Initially this was thought to mean crossroads, but bequests to repair the crosses at Goldhill, Hadlow Bridge and Palmers Street appear in Hadlow wills, suggesting that they were actual crosses. Reginald Hadecher left 20s. for the 'holing and reparation of Hadlow Cross' in 1516 (whereabouts unknown). It is probable that these crosses were visited during the traditional Rogationtide processions, and may also have been resting places where coffins were laid down while being carried to the church. (Older residents nowadays still refer to the path from Stallions Green to Bourne Grange Lane as the Coffin Path.) No trace of any of these crosses has survived and it is likely that they were destroyed in 1547/8.

A procession

1. Hasted, V, 75

2. CKS, DRb, PWr, 2, f.79

3. It is not certain that this is the same man with whom Hasted starts the family: he did not give him any dates, and allowed him only three sons; the fourth would have been Richard who died in 1488, the same year as his brother John died.

4. For his will, see NA, Prob 11, 8, 9

5. A funeral monument to a Thomas Stydolf, dying in 1457, is in Tudeley church (see drawing on page 73).

6. The family, of course, already had other branches for John's brother, Richard, who had died in 1488, was described as of Hollanden, in Leigh parish, and had the same Fane connections with Shipborne, Leigh, and Tonbridge.

CKS DRb, PWr, 5, f.152v

CHAPTER 13

SOME FAMILIES

According to Edward Hasted, the historian of Kent writing in the 1780s and 1790s, and having access to family archives, the Fane family was of Welsh origin.[1] They had arrived in Kent in Henry VI's reign, that is, some time between 1422 and 1461. Henry Vane had acquired Hilden manor in Tonbridge, part of what is now Hildenborough, and lived there. A will of one, Henry de Vane, shows his death in 1456 and burial in Tonbridge church, leaving a widow, Margaret. His donations of money for church repairs and references to land that he owned show a connection also with Leigh, Shipbourne, and Penshurst, and ownership of some Tonbridge land near North Frith.[2] The family through the generations was plainly successful in raising children, including sons, so their relationships are not altogether clear, but this Henry Vane's will shows that he had four sons, John (called John of Tonbridge), Richard, Robert, and Thomas, and a daughter, Joan, married to Thomas Reade.[3] He also had a brother, William.

Hasted then turned his attention to the heirs of the eldest boy, John Vane of Tonbridge, dying in 1488.[4] He had wide local connections, leaving money to Seal, East Peckham, Marden, Lamberhurst, Bidborough, Wittersham, and Snargate, and having land also in Ludlow, Shropshire. He too left four sons, Henry who settled in Hadlow, Richard who inherited Badsell in Five Oak Green, Capel parish, inheriting through his wife Agnes, daughter of Thomas Stidulph,[5] Thomas of London, and John of Hadlow. These four boys introduce us to the generation that brought the Fanes (the spelling now altered from Vane to Fane) into Hadlow.[6] He referred in his will not only to his brother John, having a son, Harry, but also to a Thomas Fane, without specifying the relationship. He should have been another brother. If he was, then Richard credited him with a son, John, and a daughter, Alice.

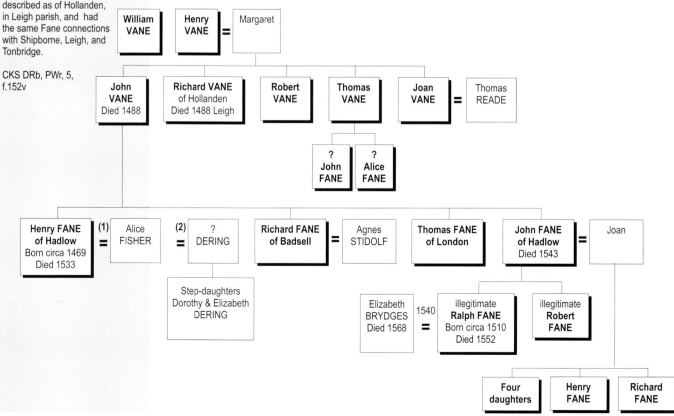

7.   Newman, 1969, 191

8.   Hasted, V, 182

The Fanes' main family home came to be regarded as Badsells, which Richard, son of John of Tonbridge, inherited through his wife. It still exists, preserving fragments of a fifteenth or early sixteenth-century house, with a moat around it, in Five Oak Green, Capel parish.[7] The family member who established the connection with Hadlow was the eldest son of John of Tonbridge, Henry (seemingly, the one called Harry in his uncle Richard Fane's will). Henry's date of birth is unknown but it may have been *circa* 1469, and according to Hasted he lived in Hadlow Place in Henry VII's reign, that is to say, by 1509.[8]

Badsell Manor

9.   Hasted, V, 182

No Fanes appear as occupiers of land in our 1460 survey, but it is perfectly possible that Henry Fane acquired Hadlow Place, which was a sub-manor, and was by 1509 a Hadlow resident. According to Hasted, he married Alice Fisher, who belonged to the Fisher family of Fishall, and, if this was so, it is quite likely that she became the heir to Hadlow Place and so had passed it to her husband.[9] Fishall and Hadlow Place lie near each other, and the Fishers were of near-gentry status. That guess is strengthened by the fact that Henry Fane referred in his will to his brother-in-law, Richard Fisher, though he did not refer to Alice Fisher as his wife. She must have died already, for his wife at his death in 1533 was a Dering, and through her he had two step-daughters, Dorothy and Elizabeth.

Henry Fane achieved considerable standing in his lifetime, at court and also in the county; he was a gentleman usher at the funeral of Henry VII in 1509, JP for Kent from 1505, sheriff of Kent in 1507-8, and subsidy commissioner in 1523-6. His will when he died in 1533, depicted a sympathetic personage, for he left legacies, in some cases substantial, to over a dozen servants, an annual payment to a chaplain until he found a benefice, and a simple request for

Coats of arms which appear on George Fanes's monument in Tudeley church

burial 'as the body of a true Christian man'. He had had no children of his own, and presumably his step-daughters were well provided for by the Dering family, for the Derings were well-endowed Kent gentry. So he chose as his heir, Ralph Fane, the illegitimate son of his brother, John.

The Oxford DNB is in error, along with many other authors, in saying, that Henry Fane was father of Ralph Fane. He was not. John Fane made this clear in his own will in 1542. John recognised Ralph as his bastard son and bequeathed to him a house and lands in Southborough, with remainder to another bastard son, Robert, though of Robert nothing further has been found. John went on to marry, and referred to all his legitimate offspring in his will, expressing his last wishes in Catholic rather than Protestant, terms. He had married Joan, and by her had had four daughters, not yet married, and two sons, Henry and Richard. He showed concern that Richard should be put to school and university, 'if he had sufficient learning'; and he left him land in East Peckham and Nettlestead. Henry, the older boy, was to have lands in Tonbridge, Seal, Leigh, and Shipbourne, and was made

10.   NA, Prob. 11, 29, 15

executor of his father's will along with John's wife, Joan.[10] Henry Fane's will in 1533, bequeathed his 'manor house at Hadlow' and some small lands to Ralph Fane along with all his lands in Hadlow and Capel. So this was Hadlow Place, which had once been the house of Anne, Duchess of Buckingham, until her death in 1480. We have to guess that it came somehow to the Fishers after Anne died in 1480, and was in due course inherited by Alice Fisher. Therefore, at some date between 1533, when Henry Fane died, and 1540 when Ralph Fane married, Ralph moved into Hadlow Place.[11]

11.   NA, Prob. 11, 25, 4

Ralph Fane's date of birth is unknown, but is thought to have been about 1510.

Effigies of Thomas and Alice Stidulph, based on the brass monument in Tudeley church

He was later described as having rough manners, and he may well have had a deficient education, at least in foreign languages, for he later lamented his incompetence in French and German. But he had entry into governmental circles as a young man, for he served Thomas Cromwell from 1531 until 1538, and was commended by him to the king. In 1540 he became a Gentleman Pensioner at court, accepting the duty of attending Henry VIII on ceremonial occasions. He also accompanied him to war in France and Scotland, and was knighted at Boulogne in 1544. In the 1540s he received some considerable grants in Hadlow, Tonbridge, and Shipbourne of land that had been forfeited by the Duke of Buckingham, as well as acquiring Fishall from the Fishers. In 1542 he was appointed Chief Governor and Keeper of Cage and Postern Parks, and we may suspect that as a Gentleman Pensioner he made good use of those parks and North Frith Park as well for the purpose of breeding fine horses. It became one of Henry VIII's dedicated policies to improve the breed of English horses; they had proved so weak in bearing burdens when compared with Dutch horses.[12]

12. Thirsk, 1984, 383-6

Ralph did valiant service for Henry VIII between 1543 and 1546, being deputed to go to Flanders to hire mercenaries to fight for England in alliance with the Emperor against France. His letters back and forth to the king survive for these years, vividly showing what a harassing experience it was as he entered into a contract with the mercenaries, they milled restlessly and threateningly around the area of Aachen, and he waited for the money to arrive in Antwerp to pay them. These negotiations concerning the hiring of 4,000 footmen and 1,000 horsemen dragged on for months.

The Tudeley monument to George Fane

Subsequently, at the siege of Boulogne Ralph acquitted himself with honour, and was knighted by Henry VIII. He was back at home for the winter of 1544, in royal favour, and received a grant of lands in Shipbourne and Tonbridge. In 1545 he was promoted to be a Lieutenant of the Gentlemen Pensioners, and at some time in the same year he was ordered back to Flanders all over again, this time to muster German troops and lead them through France to Calais and Boulogne. Again he faced the agony of having settled to pay the soldiers for three months, and finding that they demanded four months' pay, since they had been kept idly waiting for one month already. Three months' pay left them with only one month's campaigning and another month to get home; had they known how things would turn out, they said, they would never have agreed to such a short contract. At one stage Fane was threatened with mutinous men wanting to kill him: 'God send us good riddance out of these wild beasts' hands', he wrote.

In the course of this correspondence, it is revealed that a Henry Fane, described as his cousin, was in company with Ralph in October, 1545. They were at Florines, and he is likely to have been Ralph's half-brother; Lord Cobham's son was also there. It gives us an insight into the way younger sons of gentry in Kent were introduced into adult life, getting access to a circle in which they might find a patron, and end up in court or in government service.[13] Henry had been the executor of his father John's will, when he died in 1543. He had inherited John's main lands in Tonbridge, Seal, Leigh, and Shipbourne.[14] John was, of course, Ralph's father also. But by this time Ralph, by another route, had become a fairly wealthy man too; he was rated in the 1543 subsidy as owning lands to the value of £320. Ralph returned unharmed to England by early 1547, then fought in Scotland, and in the same year was recorded as a JP for Kent, and MP at

13. L&P, Hen.VIII, 1545, XX (ii), 292

14. NA, Prob. 11, 29, 15

73

Westminster. In the new reign of Edward VI, he looked to Somerset for patronage and favour, but when Somerset was overthrown by the Duke of Northumberland, Ralph was accused of conspiring against him. At the trial, he was said to have been 'answering like a ruffian',[15] and was condemned and hanged in February 1552.

A vestige of Ralph's career survives in Hadlow Place which has a wooden frieze of carved heads over a stone fireplace. John Newman in Pevsner's *Buildings of the Western Weald* says that they are plainly German heads, dating from the period 1530-40. Ralph must have brought them back from the Low Countries, possibly when he attended on Anne of Cleves when she travelled from Düsseldorf to Calais for her brief, ill-fated marriage to Henry VIII, or, more likely, when Ralph was negotiating the hire of mercenaries in Flanders between 1543 and 1546. Perhaps the citizens of Aachen presented them to him, while begging him to take the mercenaries away from marauding their neighbourhood!

When Ralph Fane died in 1552, Elizabeth, his wife, did not continue living at Hadlow Place. She was Elizabeth Brydges, daughter and heir of Roland Brydges of Clerkenwell, Middlesex, and of The Ley, Weobley, Herefordshire, and had had no children by her marriage. She was a fervent Protestant who translated some of the psalms, and was deemed a 'liberal patronness' of Robert Crowley, a poet and cleric who insisted on the need to curb avarice and help the poor.[16] She was also 'a great and helpful supporter of imprisoned Protestants', persecuted under Queen Mary; she corresponded with them and was herself obliged at one stage to go into hiding. She moved to London at Ralph's death, and died in Holborn; she was buried in St Andrew's

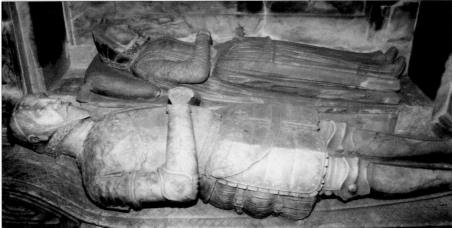

church on 11 June, 1568.[17] Scattered references to the earlier Protestant sympathies of some other Hadlow residents have been noted above in Chapter 7. Sir John Rivers and his wife, Joan, who moved into Hadlow when the Fanes departed, perpetuated the same tradition.

The next episode in the Fane story emerges from our Hadlow survey when analysing the additional notes that were inserted by the steward in 1581 when he copied out the survey of 1460. He inscribed in the margin the names of many of the new occupiers of the tenements. Now Henry Fane, Ralph's half-brother, featured noticeably, having acquired one fifth of a knight's fee of Hadlow manor, and holding sixteen named pieces of land, plus three that were shared with another. The total amounted to some 66 acres, that had been negotiated through some nineteen transactions with people occupying eight different tenements. An unidentified Colyer Fane also held a fragment of one acre. These two Fanes may, of course, have held land in other Hadlow manors also, but the Fanes were not destined to remain long in Hadlow, and as leading gentry in the parish, they would be replaced by the Rivers family.

The Fane story offers many insights into the fortunes of Kent's gentry, all of them starting modestly, but accepting the rules of gavelkind to provide for all their sons. Opinions about this system of inheritance would begin to change in the sixteenth century, and some gentlemen would procure acts to disgavel their land, enabling them to promote the eldest son at the expense of the rest. Families like the Culpepers, the Cottons, and the Fromonds were all agents and victims in Hadlow of this changing world. Some of their offspring would be content to be diligent, conscientious, local administrators without

15. ODNB

16. ODNB

17. ODNB

Monument to Thomas Fane and his wife Helen in Hunton church, who died in 1606.

The Fane family's grief is here set in stone, when their only child, Mary (above), died in childbed, and their only grandchild and heir Thomas (right) died soon after.

aspiring to great heights in national life. Others had greater ambitions. Experience in the first half of the sixteenth century taught some sharp lessons about the fortunes that might be made, but also about the risks that they ran of premature death, if once they entered politics or found a footing at court. One branch of the Fanes prospered exceedingly, becoming landowners in Mereworth, building Mereworth Castle, and becoming Earls of Westmorland. The first earl was Francis Fane (1583-1628), son of Sir Thomas Fane who died in 1589. Hunton church has a fine memorial in the chancel to another Sir Thomas Fane who died in the same year as his wife, Helen (described on the tomb as Dame Helen Somerset), in 1606. It shows them recumbent alongside one another, with a figure in the front of their only daughter, Mary, who died in childbed, and her son, Thomas, who died soon after her. As this Sir Thomas had no other children, he made Sir George Fane, second son of Sir Thomas Fane of Badsell and of Dame Mary, Baroness Le Despencer, his heir. A brass plate on the wall of the church also commemorates Francis Fane, grandchild of Baroness Le Despencer, and son of the above Sir George Fane. Another earlier monument of a George Fane is a tomb-chest with canopy, but without effigy, dated 1571 in Tudeley church (see photo on page 73), the church that also has several windows by Marc Chagall.[18]

Monument brass in Hunton church to Francis Fane

We are most grateful to Dr Michael Zell for the use of his notes of the Fane wills.

18.   Newman, 1969, 552

THE RIVERS FAMILY

The Rivers family were the leading gentry in Hadlow around 1600, having succeeded to the role that had been played by the Fane family until Ralph Fane was hanged for treason in 1552. They settled in slowly, but some members of the family remained to the end of the seventeenth century.

When the Rivers family arrived in Kent, their main home was in Chafford. According to Hasted they acquired Chafford Place, in the parish of Penshurst, in Henry VIII's reign, having come originally from River Hill in Hampshire. Richard Rivers was steward of the lands of Edward, Duke of Buckingham. As the Duke was executed in 1521, Richard Rivers could have been introduced to Hadlow early in the sixteenth century, visiting it as an official in charge of the Duke of Buckingham's lands. But no trace of the family is found in Hadlow documents until the 1580s, when a rental of Hadlow manor in 1586 mentions one Rivers, a widow, as a tenant, and also names the heirs of Sir John Rivers as having an interest in a piece of Hadlow land called Lowlings. In the same document, Sir John Rivers is also shown holding a knight's fee for Pechams manor, along with Henry Fane esquire. More than one member of the Rivers family was now settled in Hadlow, for in a subsidy list of taxpayers in 1589 Lady Rivers was paying more than anyone else in subsidy on goods (at 41s.8d.), and Richard Rivers, esquire, (relationship unknown) paid on 8s.4d; no member of the family at this date, however, was taxed on land.[1]

Monument in St Mary's, Hadlow to Sir John and Lady Joan Rivers

1.   Hasted, 1798, III, 250; BL, Add MS 16279, f.383; CKS, U38/M1

The scattered places with which the Rivers family showed a connection included Leigh and Tonbridge in Kent, Chafford in Sussex, and London, suggesting that they had no overpowering attachment to Hadlow. But their loyalty increased over the years, and in the 1690s Clement Rivers was at Fish Hall. Around 1600 it is Sir John Rivers and his wife who attract most notice, for Sir John had been Lord Mayor of London in 1573, and a member of

2.   Dietz, 7, also 45, 112, 234

3.   NA Prob 11 / 66, f.37

4.   CKS U 1475, E55 / 1

5.   NA Prob 11 / 133, f.504ff

the Grocers' Company. London port books in 1567/8 show him as John Rivers, alderman of London, importing ginger and pepper from Antwerp.[2] A memorial commemorates both husband and wife on the south wall of the chancel in Hadlow church.

No family archives for the Rivers are known to exist, and no traditions of their living in Hadlow survive. But we learn something about them from their wills. Sir John Rivers's will was dated January 5, 1581 and he was buried on 17 March, 1584.[3] Words in his last testament showed his strong Protestant beliefs, hoping to rise with the Elect at the end of a transitory life, and wishing to be buried in the chancel of Hadlow church on the right hand side, near the wall. He left money for preaching four times a year for five years in Hadlow church, and made similar provision in Little St.Bartholomew's church in London. Among bequests to the poor he gave sums to prisoners in Newgate prison and King's Bench prison in Southwark. He also provided for a dinner on the day of his burial for members of the Livery of the Grocers' Company, and allowed for innumerable black coats to be given to his relations, all his servants (but gowns for the women), and certain friends in Penshurst, and in Withyham, Sussex. Significantly, members of the Willard family, including David, the thrusting entrepreneur in the iron industry, received black cloaks rather than coats, while others, including closer relations, received gold rings. Sir John owned property in Tonbridge, Groombridge, Withyham, Ashurst, and London, and was owner of the manor of Chafford. In a codicil he arranged for his woodlands, without stating where they were, to be used to make coals, the profit going to his wife. (In 1559 John Rivers, not yet knighted, had bought from Sir Henry Sydney woodland in Penshurst in South Park 'to be taken and felled within 21 years', but he sold it back to him in 1569.[4]) The development of the iron industry in and around Tonbridge was clearly still in full swing in the 1580s and Sir John evidently had no qualms about his collaboration with David Willard. Was it perhaps David Willard who had nudged him into inserting this codicil?

Sir John's widow lived for another twenty-five years, being buried on 30 May, 1619. Her will was made when she was in good health, and had perfect memory, but it plainly showed how she had disapproved of her husband's expenditure on all those black coats and cloaks.[5] She, in contrast, wanted to be buried 'in some convenient place without vain show of black or other extraordinary funeral expenses'. In their stead she gave away a number of gold rings. The preamble of her will was considerably more impassioned than her husband's in proclaiming her belief in an afterlife. The ranking of her feelings towards local places was revealed in her bequest of £6 to the poorest and eldest people of Hadlow, £5 to the poor widows and the eldest poor of Westerham, and £4 to the poor of Penshurst. She also left £5 to build a stone porch at Ashurst church, when the parishioners 'shall go about the new building of it', and like her husband she left money for poor prisoners in three prisons in London. She had warm words for her husband, calling him 'most kind and loving', and asked for a monument to be erected in memory of them both and their children in Hadlow church, like the one erected to her own parents in St Bartholomew's church near the Exchange in London. She left quite a few pieces of silver ware to kinsmen, and in a way that was more characteristic of women than men, she listed many personal possessions, such as items of furniture, tapestry, and kitchen pots, and one long needlework carpet with arms that had once belonged to her father, Sir George Barnes. This property was evidently located at Chafford, which was clearly a substantial house with a great hall and gallery; it was pulled down in 1743. Echoing her husband, Lady Elizabeth expressed the hope that her family and friends would be contented with her will; it was certainly a detailed one that must have taken her much time and thoughtful consideration, for she had a large family of children and grandchildren to consider. She had given birth to at least six sons and three daughters.

Edward Rivers, one of Lady Joan's younger sons, was executor of her will, and in 1632 when he made a will, and was unmarried, he was described as a merchant; judging by his connections, he worked in London. He had become owner, seemingly, by inheritance from George Rivers, esquire, (see below) of what he called 'the manor of

6. NA Prob 11 / 160, f.100

7. NA Prob 11 / 162, f.69

8. NA Prob 11 / 273, f.54

Fishall', though Fishall's status as a manor is not proved in any manorial documents, and he wished to be buried in Hadlow near his mother. He did not die until 1660, however, and no monument to him is visible in the church.[6]

The concern that Sir John and Lady Joan Rivers showed in the words of their wills to avoid disputes is reflected in the will of another member of the Rivers family. George Rivers, esquire, of Hadlow was a younger son of the late Sir George Rivers of Chafford, and was the owner of Fishall when he died in 1632. He lived, he said, 'in the messuage in Fishall', and he too deemed it a manor. Lady Joan was his grandmother, and it seems that she had exerted great influence over her family, for he wished to be buried in Hadlow church near her and his uncle, and he was as fervent a Puritan as she had been.[7] His anxieties were expressed thus in his will as he lay on the brink of death, 'knowing how much it concerns every man in his life to settle his estate so that after his death it may be enjoyed by such to whom he intends it without controversy or suits, which otherwise often happen between persons near in blood, to the breach of all bonds of amity and the corruption of many estates'. A momentous story obviously lay behind those words, perhaps involving a local family, or stirring gossip in London. Significantly, he gave to his wife, Rose, in her widowhood his whole estate, rather than just the half to which she was entitled, though if she married he reduced it to a half, without, he said, wishing to restrain her from marrying, according to her 'good liking'. His prime concern was for the education and maintenance of his children.

The strong sense of kinship in this family permeated other wills, such as that of Sir Thomas Rivers in 1657, owner of a manor in Hadlow, which may have been Pechams because he held a farm called Peckham Place. He was evidently unmarried, without children, and all his property was destined for his brothers and sisters.[8] In Hadlow's social hierarchy, the Rivers family replaced the Fanes, but only gradually did they establish a firm bond with Hadlow, and they left no elegant buildings in the village by which we might remember them.

THE FROMOND FAMILY

The Fromond family was of near gentry status, at one time owning lands totalling only slightly less than a knight's fee. However, by the time of the survey some branches of the family were humbler and played their part in Hadlow life alongside families such as the Bishops, Bealdes and Fishers. Although they had connections with Tonbridge castle and business dealings with London, Maidstone and other areas of Kent, there is no evidence that they took any part in national politics.

The family name first appeared in the area in association with the 'Manor of Thomas Fromond in Hadlow'. Court Rolls for that manor, beginning 20 July 1294, cite Thomas as lord. In 1339 his son Nicholas succeeded him but by 1349 Nicholas's widow, Alice, was holding the court. In December 1350 Thomas Fromond junior was lord, but in 1352 the lordship passed to Richard at Weald and by 1378 it was in the hands of the Godyng family where it remained for more than a century. In spite of the change the court was still said to be 'held at Thomas Fromonds'. However, Thomas Fromond 'of Fishall' and his son Thomas Fromond 'of Goldhill', continued to owe suit of court in the manor, and court rolls and rentals of the manor continued to record members of the family holding land there.[1]

1. CKS, U55, M360

Numerous other documents, apart from the survey, refer to the family. The most useful of these are nine early wills, dating between 1447 and 1488. Because they cover a far shorter period than the Bishop wills it is more difficult to discover a line of descent, but more branches of the family are included. Members of the family appear as litigants in the manor court rolls and, in various capacities, in the wills of others. Perhaps because of their higher status there are also early references in the Patent and Close Rolls and among Kent Feet of Fines.

As early as 1320, a case between Thomas, son of John Fromond of Goldhill senior, plaintiff, and John Fromond of Goldhill, defendant, shows that the branch of the family that called itself 'of Goldhill' as opposed to 'of Kempinghale', or 'atte Water', was established. The case also listed the property involved; one messuage, fifty acres of land, thirteen acres of meadow, and a weir in the water called Knokewere (Oak Weir), with its appurtenances. The lands were eventually granted by Thomas to John for life, 'for service of a rose', to be paid at the feast of the Nativity of St. John the Baptist.

Another document of 1320 demonstrates that the Fromonds were not only land owners but also shop owners and that their holdings extended beyond Hadlow. Gilbert Fromond owned one messuage, one shop, twelve acres of land and one of pasture in East Peckham, Hadlow, Tudeley and Maidstone. In 1337 Gilbert Fromond was in debt and in 1346 Johane Fromond paid 20s. in an aid to the Black Prince for a demesne in Hadlow.

In 1358 there was a reference to 'John Fromond Receiver, the Earl of Stafford's Lordship of Tonbridge'. As Receiver, John would have come into the orbit of Tonbridge Castle and the family must have had connections with other minor and even major figures in the Earl's household. A payment by John in 1362 to the Prior and Convent of Tonbridge of 10 marks indicates a man of some substance. The Close Rolls have another reference to a John Fromond in 1398, the last of the century. He made a quit claim of all his lands in Hadlow, a way there called 'the Forde' and two bridges, to Thomas Sibseye, tailor, of London, again showing that the family had more than just local connections. The lands included pieces called Nuemede, Smeltes Meede, Warde and Bothegate.

Probably the most important early document which mentions the Fromond family is the Inquisition Post Mortem into the estates of Gilbert de Clare in 1315, after the death of Gilbert at the battle of Bannockburn. This shows that a John Fromond had half a knight's fee in Hadlow called Fromonds while Thomas Fromond held one fifth of a knight's fee called Goodmans (Godyngs?). A later Inquisition, on the death of Hugh de Audeley who inherited part of the Clare estates through his wife, Gilbert's daughter Margaret, updates the situation. At this time a John Fromond still held half a knight's fee while Gilbert Fromond held an eighth of a fee, and a sixth with John atte Weald, and a sixteenth with William de Pympe. Nicholas Fromond held a fifth of a fee. While John's fee was said to be 'held of the King in chief', the fees of Gilbert and Nicholas were presumably held through the Archbishop like other lands in the Lowy. By 1398 a Thomas Fromond was in possession of the half knight's fee and a John Fromond had inherited Nicholas's fifth. The fractions of fees which Gilbert held were no longer attributed to the family. In 1405 a list of the dower lands of Anne, late wife of Edmund, Earl of Stafford, included the fifth part of a knight's fee in the hands of Thomas Fromond.

An inquisition at the time of the death of Humphrey, Duke of Buckingham, in 1460 states that a John Fromond still held a half fee in Hadlow. However, our survey only assigns him, 'one sixteenth part of a knight's fee in his own capital messuage, with lands called Kings adjoining, formerly of Richard Bealde', in Hadlow Manor itself. Lady Margaret Fromond held a sixth of a knight's fee, formerly of Richard Broomfield, at Edmund, Fromonds and Collesstokes. At the same time Sir Richard Culpeper held half a knight's fee, 'lately of John Fromonde next Barns Street in Hadlow' and John Goding held a fifth part of a knight's fee formerly of Thomas Fromond'. This would indicate that the Fromonds were alienating as well as acquiring land and that the original half knight's fee did not remain the core of their holding. Thomas Fromond's will of 1447 mentions 'my capital tenement with garden adjoining, in total one messuage, garden and two pieces of land adjoining called Kings', which contained fifteen acres, about one sixth of his total holding of approximately eighty eight acres. The survey is quite clear about the obligations which came with a knight's fee, or part knight's fee. Lady Elizabeth Culpeper, for instance, 'owes castle guard in time of war in the fashion of a knight' and scutage and suit of court every three weeks. But the survey does not describe the lands which went to make up the parts of fees it mentions. Did they actually consist of lands or did lands already held create an obligation to knight's service, compensated for by some privileges and prestige? [2]

2. Knights' fees are most helpfully discussed in Harvey, 1970.

By the time of the survey seven members of the Fromond family, four of them women, held land in Hadlow Manor. The holdings were in ten different tenements, most to the south of the Goldhill to Tonbridge highway, some bordering on the Medway, adjacent to, even interspersed with, land in the Manor of Fromonds. (See photo map on page 61 for orientation of Goldhill.) John Fromond of Goldhill was credited with a sixteenth of a knight's fee and approximately forty acres concentrated in Brook tenement. Lady Margaret Fromond held fourteen acres distributed between Lake, Brooke, Eastwosys and a tenement formerly of William at Lake that was held to be one sixth of a knight's fee. Gilbert Fromond held less than two acres in Brook tenement and his wife Alice four acres in Stoperfields. Another Alice Fromond, widow of Peter, held over five acres in Hamenetts, over three in Alynslove, and four in Stoperfields. Joan Fromond atte Water held approximately sixteen acres distributed between Jopes, Fishland, and Odamys tenements. John Fromond of Kempinghale had just over sixteen acres in Lake and Lotewood.

Women digging in the herb garden

Joan Fromond atte Water was left a fairly wealthy widow by the will of her husband Thomas. According to the survey she had two houses, 'a garden with a house built upon it called Hentlove' in Jopes tenement and 'her messuage in which she lives with a small piece of land adjoining' in Odamys tenement. Alice, the widow of Peter Fromond atte Water, Joan's daughter in law, does not appear to have lived in the manor as there is no house recorded on her lands there, unless she lived in one of Joan's houses. However, Alice, the wife of Gilbert Fromond, held, in her own right, a messuage and garden called Robards, near to the Goldhill to Malling highway. John Fromond of Goldhill, also had his 'capital messuage' within the manor but his mother, Lady Margaret Fromond, unless she shared his house, lived outside the manor, possibly outside the parish, as she had holdings in Tudeley, East Peckham, Hunton and Linton and even in Romney Marsh. The last member of the family to appear in the survey, John Fromond of Kempinghale, had a 'messuage in which he lives with a barn, land and garden' called Clob Croft, near to the lane to Gibbons Lake and also 'one parcel of land with a house built upon it, called Thomas at Grove, lately acquired of Richard Knight'.

The Fromonds of Goldhill

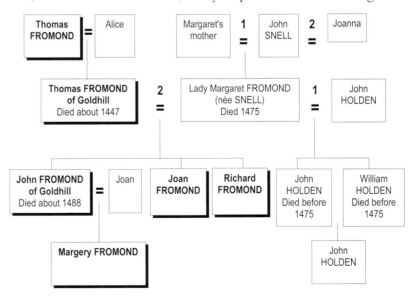

The wills help us to make some sense of family relationships. The first of the wills is that of Thomas Fromond of Goldhill, written in 1447. This will firmly connects him to his son, John Fromond of Goldhill, and to his wife, Lady Margaret Fromond. In it numerous pieces of land are named, including the part knight's fee and capital messuage, which then appear in John's name in the survey. A piece of land ordered to be sold to pay for masses, 'Bounds', appears in the survey under Walter Martyn's name 'lately purchased of Lady

Margaret Fromond'. Not only did both Thomas and Margaret acknowledge an heir, John, in their wills, but also a younger son Richard and a daughter Joan or Joanna. Provision was also made in Thomas's will for an unborn child with which Margaret was pregnant; if it was a girl she was to have 20 marks like her sister Joan, if a boy he was to share Margaret's dower lands with his brother Richard on her death. Margaret left nothing to this child in her own will, so presumably it died. Thomas is not given a title so perhaps Margaret's title was in her own right or that of her first husband. Thomas's will also takes us back a generation as he provided for masses to be said for the souls of his parents Thomas and Alice.[3]

3. CKS, DRb / PWr 1

The next will, that of Roger Fromond in 1448, was that of a less affluent man if we can judge at all from his tithes. Whereas Thomas and Margaret each left 6s.8d. for forgotten tithes, Roger left only 12d. It was not that he was lacking in piety, he left many bequests to the church and pious causes as he did not seem to have had a wife or children. He did, however, leave bequests to the Watte family, particularly Julia and Robert, possibly a daughter or niece and her husband. Julia Watte is in the survey owning land close to the Fromond family.[4]

4. CKS, DRb / PWr 1

Peter Fromond must have died shortly before the survey was made. In his will, dated 1462, he left only 12d. for forgotten tithes but also left money to pay for white bread to be made and distributed to the poor on the day of his burial. His mother (or stepmother perhaps as she is referred to as 'formerly my father's wife'), Joan Fromond atte Water, had been left well provided by his father Thomas. His own wife, Alice, the 'widow of Peter Fromond' in the survey, was in possession of fourteen acres. His will specified that on Joan's death the profits from all her lands, as set out in his father's will, were to go to Alice until their son Richard came of age to inherit, at twenty one

The Fromonds atte Water

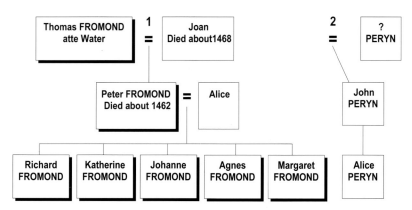

years. Katherine, Johane, Agnes and Margaret, his daughters, seem to have been left at the mercy of their mother and brother, only to inherit if Richard died without 'heirs of his body lawfully begotten'. In common with other testators, Peter indulged himself in pious fantasies of what should be done with his estate if all his children were to die without heirs, (somewhat unlikely even in the fourteen hundreds). His lands were to be sold and the money used for repairs to the church wherever most needed. However he provided that any member of 'the blood' (the family) would have first refusal at the sale.[5]

5. CKS, DRb / PWr 2

In his will of 1468 John Fromond of Kempinghale also left a modest sum of 12d. for forgotten tithes, and only 4d. for the priest and for each of his godchildren. His wife, Margaret, was to have half of all his lands, tenements goods and 'utensilium', if she chose to remain in the house. 'Utensilia' is variously translated as 'appurtenances' or 'looms' and in the context of 'dimidiam bonorum et utensilium meorum', looms would seem possible. John had only about seventeen acres of land, at least in Hadlow Manor, and may well have needed another occupation as well as farming. If Margaret died or if she chose to leave the house, then everything was to remain to his son Richard and his feoffees, who had to pay Margaret 20s. a year till the end of her days. Presumably the house in question, 'mansum' was the main dwelling house and not one he had 'lately purchased of Richard Knight'.[6]

6. CKS, DRb / PWr 3

The Fromonds of Kempinghale

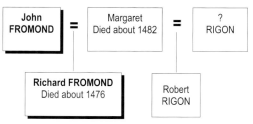

```
John                  Margaret              ?
FROMOND      =        Died about 1482  =   RIGON

              Richard FROMOND            Robert
              Died about 1476            RIGON
```

Joan atte Water also left a will dated 1468. The only named piece of land mentioned in it, Northmessteye, does not appear in the survey, making it difficult to place her in the family with certainty. However, it would seem likely that she was the Joan atte Water of the survey, widow of Thomas and owner of two houses and about sixteen acres of land. In Peter at Water's will, lands were referred to which his wife Alice should inherit on the death of 'my father's wife Joan'. Presumably these were dower lands and passed automatically back to the family and were therefore not listed in Joan's will. However, she made provision for the piece of pasture, Northmesteye, to be sold and from the proceeds £4 to be paid to Agnes Peryn on her marriage and 13s.4d. to 'John Peryn filium meum'. It is possible that John Peryn was a son-in-law, but more likely he was a son from a previous marriage and Northmesteye was either Joan's in her own right or inherited from this earlier marriage. Her executors were John Peryn and Richard Fromond of Kempinghale.[7]

Gilbert Fromond who died in 1471, left 3s.4d. for his 'forgotten tithes'. This is slightly surprising as he held only two acres in the manor, in Brook tenement. Perhaps he held more land in other manors of the parish. His wife, Alice, held four more acres in her own right. His will was simple, all his lands were to be sold and after Alice had been paid ten marks, the rest of the proceeds were to be disposed for the health of his soul. Neither his executors, nor his feoffees were members of the Fromond family. This can perhaps be explained by a law case between him and Joanna Henley, née Fromond. She maintained that her uncle William had paid Gilbert for eight acres in Hadlow but that before ownership was transferred William, 'so visited by sikness that he doubted him to dye', willed the land to his brother Robert, Joanna's father. By the time of the case the said Gilbert had 'utterly refused and still refuseth' to give up the land.[8]

Lady Margaret Fromond followed her husband Thomas to the grave in 1475. Like many wealthy widows, she indulged herself with numerous small bequests, which show a more human side of the society of the time. She left, in total, about fifteen marks to various churches, including the Friars at Aylesford, (popular beneficiaries among Hadlow donors), the prior and convent of Tonbridge, and Hadlow and Hunton parish churches, for repairs but mostly for funeral and memorial masses. She did not specifically mention her first husband among those to be prayed for but included her two sons, William and John Holden. She also left 12d. to each of her godchildren and 1d. to 'poor people' to pray for her soul. She used the phrase 'corpusque meum sepelendum et tumulendum in ecclesia de Hadlow' rather than the more usual 'sepelendum in cimiterio ecclesie de Hadlow,' possibly indicating a burial in a tomb in the church rather than outside in the churchyard.[9]

After her soul, Lady Margaret's next most pressing concern seems to have been for her son, or more likely, grandson, John Holden. She left her younger son, Richard Fromond, all her lands, tenements, rents and services to him and his heirs in perpetuity, including lands in Yalding to which Margaret was heir on the death of Johanna Snell, her father's widow. But it was only on condition that 'Ricardus Fromond custodet.... Johanem Holden, fratrum suum bene et honeste'.[10] She obviously did not entirely trust Richard's good will and honesty towards his half brother's child because she spelt out the care and maintenance expected in equipment, clothing, bedding, food and drink. There were numerous legacies to others, not obviously family members, including two of her servants: 20d. to John Brown and a two year old heifer to Agnes Peneale to 'pray for my soul'. As a footnote, and as further evidence that family arrangements did not always go smoothly, Margaret and her son Richard went to law with Nicholas Stoperfield for the

7. CKS, DRb / PWr 3

8. CKS, DRb / PWr 4; NA, C1 / 33 / 151

9. CKS, DRb / PWr 3

10. The word 'fratruum' is abbreviated, and in view of the fact that Margaret had provided for masses for the souls of her sons, William and John Holden, and the sort of care to be provided for this John, the word fratruus, meaning, at this date, nephew rather than brother would seem more likely.

11. NA C1 / 33 / 121; NA C1 / 44 / 135

release of lands he held of Thomas Fromond, Margaret's husband and Richard's father, and also with John Snell and Richard Cob for lands due to her from her first husband, Richard Holden.[11]

The Margaret Fromond who died in 1482 does not feature in the survey as a tenant but the lands which she left in her will were there, held by John Fromond of Kempinghale. She was presumably his widow but she either remarried in the fourteen years following his death or she had been married previously as all the lands at her disposal on her own death were left to her son Robert Rigon. These lands totalled over nine acres out of the sixteen listed in John Fromond of Kempinghale's name in the survey, so his own son Richard either did rather badly or inherited land in another manor. Robert Rigon was also made her executor, but Richard Fromond, with John Fromond and Thomas Stoperfield, were her feoffees with Robert. She left Alice Fromond and John son of Thomas Stoperfield 12d. each, 12d. to the church for her tithes and 12d. to repair the road between the houses of John Fromond and John Polley. Robert Rigon was to pay 3s.4d. out of his inheritance for church repairs.[12]

12. CKS, DRb / PWr 5

The last will of the series, that of John Fromond in 1488, is both interesting and tantalising because it only mentions one piece of land by name and that is not in the survey. For this reason it is difficult to identify him positively. It seems likely that he was the John Fromond of Goldhill of the survey as he left his wife Joan four acres of land called Hawkynnys and land of this name appears in the will of Thomas Fromond of Goldhill, the father of a John Fromond. However, if he was the son of Thomas and Lady Margaret, he seems to have been less wealthy than his parents, who each left 6s.8d. for forgotten tithes while he only left 3s.4d. and far less in bequests to the church. As well as Hawkynnys, left to Joan in perpetuity, he also left her a life interest in all his other property. He listed the usual lands, tenements, rents and services, but added also waters, ponds, fisheries, ways, paths, weirs, banks and ditches. Clearly these constructions were an important part of his livelihood. After the death of Joan all his property was to go to his daughter Margery.[13]

13. CKS, DRb / PWr 5

The Fromonds also featured occasionally in the Hadlow / Lomewood Manor Court Rolls. Usually John Fromond of Goldhill was fined for non-attendance at the court or paid in advance for remittance of his suit. Occasionally Richard Fromond paid a similar fine of 2d. or 4d. In November 1478 John was arbiter in a suit between John Symonds at Tanners and William Fletcher, while in November 1481 he was fined, with William Bealde, for failing to take part in an inquisition between Richard Wyks and John Newman in a plea of debt. In April 1480 he was elected to the office of beadle for the tenement of Brook. Finally in January 1482 Richard Kebbyll started proceedings in a plea of debt against John and his wife Joan but dropped the case the following month.[14]

14. BL, Add.Ch. 233788—23791

By 1512 the family name had disappeared from the Hadlow Manor Court Rolls and there were no further wills nor any record of the name in the church registers. However, a rental of 1490 shows that John Fromond of Kempynhale still held land in

the Manor of Fromonds, rented from 'Richard Fromond of Barnstrete'. In 1561 Bartholomew Fromond was fined for not attending the court of that manor. It was presumably he who moved that branch of the family to Surrey, as when he died in 1579 his will (proved in the Prerogative Court of Canterbury) recorded him as 'of Cheam in the county of Surrey'. He still held lands in Hadlow and Hunton, however, which he left to his son William who in 1586 was paying Sir George Carey 2s.8d. rent for Barnes Place.[15] The name did not appear in the subsidy rolls of 1589 for Hadlow or the nearby boroughs and there is no further reference to the name in the

15. CKS U38 / M1

Sources.
Calendar of Close Rolls
Calendar of Patent Rolls
Calendar of Fine Rolls
Calendar of Inquisitions Post
    Mortem

manor of Fromonds. William and, later, Bartholomew Fromonds do, however, appear in the Causton Manor court rolls, the last reference being in 1661. It is impossible to say whether the male line died out after this or if the family simply retreated to their Surrey estates.

THE BISHOP FAMILY

The Bishop family, while not of knightly or even gentry status, were certainly important landowners with considerable holdings and influence in both the manor and locality. Like the Fromonds and Fishers they were members of a closely linked group of local families with marriage and business connections, some of whom were prospering while others were 'mouldering away'. Apart from references to the family in the survey itself, eight family wills date from the period relevant to the survey, and family members appear as beneficiaries, executors, overseers and witnesses in the wills of others. Bishops also feature in manor court rolls and other miscellaneous documents such as deeds and legal cases. From these materials it is possible to construct a rudimentary family tree and to gain some idea of family relationships and of the family's influence in the parish.

Gervase Bishop was possibly the common ancestor of the various branches of the family which appear in the survey. He is recorded as the former holder of the tenements of 'Freferding', 'Peacocks', and 'Woodmaneys', which by the time of the survey were in the hands of John Bishop, son of Robert, and his associates. However, his relationship to John is not made clear. Another tenement, 'Broomfields', at the time of the survey held by John atte Stable and his associates, was 'formerly of Walter Bishop'. Again there is no clear connection to the Bishops of the survey.

By contrast, William Bishop is mentioned in a way which implies that he is fairly recently deceased, and sons and grandsons are recorded as now holding his land in a way that links him to the next generation, the generation of the survey. His name is also recorded in a rental of the nearby manor of 'Caustons', dated 1406-7, holding jointly with William Coiffe, 'land lately of John Bishop and the heirs of Richard Bishop'. These references, to Gervase, Walter, John and Richard Bishop, imply that the family was well established in the area before the beginning of the fifteenth century.

At least four Bishops appear in the survey, holding approximately 169 of the manor's 1287 acres in nineteen out of the fifty-nine tenements. These were; Robert, son of William, Thomas, son of William, John son of Robert and John son of Richard (also William's son but by this time dead). John, Thomas and Robert Bishop also feature without the qualification 'son of', almost certainly the same men, but it is impossible to be sure or to know whether it is John, son of Richard or John, son of Robert. Within the Manor of Hadlow, John, son of Robert, was the family member with by far the largest amount of land, and he is named as the chief tenant in eight tenements, but this may not reflect the situation in the parish as a whole. The survey also describes the location of some of the family's houses. John, son of Robert and John, son of Richard, almost certainly cousins, had houses on the North side of the Hadlow to Tonbridge highway, at Stairbridge. The house of John, Richard's son, is described as 'his capital messuage with garden adjoining'. On the south side of the road, John, son of Robert, had another house called The Mill House, with a piece of land called 'Seatons'. The survey does not state that he lived in either of these, but he does not appear to have owned any other house in the manor. Near by if not adjacent to the Mill House, Robert Bishop, son of William, held 'one messuage in which he lives, formerly of John Kene, with a garden and three pieces of land'. (See map on page 10, and plan on page 12.) He also had another messuage 'by the right of his wife Agnes, for the term of her life' in the tenement of 'Wekerylds'.

BISHOP WILLS Unfortunately *William Bishop's* testament, made in 1456, contains only details of charitable bequests to the church, repair of the road, and to various friends, or possibly servants. The rest of his appurtenances he left to his son Richard and his 'goods unbequethed' were divided between sons Richard and Thomas. Both were named as executors, so must have been adult by this date. No will is registered with the testament and therefore there is no mention of any land. Nor is there any reference to a son Robert, although Robert, son of William, is one of the Bishops who feature in the survey. Perhaps Robert was the eldest son and had already taken charge of the lands of an elderly father. It is safer to assume that custom and/or his wishes were well understood and a formal will was unnecessary or at any rate not registered. Conversely, there is no mention in the survey of a Richard, son of William, so presumably he had died by the time the survey was made and his son John had already inherited.[1]

Another problem is posed by a will of 9 August 1459, that of **Robert Bishop** senior. He had a son John, and grandsons Richard, John and Robert, fitting neatly with information in the survey and other family wills. However, if the dating of the survey is correct, he must have died before it was made and cannot be the Robert son of William to whom it refers. Perhaps he was a brother of William Bishop rather than a son.[2]

In 1483, **John Bishop**(1) senior made a will. It seems likely that he was the John, son of Robert, who featured in the survey, but apparently he had only one son John (2). The will shows that, as suspected, he had holdings not only outside the manor of Hadlow, but outside the parish. He left his wife Alice 'for term of her life', two pieces of land in Hadlow, 'Larkhale' and 'Buntanhale'. Although neither of these pieces of land was listed among the Bishop lands noted in the survey, the names appear attached to other occupiers in tenements, 'Lark' and 'Buntyns', on the edge of the manor. 'Buntynhale' was bordered by John Bishop's piece of land called 'Vicars Field', which lay within the manor. In the next tenement (Lake) there is a reference in the survey to land bordered by 'Katherine Bishop's land'. Presumably this lay in the next manor as she does not appear in the survey holding land in Hadlow manor.

John also left his wife 'all his lands and tenements in Bitberea' (Bidborough). His son John was to inherit all his other lands in Hadlow, Tonbridge and elsewhere in Kent. In his will he made arrangements for his executors, Alice and John, to pay heriots to Henry, Duke of Buckingham, Richard Culpeper, knight, and George Chown of Leigh. It was a quirk of Kentish tenure that freehold land was burdened with the payment of a heriot, unlike customs elsewhere, requiring it only from unfree land. His feoffees were John Pympe, knight, Richard Tutesham, John Welard, William Cayser and John Godyng.[3]

In 1512 another **John Bishop**(2) made a much more helpful will. He was apparently a fairly young man at the time of his death as he left at least two unmarried daughters. He left his wife all his goods, 'moveable and

1. CKS, DRb / PWr 2

2. CKS, DRb / PWr 2

3. CKS, DRb / PWr 5

84

immovable', and all land in corn 'until it be inned and in my barns until it be outted'.

Perhaps the most interesting part of the will is the light it throws on the size and arrangement of his house at Stair. Originally a simple hall house, it would have been timber framed with a central hall open to the roof with a kitchen at one end. The wills add a great deal to this basic information. John's widow and executor, Joan, was to have

'the east part of my house with the parlour chambers and kerchyn with free comyng and goyng to the well, oven and garden lying over the east-side of the parlour', so some extension and modification had already been made. Reasonably enough she was to leave the house if she remarried and 'release the keepyng of her keene'. The will does not mention giving up her annual supply of kitchen wood, however, nor her lands.

These lands included 23 acres in 'Buntinghale' which suggests that this John Bishop was the son of the John Bishop(1) who died in 1483, and that he had inherited them on the death of his mother, Alice Bishop. If so John Bishop(1) was almost certainly the 'John son of Robert' of the survey as he was then the occupier of the other pieces of land left to Joan, widow of John(2). These included 'Richetts', 'Brodfeld', 'Steyre Barn', 'Mottes' and land in 'Jopismede'. The fact that John(1) also left 6s.8d. to 'Johane, uxore Johii filii mei', would seem to confirm the relationship as Joan was the name of John(2)'s wife.

John(2) left all his tenement at Stayre and all other lands in Hadlow to his son John(3). On Joan's death his son Robert was to have the 'lordship of my lands Sharynden in Capel and Tudeley', (Sherenden Farm still exists) and his lands in Bidborough plus 'five acres of meadow I had of John Cayser'. From this inheritance he was to pay his sister Joan ten marks unless she died before her marriage in which case it would revert to him and his heirs.

There were bequests to two married daughters, Margaret and Elizabeth, provided their husbands fulfilled certain conditions. John(3) was to deliver five marks to another unmarried daughter, Marion, 'within a year of my decease', and she was also to receive ten marks from her mother 'if she be ruled by her'. Presumably she was more troublesome than her sisters. John Fisher, John Chown and John Berde were his feoffees, charged with delivering 'a state' in the croft 'The Bear'.[4]

4.   CKS, DRb / PWr 6

'to fynde hym to scole for to have his lernyng

The next **John Bishop**(3) who made his will in 1515 was certainly John(2)'s son. He was still a young man and left his brother Robert the 'custodie and rule' of his son John (4), and of his lands, 'to fynde hym to scole for to have his lernyng'. John(3)'s mother, Joan, was still alive and presumably still in occupation of the parlour chambers and kitchen of the Bishop house at Stair (her will was made in 1530 and probate granted 1541). His wife, Margaret, was to have 13s.4d. a year above her jointure and occupation of the 'new chamber' over the kitchen. This was probably because chimneys had been built, as the end of the use of an open hearth meant it was possible to insert an upper storey. Like her mother in law Joan, she too had access to the oven and keeping of two cows 'so long as she remain widow'. It is to be hoped the two women got on well as Joan did not die until 1530.

Margaret's unborn child was to inherit twenty marks at twenty one, if it lived so long. If 'God defend', John(4) should die before the age of twenty one, the lands were to go first to his uncle, John(3)'s brother Robert, for his life time, then to Robert's son Richard for his life, then Robert's son Thomas for his life time. On Thomas's death the lands went to 'the next heir male lawfully begotten of the bloode of the foresaid Bischops'. Presumably this would include his own unborn child if it survived and if it was male. Failing a male heir, his land was to be divided between his four sisters and we are given their married names: Elizabeth Goldsmyth, Margaret Cokks, Joan Lane, and

Marion Basset. His witnesses included John Cokkes, parchment maker, Simon Goldsmyth (his brothers in law?), and Robert Hampton, notary. He must have spent time in London on business because he stipulated that he should be buried in St. Olave in Southwark 'if I die there', otherwise in the church yard in Hadlow. There is a note in the register that he was in fact buried at St. Olave.[5]

5.   CKS, DRb / PWr 7

Unfortunately, we do not have his son John(4)'s will, but we do have his mother Joan's, made in 1530. She distributed personal possessions, pots and pans, kertles, caps and gowns to god daughters, Johane Bishop, Elizabeth Bishop, Margaret Bishop, Eme Forman, Joane Harman and 'post wife', and two other women. No jewellery was mentioned and only three gowns, so she does not appear to have been very rich.[6]

6.   CKS, DRb / PWr 9

By contrast the last will of the series, that of **Richard Bishop** in 1559, was the will of quite a rich man, but although five pages long it does not mention any land. Richard, apparently, had only goods and the proceeds of a house in Tonbridge to distribute among his friends and relations. He was almost certainly the nephew of John(3) which would explain why land was not mentioned, as by the terms of his uncle's will the land automatically passed to his brother Thomas Bishop.

Although Richard had a wife (her best gown was left to Margaret Inge, so presumably she was dead by 1559), no children were named in the will. His brother Thomas and cousin Hughe Sydene were the main beneficiaries, but twenty one people, including Robert Bishop the 'the tyler', received bequests. The furniture left gives us some idea of the interior of a Bishop house. It was very simple consisting of chests, 'my great chest' and two others, and four feather beds with their bedding and hangings. But Thomas's meal table was elegant. He left pewter dishes, basins, platters, saucers and candle sticks, what must have been a handsome set (called a 'garnish') now divided among his nieces. His brother Thomas received a silver salter with a cover, two masers, and nineteen silver spoons. The odd number was probably because he left a silver spoon to each of his godchildren. Women, including Hugh Sydene's wife Margaret, and Mary, Margaret, Elizabeth and Dorothie Bishop, his sister Turner, Alice Turner and Margaret Inge, also

Another elegant table!

received considerable quantities of brass, wool, cloth and animals. George Bishop was to have his mare, Stagg and Hugh Sydene his grey mare, and they were to share four flitches of bacon.[7]

7.   CKS, DRb / PWr 12

The link between the will of John Bishop(3) and that of his nephew Richard is provided by the will of John's brother, and Richard's father, Robert Bishop, in 1535. Although he had lands in Hadlow, Capel and Bidborough he was 'of the parish of Tonbridge' and that is where he was buried. The relative value of the lands he held in the four adjacent parishes is probably indicated by the amount he left to the high altar of each church; 12d. to Tonbridge, 40d. to Capel, 4d. to Bidborough and 12d. to Hadlow. He had inherited the lands in Capel (the 'lordship of Sharynden') and Bidborough from his father John Bishop(2) after the death of his mother Joan, but the lands in Hadlow he must have inherited on the death of his nephew John(4) before the latter was able to produce an heir. By his will Robert passed on these lands in Hadlow to his own son Richard, as had been ordained by his brother John(3)'s will, but all the rest of his lands went to his son Thomas. In the end, Thomas inherited the Hadlow lands as well when Richard died in 1559, although they were not actually mentioned in the will.[8]

This fairly complicated series of wills shows many features in common with the wills of families of a similar status. There were several branches of the family, some wealthier than others. The main concern was to provide for wives and children. Where children were concerned the male line ('the bloode of the Bishops') was important and there was an effort to provide adequately for younger sons. Daughters fared worse although the obligation to provide marriage portions for sisters must often have been quite a drain on an inherited estate. In some wills, for instance those of Robert Bishop in 1534 and Richard in 1559, considerable quantities of 'chattels', including animals, wool, food, clothing, bedding, brass, pewter and silver were distributed among the wider family, friends and even servants. Richard Bishop left 'Hilles, my man, my cote, a payre of hose & a two monthling bullock' and 'to Skynner, a bushell of wheat'.

BISHOPS IN THE MANOR COURT ROLLS

John Bishop also features in the manor court rolls of both Lomewood (1478-82) and, later, Hadlow (1512). Between October 1478 and June 1482 the Lomewood court was held at Stair on five occasions and on each of these John Bishop was either a member of the Grand Inquisition or an Assessor or both. On the other hand, John Bishop, John Bishop junior and the heirs of Richard Bishop paid fines for the remittance of their suit of court at Hadlow on several occasions. Apart from these routine fines John Bishop was also

involved in a plea of debt against John Symonds at Tanners which was never settled, the defaulting Symonds eventually being ordered to be distrained by the beadle. John Bishop senior (the same man?) made fidelity to the Lord for two acres of land and four dayworks alienated to him by Thomas Fisher and Henry Walter. John Bishop, Richard's son, was not such a pillar of the community, appearing twice in the rolls, once to be amerced for non-attendance at an inquisition into debt, and once fined for not repairing his ditches and thus making the highway unsafe in Well Street. Robert Bishop was similarly fined for his ditches on Palmer Street. Even less reputable was Thomas Bishop, fined twice, once that he 'offered insult to John Galton with a biniculus called a stick and thrashed him contrary to the king's peace', and once that' he offered insult to Nicholas Taylor with a round staff contrary to the king's peace'. On the first occasion Thomas Fisher and Richard Kebyll stood sureties for him but on the second he placed himself on the favour of the court and was fined 2d.

In the Hadlow manor court roll of 1512 John Bishop senior and John Bishop junior are mentioned in connection with the transfer of land from John senior to John junior through the older John's feoffees, John Chown and John Berde. They were ordered to pay 2s.8d. half a penny and half a farthing, as relief. This ties in with the appointment of John Chown and John Berde as feoffees in John Bishop(2)'s will of 1512.

BISHOPS IN THE COURTS

In the wider world beyond the manor, the Bishops also became involved in several court cases and a pardon. John Bishop, yeoman of the Lowy of Tonbridge, who was pardoned for his part in 'the recent risings' of 1471 may have been a younger, more hot headed John(1) or (2) or merely a relation. A law case earlier, in the first half of the fifteenth century, between Robert Torkesey of Lingfield on the one part and Robert and John

Bishop, his father and brother in law respectively on the other, add two small pieces of information. Robert Bishop had a daughter as well as a son, and also he had sufficient status to marry that daughter to a man outside Kent who held land in at least three counties (Kent, Surrey and Sussex) and this land was in dispute between them. Another case in the

early sixteenth century features Richard and Thomas Bishop, plaintiff and defendant, in a case of seizure of crops. Richard Bishop had leased some land to Thomas Somer who 'set it in coppice'. Thomas Bishop took exception to this and 'with divers riotous and ill disposed persons', eight in all, 'arrayed with divers weapons, swords bucklers, staves and pitchforks', entered the premises and did damage to the value of twenty marks. The bellicose Thomas of the court rolls was in trouble again.[9]

9. NA, STAC 2 / 5

BISHOPS IN REGISTER & RENTALS

Church registers and rentals continue to record the Bishop name well into the seventeenth century but as with the very early Bishops it is difficult to connect these individuals directly to the families of the survey.

THE BEALD FAMILY

The Bealde holding in Hadlow manor totalled less than fifteen acres suggesting a modest family of the husbandman class. The family was typical of many, with inconveniently scattered holdings over several manors of the area showing evidence of the past effects of inheritance by gavelkind. However, there is no hint in the wills that they had any wish to depart from that custom and the arrangements they made were typical of the age. By the time of the survey we know that one of the members of the family was a carpenter and others were involved in the manor court, one elected as a reeve. They were also part of a group of families, linked by ties of marriage and friendship, which supported and trusted each other, acting as executors and witnesses to wills and as feoffees to ease the transfer of property. They also went to law with one another, showing that the trust was not always justified.

In his *Kent Surveyed and Illustrated* of 1659, Thomas Philipott pointed out that the family had had more exalted origins. He looked on 'Goldhell' as a manor and 'a place of some importance since some Families of Estimate have been possessors of it; so first it was the possession of the Beals; ... and when this Family began to moulder away the Title by sale shifted itself to the Fromonds'. This manor was later known as Fromonds and it is here, not in Hadlow manor itself, that we first find a specific reference to the Bealde/Beal/Bele family in the parish of Hadlow. John Beald at 'Skoclyns' is said in the court roll to owe fealty for his lands there to the lords of the manor, William Goding and John Lawrence. The family is also recorded in a rental of another of the parish's manors, Caustons, in 1407. John Bealde, junior, and John Tanner owed 18d. for land formerly belonging to Johanna daughter of Lawrence Tanner. John Bealde on his own owed 3½d. and half a hen for land 'late of Emme Bealde'. In 1432 'John Beald of Skoclyns' was in default of his attendance at the Fromonds manor court, and a rental for the same manor the following year records lands held by 'Richard Beald, brother of John' and 'John Bealde, senior, brother of Richard'. Some of these holdings, for example, Skoclyns and Newmede, appear again at a later date, helping us to identify a line of descent. Deeds of 1453 referred to land 'late William Bealde's', and to lands conveyed from John Kinge to Richard Bealde, among others, and a rental of Caustons manor in 1446 credited ' John Beald, carpenter' with four acres in 'Le Greteberne field'.[1]

1.   CKS, Stoneley Documents, U309 / T1; Maidstone Museum, Larking Transcripts

In the Hadlow manor survey of 1460, two John Bealdes are recorded. John Bealde of Wrotham held just over seven and a half acres of land in two pieces, one in Lockbridge and one in Grove tenement. John Bealde, sometimes referred to as 'carpenter', and unlikely to be the same man, owned just over three and a half acres in five small plots located in Wells/Bowlere, Holmans and Tannerys tenements. Neither had a house in the manor, though John Bealde did own a garden in Hadlow Street called Walters Haugh. This piece of land appears in the will of the John Bealde of Hadlow who died in 1475 and who was therefore almost certainly the same man. From this will we know that he had a house in Hadlow Street, presumably on land of another manor, and that he owned land in Goldhill including the previously mentioned 'Skoklyns'. Unfortunately, John of Wrotham did not leave a will which might have made clear his relationship to the rest of the family but Jane Semple, in her work on Wrotham[2], makes several comments about him and the Bealde family.[2] As in Hadlow the family disappeared in the early sixteenth century, between two rentals, one of 1495 and one 1538. She considers the most likely reason to have been failure of the male line in a time of severe epidemics.

2.   Semple, 1982, ' The Manor of Wrotham in the Early Sixteenth Century '

However, not only John Bealde of Hadlow but two Richards, a William and a Lawrence also left wills and these make clear that the Bealdes were richer than would be guessed from their holdings in Hadlow manor alone. We have already seen that they held land in the manors of Fromonds and Caustons, but other evidence[3] shows the family had connections with Sevenoaks, East Barming, Speldhurst, Shipbourne and Hoo. While one of the survey's John Bealdes is said to be 'of Wrotham', the wills themselves show the family had an interest in the churches of East Peckham, Tudeley and Tonbridge as well as Hadlow.

3.   Jean Fox, CD Rom, Index to West Kent Wills

Nevertheless, even in Hadlow the Bealdes were quite influential. Like the Bishops, Fishers and Fromonds they appear frequently in the wills of others, as executors, witnesses, beneficiaries and feoffees. Feoffees enjoyed considerable power and those chosen must have been well trusted and well-to-do. Most wills were made to either supplement or diverge from the normal customs of inheritance. 'Feoffment to uses' was a device by which the will maker could enjoy greater control over the disposition of his property. It was a form of trust, not unlike the trusts formed by those seeking to avoid inheritance tax today. The feoffor, the landowner, could transfer the title of his property to a person, or more usually more than one, known as 'feoffees to uses' who legally owned the property but held it for the 'use' of the feoffor or his heirs. After the death of the feoffor, the feoffees could transfer the property back to his heirs in accordance with his wishes which might not be in accordance with the customary laws of inheritance. If the heirs were minors, the transfer often took place when they reached twenty one.[4] In most areas of the country it was a way to avoid the inequities of primogeniture (when the eldest son inherited all the land) but in Kent, where gavelkind was the norm (land was divided equally between all sons) this problem was less pressing. It was often used when there was no immediate family, or a widow was left alone or with under age children. Such children and their lands would otherwise come into the wardship of the lord of the manor, and so many landowners preferred to appoint friends and relatives as their feoffees.

4   Judith Ford, Open University, Internet article

BEALD WILLS

The testament of **Richard Bealde** written in 1456 is that of a wealthy but apparently childless man. He was also a very pious one in the orthodox tradition, leaving large amounts of money for his funeral and for masses in Hadlow and Aylesford for the health of his soul and those of his relations and benefactors. Considerable sums also went towards the repairs of various churches; Hadlow itself, Tonbridge, Tudeley and East Peckham. He only mentions two members of the Bealde family in his will, Agnes, widow of William Bealde, and Agnes, daughter of John Bealde at Tanners. 'Our' John Bealde of the survey and will of 1475 owned land in Tannery's tenement but there is no reference to a daughter Agnes. Other female beneficiaries like Larete Rabette and Agnes Maysterer who, like Agnes, each inherited five marks, may well have been family too. There were several other smaller, but still significant bequests, mostly to women. He also left money to several of the gentry of Hadlow, John Berton, Nicholas Stoperfield, John at Stable and Thomas Fisher and, at the other end of the social scale, to his servant John Salams. No will exists to show the disposition of his lands. Perhaps he had already sold them or perhaps they had been or were to be divided among his sons according to custom. However, it would be unusual not to make adult sons executors and his 'supervisors' were John Berton, Thomas Fisher, John at Stable and Nicholas Stoperfield, none of them obviously family members, so probably he had no children. One section of the will suggests that his affairs were in some confusion, possibly with lawsuits pending or claims against him still unresolved. If the prosecution of these cases involved them in expenses, his executors could claim up to a tenth of the money left for the church tower, provided proper accounts were submitted.

John Bealde, by contrast, showed himself very much a family man. When he made his testament in 1475 the only bequest he made to the church was 12d. for his forgotten tithes, an unavoidable impost rather than a generous donation. There is nothing in his will for masses at his funeral or 'month's mind' or for lights to burn before the images of the saints. He made his wife Margaret and son Lawrence his executors and, after his debts had been paid, the residue of his goods were to be divided between them. In addition, Lawrence was to have two oxen. His son Richard was not included at this stage. The division of his lands, 'in Hadlow or Hoo', was also rather unequal. Margaret was provided with a messuage in Hadlow Street, purchased from John Colyn, and a piece of land, Cattysbrayn, which were to revert to Lawrence on her death as was a garden, Gandychaugh, which they were to share during her life. Lawrence was also to inherit the family land 'Skoklys'. John had enfeoffed James Gosse in this land, perhaps because he did not want it divided between Lawrence and his brother Richard as custom would dictate. But it came on a condition; that he look after his sister Johanne for life. Perhaps the unfortunate girl was handicapped in some way. Richard was to inherit the garden, Walters Haugh, in Hadlow Street, which appears in the survey in John's name. All John's other lands were to be divided equally between his two sons. His witnesses were the vicar of Hadlow, Brother David, John Somer his neighbour in Hadlow Street, and John Goding.

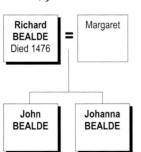

Richard Bealde was the father of a younger family when he died in 1476. Whether he was John's brother, as recorded in the rental of 1432, or a younger cousin or nephew is impossible to say. Like John he left no money for lights and only 2d. to the priest. His wife Margaret and John Gates were his executors. He left 26s.8d. to his daughter Johanna on her marriage to be paid by his son John 'if he lives then'. He had three feoffees, James Gosse, John Berton, and Peter Fisher. His will states that immediately after his death they should 'devise and grant' to his wife half of a messuage in Hadlow and that John Berton and Peter Fisher should deliver five virgates of meadow (This seems too much.) which they held. It makes no mention of when the rest of his lands were to be delivered to his son, implying that he was young and the feoffees would have to be responsible for the lands for some time. Richard also seemed to be rather dubious about whether John Berton and Peter Fisher would be willing to hand over the meadow when it came to the time, as he made

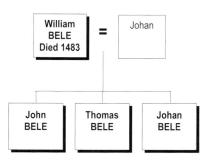

```
William
BELE          =      Johan
Died 1483

   |                    |
-----------------------------------
|              |                  |
John          Thomas            Johan
BELE           BELE              BELE
```

provision for his other feoffee to see that, if necessary, lands of a similar value were substituted. That such arrangements did not always go smoothly is attested by the number of law cases involving feoffees. He may have hoped for safety in numbers because he had no less than six witnesses to his will.

William Bele also had under age children when he made his will in 1483. He left all his goods to his wife 'that she may dispose of them in legacies better than I'. The only specified bequest to the church was for his forgotten tithes, though at a later stage in the will he arranged that, after his wife's death, lands should be sold and the profits devoted to works of charity. These included 'necessary warkes of the sayde church of Hadlow' and 'prestys syngyng', but also 'fowel weys and maydynes maryages'. Foul ways, or bad roads, and dowries for poor girls became increasingly popular objects of charitable bequests while, in the Beald family at least, elaborate funeral arrangements and masses for the dead no longer featured.

By the time he made his will William's lands were already in the hands of feoffees, Thomas Gerthe and William Marny esquires and John Wettenstall and Walter Mildmay. These men, after his death, were to pass the lands they held to Thomas Fisher and John a Borne, presumably to administer for his sons. The sons, John and Thomas, were to enjoy 'the resnabill yssues and profettes above al charges and reprises'. In other words Thomas Fisher and John a Born were expected to charge reasonable 'expenses' for their work, more or less according to their commitment to, or affection for, their charges. The lands were to be equally divided between his two sons when they came to the age of twenty one, or if one died the 'overliver' was to inherit.

Apart from inheriting all his goods no specific provision was made in the will for his wife Joan. By custom, in Kent, she was entitled to half his lands for life as long as she remained 'chaste'. Probably lands were already set aside for her as part of a marriage settlement. His daughter Johan, however, was left two pieces of land, Bunyards, 'wen she comyth to marriage'. If all the children died without issue, his wife was to inherit everything, and on her death the lands were to be sold and the money disposed for charity.

A simple burial scene

We do not know what happened to *John* or *Thomas Bealde*. No wills were registered in their names and they do not appear in any subsequent court rolls or rentals in the area, although the mention of 'land purchased of Thomas Bele', in the will of John Somer of 1529, indicates that at least Thomas survived to adulthood. He may have moved to a neighbouring parish where we know the Bealds also held land. We can, however, surmise what happened to Johane. In the will of John a Born, dated 1544, he leaves 'my mansion Scokklls als Scokkllis or Bealde', with other lands in Hadlow, to his son Thomas. His wife was called Johan and it seems too much of a coincidence for her not to be the daughter of William Bealde and for him to have inherited that piece of Bealde land through her. He may have been William's feoffee, John a Born, but more likely John a Born exercised his influence as feoffee to marry the heiress Johan/Johanna to one of his relatives. The other possibility is that the Joanna concerned was the sister of Lawrence Bealde and that he had used the family mansion as her dowry.

The last will of the series, that of *Lawrence Bealde* in 1491, appears to be that of a relatively poor man. He left the bare minimum to the church for his tithes and 'a light for the herse'. If all his heirs were to die without issue, his lands were to be sold and the money devoted to works of mercy. No mention was made of elaborate funeral ceremonies or masses for the dead. His wife was called Mercy, again perhaps an indication of reformist sympathies. He left Mercy a messuage and three pieces of land and 'an

Eylonde late purchased of Thomas Crudd'. The island was to be sold by his feoffees to pay his debts but Mercy was to enjoy the rest of his property for life. On her death it was to be equally divided between his sons, Richard and John.

BEALDS IN THE MANOR COURT ROLLS

Three members of the Bealde family appear in the Hadlow/Lomewood court rolls. The William Bealde of the will of 1483 was almost certainly the William Bealde who appears in the court roll where he is last mentioned in an entry for November 1481. He was twice fined 2d. for not attending the court and twice 6d. for failing to take part in an inquisition, once between John Newman, maltster, and John Wyks in a plea of debt and once between John Crud and Richard Haycher in a plea of trespass. On July 20, 1479, he was elected reeve for the tenants of Palmer and in the View of Frankpledge of October 1481 he was a member of the Grand Inquisition. Lawrence Beald and Margaret Beald, probably his mother and the widow of the John Beald who died in 1475, were both fined for not clearing their ditches. In Margaret's case her failure resulted in the obstruction of 'the common water course in Hadlow Street' where we know she was left a house. Lawrence's ditches were along the New Way, beside his land 'Long Field'.

After Lawrence's will of 1491, the Bealde name seems to disappear from Hadlow. There is no reference to them in the later manor court rolls, nor in the parish registers when they begin. We know that other members of the family had land in nearby parishes, so perhaps Lawrence's sons moved, probably to East Peckham. Perhaps the family known variously as Beald, Bealde, Beal, Beale, Bele, and Beel, finally became Bell.

THE STOPPERFIELD/STUBBERFIELD FAMILY

The Stubberfields first appear in documents in Kent in the Lay Subsidy roll of 1327/9, when they were living in Brenchley Hundred, perhaps in East Peckham parish, and in the Lowy of Tonbridge, possibly already in Hadlow parish. No other record for a century shows

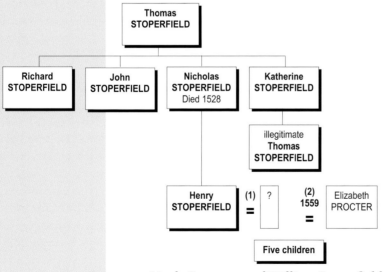

the family continuing there, whereas many were in Brenchley Hundred. But plainly they had a continuing connection with Hadlow for in 1446 and 1447 a William Stoperfield was named in two wills of people belonging to Hadlow and Tonbridge, and in the second case, he was mentioned as having land near one of the Fromond family who certainly lived in Hadlow.

In our survey of 1460 the same man's name was given to a Hadlow tenement, though he was not then occupying any of its land. Stoperfield tenement as it was called was, unusually, said to have belonged formerly to two men, Hugh Coustone and William Stoperfield, though this did not necessarily refer to the William Stoperfield then living. The holding had become considerably subdivided, into twelve pieces among seven people. But its original composition gives the impression of having been put together in a somewhat makeshift fashion at some time in the past, for the details showed that it had consisted of five separate units when Coustone and Stoperfield acquired it, namely, 4 acres from William Usserey, 3 acres from Nicholas Tanner, 6 acres formerly of Geoffrey at Grove, one messuage and 2 acres, formerly of Robert Pudding, and a fourth part of half a ferling, lately of Nicholas Tanner. None of these surnames was current on the manor in 1460, suggesting that this history went back into a somewhat distant past. The land described amounted to only 19 acres plus the fragment of a ferling

1. Witney, 2000, 343

which, theoretically, since a ferling was about 10-13 acres, should have meant about one and a half acres.[1] Did the tenants in 1460 know what a ferling was, since the term had fallen into disuse by the mid-fifteenth century, and is hardly used anywhere else in our document? At all events, this made just over 20 acres put together from five lots, whereas the current tenants showed themselves to be holding 36 acres, which was the size of a standard holding. It must at some time have been increased in size. The present tenants claimed to hold by an old charter granted by the Earl of Stafford, and the holding was evidently referred to in an old rental; the surveyor seemed to view all this with scepticism, but as he had not seen the old rental, he could not dismiss their claim.

One is tempted to think that this holding's history sheds some light on disordered circumstances at the time of the Black Death, though that is pure guesswork; one piece of land bordered *Cotlands*, a name which designated land that in the past was allotted to serf-like labourers working mainly on the manorial demesne. Cotlands itself by 1460 was now distributed among tenants like most of the rest of the manorial land, and the existence of cottars as a class of tenants was nowhere suggested in the survey or in any other documents of the time. The rest of the land lay in the vicinity of Robards Went, Skeyffe Lane, and the road from Goldhill to West Malling, in other words Victoria Road. Some of it lay near Caustons manor, the main Caxton property in Hadlow that had also been partly dismantled by 1460. In short, we may here catch a glimpse of a part of Hadlow parish that had undergone more than usual turmoil in the fourteenth century when compared with the eagerness for land already hinted at down by the Medway. Perhaps the first William Stoperfield had arrived on the Hadlow scene at an opportune moment, and with Hugh Causton assembled a new tenement from vacant bits and pieces at a time when the lord was grateful to find tenants for unoccupied land, of which some lay amid the lord's own demesnes.

Two descendants of the Stoperfield family feature in Hadlow documents from the 1440s onwards but only one had land in this Hadlow manor. This was Nicholas, with a wife called Alice, and a daughter, Margaret. He was then the principal occupier of Gibbons tenement. He held just over 33 acres, which included the house and garden where he lived plus two other pieces of land, making nearly 42 acres in all. It lay on the north side of the main road from Tonbridge to West Malling in the neighbourhood of the vicarage, rectory land, and Fullers Field; in addition he held 6 acres in Coswyns tenement. This was evidently not all the land that he occupied, however, for he held some in other manors bordering on pieces of Coiffe's tenement. (Eight manors in Hadlow meant that the manor lands were somewhat intermingled.) So his name appeared as a neighbour of people in Coiffes tenement, and that holding lay at the centre of the village among the shops, and bordered the high street leading to West Malling. Altogether Nicholas Stoperfield held 48 acres on our manor, plus more in other manors, giving him sufficient land for a decent living for his family, and conceivably enough to claim the status of a yeoman. One daughter Margaret was his only recorded descendant, and she either died childless or married and lost her family name; so we cannot follow that branch of the family any further.

The other Stoperfield in Hadlow at this time was Thomas, though he did not occupy any land of our Hadlow manor. But he was the one whose offspring maintained the connection with Hadlow for another two generations. He had three sons and one daughter. His daughter, Katherine, had an illegitimate son, called Thomas, for whom the older Thomas, his grandfather, made provision in his will. Two of his three sons were Richard and John, but their history has not been traced. The third son was Nicholas, (his first name suggesting that his father, Thomas, was the brother of the Nicholas occupying Gibbons tenement in 1460 - see above). Nicholas II became a conspicuous member of the Hadlow community, witnessing wills, and signing documents in which, significantly, Henry Fane, gentleman, was often also a signatory. The Fanes were gentry, having their main house at Badsells in Tudeley, a next door parish, and Nicholas evidently established a sufficiently close relationship with Henry Fane for Fane to become godfather to his son, Henry, (probably explaining also the choice of the baby's first name). Nicholas Stoperfield, the father, lived in Sole Street, i.e. Three Elm Lane, and died there in 1528. This was close to Hadlow Place where Henry Fane lived until his death in 1533. So they were close neighbours, and Henry Fane, who had no children of his own, left some land to young Henry Stoperfield when he died. (For more on Henry Fane, see pages 71-5 on the Fane family)

Nicholas Stubberfield died in 1528, but the connection of his son Henry with the Fane family surfaced again when the nephew of Henry Fane, was involved in the Wyatt rebellion in 1554. This was a protest against Queen Mary's planned marriage to Philip of Spain. The younger Henry Fane was involved but he was pardoned, and in a pardon roll of 12 January,1559, pardon was also granted to Henry Stubberfield (the surname having been changed to this form around 1550). This suggests that Henry Stubberfield had Protestant, rather than Catholic sympathies. Yet in 1559 Henry married, as his second wife, Elizabeth, the widow of John Procter; and John Procter, a schoolmaster at Sir Andrew Judd's newly built school in Tonbridge, had been the pro-Catholic author of a book about the Wyatt rebellion. So Catholic sentiment had brooded in the Procter household in 1554, whereas we know that Protestant loyalties were strong at Hadlow Place. Ralph Fane's widow Elizabeth, née Brydges, succoured some of the radical Protestants when they were persecuted and imprisoned by Mary, and she herself had to go into hiding near Reading. Henry Stubberfield's pardon after the Wyatt rebellion hints at his Protestant loyalties, so perhaps we stumble on former religious disagreements in the Procter family when we find John Procter's widow marrying Henry Stubberfield. Moreover, she did so somewhat speedily, two days before her first husband's will was proved, in July 1559.

Elizabeth Fane's husband, Ralph, had been charged with high treason in 1551 and was hanged in 1552. (See under the Fane family.) So his home at Hadlow Place was inherited by Henry Fane, the nephew of the first Henry Fane, and Elizabeth Fane probably moved out when Henry moved in. She granted to Henry Stubberfield Tonbridge rectory and its lands in 1556. London thereafter became Elizabeth Fane's home, and she died in Holborn in June 1568.

Henry Stubberfield's five children found their way into trade in Tonbridge, into law, teaching in Sussex, and into the church. But one of the occupations of their descendants that extended Hadlow's links with the fish trade was as rippiers, transporting sea fish swiftly from Rye and Hastings on the coast to London.[2] Rippiers stopped to change horses, and sell some of their fish to the locals, in this case, at Goudhurst in the Weald, and then at Chipstead in Chevening parish, Surrey. So Stubberfields are found at Chipstead in the 1540s, (they must have passed through Tonbridge en route) and one Stubberfield lived intermittently at Chipstead and Southwark, while another lived at Goudhurst. In short, this family tree shows a far-flung network of kin in one trade, exactly like those found in the horse trade Branches of the same family cooperated with each other, formed partnerships, and some became wealthy men.[3]

THE PLAYNE FAMILY

Among the new faces appearing in Hadlow after 1550 were members of the Playne family. They possibly have some significance in the Protestant history of the Weald, but absolutely nothing is proven about the Tonbridge branch; it is simply worth bearing them in mind should other evidence turn up.

No one having the Playne surname appears in the 1460 survey, nor has anyone of that name been found in other Hadlow documents before 1550. But the family lived somewhere in the vicinity, probably in Tonbridge, and more than one of them were friends of the Fanes, for Henry Fane's will in January, 1456 shows Thomas A.Plane as a witness.[1] Another will, of Thomas Fane, gentleman, of St Peter the Poor, London, and Tonbridge (for he had lands there) was made on July, 1532, leaving a gelding to Thomas

2. On 'rippiers', see Prior, 1982, 60-61

We are deeply grateful to Mr Tim Mitchell for details of the family history of the Stubberfields.

3. Edwards, 1988

1. CKS DRb, PWr / 2 fo. / 79

2. NA Prob, 11 / 24 / 19

3. NA E178 / 1093
4. CKS U38 / M1

5. NA, CKS DRb / Pwr 18 / v

6. We are most grateful to
Catharine M.F.Davies and Professor
Susan Wabuda for information about
William Playne.

Plane, yeoman, his feoffee.[2] We see many connections in the sixteenth century linking Tonbridge and Hadlow people with traders in London, and this is another example.

On a cold day in December 1570, several Hadlow men and others were called to a meeting at South Frith to inspect its timber, furnace, and finery for the iron mill, and asked to judge the value of any future lease, for the existing lessees were minded to surrender theirs now that the area had been shorn of its timber for burning charcoal. Among those called to this task were Wyatt Playne, and two Michael Playnes, senior and junior.[3] In a Hadlow rental of 1586 Wyatt Playne is shown occupying Court Lodge and farmland.[4] It is the first intimation that Hadlow manor had a manor house, evidently something considered apart from Lord's Place in Church Street. It probably lay somewhere on land that was later occupied by Hadlow Castle, for a document of 1856 says that the Castle was built near Court Lodge, but we have no information on when that first house was built. As Wyatt Playne also had farmland, it may mean that he was the lessee of the home farm of the manor; in other words, he had quickly achieved the status in Hadlow of an inhabitant commanding authority and respect.

The first name, Wyatt, prompts speculation. Did it indicate friendly connections or kinship with the Wyatt family of Allington? Sir Thomas Wyatt had been a leader in 1553-4 of the Wyatt rebellion, sparked off by opposition to the planned marriage of Queen Mary to another Roman Catholic, King Philip of Spain. She married him, the rebellion failed, and Wyatt was executed for high treason. The first name, Wyatt, was preserved in this family until at least 1638 when another Wyatt died whose burial is recorded in the Hadlow parish register. Was anti-Catholic feeling expressed in the forename Wyatt, or was it just a popular name at this time?; the Hadlow parish register shows ten children given the name of Wyatt between 1561 and 1611.

Opposition to a Spanish Catholic marriage might also betoken a stout devotion to Protestant beliefs, and certainly those are shown in the preamble to Wyatt Playne's will in 1599. He married Rebecca Jones on October 6, 1570, and she proved to be a strong and healthy wife after her first child, Henry, died in 1572. After that, she produced children almost every year, Thomas in 1574, Wyatt in 1575, Francis in 1577 (he died in 1619), Rebecca in 1579, Mary in 1580, and at an unknown date two more, Michael who died in 1599, and Agnes who became the wife of Wyatt Paule (possibly intended as Pawley, another Hadlow surname). Rebecca's many pregnancies, following so soon after one another, suggest that she did not breastfeed her children but employed a wetnurse, a practice of gentlefolk rather than yeomen. Other information about Wyatt Playne is meagre, apart from words in his will in 1597 describing him as a yeoman, showing him to have been literate, since he signed his own name, and being concerned for the upbringing of his six younger children. He entrusted this task to his wife 'according to the trust I have always placed in her, and as she will answer before God at the day of judgment'. His property comprised land in East Peckham that included 5 acres at Chidley Cross and a messuage in Hale Street, where the butcher lived, though Wyatt kept its orchard for himself; in Hadlow he held 8 acres 'beneath Branbridges', 8 acres 'above Branbridges', and 2 houses in Hadlow Street.[5]

It is tempting to wonder if this Playne family was in any way related to the William Playne who was persecuted for his association with fervent Protestants in Mary's reign. The story of this other William Playne was told by John Foxe, the martyrologist, because he died three years after being tortured, imprisoned in the Tower of London, and having his health ruined. He had delivered a message from someone else to a Dr Crone urging him not to recant in public for strong words uttered against Papists when he was preaching in his London church. For this simple, message-carrying service William Playne received the harsh punishment that brought on his death. The records found so far do not reveal any connection between this William Playne and Tonbridge or Hadlow.[6] He was a member of the Skinners Company, and his will and that of his wife show only a home in London, and a son, Apollo, living in Suffolk. The fact remains that the Skinners Company had some distinguished members around Tonbridge, including Sir Andrew Judd who was six times

Master of the Company and founded Tonbridge School in 1553.

Many Playnes lived in the Tonbridge area: wills exist for John Plane of Tonbridge (d.1511), Thomas, senior of Tonbridge, and Thomas, senior, yeoman of Tonbridge.[7] The Hadlow parish registers continue to record baptisms for seven Planes between 1572 and 1582, and another six between 1610 and 1692. Seven marriages of Playnes were celebrated between 1570 and 1622, including one in 1605 of Mary Playne to Thomas Stubberfield (a separate account here deals with the Stubberfield family). So it would be worth keeping watch for a family relationship that might link the persecuted William Playne in London with the Protestant network known to exist in the Weald of Kent.[8]

7. Duncan, 1924, Kent Records IX, Rochester Wills, 1440-1561

8. Wadmore, 1902, 159, 225

CHAPTER 14

TOPOGRAPHICAL PROBLEMS

HADLOW STAIR

In analysing the Sewer Commissioners' report on the Medway it becomes clear that although they mention the branch of the river that runs 'with its compass northwards' from Walmsley's Weir, there is no mention of a landing place at Hadlow Stair. The report tells us that this course passes through ancient Cranborrows Weir which had paid 'certain Sticks of Eels unto the Castle of Tonbridge' but nothing more. It therefore seems likely that this 'stair' or landing place had long since fallen into disuse. The word (de Steghere) is first found in a document of 1327[1], but that does nothing to prove when the stair was actively in use as a landing wharf. However, in a manor document of 1334 Walter at Steyre was said to be aged 50 or more – thus taking the name back to at least 1284.

There are no clues as to the exact position of the landing place on any available maps so some imagination has to be used. However, geographically this is the one place in the parish (and manor) where the contours guarantee that the landing of goods would still be possible at high water.

1. Wallenberg, 1934, 178

In Kenes tenement we are told that the Medway lies south of Robert Bishop's messuage at Stair Bridge (the bridge where the highway from Hadlow Street to Tonbridge crossed over the Pen Stream) and in Freferding tenement it lay north of his 'cott in the payne of eyland'. Dumbreck tells us of two names for this land - 'Fishers Lease' or 'Paines Island' - so it is possible to identify its position. In the Tithe map apportionment it is reduced to the mundane 'Five Acres' – the acreage being 4a.1r.30p. Robert's part lay on the west side of the field, the larger part was held by his neighbour Thomas Crudd, their joint holdings adding up to 4a.1r. Thomas Crudd was bequeathed the land, including his messuage, by Thomas Walter in 1448 and Paynes Island was said to lie next to the land of the Duke of Buckingham. In 1476 Thomas Crudd bequeathed Paynis Eyland to his wife Alice and thence to his son John.

Reconstructing the layout of holdings at the Stair from our survey we can establish the position of the 'lane to the Medway' and therefore state with reasonable confidence the rough position of a landing place. Although we cannot say what the structure was like and whether constructed of wood or stone, the illustration above is an attempt to portray its possible appearance.

From the Dumbreck maps we are able to establish the old course of the ancient Medway which gives us a better idea of the orientation of tenement holdings in this part of the manor. It seems reasonable to believe that Cranborrows Wear must have belonged to the sub-manor of Crombury. A document of 1590 tells us that Thomas Barton held Coulton Mead with one island and a wear 'sometime in the tenure of David Willard' and we can be sure he knew the best navigational stream! Coulton Mead lay adjacent to Weir Meadow and can be identified on the Tithe map.

ROADSIDE CROSSES

Seven 'crosses' are mentioned in our survey.

Wayside crosses were a common feature in the medieval landscape although only 350 are now known nationally and these are principally concentrated in the south-west of England in Cornwall and on Dartmoor and a small group on the North York Moors. There are plenty of examples in Eire but it was during the Reformation and the Commonwealth that the majority in England were lost.

Crosses had several origins and functions. The original 'preaching' crosses pre-dated churches and indicated meeting places for the preaching of Christianity in Anglo-Saxon times. Hunebere (the Anglo-Saxon nun) said '…. on the estates of the nobles and good men of the Saxon race it is the custom to have a Cross, which is dedicated to Our Lord and held in great reverence, erected on some prominent spot, for the convenience of those who wish to pray before it.'

Positioning the cross at the crossroads

Holy crosses were placed by the sides of roads especially in wilder places as an indication of the way to a church, and probably some were related to pilgrimages along routes such as those to Canterbury and Walsingham. Boundary crosses marked the limits of monastic and other estates and guide posts were known as crosses when they stood at cross-roads. In any case we can safely assume that their presence reinforced the Christian faith and reassured the traveller.

It may be, of course, that our 'crosses' were merely where two pathways crossed – a perfectly feasible explanation, and they may well have had standing stones as well. It is only through the monies left in wills for repairs that we can be sure that an upright cross existed; Agnes Gambon gave money for the repair of Goldhill cross as did John Symond, and Thomas Fisher and Reg Hadecher left a bequest for the Palmers Street cross.

Following the path of our survey, one acre called The Dene (in Freferding tenement) was 'next to **Longshots Cross**' and lay on the south side of the Hadlow Street to Tonbridge road. The cross must have been close to the land called Longshots which lay in the same tenement and was probably next to the junction of the highway and Longshots Lane. A 'commonway to Longshots' was mentioned in Kene's tenement and when the north lodge to the present Stair House (formerly the site of William Homewood's dwelling) was built, the first part of the path was moved further east next to the tin church on the main road. Thomas Walter left monies in 1448 for the repair of the road between Longshots cross and the mansion of Stephen Frutar. In our survey Stephen's widow Joan was living in what is now called Hogs meadow, Hoggs tenement, at the corner of Three Elm Lane and the main Hadlow road.

In Wells tenement a highway led 'from the cross called **John at Stable's cross** as far as Jopis mead'. John left monies in his will of 1476 for the repair of the road at 'Shroppstyle and Malyncrowch'. Shropsfield was in Tanners tenement which lay between Three Elm Lane and the Hadlow to Tonbridge Road, 6½ acres called Malynred lay in Pococks tenement on the opposite side of the road, but neither piece was held by John in our survey although he held 1½ acres in the adjacent 'Broadfield'. The will alludes to 'step stones', so was this a crossing of the highway or a standing cross? Many years later the Hadlow court rolls of 1844 stated that the bridge at the end of the Causeway at Three Elm Lane required repair; perhaps a quick prayer was required after all. Curiously, in Hoggs tenement, the survey speaks of 'the common way…leading from John at Stable's dwelling house towards Fish Hill' and John Bishop, in his will of 1483, gave money for the repair of the King's highway 'from Le Cage Gate to the cross adjoining the mansion of John at Stabyll'.

John had a messuage called Parrocke's in Fletchers tenement which is mentioned in his will but the survey gives no hint of his house in this part of the manor. However, there is land here which is not measured in our survey and John's house may very well have been near the site later known as Greentrees, one of the gates to which was opposite the lane leading to present day Little Fish Hall. This would fit in nicely with our mapping.

In Wells tenement a common way is mentioned 'leading from **Revecocks Cross** as far as Fish hill' but whether this is the same cross is not clear.

The survey indicates that **Palmers Street Cross** was on the junction of Palmers Street (the present day Ashes Lane) and the Tonbridge Road. Ashes Lane continues across the road as a track to Three Elm Lane to the south. The survey, at this point, mentions a messuage and land called 'Bacris Cross or Barris Croft' (now The Ashes) next to Palmers Street cross in Wekerylds tenement. On the opposite side of the road six acres in Crouchland tenement are identified as being next to Palmers Street cross. In 1509 Thomas Fisher left monies for repair of the cross.

An old engraving showing the view into the village, looking west from the Maidstone Road. Note the stream flowing down the road which has caused so many problems in the past.

Dorants was a house and 8 acres of land held by William Hogett in Coswyns tenement, now called James House and farm. 'The highway from **Dorants Cross** to Goldhill' ran to the north of the farm and described either the present day Cemetery Lane or a footpath that runs from the main road by the cart pond over towards Goblands Farm. The pond is the northern vestige of the watercourse that ran down the main road from Lonewood Common through the village to the River Bourne. It is where the traveller left the village to cross the common and had another 2 miles to go before the next village – Mereworth. Perhaps another swift prayer was called for! In 1461 Denise Ippenbery left money for the repair of the footway between Dorant's bridge and Lomewood.

'Robards went' marks the point where 'Skeyffes Lane' (now known locally as Dog Kennel Path) crosses the highway from Dorants cross to Gold Hill (Victoria Road) and leads to Caustons Manor and lands at Buntanhall. Robert Wotton, who held Caustons Manor, held 8 acres in Stoperfield tenement called 'the field at **Caustons cross**' to the east of the highway. In the adjacent 'Crouchlands', in Puddings tenement, he held another 8 acres. John Robards' messuage lay on the third corner of the crossing and on the fourth lay 'Park Field' part of Hadlow Court lands belonging to the lord of the manor.

Borne cross is the last cross to be mentioned in the survey. This is a puzzle. The first clue to its position is in Fishland tenement where Joan Fromond 'formerly Thomas Fromond At Water's wife holds for the term of her life two pieces of land lying together at the Borne called the Cross at Borne' (3a.2r.). It could be thought that 'Borne' refers

16th century Rose Cottage, Three Elm Lane, which was part of Fish Hall estate. It lies next to the supposed site of Borne Cross where John at Stable held a croft.

to the local river Bourne. However, the survey tells us that the land lay south of the highway leading from Goldhill towards Tonbridge (Three Elm Lane) and, by definition, south of that river. It could, of course, relate to a smaller brook but this seems unlikely. The word 'borne' is French for 'boundary marker' and so could well refer to the limits of an estate or manor. By piecing the tenement together, it appears that the 'cross' lay on Three Elm Lane at the junction of what is now a footpath leading to Fish Hall. To the west of the path is a ditch and bank which may have delineated the boundary. To the west of the bank lay John at Stable's 'Croft at the Borne' in Hoggs tenement.

LAW DAY PLACE

References to lawdays are quite common in medieval records, and the word could mean any meeting at which a parish or manorial population assembled to discuss common matters, including the three-weekly meeting of the manorial court. In other cases, a 'lawday' refers to the views of frankpledge, that were held only once in six months. A Statute of 27 Henry VIII also refers to 'lawdays' twice a year, and at Wateringbury, along the Maidstone Road, the locals expected them twice a year.[1] Another Kent document, relating to Sturry, equates 'the lawday' with 'a view of frankpledge'; and at Hunton, the parish next door but one to Hadlow, the business on a 'lawday' lasted all day and people complained because the lord offered no food. Apart from holding a view of frankpledge on lawdays, other august occasions might be so deemed. Professor Duffy has described one in Morebath, Devon, at the beginning of Mary's reign, when a new lord had taken charge, following the death of the old lord in 1551, and there the parish debts were examined, a collection was agreed to pay them off, and since Catholic ritual was also about to be restored, he implied that the occasion was a notable one for the community, conveying a sense of a meeting in order to make a fresh start.[2] Another special occasion is implied in a notice about a lawday feast in 1497(?) in Huddersfield at Cutthorne Cross (the word 'Cross' could also have significance here), when a perambulation of the boundaries was undertaken.[3]

In a place like Hadlow having eight manors, meetings to discuss contentious issues must frequently have been necessary, and so it is no surprise to find an open-air site actually allocated for such discussions, allowing room for many people to assemble. That is the meaning to be attached, then, to a piece of land in Hadlow called Lawday Place, mentioned in the survey on folio 64. To the south Richard Nepaker of Lomewood had a house in which he lived, with a piece of land called Swaynes, which formerly belonged to the Fromonds. Lonewood common lay on the west and north, land of John Elliott (formerly John Mounssey) on the east. Although we cannot fix firmly on the exact site, we know enough to say that it lay towards the boundary of Hadlow parish, and furthermore at a point where the three parish boundaries of Hadlow, West Peckham, and East Peckham met. In a much later document of 1815, Lawday Place was named again, but now shown to the west of Swaines, then belonging to the Hon. Catherine Fermor, widow of the late Rev. I. S. Fermor (compare Swaynes above in 1460), with Lonewood common on the east and north sides.[4] Such a site, almost surrounded by commonland, and near the junction with two other parishes, was certainly appropriate. The site that we authors favour for it even has a slight mound!

Sites for common assembly meetings have long been known through place names, though the subject has not recently received the attention of many scholars. In 1999 a researcher, writing from St Hugh's College, Oxford, Aliki Pantos, published a list of some thirty such medieval assembly places in Nottinghamshire, Leicestershire, Lincolnshire, and Rutland. She described them as hundred and wapentake meeting places, adding some further sites that were identified through field names. She was then compiling a photographic and documentary record.[5] Much earlier than that, in 1880, George L. Gomme wrote a wide-ranging book on the subject of *Primitive Folk Moots: or Open Air Assemblies in Britain*, and traced such assembly places back into antiquity. Indeed, he argued that all human societies across the world started in this way, beginning with examples from the North American Indians, African tribes, and India, and moving across Europe through Scandinavia, Germany, Switzerland, Holland, and France, before focusing on English examples in shire moots, hundred moots, forest courts, courts of dens, evolving locally into manorial courts.[6] These meeting places were 'under the light of heaven' and often at distinctive sites like an oak tree, a lime tree, an ancient burial place, a river ford, stone circle, churchyard, or at a boundary point between parishes. A notable one in Kent was Pennenden Heath.[7]

We shall continue to search for more evidence on Hadlow's more modest site.

1. Furley, 1871-4, II (i), 130

2. Duffy, 1992, 155

3. Notes and Queries, 2nd ser., X, (Dec.8, 1860), 258

4. CKS, Stoneley documents, U309 M1

5. Pantos, 1999, 33

6. A notable example of a court of dens at Aldington was attended by Sir Roger Twysden on September 18 1655, and September 16 1656. It took responsibility for collecting payments from 32 dens, and Furley admitted that people no longer knew where these dens were!

7. Furley, 1871-4, II (i), x, 4,122; Gomme, 1880, 75-83

NORTH FRITH PARK

North Frith in 1460 was a hunting park, much larger than now, which had long been in the possession of the Clare, and then the Stafford, families. Much of it lay in Hadlow parish, but it spilled well over into the parishes of Shipbourne, West Peckham, Tonbridge, and Hildenborough, and its full extent is never estimated by contemporaries. One document referred to its extent as seven miles but did not make clear if this meant seven square miles or seven miles in circumference. In Hadlow parish, we may perhaps guess at somewhere around fifteen hundred to two thousand acres, but Mick Rodgers, farming at North Frith Farm, reckons its full extent to have been nearer five thousand acres. Towards Tonbridge it stretched as far as Cage Green, so that courtiers at Tonbridge Castle had a readily accessible entrance into the park at Cage Gate. It extended north-west to Trench Wood, Coldharbour, and Kiln Wood, getting near to Shipbourne village, then turning east (the place-name Claygate seems to suggest another entrance), then veering south of Oxenhoath back to High House Lane, along a boundary with Hadlow manor.

Both North Frith park and Hadlow manor were in the hands of the same owner, so while North Frith lay outside all Hadlow's sub-manors, it must have lain within our chief Hadlow manor. So long as it belonged to the Clare and Stafford families, nothing about it has been found in their archives for they became scattered and are meagre when compared with the size of their great estate. But when once the Duke of Buckingham

This map in Hasted's History and Typography of the County of Kent 1799 shows the extent of woodland in Hadlow in that year but not the full extent in 1460.

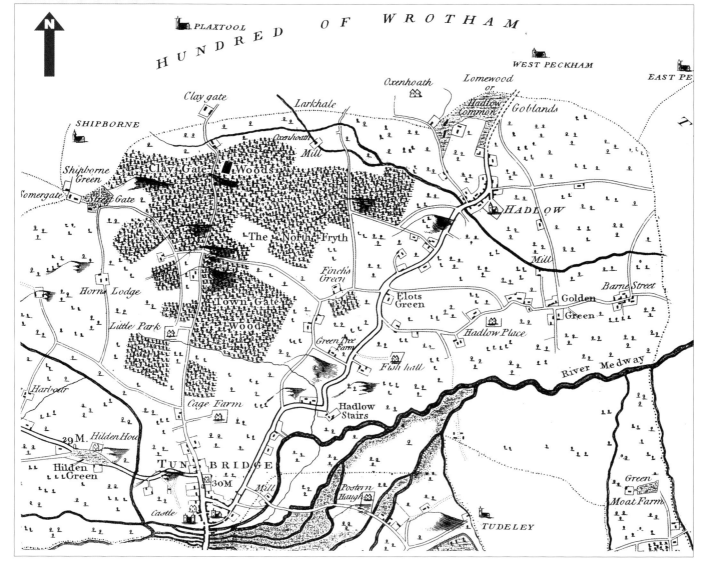

1. L. & P.,Hen. VIII, XVIII, ii, 59

2. Thirsk, 1984, 384-6

3. L. & P., Hen. VIII, XVI, 499

4. Hasted, 1798, V, 180

5. L. & P., Hen. VIII, XVII, 30

6. L. & P., Hen. VIII, XVI, 622

7. NA C3 / 42 / 83

was executed for treason, and all his lands were surrendered to the King in 1521, more about its management is learned from the national records. Grants of North Frith were made by Letters Patent, and one additional document records Thomas Culpeper, esquire, holding courts in Hadlow. Moreover, some Hadlow manor tenants, as our 1460 survey shows, had rights of pannage in North Frith (i.e. rights to graze pigs there); also Richard Fisher, being lessee of Hadlow manor for 21 years from 1543 onwards, claimed for himself pannage for thirty swine.[1] North Frith must have been part of Hadlow manor.

The first grant of the hunting park after 1521 was made to Sir Henry Guildford, who was Master of the King's Household and also Master of the Horse. At the dissolution of the monasteries, it is noticeable how often parks were granted to gentlemen who had some obligation to produce horses to ride with the king, either to war or on formal occasions; this last obligation was laid on Gentlemen Pensioners, and Sir Ralph Fane of Hadlow was one of them. So many grants of parks savour of official policy, designed to encourage gentlemen to breed better horses in them, thereby supporting one of the king's campaigns at this time to improve the breed of English horses.[2]

Sir Henry Guildford held North Frith until his death in 1532, and his widow sold it back to the Crown in 1541.[3] Then Hadlow manor and North Frith passed in Edward VI's reign to John Dudley, later Duke of Northumberland, a powerful figure in the young king's reign who exchanged it for properties in other counties.[4] He himself lost his life for resisting the succession of Catholic Mary. North Frith now passed through an unsettled period of grants, forfeitures, and re-grants, leaving us to speculate on how Hadlow people experienced it all, for they undoubtedly picked up the gossip about the standing of local gentlemen at court. In Chapter 15 below we note some of the banter passing among the poachers in 1538 about local gentry, in that case, the Boleyn family, when they were in bad odour with the king. The herbage and responsibility for the deer were bestowed on various local gentlemen until they, one by one, fell from favour, and were attainted, some forfeiting all their property. Thus Sir Edward Neville at Mereworth (whom we encounter in 1538 reporting on deer poaching in many nearby parks (see Chapter 15)) had been made keeper of North Frith park at some unknown date, and was then attainted. Thomas Culpeper, esquire in 1541 held the grant of the herbage of North and South Frith, and in his turn too was attainted.[5]

Thomas Culpeper's accounts shed some further light on the management of North Frith, for he was paying two men £3 for ten weeks to watch an eyrie of goshawks, as well as repairing the park pales and gates, and making a hedge about the 'hawksege', costing him 3s. 2d. He held courts for the manor, and paid three keepers of North Frith £10 for their year's wages.[6] We noted above in Chapter 8 the generous rights given to these three keepers for grazing a number of their own bullocks in the Frith. As the Tithe map of 1842 shows, some meadow land by the Medway was actually called North Frith Meadows; we may wonder if the keepers routinely took them down there to fatten in the summer.

Culpeper's responsibilities in North Frith seem to have arisen out of the grant made to Sir George Harper, in 1542, for he and Thomas Culpeper were partners. A lawsuit in Chancery reveals a tangle of family relationships and influences exerted at court that bound together many of the beneficiaries of Crown grants in the sixteenth century when they scrambled for favours; their personal ties were crucial for success.[7] So Sir George Harper who got the grant of South and North Frith was married to a Harper kinswoman who was also the sister of Alexander Culpeper; Alexander Culpeper went to Spain in the service of 'the prince', while two other Culpeper brothers of Thomas acquired a material interest in North Frith, one as a solicitor handling Alexander's affairs when abroad, the other by inheritance. Unfortunately, we lose sight of the way that dispute was settled.

Going back to Henry VIII's reign, Sir Henry Isley of Sundridge became keeper of the park of North Frith, master of the hunt, and chief steward and bailiff of Hadlow manor in place of Sir Edward Neville, who was beheaded in 1538 for conspiring with the Pole family.[8] Isley was the next to be attainted for being concerned in Wyatt's rebellion, 1554-5.[9] Finally, in 1558, Elizabeth granted the park, with the manor, to her first cousin, Sir Henry Carey, without requiring him to pay any rent.[10] Sir Henry Carey (1524?-1596) was the son of Anne Boleyn's sister, becoming Lord Hunsdon in 1559. In 1587 he set to work to find out what rents were owed him, raising the rent paid by David Willard for his furnaces, foundries, iron mill, and a pond for his ironworks.[11] But he had no personal connection with Kent, and his descendants in James I's reign sold their interest.

For over a hundred years of the fifteenth century Hadlow people had had a rich nobleman (living at home in Thornbury, Herefordshire), as the lord of North Frith. It must have been very different when the park came to the Crown under the Tudors, and numerous different grantees took over, appointing their own sub-lessees, and all no doubt taking their pickings from the woodland. The lease given to Sir George Harper and Thomas Culpeper, esquire, in 1553, allowed them for forty years to take timber freely for charcoal to make iron. They paid £500 p.a. for the right, but by 1570 the woodland had been stripped and it was no longer worth the rent. They surrendered the lease in 1574, after only 21 years, and when Hadlow people were summoned to revalue what was left, they counted South Frith and North Frith together, and reckoned it to be worth no more than £33 16s. 8½d.[12]

Two generations of Lord Hunsdon's heirs held North Frith and then sold it to a London physician, who conveyed it to the Rivers family, gentry whose story is told in Chapter 13 among local families since one branch of the Rivers settled in Hadlow.[13] They have left no estate archive, so the subsequent history of North Frith is not easy to follow. Ironworking in the Weald declined in the first half of the seventeenth century when such industrial activities moved to the West Midlands and South Wales in search of better quality iron and more timber.[14] Early in the 1600s, a growing enthusiasm for improving land in the Weald for agriculture was made clear in the published work of Gervase Markham (discussed in Chapter 8), and some of North Frith's land that had been irredeemably cleared of wood was accordingly laid out in farms. Dr Chalklin has

8 & 9. L. & P., Hen. VIII, XVII, 159

10. BL Lansdowne MS., 165, f.42

11. CKS U38 / M1

Traces of a substantial old road with ditches in the woods at North Frith

12. NA, E178 / 1093

13. Hasted, V, 180-81

14. Chalklin, 1965, 131-2

Hunting in the Frith

15. CKS U38, M1

16. Chalklin, 1962, 35

17. Jessup, 1985, 124; Cook, 1938,
118, 120, 125, 127, 130, 132-4;
Chalklin, 1962, 42

written about the changed layout of farms in Tonbridge parish that resulted between 1650 and 1750, and although he does not separately describe the reshaping of the parkland of North Frith, one of the large farms newly created in 1674-6 was Old Trench Farm, which must have been part of the hunting park since Trench Park of North Frith was listed in 1586 as part of the manor.[15] The farm was measured at 275 acres, and was sold at first to a syndicate of eleven local people, but then it was immediately resold to one yeoman tenant. Dr Chalklin's tabulation of farm sizes on the demesne land of the manor in South Frith shows other large farms being laid out by this time, 24 per cent of holdings being between 100 acres and 320 acres apiece.[16] In short, some large farms appeared in this part of the Weald which had formerly been the more congenial home of smallholders.

As for the woodland, we can reasonably guess that some of North Frith's trees began to be more carefully coppiced again, for experience shows how a revival of interest in coppicing regularly returns after a long period of neglect; it is happening today. Sir Roger Twysden at Roydon Hall in the next door parish of East Peckham showed extreme concern for preserving woodland by coppicing, after his estate suffered severe despoliation during the Civil War. Replanting must have taken place at some time since some woodland in North Frith survives to this day.[17]

Speed's map of 1611.
It shows Hadlow in the
Lowy of Tonbridge and
the pale round North
Frith park.

CHAPTER 15

HADLOW IN A WEALDEN CONTEXT

The history of early settlement in Kent, especially in the Weald, is distinctive, and has left a deep impress on its history, some of it visible still. So in this last chapter, the broader Wealden context in which Hadlow lay is the focus of attention. Subjects discussed here could alert those who study other Wealden parishes to identify more evidence, which may strengthen some of the observations made here about Hadlow.

We are accustomed these days to reading about 'the panoramic beauty of the Weald, unsurpassed in any part of England', and some descriptions of it are lyrical; for Peter Brandon, it 'delights the eye, warms the heart and feeds the soul'.[1] But the Weald was not always seen in this attractive light. Professor Richard Bradley in 1729 printed a sobering story of a man from the Weald of Kent accused of poisoning several wives. In less than twenty years, he buried fourteen of them, and with each one gained a fortune. He went for trial, and said that he married women from hilly countries, but the difference of air and diet probably explained their deaths. Physicians confirmed that view, and he was acquitted.[2] In other words, the Weald was not an alluring countryside in the past when compared with the downs and vales in the east and north of the county. Our understanding of its early history owes much to the careful work of Kenneth Witney in his book of 1976 on *The Jutish Forest*, studying the Weald from AD 450 to 1380. Kenneth Witney's parents were missionaries in India, and he spent much of his childhood and his holidays in Kent, going on to live during his working life in Tonbridge until his death in 1999. He knew Hadlow and the district very well indeed.[3]

The Weald of Kent in Witney's book starts off as a primeval forest, though bearing traces of ironworking and associated tracks from Roman times. The new settlers in the fifth century were a Frankish people from the Middle Rhine, who brought a different culture from that of the Anglo-Saxons who settled elsewhere. Their ordinary freemen enjoyed great freedom, and they followed the gavelkind custom of inheritance, not passing property on death to the eldest son alone but dividing it equally between sons, or, if no sons, then between daughters. They were accustomed to settling in scattered farms or small hamlets, not in villages. Even when the invaders later had to submit to Anglo-Saxon rule, they preserved these old customs and tenures.[4]

1. Brandon, 2003, 219, xv

2. R.Bradley, 1729, 21-3

3. The Foreword in Witney, 2000, pays tribute to him

4. Witney, 1976, 3-5

Kentish territory was divided into lathes, each lathe being headed by a royal vill, situated on the more readily cultivable land north of the Weald; in the Hadlow case this royal vill was at Aylesford, extending over a very large domain which would subsequently become divided between many manorial estates. Hadlow lies on the outer rim of the Weald, and benefited from the fact that the continuous forest belt of the Weald running from west to east was broken by the Medway. This river deposited alluvium on the terraces and so ameliorated Hadlow's soils at its southern end. Each lathe at the beginning owned a corridor of land running into the forest along which farmers drove their swine in autumn for fattening on acorns and beechmast. The drove roads became settled routes into the forest's recesses, and in the vicinity of Tonbridge and Hadlow, used two ancient crossings over the Medway at Branbridges and Twyford.[5]

In every lathe the king had a scattered demesne, of which some land was let to

The ancient crossing at Twyford, Yalding

5. Witney, 1976, 11-13, 13, 39, 41, 49-51

tenants, known as 'inmen', owing suit of court and some labour services to their lord. Other land in the lathe, known as 'outland', was let to freemen, and gave them individual farms, scatttered singly or in small hamlets, out of which they created their arable, meadow and pasture. In the pannage season all drove their swine into the forest, sharing its resources with the king and his 'inmen'. As time wore on and the settled population increased, a distinction developed between woodland belonging to the crown and the common woodland, the king holding on to places on the northern margins of the Weald - Witney names the Mereworth woods and Oxenhoath, in West Peckham, as two such areas - while leaving the deeper woodland to the freemen[6] Further adjustments and changing usages to accommodate yet more people resulted in the king granting substantial estates to courtiers around him, and such landholders in turn let smaller estates to their retainers which became submanors. In providing some Wealden common to all such grantees the chief lord broke up the continuous woodland into a series of dens, and so single manors acquired a chain of such halting and feeding places, necessarily lying at a distance from their parent base.[7] The resulting topography became a tangle of intermingled manors, dens, and farms, whose farmers enjoyed great freedom without accepting any strong necessity for the regulation of common assets such as evolved in areas of Anglo-Saxon settlement. In course of time, manorial conventions hardened and moved people increasingly towards an administrative conformity in Anglo-Saxon territories, and inexorably these trends exerted influence in Kent too, for manorial stewards trained in the law were bound to promote notions of conformity wherever they took office. But in some respects, though not all, people in Kent succeeded in resisting these tendencies. It is true that Kent's distinctive lathes, and the lesser units, called hundreds, adapted to accommodate manors, while the church everywhere divided Kent communities into parishes. But the pattern of farms and communal usages remained different in Kent, and continue to be difficult for us to disentangle and explain.

As Hadlow lies on the edge of the Wealden forest, and not on the more fertile soils around Aylesford, where lay the original royal vill of the lathe, the improvement of ploughland and the making of self-sufficient farms with adequate cornland to feed a family was doubtless a slow process, carried out over many generations as the population gradually increased in the neighbourhood. Until the Norman Conquest, we know almost nothing in detail about the shaping of that landscape. We first learn the name of a grantee of land in the Tonbridge area in the time of William the Conqueror, when Richard, son of a Frenchman called Gilbert, Count of Eu or Brionne of Normandy, received a major grant. He was known sometimes as Richard of Tonbridge, for that strategic place on the Medway was already important, though Gilbert actually founded his fortunes on a larger estate at Clare in Suffolk, from which he took his surname. Some land appendant to Tonbridge was called a lowy, granted to him in an exchange arrangement, and as it extended into Hadlow, Richard Clare was lord of Hadlow's land. After that the Clare family rose in wealth, estates and influence, building up a strong presence around Tonbridge, and taking increasing pleasure in the use of the surrounding woodland for hunting.[8] Early in the twelfth century North Frith and South Frith woodlands and all the land between were turned into a large hunting chase with deer parks in Postern and Cage. It stretched over some forty square miles from Shipbourne to Tunbridge Wells.[9] The Clares' attachment to Tonbridge may be gauged by the fact that Richard Clare who died in 1263 gave instructions for his body to be buried at Tewkesbury, his bowels at

Branbridge in the early 1900s. Compare with the etching on page 56

6. Witney, 1976, 166, 57-63

7. Witney, 1976, 37-55

8. Witney, 1976, 164-168; see 135 for the plan of the Clare estates in the 13th century.

9. Witney, 1976, 166-167

10.   Witney, 1976, 297, fn.61

11.   Witney, 1976, 139

12.   Hasted, V, 180-88

13.   Golding-Bird, 1990, 147

Canterbury and his heart at Tonbridge. It was surely the hunting around Tonbridge that had captivated him.[10]

When Richard Clare died in 1263 the land around Hadlow was taking on the appearance of a farmed countryside. Kenneth Witney judged that the balance had tipped during the twelfth century from pannage (using the woodland to feed swine) to crop cultivation and the exploiting of timber, but the absence of documents prevents us from tracing out the process until the thirteenth century.[11] Nevertheless, something of the zest for owning land around Hadlow, which offered access to courtiers at Tonbridge castle and hunting facilities round about, may surely be detected in the existence of seven sub-manors in the parish of Hadlow, all in place by 1460.

Manors in the parish that are named in the documents are Hadlow Place, Goldhill, Crombury, Fromonds, Caustons, Fish Hall (called 'a reputed manor' in 1694, but almost certainly never a recognised manor, and not counted here), Lomewood and Peckhams.[12] They are likely to have been small, at the very most 200-300 acres apiece, and some perhaps smaller still (a historian of Meopham in Kent identifies one manor there of only 50 acres).[13] But if they were all manors, we have to assume that they all held manorial courts. The court rolls of some do survive, although they are fragments only, and they exhibit a conformity with conventional procedures. (Discussed in Chapter 6 above).

THE SUB-MANOR OF CAUSTONS

Among the sub-manors, Caustons calls for special mention for Hadlow was one of the homes of the Caxton family, and Hadlow, may have been the birthplace of William Caxton. The evidence is circumstantial and certainly not proven, but it deserves attention.

The Causton family's origins are thought to lie in Cawston, North Norfolk and possibly in Caston, West Norfolk. The family is then found in Cambridgeshire, associated with Caxton, which lies west of Cambridge, with London, Kent, and Suffolk. The Clare family were prominent landowners in Suffolk, and it is guessed that a Causton arrived in the Weald of Kent in the service of the Clares, at a time in the later twelfth century when they were developing their estates along the Medway. The one Cawston who was best remembered around Hadlow was Hugh de Causton, and he features in our Hadlow survey as a past owner of Caustons manor. The fact that the same first name was borne by more than one generation, however, makes for difficulties in establishing any firm chronology.

William Caxton

Documents in the National Archives show a William de Causton in 1291/2, having a son called Hugh de Causton who granted away land in Causton, Norfolk. Then, a Hugh de Causton, who could well have been the same person, having sons Francis and Roger, was engaged in land transactions relating to West Peckham, Tonbridge, and Mereworth in 1306, 1310 and 1324. So a landed interest in Kent had been established, and in an Inquisition Post Mortem of 1315 the same Hugh was also shown holding the manor of Causton in Hadlow, deemed to be one-eighth of a knight's fee and held from Gilbert de Clare, Earl of Gloucester. At the same period another family in Hadlow, who would show a significant connection with the Caustons, bore the surname atte Berne or Barne, and in 1306 Richard atte Berne was mentioned in connection with woods in West Peckham that had come into the possession of Hugh de Causton. A second connection between the Atte Bernes and Caustons was the marriage of William de Causton, who died in 1354, to Cristina, who then took John ate Berne as her second husband. In 1352 Hugh de Causton of another generation sold the manor because his eldest son, John, had become a friar in 1334 (he was later to become prior of Dover), and his brother William assented to the sale. Was this perhaps the same William who had married Cristina?

The date of birth of William Caxton, the printer, is unknown, but it is reckoned at somewhere between 1415 and 1424.[14] This is some sixty years after the last firm evidence of the Caustons in Hadlow. But he nevertheless clearly said that he was born and learned his English in the Weald of Kent, and that must mean that he went to school there.[15]

14.   ODNB under Caxton

15.   Larking, 1859, 231-3

William Caxton's imprint

16. NA E178 / 4118

17. Duncan, 1924

18. Tenterden Exhibition of Books Catalogue, 22 July-4 August, 1951, 7-10; on Caxton,s father, see also Blake, 1962

William Caxton was then apprenticed to a London mercer, and turning to the records of the Mercers' Company we find that the first warden's accounts in 1347 name no less than eight Caustons as members. The William de Causton, mentioned above as the brother of the friar, could well be the mercer who died in 1354, for he showed a Hadlow connection by naming his late apprentice, John atte Berne, as his executor. This John atte Berne evidently remained in Hadlow for he owned, and possibly himself built, Barnes Place, a fine medieval house existing still in the parish at Barnes Street, east of Golden Green. It is listed Grade 1*. In a much later document in James I's reign, in 1613, this John Barnes was again mentioned as a mercer and an executor of William Causton's will; he set up a chantry in London for him.[16] In 1393 a John atte Berne (the same man possibly or, more likely, a descendant) bought some of the Causton manor lands in Hadlow adjoining his own.

It might seem that the Caustons, arriving around 1300, had severed their connection with Hadlow by 1352 when selling the manor. Yet their second link with Hadlow survived, namely, as owners of that one eighth of a knight's fee in Hadlow, mentioned in 1315. In 1403 it still belonged to heirs of Hugh de Causton, though we are not told that they still bore the Causton name, nor are we told where they were living. A Richard atte Berne also held one sixth of a knight's fee in Hadlow. Thereafter, some of the Causton family members are found in West Wickham, Kent. The wills showing this are dated considerably later, between 1490 and 1560.[17]

More on William Caxton, the printer, came to light in 1922, when Richard Holworthy found deeds fairly certainly showing that William's father was called Philip, and his wife, Dionisia, and they had two sons, William and Philip.[18]

One of the missing links in William Caxton's connection with Hadlow, then, is evidence that any members of the Causton family continued to live in Hadlow when Hugh sold up in 1352. He had first received the agreement of his sons, John, the friar who went to Dover, and William, the mercer who worked in London. But William, the mercer's offspring, could well have kept a home in Hadlow for many important and influential members of London companies in the sixteenth century did exactly the same, maintaining connections with their native places; two of those doing so in Hadlow, while making their livings in London and abroad, were the Fanes, remaining in the parish registers until at least 1616, and the Rivers until, at least, the 1660s. Their histories are discussed in Chapter 13.

Above: The reputed birthplace of Caxton in Hadlow's High Street. The house was demolished in 1936 and re-erected at Forest Row, on the northern boundary of the Ashdown Forest (left), although it appears that it took more than one house to make this new building!

So evidence about William Caxton's early years eludes us still, but Hadlow people preserved a vague oral tradition about the family, and an old house in the High Street, now gone, was said to have belonged to them. A further link may yet be found, when pursuing the Caxton surname in public archives, or when exploring the Causton association with the mercers. The link with mercers in trade seemed to endure into the printer's youth for William was apprenticed in 1438 to Robert Large, one of the influential and rich members of the Mercers Company, who in due course became sheriff and mayor.[19] The recognised authority on Caxton, N.F.Blake, has written the most recent account of Caxton's life for the Oxford DNB, and expressed the opinion that views on his birthplace 'lack conviction'. But he did guess that William's father 'may have been a prosperous merchant, since it cannot have been easy to

19. Dumbreck archive, CKS TR 1335 / 3,5,12; 1336 / 6A; Lambert Larking, 1859, 1862-3-

apprentice a son to an important man like Large'. So it might well be fruitful to look for other influential mercers around Tonbridge who could have helped William Caxton into his apprenticeship. Meanwhile Hadlow people cling to the story that William was born in Hadlow, since the circumstantial evidence makes it the most reasonable suggestion so far.

Returning to our survey, we note that Hugh de Causton was well remembered in 1460 as the one-time lord of Causton manor, while we have to assume that those other pieces of land occupied by him in our survey belonged to the principal manor of the Staffords, for we are not conversant with any convention whereby one manor's land could be severed and passed to another manor. However, it is not inconceivable that it happened at the time of the Black Death, causing part of Caustons manor after 1352 to be joined with the principal manor of Hadlow. A Caustons manor remained in existence, its centre being known to have lain in the vicinity of the present Style Place. Houses recently converted from the old nineteenth-century maltings and brewery buildings of Style Place have been given the name of Caxton Place.

SUB-MANORS IN THE WEALD

Hadlow manor was unusual in having seven sub-manors in the parish along with the main manor of the Clares and Staffords. Many practical questions come to mind concerning the way they co-existed peaceably. Their lands were intermingled; so disputes between them were bound to arise, particularly about boundaries. How were they settled? In some counties like those in the Midlands, where one manor often extended over a whole parish, it is possible that disputes with neighbouring manors were rare. Even where two or three manors co-existed in a parish, problems might be amicably settled by gentlemen owners conferring with each other. But eight manors in one parish suggest problems on a quite different scale; yet we find no documents to suggest how they were dealt with. One place-name only in our survey prompts speculation about the existence of a possible meeting place in the manor where contentious issues could be thrashed out, for it was called Lawday Place. Nothing has been found in any Hadlow documents explaining its use, but it is briefly discussed in Chapter 14, as a *Topographical Problem*.

What is made clear in this puzzle about practicalities in a parish with so many manors is the unceremonious way in which the manors themselves were created. If that impression is correct, then we should not be surprised to find unceremonious administrative procedures being followed thereafter. The records of manors usually studied by historians relate to great landowners served by stewards, bailiffs, reeves, beadles, and others; but educated and trained administrators were not always at the disposal of our small Wealden landowners or their manorial lessees. An episode in 1598 at Hunton (a parish next door but one to Hadlow, with Yalding parish lying between) illustrates this situation. The tenants took to the Exchequer Court in Westminster a complaint about their manorial lord. He was not the owner but the lessee, but he did not occupy the manor house, did not relieve the poor, did not keep a bull or boar for the use of the tenants, did not allow them hedgebote or stackbote, and did not give them a dinner every lawday. When they attended court on one occasion from 8 a.m. until 5 p.m, they were offered neither meat nor drink, had to assemble under some trees, and the steward was obliged to write his notes sitting on a log. The tenants knew the correct manorial procedures but the practice could be somewhat different.[20]

In Hadlow, we come close to similar makeshifts in 1587 relating to Fromonds sub-manor. In a dispute about whether Fromonds was held by knight service, all seventy-year old witnesses agreed that 'they took Fromonds to be a manor,' for it 'had demesnes and services'. They were also aware of how the manor had descended by inheritance. But they also knew that the demesne lands had been sold away from the services, so that the lord, Mr William Cotton, 'left not any piece whereon he might hold a court'. Notwithstanding this difficulty, Sir Thos Cotton, his son, held divers courts for the manor 'in a part of the highway near the same'. The rents of Fromonds were known to another witness, Walter Trice, a mercer of Hadlow; they consisted of 9s. in money, certain peppercorns, certain hens, and one red rose. A rickety manorial structure comes into view, though it was held together by the tenants recognising their duty to gather the lord's rents and uphold the customs. To that end, they said, a customary book had been produced in 1464-5, more than a century before, to show what they owed, and after the death of Sir Thomas Cotton (evidently a recent occurrence) the homage of the manor had made a presentation of the rents and services. Testimony in this lawsuit is shot through with some knowledge of court procedures, and an awareness of ancient customs. Indeed, it goes further, showing deep respect and obedience to the customary book. The testimony of Walter Trice brings us face to face with a peaceable community, accepting their manorial duties, while also very carefully watching their manorial rights, yet content to let the customary book (of 1464-5) have the final say. We learned from other evidence that Walter Trice occupied Court Lodge; that suggested that he possibly cultivated the home farm as well. He was 72 years old in 1586 and had held a copy of the customary book for some thirty years, having had it 'faithfully' copied for him by Stephen Austen; he believed it to be an exact copy of the one held by George Bishop, once of Hadlow, now of Tonbridge. The customary book, he said, 'was of very great credit amongst all tenants of the manor, insomuch that upon any question arising about the rights, rents, and services of the tenancies there, they used to repair to him for search in the said book of his, and did hold themselves quieted and satisfied with that which was found there, as he hath very often known and seen'. The episode conveys a sense of people's contented adherence to very old practices though without the bureaucratic efficiency and consistency expected of a chief manor. Small sub-manors often changed hands; in such circumstances, they might, or might not, long endure.[21]

Professor Nellie Nielson contributed an extremely well-informed and perceptive essay on this question in 1928-9, having closely studied the medieval manors of Bilsington in Kent, Fleet in Lincolnshire, and others more cursorily. She was very conscious of the diversity of manorial forms across the kingdom, and in what she called 'desultory reflections'[22] she protested against 'the somewhat insidious temptation' to cover England too generally with the types of manorial organization described by Frederic Seebohm. He was the authority writing in the 1880s, much respected in her day. Such types were common in parts of the Midlands and the south, but not necessarily elsewhere. Professor Neilson was well aware of all the past discussions about racial influences on manorial forms, but she herself gave more weight to agricultural explanations, and was inclined to give priority to Continental influences since Kent lay so near to the European mainland, and contacts could have conferred 'an early self-consciousness and entity that enabled her (i.e. Kent) to withstand the equalizing and standardizing influence of the Norman conquest'.

Professor Neilson was familiar with unusual manorial practices like the coalescence of small manors to make larger ones, and the fission of vills to make new manors. She expected newly created manors to adopt tenurial styles, like gavelkind, to match the practices of neighbours, thus strengthening the drift towards ever more local conformities. But she harked back also to an older, pre-Norman past when the manor had not been the vital administrative unit but the village had reigned supreme, so that where village boundaries met, it was the village that claimed rights over common alongside other villages, thus explaining the widespread existence of non-manorial commons. She looked forward to someone writing a 'great work on early commons' which would differentiate between commons within manors and inter-village commons, and would also establish a chronology relating to the status of tenants, starting with ancient tenants all of whom turned onto the commons all their cattle throughout the year, while tenants coming later had to pay for the right, and were restricted to a certain number of animals only. A varied array of individual rights and privileges would accumulate, which she found embedded in the names used for classes of tenantry. She gave some examples from widely scattered

21. NA E134, 29 Eliz., Hil. 19

22. Neilson, 1928-9

documents, embracing sub-tenants, and, seemingly, transhumant people, i.e. those bringing their animals, like pigs into woodland, for only one season of the year, a group to which other historians pay no attention; all would require explanation.[23]

23.   Neilson, 1928-9, 730-31

Similarly, Professor Neilson scrutinized the varied terms given to tenemental units, mentioning yokes and dayworks, though she did not refer to the ferlings that appear in our survey. Labour services were yet another subject for infinite variation; these obligations in course of time would take on subtle, fresh meanings in identifying status. In short, Professor Neilson depicted an extremely fluid manorial scene in time and space in the Middle Ages, helping us to adjust our vision when confronting, for example, all the puzzling mismatches of rents, dues, and services that were owed in Hadlow in 1460. Perhaps, they did constitute one layer piled on another and another of changing practices, without any attempt at spring-cleaning ever having taken place. So in remarking finally on the 'far from conventional manorial type' found in Kent, and while allowing, even so, for some conformity of procedures, she enables us to consider the possibility of conformities in the Weald that were unique to the region and identify a distinctive Wealden type. Significantly, Professor Neilson recognised with other medievalists how little embarrassed were our forebears in accepting the co-existence of pre-feudal and feudal custom.[24] We are prompted to wonder if this prepared them mentally for the new age in the sixteenth century when a fresh administrative revolution would descend.

24.   Neilson, 1928-9, 739

ADMINISTRATIVE REFORM

We take it for granted that administrative routines throughout the kingdom were profoundly disrupted by the calamity of the Black Death. The population of the kingdom was reduced by about a half, and manorial officials died along with tenants. The bulk of our estate records in the Middle Ages relate to religious houses, nobility or richer gentry, and such landowners kept the best records. Those lying in the most fertile areas of the country show vacant holdings being speedily filled. But this did not necessarily happen in the Weald. It did not have the attraction of loamy soils in sheltered valleys. Rather, its residents were more likely to move elsewhere if other districts offered more alluring prospects. So we may reasonably assume that different circumstances in the farming routines and the social structure of the various provinces of the kingdom constrained landowners, and demanded some flexibility rather than producing a uniform adherence to standard rules. So what variability emerges?

Eleanor Searle, studying the estates of Battle Abbey in Battle in the High Weald of Sussex, shows the lord seeking fresh tenants in the 1450s and still accepting low rents and low entry fines. The abbey allowed a variety of tenures in its efforts to get tenants at all costs.[25] But gradually, everyone's spirits lifted, and a more optimistic phase of economic development came into view, causing landlords to value their land afresh, and to take more trouble to check what they owned. In support of these propositions, we notice in Kent, among more considerable landowners in the mid-fifteenth century, an interest in compiling fresh surveys. A fifteenth-century terrier of priory lands (not more closely dated than that) survives for Bilsington, situated on both Weald and marsh. A survey of Wye on the downlands was taken in 1452-4.[26] The Hadlow manor survey in 1460 reflects the same economic mood. A rental and survey for the archbishop's manor of Wrotham, next door to Hadlow, taken in 1495, but on downland rather than in the Weald, represented yet more local stocktaking [27]; and in the course of the sixteenth century a much more commercial attitude towards landownership would spread all over the kingdom.

25.   Searle, 1974, 372, 374

26.   Neilson, 1928-9; Muhlfeld, 1933, repr. 1974

27.   Semple, 1982, 1-3

The Wealden evidence encourages the notion of a drive towards greater efficiency in manorial management, building up steam from the 1580s onwards in this area. Looking at the kingdom more generally, historians have identified a slow build-up of the desire for instruction in record-keeping, starting from the thirteenth century but positively surging in the early sixteenth century. The written treatises about managing courts were first written by monks and laymen, and historians have dated them by the legal precedents that they cited, starting around 1265, with more following around 1307 and 1342. Consonant with Professor Neilson's arguments, different local conventions were acknowledged by contemporaries. A treatise dated to 1269-80 instructed officials to know the customs of the county, the hundred, the court or manor, and the franchises, 'for laws and customs differ in divers places', it said. When printing four such treatises, F. W. Maitland concurred by seeking clues to the regional affiliations of authors, saying that the literature was at an early stage of growth and was of a novel kind.[28]

As time passed, more and more of the people needing to know the rules for the governing of manors were trained at the Inns of Court in London, and so policies and conventions began, to some extent, to converge across the kingdom. But the compelling logic of that situation means that change will have been gradual, rather slower in the Weald than elsewhere for it was a late settled area, and we have already suggested that some of its manorial lords were modestly endowed, with short experience and limited means for managing their lands efficiently. Even our Hadlow manor survey, belonging to a great lord, does not shine as a model. When it was made in 1460, it was markedly careful in some respects, but markedly sloppy in others. It took much trouble to give the names and enumerate the location north, south, east, and west of every piece of land , but it entirely failed to define the tenures, whether free or unfree, by which it was held.

The arrival of the printing press made it possible to publish in book form treatises on manorial administration, and they appeared thick and fast. F. W. Maitland listed their dates of publication as 1510?, 1515?, 1520?, 1530?, 1534?, 1539, 1542?, 1544, and 1546. From the 1540s they could be securely dated. Another significant contribution was made in 1523 by John Fitzherbert (almost certainly helped by his lawyer brother, Anthony), urging the more assiduous surveying of estates by lords.[29] That these words were heeded is borne out by the many manorial surveys that survive from the sixteenth century, and furthermore by the many lawsuits set in train to adjudicate on disputes that broke out about the ancient customs of manors. Wrotham, having been surveyed in 1495, was surveyed again in 1538 and again in 1568. But we should remember that that manor belonged to the archbishop of Canterbury, so we would expect administrative zeal in that quarter. The many changes in ownership of Hadlow manor, following the confiscation of the Duke of Buckingham's estates in 1521, precluded fresh surveys there, though elsewhere by mid-century they were numerous all over the kingdom.

The timing in 1581-3 of a fresh copy of the 1460 Hadlow survey fits well into a late phase of the new era when a review of tenancies, rents, and land use had come to be recognised as an essential tool of manorial administration. We can further illuminate the background to this development in the Weald by recording what happened at Wrotham at much the same period. George Segars became the steward of the manor there in 1618 and remained in that office until 1631. He had been resident in Wrotham since at least 1600, recording the births of his seven children there between 1600 and 1623. He was also evidently a man with a long-standing interest in historical matters, for when he came into possession of the 1495 survey of the manor, presumably as steward, possibly before 1610 and certainly before 1618, he wrote a note on the cover saying: 'This book I wrote with my own hand out of an old rental of Mr Richers long before I was steward of Wrotham. George Segars'.

Of the 1538 survey of Wrotham two copies survive, one being a roughly written copy that is incomplete, and another a good copy. The good copy contains on its cover yet another note by George Segars, saying: 'This book I bought of Robert Wybarne, senior, and paid a valuable consideration for the same, before I was steward of the manor of Wrotham divers years'.[30] The Wybarne family were gentry of old standing in the neighbourhood; John Wybarne, esquire, featured in our Hadlow survey, though holding only a small piece of land of less than one acre on the main street in Ralph Kene's tenement. But Anthony Wybarne appeared in Henry VIII's reign in a list of rentals and surveys, holding Duke of Buckingham lands in Tonbridge; he also held a knight's fee,

28. Maitland, 1888, 3-18, 68

29. Fitzherbert, 1523

30. Semple, 1982, 3-4, 53-4; CKS U55, M59; U55, M60 / 1 / 2

31. NA SC12, Portfolio 2, no.56;
Semple, 1982, 15-16

32. Tite, 2003

33. Lambarde, 1970; Warnicke,
1989, 74-5

34. CKS U38 / M1

35. For an instructive county-wide
investigation in Somerset, 1500-
1623, see Havinden, 1998-9.
The author's text and maps, nevertheless, invite further geographical
and chronological refinement.

and a Wybarne held land in Wrotham in 1495.[31] So our local Wealden gentry and their stewards were evidently collecting old documents with much the same enthusiasm in the late sixteenth century as the more illustrious antiquarians in London like Sir Robert Cotton. His massive archive has recently been analysed with great care for the British Library.[32]

We begin in the sixteenth century to assemble the surnames of gentlemen living in and around Hadlow with a more conscious interest in its landed potential. Quite certainly it was sparked by the forfeiture of the Duke of Buckingham's great estate in 1521, coming at just the time when economic hopes were reviving more generally. Within a couple of decades after 1521, we find evidence of ironmasters exploiting iron at Somerhill and casting greedy eyes on Hadlow's timber. Gentry like the Fanes and Culpepers had official duties in caring for the hunting in North Frith, and were picking up land in the parish at the same time. It all builds up into a social image on this fringe of the Weald of a countryside becoming well populated with up-and-coming gentlemen, whose activities deserve closer scrutiny. The most illustrious and best known was William Lambarde, a leading antiquarian, who prepared a *Perambulation of Kent*, which he finished in 1570 and published in 1576. For this he had scoured the archives for legal documents about the county. He married in 1570 Jane Multon of Ightham, a parish next door but one to Hadlow, where she died in 1573. When Lambarde remarried in 1583, he moved away to Halling, near Rochester, where his new wife held property, but his continuing connections with the Hadlow neighbourhood may be assumed since his first son by his second wife was called Multon, thus honouring his first wife's father in Ightham, and one of his twin boys born in 1587 was called Fane, thus connecting the Lambardes with the Fane family who became conspicuous in Hadlow in the first half of the sixteenth century. Retha Warnicke suggested that this denoted friendship with Sir Thomas Fane of Badsell, in Capel parish next door to Hadlow parish. But the Fanes had other branches, in Mereworth, Hadlow, and later at Fairlawn in next-door Plaxtol.[33] In short, the network of interconnected families hereabouts spread widely. It further encompassed the Cotton family who held Fromonds manor in Hadlow, and the Culpepers at Oxenhoath in West Peckham. In 1586 one document listed Hadlow's gentry as Dorrells (= Darrell?), Fishers, Fromonds, Keysers, Multons, and the Whettenhalls of East Peckham.[34] We are entitled to conjure up a picture of many meetings between local gentry, not only socially but in connection with their duties in local government, when they freely discussed with each other the problems of estate management, and among other things urged each other to keep good records.

At this period, then, we may expect a steady movement towards more uniform procedures in manorial administration, especially since gentlemen sent more and more of their sons to be educated at the universities and, for legal training, to the Inns of Court. But we should also remember that a district almost overflowing with modest gentlemen was not characteristic of the whole Weald. In the later eighteenth century parts of the deeper Weald were still deemed to be lying in a wilderness, and in the kingdom generally gentrification was patchy, very noticeable in some places, but not in others.[35] A conjuncture of special circumstances are to be expected wherever many gentry congregated. We do not find it happening in, say, Romney Marsh. We know that it would begin to happen in the fens of East Anglia in the seventeenth century, but not yet. The forest country of east Northamptonshire invites comparison in this respect with the vale land of west Northamptonshire, next door. Indeed, a more questioning, investigative enquiry into the social structure of regions all over the country could one day produce an instructive social atlas. It would almost certainly shed light on gentrification in a certain explicable chronological order. Its beginnings in the Hadlow area should surely then be traced back to the existence of the castle at Tonbridge, the build-up of enthusiasm for hunting in the later Middle Ages, and the comparative ease with which kings and courtiers could ride there from Greenwich Palace. The custom of gavelkind in Kent nurtured a more than usual number of young gentlemen of birth and

The impressive gateway of Tonbridge Castle

36.   CKS U38 / M1, 1586

37.   Chalklin, 2004; Cleere and Crossley, 1985

38.   Anon, Magna Britannia, II, 1084-5

breeding, having only modest estates that needed somehow to be augmented. The grand opportunity came their way with the forfeiture of the vast estates of the Duke of Buckingham in 1521; a swarm of bees was soon buzzing round that honeypot, receiving grants, selling on the land, issuing profitable leases to traders in iron and dealers in timber. A splendid illustration of the trend is given in a note at the end of a survey in 1587 concerning rents 'increased upon agreement' with Sir George Carey on June 25,.1587[36] The settlement pertained to the lease of the iron mill, the pool of the mill (lying either in Tonbridge or in Hadlow - it is not made clear where they lay), and some land in Shipbourne next to the paling of North Frith park. It showed the Queen's cousin, marshall of her household, having received from this friendly patron a grant of Hadlow manor, immediately seizing the opportunity to collect some of the profits from David Willard's commercial operations. We have mentioned him already, heavily engaged in shipping iron down the Medway while other confederates were felling timber in North Frith for iron smelting.[37]

The social consequences of gentrification round Hadlow were evidently still conspicuous in the early eighteenth century, for in a work of 1720 entitled *Magna Britannia et Hibernia Antiqua et Nova, or a New Survey of Britain* its author laid emphasis on the many gentry originating and still living in Hadlow and Mereworth parishes. Mereworth parish, next door to Hadlow, he said, was filled with gentry, 'who dwell thick for ten miles around, and often have their meetings here for business and diversion'.[38] By that time, of course, another magnet was attracting and holding gentry in the area, namely the spa at Tunbridge Wells, fostering a fashion for taking the waters and joining in the social round.

THE SOCIAL LIFE OF ORDINARY FOLK

Our documents tell most about the life of rich people for they kept records. Working people are mostly invisible, and women especially. Only one woman comes to life in these pages, namely, Anne, Dowager Duchess of Buckingham; others in the shadows were those women brewing ale in their kitchens for sale to the locals, while all the rest are unseen. But a precious insight into men's lives is vouchsafed in 1538 when Thomas Cromwell took action to crack down on poaching.

This district of the Weald was a countryside of many parks. We have already referred to Postern and Cage parks, but there were many more. Poaching deer in the parks of the Weald was evidently a joyous male pastime. Men undertook it as casually as we would go for a walk. We cannot be sure that the same carefree attitude prevailed everywhere in the kingdom; it depended on how effectively lords and parkwardens guarded their parks and deer. We know of the harsh attack on poachers in the later seventeenth century and early eighteenth centuries, when tough legislation was enacted against poachers. But in the first half of the sixteenth century, Wealden evidence, at least, strongly suggests a tolerant, lax attitude, and it may have existed there for so long that local people had almost forgotten that it was against the law. Around Hadlow, we find people, who in other respects would have valued their public reputations, happily joining in. So much hunting country lay around that visits by courtiers and kings were routine experiences; Henry VIII was a visitor at Hever Castle, doubtless hunting there as well as courting Anne Boleyn at Hever. For the gentry living in the vicinity, parks were a conventional adjunct of the house. For a brief period, then, poaching enjoyed a heyday, though it did not last; when

39.   Lambarde, 1970, 9

William Lambarde was writing in 1570, he claimed that within memory deer parks had been reduced by almost a half.[39] But the parks themselves did not disappear; rather, the commercial aspirations of landowners resulted in their being turned into grazing pastures for cattle.

A sharp shock was administered to the locals when Thomas Cromwell suddenly cracked down on poaching in 1538. Many poachers were caught and questioned, and a long account of their examinations, running to 31 pages, survives among Cromwell's papers giving their answers. An accompanying letter suggests that the prodding to prosecute came from Sir Thomas Boleyn, the Earl of Wiltshire at Hever Castle, father of Anne Boleyn. He would die in the following year. Nor shall we be surprised to discover that he was much hated locally; perhaps gossip in the neighbourhood had already made everyone aware that he was instigating their prosecution.

40.   An enigmatic statement by one Anthony Lee to Cromwell in 1537, in the year before the date of those poaching testimonies, suggested that it was Sir Edward Neville's men 'who so commonly hunted my lord of Wiltshire's grounds'. Lee added that Mr Fane (possibly Ralph Fane?) had likewise suspected the same. Yet, Sir Edward Neville conducted the enquiry! - Brewer, ed., L.& P., Henry VIII, XII (ii), 287.

Those conducting the investigation included Sir Thomas and Sir Edward Neville,[40] brothers of Baron Bergavenny, who was lord of Mereworth; members of the same family would become Earls of Westmorland at Mereworth and build Mereworth Castle. The Nevilles were already influential men in Kent: Sir Thomas Neville was MP for Kent and Speaker of the House of Commons, deeply embroiled in the enforcement of the law against small men since he was a member of the Council of Star Chamber; Sir Edward was a courtier who attended the marriage of Anne Boleyn to Henry VIII, but was found guilty of conspiracy, along with the Pole family, in opposing Henry's divorce from Catherine of Aragon, and was beheaded in 1538. The Nevilles collected together the examinations of the poachers and submitted them to Cromwell in 31 pages in what they termed only an *Abridgement of the Evidence*. Would that we had it all! This makes plain that it only required one man to knock on the door of his crony and suggest a night out for word to spread like wildfire among a whole gang who then met at a prearranged park, muffled, hooded, or enveloped in cloaks. Some brought nets (one admitted to having 4-5 small nets and one other long net, 40 ells long and a fathom deep), others carried bows or deer harness, a reference being made to one man who actually made the deer harness in his own house. Because of their disguise few men admitted to recognising anyone except their immediate friends. Yet they did not seem to be too scrupulous about concealment, for they brought their dogs as well, and some raids were carried out in broad daylight. Few could remember how many deer they caught on any particular occasion, but the number of bucks caught ranged from two to ten, and their parties (15 or 16 people on one occasion, 20 on another) gathered together a motley assortment of local men, including parsons and schoolteachers, even a keeper of North Frith Park, George Penhurst, who went hunting in Knole park with the poachers, and stood guard for the rest. 'Keeping the lodge' seems to have been a euphemism for keeping watch for the others. The parks that were named in the depositions were North Frith, South Frith, Cage, Postern, the North Park of Leigh, Knole, Otford, Wrotham, Penshurst, Hevynden (= Heverham, part of the Boleyn estate at Hever?), Ashore (called Eshores by Hasted), Wallers (of the Waller family in Groombridge and Speldhurst?), and Frankams (Frankfield, SW of Ightham?) - the last four not as yet positively identified. Those known to have been Hadlow men were Thomas Symonds, Thomas Godfrey, husbandman, Richard Fisher, Thomas Boucher of Hadlow, labourer, (though in one place his name was crossed out), Thomas Meyrick of North Frith, and Thomas Plane, probably of Hadlow for that was a Hadlow surname, though he was also described as a serving man at Knole, and by someone else as a servant of Sir Thomas Wroth (perhaps a visitor at Knole on that night?). Familiar Hadlow surnames in addition were Willard, Bishop, Fisher, Somer, and Rivers, while other poachers came from Tudeley, Birling, Leeds, and Yalding. Some identified by occupation or place were John Walker, who was nevertheless keeper of Otford park and disguised himself with a nightcap, Richard Potter, deemed a gentleman, Henry Somer now gone to Ireland, Thomas Atwood, a schoolmaster of Sevenoaks, William Denman of Seal, yeoman, one Garbett of Birling, also called a keeper, Birling being somewhat distant beyond West Malling, George Wekes now a paler at Hampton Court, John Basset of Tonbridge, yeoman and servant of Sir Edward Neville, Thomas Price, vicar of Frant, Edward Hart yeoman of Pepinbury, and John Domewright of Chevening, brasier. For each park, lists of names was given of those who confessed, those who were detected, and those newly detected but not yet examined.

These men had some firm views about the local gentry which coloured their attitudes towards the poaching of the deer. Edward Rivers's master was Lord Wiltshire himself. Another man referred to Queen Anne and her brother, Lord Rochford, both having lately suffered, he said (Viscount Rochford was executed two days before his sister). He also added that my lord of Wiltshire was not beloved in the country, so he was 'gladder' to hurt his park. Another was 'the more willing to make those huntings because my lord of Wiltshire was so extreme a man among them and was supposed then to be out of favour with the king's grace that men might also perceive that he had no love of the country neither'. It is illuminating to realise how much gossip people in the Weald picked up about the feuding and conspiracies at court in the reign of Henry VIII.

Finally, and indirectly, this record of poaching tells us how dramatically life changed for ordinary folk in Hadlow when once North and South Frith were turned into farmland. The deer made way for cattle in the parks. Our Hadlow menfolk lost a pastime. The women lost all the venison that had varied the bacon in their pottage for family dinner.

BIBLIOGRAPHY

ABBREVIATIONS

AC Archaeologia Cantiana
BL British Library
CKS Centre for Kentish Studies, Maidstone

KAS Kent Archaeological Society
NA National Archives, Kew

BIBLIOGRAPHY

Addison, William
1980 *The Old Roads of England.*

Altschul, Michael
1965 *A Baronial Family in Medieval England. The Clares, 1217-1314.* Baltimore, USA

Anon
1720 *Magna Britannia et Hibernia Antigua et Nova, or a New Survey of Britain*

Bailey, M.
1989 *A Marginal Economy?: East Anglian Breckland in the Later Middle Ages.* Cambridge Studies in Medieval Life and Thought, Fourth Series, 12, Cambridge

Bradley, Richard
1729 *A Philosophical Enquiry into the Late Severe Winter, the Scarcity and Dearness of Provisions, and the Occasion of the Distemper Raging in Several Remote Parts of England*

Brandon, Peter
2003 *The Kent and Sussex Weald.* Chichester

Brewer, J.S., editor
1862-1910, Letters and Papers, Foreign and Domestic, of the Reign of Henry VIII

Campbell, Bruce M.S.
2000 *English Seigniorial Agriculture, 1240-1450.* Studies in Historical Geography, 31, Cambridge

Chalklin, Christopher
1961 'Navigation Schemes on the Upper Medway, 1600-1665', *Journal of Transport History*, V (2)

1962 'The rural economy of a Wealden parish, 1650-1750', *Agricultural History Review*, X(i)

1965 *Seventeenth-Century Kent. A Social and Economic History.*

2004 *Iron manufacture in Tonbridge parish, with special reference to Barden furnace, 1552-1771.* AC, CXXIV

Clark, Peter
1977 *English Provincial Society from the Reformation to the Revolution.* Hassocks

Cleere, Henry and **Crossley, David**
1985 *The Iron Industry of the Weald.* Leicester

Cook, A.R.
1938 *A Manor through Four Centuries*

Dietz, Brian
1972 *The Port and Trade of Early Elizabethan London. Documents,* London Record Society, VIII

Du Boulay, F.R.H.
1966 *The Lordship of Canterbury*

Duffy, Eamon
1992, new edition 1994 *The Stripping of the Altars: Traditional Religion in England, 1400-1580.* New Haven
2001 *The Voices of Morebath: Reformation and Rebellion in an English Village.* New Haven, Conn., USA and London

Dumbreck, W.V.D.
1958 *The Lowy of Tonbridge.* AC, LXXII

Duncan, Leland
1924 *Kent Wills, 1440-1561*. Kent Records, KAS IX

Dyer, Alan and **Palliser, D.M.**
2005 *The Diocesan Population Returns for 1563 and 1603*. British Academy, Records of Social and Economic History, New Series, 31

Dyer, Christopher
1980 *Lords and Peasants in a Changing Society*. Cambridge
2005 *An Age of Transition? Economy and Society in England in the later Middle Ages*. Oxford

Edwards, Peter
1988 *The Horse Trade in Tudor and Stuart England*. Cambridge

Elton, C.I.
1867 *The Tenures of Kent*

Ekwall, Eilert
1936, 4th Edition 1960 *English Place-Names*. Oxford

Fenton, F.H. editor,
1960 *Tottenham Manor Court Rolls, 1510-1531*, Vol.6. Manor of Tottenham Series, Tottenham

Foard, Glenn, Hall, David, and **Partida, Tracy,**
2005 'Rockingham Forest, Northamptonshire: the evolution of a landscape', *Landscapes*, 6 (2).

Fox, Jean
The History of Sevenoaks up to 1650…with Database of West Kent Wills to 1650. CD Rom (ISBN 0-954331-90-7)

Furley, Robert
1871-1874 *A History of the Weald of Kent*, 3 vols. Ashford

Golding-Bird, C.H.
1934, reprinted 1990 *The History of Meopham. A Kentish Village from Saxon Times*.

Gonner, E.C.K.
1966 *Common Land and Inclosure*

Griffiths, Matthew
1980 'The Kirtlington manor court, 1500-1650', *Oxoniensia*, 45

Harris, Barbara J.
2002 *English Aristocratic Women, 1450-1550. Marriage and Family, Property and Careers*, Oxford

Harvey, P.D.A.
1984 *Manorial Records*. Archives and the User, No 5, British Records Association

Harvey, Sally
1970 'The Knight and the Knight's fee in England', *Past and Present*, 49

Hasted, Edward
1798 *The History and Topographical Survey of the County of Kent*. 12 vols. Canterbury

Hilton, John
1971 *A History of the Medway Navigation Company, Compiled from Various Sources*. Privately printed by John Hilton

Jessup, F.W.
1984 *Sir Roger Twysden, 1597-1672*

Jewell, Helen M.
1981 *The Court Rolls of the Manor of Wakefield from September 1348 to September 1350*. Yorkshire Archaeological Society, 2

Lawrence, Margaret
2004 *For All the Saints. St Michael's Church, East Peckham, Parish and People*. Privately printed by Margaret Lawrence, East Peckham

Lock, Ray editor
2002 *The Court Rolls of Walsham le Willow, 1351-1399*. Suffolk Records Society, 45, Woodbridge

Maitland, F.W. editor
1888 *The Court Baron, being Precedents for the Use in Seigniorial and Other Courts*. Selden Society, IV

Markham, Gervase
1625 *The Inrichment of the Weald of Kent*

Miller, Edward
1978 *Medieval England. Rural Society and Economic Change*. Cambridge

Muhlfeld, Helen E.
1974 *A Survey of the Manor of Wye.* New York, USA

Newman, John
1969 *The Buildings of England. West Kent and the Weald.*

Pantos, Aliki
1999 'Early medieval assembly places'. *Annual Report*, Medieval Settlement Research Group, 14

Petrie, Sue
2004 'The religion of Sir Roger Twysden (1597- 1672): a case study in gentry piety in seventeenth-century England'. AC, CXXIV

Prior, Mary
1982 *Fisher Row. Fishermen, Bargemen and Canal Boatmen in Oxford, 1500-1900.* Oxford

Rawcliffe, Carole
1978 *The Staffords, Earls of Stafford and Dukes of Buckingham, 1394-1521.* Cambridge

Seebohm, Frederic
1883 *The English Village Community*

Schofield, John
1994 *Medieval London Houses.* New Haven and London

Semple, Jayne L.
1982 *The Manor of Wrotham in the early Sixteenth Century. Some Aspects of Land Holding and Population.* Unpublished thesis, University of Kent at Canterbury

Thirsk, Joan
2000 'Agriculture in Kent, 1540-1640', Chapter 3 in **Zell, Michael**, *Early Modern Kent, 1540-1640.* Woodbridge

1984 'Horses in early modern England: for service, for pleasure, for power', *in* **Thirsk**, *The Rural Economy of England. Collected Essays*

Thomson, John A.F.
1965 *The Later Lollards, 1414-1520*

Virgoe, R.
1960 *Some Ancient Indictments in the King's Bench referring to Kent, 1450-1452.* KAS, Record Publications

Wadmore, James F.
1902 *Some Account of the Worshipful Company of Skinners of London*

Wallenberg, J.K.
1934 *The Place-Names of Kent.* Uppsala, Sweden

Williams, Alison M.
1985 *Aspects of a Community. Tonbridge and the Surrounding Parishes in the Period 1500 to 1560.* Unpublished thesis, Diploma in Local History, University of Kent Canterbury

Williamson, T.
2003 *Shaping Medieval Landscapes. Settlement, Society, Environment.* Macclesfield

Winchester, Angus J.L.
2000 *The Harvest of the Hills. Rural Life in Northern England and the Scottish Borders.* Edinburgh

Witney, Kenneth P.
1991 'The woodland economy of Kent, 1066-1348', *Agricultural History Review*, 38 (i)

1976 *The Jutish Forest. A Study of the Weald of Kent from 450 to 1380 A.D.*

2000 *The Survey of Archbishop Pecham's Kentish Manors, 1283-5.* KAS, Kent Records, XXVIII.

Woolgar, C.M.
1999 *The Great Household in Late Medieval England.* New Haven

Zell, Michael
1984 'Population and family structure in the sixteenth-century Weald', AC, C

1994 *Industry in the Countryside. Wealden Society in the Sixteenth Century.* Cambridge

THE SURVEY OF HADLOW MANOR, 1460

'RENTAL OR CUSTUMAL OF HADLOW', Kent, copy of 1581

Hadlow Rental or custumal of all the lands and tenements being there within the demesne of Hadlow, compiled and made and delivered before a full court held there 18th day of December in the year of the reign of king Edward IV after the Conquest of England drawn up from the information of John Godinge, John Bishop, John Fromond, Laurence Farman, John Stable, John Barton, Richard Fisher, Thomas Fisher, John Fromond of Kempinghall, Robert Bishop, John Simond senior, John Martin senior, Nicholas Alorne, John Newman maltster[1], Richard Nepaker, John Somer, Richard King and John Andrew, Richard Pynchon, James Gosse, John Beald, Peter Fisher, William Martin, Walter Martin, Walter Burgeys and Thomas Knight men having office at the inquiry for the renewal of the rental or customal of the matters presented within the demesne and those men having been elected, were returned and sworn at the court. These sworn men state upon their oath that information was presented in the rental or customal about each tenant of the said demesne as relating to all their tenures which were situated within the aforesaid demesne as here written and this was assessed efficiently, publicly, clearly and faithfully, both with regard the rent as with the customary payments owing and how and in what way the security of each tenant's tenure was determined and it shall be stated by what customary service each tenant of the aforesaid demesne has tenure within the aforesaid demesne and the measurement is made by the linear measure of sixteen feet of assize etc. as follows

1 In the original Latin text the word Polenter / pollenter is used when describing John Newman's occupation. This poses problems. Medieval scholars maintain that there was no such profession as poulterer (which seems to be the obvious translation). The suggested alternative is maltster. That has been used here but the problem is, in fact, unresolved.
The Latin word 'polentarius' is known for a maltster, c.1200, 'polentarium' as a brewery, and 'polenta' as barley in 1367. The translation cautiously offered here, therefore, (folios 58, 59, 60, 61, 62, 67) is maltster, which would fit the Hadlow scene.

Folio 1

Margin: left hand: *Kent Hadlow manor.*
Firstly they state that the **lady Elizabeth Culpeper** holds during her lifetime half a knight's fee, lately of John Peckham and a tenth part of a knight's fee, as is shown in the ancient rental and for her portion she must provide castle guard in time of war after the manner of a knight and she owes scutage according to the account and suit of court every three weeks
Item **Richard Culpeper esquire** holds half a knight's fee lately of John Fromonde next to Barn Street in Hadlow and he owes guard as above and suit of court
Margin: left hand: *now of Thomas Peckham*
Item **William Watton** holds a sixteenth part of a knight's fee formerly of Hugh of Caustone and he owes as above for his portion and suit of court
Margin: left hand: *now of Henry Fane*
Item **John Goding** holds a fifth part of a knight's fee formerly of Thomas Fromond as is shown in his charter made and sealed through the lord Richard of Clare while he was the earl of Gloucester, paying each year for this two capons or 12d. in rent at the feast of Michaelmas for all services and secular charges
Margin: left hand: *and Fane*
Item **Walter Robarde** holds a sixth part of a knight's fee formerly of John Tetlongby and he owes as above and suit of court
Margin: left hand: *now of Thomas Burgeis*
Item **Richard Baker of East Peckham** and **Alice Stretende with their associates** hold an eighth part of a knight's fee called **MOTELANDS** and he owes for the portion as above and he owes suit of court; this particular fee was in Richard Swift's tenure, as in the ancient rental etc.

Item **John Fromond of Goldhill** holds the sixteenth part of a knight's fee in **his own CAPITAL MESSUAGE** with lands called **KINGS** adjoining, formerly of Richard Bealde and he owes for his portion as above and suit of court

Item the **lady Margaret Fromond** holds for the term of her life and the life of Alice Stretende and their associates a sixth part of a knight's fee and thus they owe as above for their portion and suit of court, formerly of Richard Bromfeld at Edmund Fromondes and Collestokes as is shown in the customals

Robert Latter [written above: *William Heatis*] holds **one** [un-named] **PIECE OF LAND** formerly of Simon FitzRalph lying next to Sagon Street near Tonbridge, situated near the aforesaid street there towards the east, towards the land called Upper Castle fields towards the north, towards land lately of Simon FitzRalph towards the south and west and he thus owes the lord 12d. for the same and it contains *three acres* of land by true estimation, whether it be more or less because these are not measured and then the relief is as a 4th part of the rent, that is after death or alienation 3d. only

Richard Heyward holds **one** [un-named] **PIECE OF LAND** lately of William Honewold, formerly of Simon Lawrens as is shown in the rental and it contains *one acre of land, 1 rod and 6 dayworks* lying between the Cagegates at the meadow called Bedyll towards the east, near the highway there towards the west and north and near William Honewold's lane towards the south and he then owes 7d. and a half pence at the four principal terms of the year and 2d. in relief

---

Folio 2
COWLING TENEMENT

Margin: left hand: *tenants of the tenement at The Stair: John Bishop 14 and a half acres thus 4s.2d. and a half pence each year*

John Bishop son of Robert senior and his associates hold one tenement called **COWLING** formerly in William Bishop's tenure and for this they owe the lord 4s.4d. in rent at the four principal terms of the year, 2s.9d. in aid at the feast of St Andrew the apostle,

then the aforesaid **John Bishop** holds in **a piece of land called COWLINGFIELD** lying near the highway there leading from the Kagegate as far as Penbridge towards the west, near the same John Bishop's land called Berecroft and land formerly of Richard Bishop son of William towards the east, near the highway there leading from the Stair bridge as far as Tonbridge towards the south and near the land and meadow called Cowlingmeade, Collver meade and Browncroft towards the north and they contain *8 acres, 3 rods and 3 dayworks*

and **he holds** in **the meadow called COWLING MEAD** lying near the aforesaid piece of land called Cowling field and near Richard Bishop's land towards the south near the land lately of William Honewold called Highham Broom and the said John Bishop's land called Cokelands towards the north, near the aforesaid meadow called Collver mead towards the west, near land lately of William Bishop called Le Broke towards the east and it contains *one acre of land, 3 rods and 2 dayworks*

and **he holds** in **his own MESSUAGE WITH GARDEN and 2 pieces of land adjoining called the BERECROFT and LONGCROFT** lying near the aforesaid highway leading from the Stair bridge as far as Tonbridge towards the south, land of the same John and of William Bishop east and land lately of the said William north and it contains *4 acres of land and 4 dayworks*

Margin: left hand: *John Bishop holds 2 acres and 7 dayworks, thence 9d. and a half pence each year*

Item **John Bishop** son and heir of Richard holds of the aforesaid tenement in **his own CAPITAL MESSUAGE with a GARDEN** adjoining lying at the highway there leading from the Stair bridge as far as Tonbridge towards the south, near a piece of land of the same man called The Croft under the house towards the north, near land of John Bishop son of Robert towards the west, near Lawrence Fareman's land east and it contains *1 rod and 9 dayworks* and **he holds** in the said **piece of land called THE CROFT UNDER THE HOUSE** lying at the aforesaid messuage of the same man towards the north, near the said Lawrence's land east, near land of the said John Bishop son of Robert towards the west, land of the same John [son of - omitted] Richard towards the north and it contains *1 acre and 1 daywork*

and **he holds** in parcels of land and mead and pasture called **LE MEAD ATTE WALTERIS,** lying near the aforesaid Lawrence's land east and the said Lawrence's land and land of the said John son of Richard south, near Thomas Bishop's land towards the west, land of the same John son of Richard called Walter's north and it contains *one acre of land and 7 dayworks*

Folio 3   Margin: right hand: *2 acres 1 daywork*

Item **Thomas Bishop** holds of the same tenement in a **certain parcel of land called BEREFIELD,** lying near land of John Bishop son of Richard towards the east, south and west and the said Thomas Bishop's land called The Pightle towards the north and it then contains *2 acres and 1 daywork*

Margin: left hand: *Thomas Bishop holds 3 acres and 7 dayworks thus 11d. each year.*

Item the said **Thomas** holds **one piece of meadow and pasture called LE PYGTELL** of the same tenement lying near land of John Bishop son of Robert towards west and north, near a piece of land called the Berefield and land of the said John Bishop son of Robert towards the south and land of the said John Bishop son of Richard towards the east and it contains *1 acre and 6 dayworks*.

Margin: left hand: *Lawrence Ferman holds 3 acres 3 rods and 7 dayworks thus 13d. and a half pence each year.*

Item **Lawrence Ferman** holds of the same tenement in a [un-named] **PIECE OF LAND** lately of Richard Bishop senior and there he lately resided, lying near the same Lawrence's land towards the east, land formerly of William Bishop towards the west and north, near the highway there leading from the Stair bridge as far as Tonbridge towards the south and it contains *half an acre and 1 daywork*

and **he holds** in a [un-named] **PIECE OF LAND and PASTURE** lying at the highway there leading from Hadlow Street as far as Tonbridge towards the east and south, land formerly of William Bishop towards the west and north and it contains *2 acres, 1 rod, 6 dayworks*

Margin: *William at Helle holds then 3 dayworks thence three farthings each year.*

Item **William at Helle** [written above: *John Farman*] holds one [un-named] **GARDEN** lying next to the Stair bridge near the highway there leading from Hadlow Street as far as Tonbridge towards the east and south, near Lawrence Fareman's land towards the west and north and it contains *3 dayworks*

Total of acres is: *24 and a half acres, 3 dayworks,*
then for each acre 3d. and a half and in all three farthings and half a farthing less and in relief he owes 1d. and a half pence and a half farthing for three acres

KENE'S TENEMENT   **John Bishop son of Robert and his associates** as written below, hold one tenement formerly of Ralph **KENE** and they thus owe the lord 15d. in rent at the four terms of the year, 21d. in aid at the feast of St Andrew the apostle and they must plough one acre of land, they shall harrow and they shall receive four loaves price 2d. and 8 herrings, price 1d. and a work of one acre is worth 6d., deduction having been made for food, 80 small works each work price half a penny and 16 great works each work price 2d. and one great work price 4d. and 3 boon-works with two men in Autumn price 6d. and if they shall thresh grain they ought to receive 2 and a half bushels of hard corn and 6 bushels of oats for each small work, heriot and relief and those who owe carrying service shall not give a horse or a mare thus as heriot

Folio 4 Margin: right hand: *John Bishop then holds 5 acres, 1 rod, 7 dayworks and 1 perch thus 22d. each year.*

The aforesaid **John** holds in **a house called the MILL HOUSE with a piece of land called** Setons lying near Lawrence Farman's land towards the west, near William Bishop's land towards the east, near the highway there leading from Hadlow streeet towards Tonbridge towards the north and near the same John's land towards the south and it contains *3 rods, 7 and a half dayworks*

and **he holds** in **two parcels of land lying side by side called STEGGEHILLS**, lying near the land lately of William Bishop towards the east, near the lady of the manor's land called the Bodele and the Marsh towards the west and south, near the same lady's land called Sektins towards the north and it contains *3 acres, 3 rods and half a daywork*

and **he holds one small** [un-named] **PIECE OF LAND** lying next to Heder Kagegate, near land of John Wybarne esquire towards the east, near the highway there leading from Hadlow street towards Tonbridge towards the west and north and near le Kagebodyll towards the south and it contains *3 rods except one perch*

Lawrence Fareman holds of the same tenement **one piece of land called LE SORE** lying near the highway there leading from Hadlow street towards Tonbridge towards the north, near land of John Bishop son of Robert Bishop towards the east, near John Wybarne's land towards the west and near le Kagebodyll towards the south and it contains *3 acres, 3 rods except one daywork and a half*

and **he holds** in **a piece of meadow called SEDGEHILL** lying near the lady of the manor's land towards the south and east, near the same Lawrence's land called Cardensmeade towards the north, near land lately of William Bishop towards the west and it contains *1 and a half acres, 7 and a half dayworks*

and **he holds one piece of land and meadow called CARDENSMEADE** lying near land of Robert Bishop son of William towards the east, near the same Lawrence's land towards the north, near land lately of William Bishop towards the west, near land lately of the said William and the same Lawrence's land towards the south and it contains *half an acre, 7 and a half dayworks*

and he holds **one piece of land and meadow** now of John Fisher, **called CHRISTMEADE**, lying near land lately of William Honewold east, west and north, the same Lawrence's land towards the south and it contains *1 rod*.

Margin: right hand: *He holds 10 acres, half a daywork, thus 3s.4d. and a half pence each year.*

Item the said **Lawrence Farman** holds **one piece of land called GERVASES** lying near Robert Bishop's land towards the east, William Bishop's land towards the west, near the highway there leading from Hadlow street towards Tonbridge on the north, near the same Lawrence's land towards the south and it contains *3 and a half acres and   7 daywork*s.

Margin: right hand: *John Wibarne then holds 3 rods and 4 dayworks thence 3d. farthing and a half each year*

John Wibarne esquire holds [written above: *Bishop*] of the aforesaid tenement one [un-named] **PIECE OF LAND** lately of John Picot, lying near Lawrence Farman's land towards the east, land of John Bishop son of Robert towards the west, near the highway there leading from Hadlow street towards Tonbridge on the north, near le Kagebodyll towards the south and it contains *3 rods and 4 and a half dayworks*

Folio 5 Margin: right hand: *the feoffees of William Bishop then hold 2 acres, 1 rod and 3 dayworks and a half, thence 9d and a half pence each year*

Reginald Herst and **John A. Burton** lately the feoffees of William Bishop, upon the evidence of John heir of Richard Bishop the son of the said William, hold **one piece of land called SETRENYS** lying near Lawrence Farman's land towards the east, near land of John Bishop Robert's son towards the west, near the highway there at The Stair towards the north and near the same men's land and meadow called Cardens meade towards the south [written above: *now of John Bishop*] and it contains *1 rod and 7 dayworks*

and **they hold one piece of land called SEDGEHILL**, lying near the ditches of the lady of the manor towards the south, near John son of Robert's land towards the west, Thomas Bishop's land towards the east and the land of the said feoffees towards the north and it contains *1 acre and 4 dayworks* [written above: *now of John Bishop*]

and **they hold** in a meadow called **CARDENS MEADE** [written above: *now Farman*] lying near land of the said John Bishop son of Robert towards the west, near Thomas Bishop's land and the said feoffees' land south and the said Lawrence's land and the land of the said feoffees north and it contains *3 rods*

Margin: right hand: *the lady of the manor holds 1 and a half acres, 4 dayworks, 1 perch and 1 quarter, thence 6d. and a half pence each year*

The **lady of the manor** holds of the said tenement **2 parcels of land called YERLISHELLS** [written above: *now Nepaker*] of these one parcel lies near the water there called the Rowyng lake towards the south, near Kenyspole towards the east, Lawrence Farman's land towards the north and near a parcel [of land] of the same man towards the west and 2 parcels of land lying near the marshes towards the south and near the running water there called Rowyng lake towards the east, Lawrence Farman's land towards the north and land of the heirs of Richard Bishop son of William towards the west

and the parcels contain *1 rod and 2 dayworks, 1 perch and 1 quarter*

and **she holds** in **a garden called PRETELLIS GARDEN** demised at farm to Thomas Crudd lying near the same Thomas's messuage east, Robert Bishop's land west and south and near the common way there leading to Lawrence's house on the north and it contains *half an acre of land*

Margin: right hand: *Thomas Bishop holds there 1 and a half acres, 2 dayworks, thus 6d. and a half pence each year*

Thomas Bishop [written above: *now the heirs of John Bishop*] holds of the same **one piece of land and a paddock called SEDGEHILL MEADE** lying near a ditch there called the Millditch towards the south, Lawrence Farman's land towards the east, land of the feoffees of John Bishop son of Richard towards the north and west and it contains *1 acre, a half and 2 dayworks*

Margin: right hand: *Robert Bishop then holds 4 acres and a half, 2 dayworks and a half, thus 18d. and a half pence each year.*

Robert Bishop son of William Bishop [written above: *now of Thomas Chapelyn*] holds of the same one [un-named] **MESSUAGE** in which he lives and formerly of John Kene with a **GARDEN and THREE PIECES OF LAND** adjoining at The Stair bridge lying near the highway there towards the north, near Lawrence Farman's land towards the west, near the garden called Prestelys hagh being in Thomas Crudd's hands towards the east, the water there called the Medway and Lawrence Farman's land towards the south and it contains *4 acres, a half, 3 dayworks and a half*

Folio 6

Margin: right hand: *Richard At Helle holds there half an acre and 6 dayworks, thus 3d. and a half pence and a half farthing each year.*

Richard At Hell [written above: *now of Thomas Fisher*] holds of the same **one garden called THE UPPER HAGH** lying at The Stair near land lately of William Honewold towards the east and north, near the common way leading to Lawrence Farman's land towards the south, near William Atte Helle's house towards the west and it contains *half an acre and 6 dayworks*

Margin: right hand: *William At Hell then holds 3 acres, 2 dayworks and a half, thus 3d. farthing each year.*

William atte Helle [written above: *now Farman*] holds **one MESSUAGE with a GARDEN and a SMALL PIECE OF LAND** adjoining, near William Honewold's land towards the north, the said common way leading to the said Lawrence Farman's house towards the south, near the said Richard At Helle's garden towards the east and the highway there leading from Hadlow street towards Tonbridge towards the west and it contains *3 rods, 2 dayworks and a half*

Thomas Fisher holds [written above: *now Fishers*] by right of his wife Alice, formerly William Honewold's wife for the term of his life, **one piece of land called STONELAND**, lying near the lane there leading to the messuage lately of the said William Honewold and the land called Longshot towards the east, near land of Lawrence Farman and William At Helle towards the west, the lane there leading to the said William's messuage and the said William At Helle's garden towards the south, land of John Bishop, Robert's son and land called Longshott towards the north and it contains *2 acres, 3 dayworks*

Margin: right hand: *he then holds 2 acres, 7 dayworks and a half, thus 9d. each year.*

And the aforesaid **Thomas** [written above: *now of Thomas Fisher*] holds **one small garden called STONEY HAWE** lying near Richard At Helle's garden called The Upper Hawe towards the east, near William At Helle's land towards the west and south, towards the same Thomas's aforesaid land called the Stoney land towards the north and it contains *4 dayworks and a half*

Margin: right hand: *he holds half an acre, 2 and a half dayworks, thence 2d. three farthings each year.*

Thomas Crudd holds one **MESSUAGE in which he lives**, lately of Thomas Walter **with a GARDEN** adjoining at The Stair, near the lane there leading to the Medway towards the east, the garden called Pretellishagh towards the west, Robert Bishop's tenement towards the south, the common way there leading to Lawrence Farman's house towards the north and it contains *half an acre, 2 dayworks and a half*

Total of acres is: *30 acres and a half, 5 and a quarter dayworks, 1 perch*, thence 4d. for each acre and more 1d and a half pence in all and for ten acres they owe 1d.farthing in relief

---

Folio 7
WODEMANY'S TENEMENT

Margin: left hand: *Woodmaneys* right hand: *John Bishop then holds 6 acres, 3 rods and 2 dayworks and a half, thus 3s.2d. and a half pence each year.*

John Bishop son of Robert and his associates hold one tenement formerly of Gervase Bishop, now called **WODEMANYS** tenement and they then owe 15d. in rent each year and 16d.in aid at the feast of St Andrew the apostle and they must plough 1 acre price 6d., 80 small works, price of each work half a penny, 16 great works, price of each work 2d. and they owe one carrying service price 4d. and 3 boon works with 2 men price 6d.

Thence the above said **John** holds **one piece of land called MOTTIS** lying at the highway there leading from Longhotistres as far as Tonbridge towards the south, near John A Stable's land towards the east, John A Barton's land towards the north, land lately of William Bishop towards the west and it contains *5 acres except 2 dayworks*

and **he holds** in **a piece of land** in the same tenement called **THE CROFT and STEYSBARN**, lying near land formerly of William Bishop towards the east, land formerly of Thomas Halle towards the west and north, near the aforesaid highway there and a certain lane called Wattslane south and it contains *1 acre, 1 rod and 6 dayworks*

and **he holds** [written above: *now Farman*] in **a garden called WATTS GARDEN**, lying near land lately of William Bishop west, south and north and near Lawrence Farman's land and garden east and it contains *1 rod, 8 dayworks and a half*

Margin: left hand: *now of John Bishop:* right hand: *he then holds 5 acres, 3 and a half dayworks, thence 2s.6d. each year.*

Reginald Herst and **John A. Barton** feoffees of John Fisher and of the heirs of Richard Bishop son of William hold in **a piece of land called MOTTIST CROFT** lying at the aforesaid way there towards the south, near the said John A Barton's land towards the north, near land of John Bishop son of Robert and land lately of Thomas Halle towards the west and land of the said John Bishop son of Robert towards the east [written above: *now of John Bishop*] and it contains *1 acre, 1 rod and 7 dayworks*

and **they hold in a MESSUAGE with a GARDEN and in a piece of land adjoining called WALTERS AT THE STAIR** near land of the said John Bishop son of Robert towards the west, near Lawrence Farman's land and the highway there leading from Hadlow street as far as Tonbridge towards the east, land of the said Lawrence and of the said feoffees south and the said Lawrence's land and land of the said John Bishop son of Robert and of the said feoffees towards the north and it contains *3 acres*

and **they hold one piece of land called TREYARDYN** lying near land of the said John Bishop son of Robert west, the said Lawrence's land towards the north, land lately of William Coiffe east, land of the said John Bishop son of Robert and the said feoffees' land called Walters towards the south and it contains *half an acre, 6 and a half dayworks*

Margin: right hand: *1 acre and 3 dayworks, thence 9d each year.*

John A Stable then holds [written above: *now John F*] **one piece of land called KETE CROFT** lying near the highway there leading from Hadlow street as far as Tonbridge towards the east and south, land of John Bishop son of Robert towards the west, John a Barton's land towards the north and it contains *1 acre and 4 dayworks.*

Folio 8

Margin: left hand: *note now Farman:* right hand: *he holds there 1 acres, 1 rod, 1 and a quarter daywork, thus 19d. and a half pence each year.*

John Fichet and **Thomas Fichet** hold of the said tenement one [un-named] **PIECE OF LAND** lying near the lane leading to land of John Bishop son of Robert and William Bishop's land and Lawrence Farman's land towards the south, the said John's land east, land of the same John and Thomas towards the north, moreover the said Lawrence Farman's land towards the west and it contains *one and a half acres except 1 daywork and 1 paddock*

and **they hold** another **parcel of land called HALLYSLAND** lying near land formerly of William Bishop east, the said Lawrence's land towards the west, John A Barton's land towards the north and moreover towards the south land of John and Thomas Fichet and it contains *1 acre, 2 rods, 2 and a half dayworks*

Margin: left hand: *now Farman:* right hand: *he holds there 4 and a half acres, 6 and a half dayworks, thus 2s. 3d. each year*

Lawrence Farman holds of the same tenement **one garden** formerly of Thomas Halle **called CROCHERS** lying near the highway there leading from Hadlow street as far as Tonbridge towards the east, land formerly of William Bishop towards the south, the garden of John Bishop son of Robert towards the west and near a certain lane there called Watts lane towards the north and it contains *half an acre, 9 dayworks*

and **he holds one piece of land with a small water meadow adjoining called KEYFIELD** lying near land formerly of Thomas Halle [written above: *now John Fichet*] east and north, land of the said John Bishop senior towards the west and moreover towards the south near land lately of William Bishop and it contains *3 acres, 3 rods, 7 and a half dayworks*

Total of acres is: *21 acres, 1 rod, 6 dayworks and 1 quarter*, 6d. for each acre and in all 3d. and a half pence less and then they owe 1d. farthing in relief for 7 acres

---

FREFERDING TENEMENT

Margin: left hand: *Freferding;* right hand: *he holds there 8 acres, 3 rods, 4 and a half dayworks, thus 11d. farthing each year.*

John Bishop son of Robert and his associates as written below, hold the whole of one tenement formerly of Gervase Bishop now called **FREFERDING** and thus they owe the lord 3s. in rent.

Then the aforesaid **John** holds **one GARDEN with the barn built upon it called THE STAIR BARN** lately of John Kene, **similarly with two pieces of land called BERECROFT and THE DENE** lying near William Honewold's land towards the south, the same John Bishop's land and Thomas Crudd's land towards the east, the said Thomas's land towards the north and the highway there leading from Hadlow street to Tonbridge towards the west and they contain *3 acres, 5 dayworks and a half*

and **he holds** in **a piece of land called THE SERE**, lying near land lately of William Honewold west, Richard Fisher's land [margin: left hand: *Fisher*] towards the east and north and the lane called Longshots lane towards the south and it contains *2 and a half acres and 9 dayworks*

and **he holds** there in **a piece of land called LONGSHOTT** lying near land formerly of William Honewold called Champens brook and land lately of William Bishop east, land of Bemisia Bulfinche and the said William Bishop's land south, William Stable's land and the land of the said William Bishop and of William Honewold towards the north and it contains *3 acres of land*

Folio 9 Margin: left hand: *Fisher* right hand: *Thomas Bishop holds there 1 rod thence a farthing and a half each year*

Thomas Bishop holds of the same tenement in **a piece of land called JOPISSERE** lying near the meadow Jopismeade towards the south, Richard Fisher's land called the Broke towards the north and east, land formerly of William Honewold west and it contains *1 rod of land*

Margin: right hand: *Robert Bishop holds there half an acre and 6 dayworks, thence three farthings and half a farthing each year*

Robert Bishop then holds **a parcel of land lying beyond the Medway called the COTT IN THE PAYNE OF EYLAND**, lying near Thomas Crudd's land towards the east and south, near the water called the Rowing lake towards the west and near the Medway there towards the north and it contains *half an acre and 6 dayworks*

Margin: right hand: *Lawrence Farman holds 1 acre, 3 rods and 6 dayworks there, thus 2d. and a half pence each year.*

Lawrence Farman holds of the said tenement **one piece of land called CHRIST MEADE** lying near land formerly of William Honewold towards the east and north, near the water there called the Medway towards the south and west and it contains *1 acre and 1 daywork*

and **he holds** there **one parcel of land called WIDERSTISCROFT**, lying near land lately of the said William Homewold towards the east and north, the highway there leading from Hadlow street towards Tonbridge west, William At Hell's land southand: it contains *3 rods and 6 dayworks*

Margin: right hand: *Thomas Fisher holds there 7 acres 3 rods except 1 and a half dayworks, thus 10d. and a half pence each year.*

Thomas Fisher holds of the said tenement as by right of Alice his wife for the term of his life, in **a piece of land called EASTFIELD**, near land of John Bishop son of Robert son and Richard Fisher's land towards the east, land lately of William Bishop north and west and near the lane there called Longshot lane south and it contains *3 acres*

and **he holds** in **one water meadow called CHAMPENS BROOK and in a piece of land called the WHEATCROFT** on the south part of the said piece of land, adjoining land lately of William Bishop and Richard Fisher's land east, near meadow called the Warebatere south, to land of John Bishop, Robert's son north and Thomas Crudd's land west and it contains as follows: in *Champen's brook 1 acre* and in the *Wheatcroft 1 acre and 1 rod*

and **he holds** then 2 acres of land of the aforesaid tenement **in a field** [written above: *Farman*] **called JANKMYR FIELD** otherwise **ATEYRFIELD** lying through a certain lane there leading to the water called the Medway and the said piece of land lying near

127

the messuage lately of William Honewold near the lane leading to the Wheat croft and near Lawrence Farman's land north, near the meadow called Christ's mead south, to the aforesaid lane leading as far as the Medway west and it contains *2 acres*

and **he holds** there in **a piece of land called WADERSTIST CROFT** lying near land lately of William Honewold east, John Bishop's land towards the north, Lawrence Farman's land south, near the highway there leading from Hadlow street as far as Tonbridge towards the west and it contains *1 rod, 8 and a half dayworks.*

Folio 10 Margin: left hand: *Fisher* right hand: *Thomas Crudd holds there 5 acres, 6 and a half dayworks, thus 6d. three farthings each year*

Thomas Crudd holds of the same man **one parcel of land called PAYNE OF EYLAND** lying beyond the water called the Medway, near the water of the lady of the manor towards the east, near the said lady's land called The Mistress's marsh towards the south, land of Robert Bishop son of William west and near the aforesaid water called the Medway towards the north and it contains *3 acres, 4 rods and 4 dayworks.*

And **John Bishop** holds [written above: *John Bishop now holds*] **one piece of land called THE DENE** lying next to the cross called Longshots cross, near the highway leading from Hadlow street as far as Tonbridge north, near land of John Bishop son of Robert south, east and west and it contains *1 acre, 1 rod, 2 and a half dayworks.*

Margin: right hand: *William At Hell holds 1 acre, thus 1d. farthing each year*

William At Hell holds [written above: *Farman*] **one acre of land next to his MESSUAGE** at The Stair lying in a piece of land there, situated near land late of William Honewold towards the north, Richard A Hell's garden towards the east, that William's messuage towards the south and the highway there leading from Hadlow street towards Tonbridge towards the west and it contains *1 acre*, as is aforesaid

Margin: left hand: *Fisher* right hand: *Richard Fisher holds there 1 acre, 3 rods, 2 and a half dayworks, thus 2d. and a half each year.*

Richard Fisher holds there **in a certain brook called CHAMPENS BROOK**, lying near the same Richard's land and land of John Bishop son of Robert towards the east and north, land lately of William Bishop towards the south and near land lately of William Honewold towards the west and it contains *1 acre, 3 rods, 8 and a half dayworks*

Total of acres is: *27 and a half acres, 2 dayworks*,
thus for each acre 1d. farthing and more 1d. and a half pence and half a farthing in all and for 6 acres 3 rods 2d. farthing is owed in reliefs

WALTER AT STAIR TENEMENT Margin: left hand: *Walter Ate Stair 12d. in rent*

John Bishop son of Robert and his associates hold the whole tenement formerly of **WALTER AT STAIR** and for this they owe the lord 3s. in rent and they shall plough ten acres in Winter and ten acres during Lent price 6d. as above and they shall receive as above and shall pay 21d. in aid at the feast of St Andrew the apostle, 80 small works, price of each work half a penny and 42 great works, price of each work 2d., 3 boon works with 2 men in Autumn, price 2s.6d. deduction having been made for food and 1 carrying service price 4d.

Thus the aforesaid **John Bishop** holds there in **a piece of land called LONGSHOT** lying near land lately of William Honewold called Champens brook and land formerly of **Folio 11** William Bishop east, near Binysia Bulfinch's land (f.11) towards the south, John A Stable's land and land formerly of William Bishop and near William Honewold's land towards the north and towards the west moreover the same man's land and it contains *3 and a half acres and 9 dayworks*

and **he holds** of the same in **a meadow called JOPIS MEADE** in a certain place called Westey, lying near the lady of the manor's land called le Morys towards the south, land lately of William Honewold east, land formerly of William Coiffe west and the same man's land north and it contains *2 acres, 3 rods and 3 dayworks* and **he holds** there another [un-named] **PARCEL OF LAND** adjoining land lately the said William Honewold's west, the lady of the manor's land called Lode weir south, land lately of the said William Coiffe east, Henry Hexstall's land and land lately of William Bishop north and it contains *1 acre, 1 rod and 5 and a half dayworks*

and **he holds** in the same **meadow called JOPISMEADE IN WARELAKE** one parcel lying near land lately of William Bishop called le Sere towards the north and east, land lately of William Coiffe west, land formerly of William Honewold and the same John's land towards the south and it contains *1 acre* of land

Margin: right hand: *he holds there half an acre, 4 and a half dayworks, thus 2d. and a half pence each year.*

John Fechet and **Thomas [Fechet]** [written above: *now John Fisher*] hold of the said tenement in **a meadow called WARELAKE** lying near land of John Bishop, son of Robert east and south, land formerly of William Honewold towards the west and north and it contains *1 acre, 2 and a half dayworks*

and they hold another **parcel of meadow in WESTEY** lying near the aforesaid John Bishop's land towards the east, Richard Fisher's land to the west, the same John and Thomas's land north, the same men's land towards the south and it contains *1 rod and 2 dayworks*

Margin: right hand: *he holds there 3 rods, thus 3d. each year.*

Lawrence Farman holds in **his own MESSUAGE**, **in which he lives with the GARDEN** adjoining, lying near land lately of William Honewold east and south, the lane leading to the said William Honewold's dwelling house to the north and the lane there leading to the Medway towards the west and it contains *3 acres*

Margin: right hand: *they hold 1 acre and a half daywork, thus 6d. each year.*

Reginald Herst and **John A Barton** hold there **one perch of land called LONGSHOT** lying near land lately of John Kene senior towards the south, John Bishop's land towards the west and north, land lately of William Honewold towards the east, it contains *1 acre and a half and a half daywork.*

Folio 12 **Thomas Fisher** holds by right of Alice his wife for the term of his life, **one MESSUAGE with GARDEN** adjoining formerly of William Honewold, in which he used to live, lying near a certain lane there leading to the aforesaid messuage and to a piece of land called Jankens field towards the east and a common way leading to the aforesaid messuage west, to Lawrence Farman's messuage towards the south, to a certain lane there leading to land called the Wheatcrofts towards the north and it contains *1 acre, 7 and a half dayworks*

and **he holds** in **a piece of land called LONGSHOT** lying near Byomsia Bulfinch's land towards the east and west and north, land lately of the said William Honewold towards the south and it contains [written above: *now of John Bishop*] *half an acre and 2 dayworks*

and **he holds** in **the same piece of land [LONGSHOT]** another parcel lying near the said Byomsia's land towards the east and south, land formerly of the said William Honewold towards north and west [written above: *now of John Bishop*] and it contains *half an acre and 6 dayworks*

and **he holds** of the said tenement one parcel of meadow **in a meadow called WERELAKE** lying near land lately of William Coiffe towards the east, Richard Fisher's land to the south, near a piece of land called Christ meade towards the west and near le Sawtrye there towards the north and it contains *1 and a half rods* [written above: *now of John Bishop*]

and **he holds** of the same **a piece of land called JANKENS FIELD** lying near the messuage lately of the said William Honewold, near the lane there leading as far as Wheatcrofts and to Lawrence Farman's land north, the meadow called Christ meade south, the aforesaid land called Wheatcrofts towards the east and near the lane there leading as far as the Medway towards the west and it contains more than *2 acres of another tenement called 4 Acres*

and **he holds** in the **WHEAT CROFTS with the water meadow** adjoining on the west part, near Thomas Crudd's land east, a piece of land called Jankens field west, meadow called Warelake and meadow called Christ meade south and John Bishop's land, William Bishop's land and land lately of John Kene towards the north and it contains

3 acres, 3 and a half dayworks

and **he holds** one parcel of **meadow called CHRIST MEADE** lying at the Warelake towards the east, land lately of William Honewold called Wheatcrofts and Jankens field towards the north, Lawrence Farman's land west, the lady of the manor's land and the said Lawrence's land towards the south and it contains *2 acres and 3 rods, 1 and a half dayworks*

and **he holds** in a **meadow called WESTEY**, lying near John Bishop's land towards the east and west, the lady of the manor's land towards the south and it contains *half an acre and 1 daywork* [written above: *now of John Bishop*]

Folio 13   Margin: right hand: *he holds then 3 and a half acres, 5 and a half dayworks 18 and a half pence each year*.
Thomas Bishop [written above: *now John Bishop*] holds of the said tenement in **a piece of land called JOPIS SERE** lying near the meadow called Jopismead towards the south, Richard Fisher's land towards the north and south, land formerly of William Honewold towards the west and it contains *3 and a half acres and 5 and a half dayworks*

Margin: right hand: *he then holds 1 and a half acres, 6 and a half dayworks, thus 4 and a half pence each year*
Thomas Crudd holds one **parcel of land called WHEAT CROFTS** lying towards land lately of William Honewold towards the east, west and north, meadow called Warelake in Jopismeade towards the south and it contains *2 acre and 6 and a half dayworks*

Margin: right hand: *he holds there 1 and a half acres, 7 and a half dayworks, thus 6 and a half pence each year*   left hand: *now of John Bishop*
Thomas Bulfinch holds as by right of Biamisia his wife, one parcel of land of the aforesaid tenement in a **piece of land called LONGSHOT** lying near land there formerly of William Honewold to the south and west, near land lately of William Bishop towards the east and the said Byomisia's land towards the north and it contains *1 rod, 8 and a half dayworks*

and **he holds** another **parcel of land in the same piece [LONGSHOT]**, lying near land formerly of William Honewold towards the south, north and east, land called Wheat crofts west and it contains *1 rod and 6 dayworks*
and **he holds** in the same **piece or parcel of land [LONGSHOT]**, lying near land of John Bishop son of Robert east, land formerly of the said Honewold north and west and it contains *3 rods and 4 dayworks*

Margin: right hand: *he then holds one and a half dayworks thus 20d. each year*
Item **Richard Fisher** [written above: *John Borne by right of his wife*] holds in the said tenement **one piece of land called EASTFIELD** lying near the same Richard's garden and land towards the east, land lately of the said William Honewold towards the west, John Bishop's and the same Richard's land towards the south, land lately of William Andrewe and the same Richard's land towards the north and it contains *3 acres and   3 rods*

and **he holds** of the same tenement in **a meadow called WESTEYE** lying near the lady of the manor's land towards the south, land lately of William Coiffe towards the east, moreover William Honewold's land towards the north and west, it contains *1 rod and a half daywork*

Total acres is: *36 [acres], 1 rod, 9 dayworks,* thus 3d. for each acre and for 4 acres they owe 1d in reliefs

---

WELLS TENEMENT

Margin: left hand: *Bowlere 7s.4d. and a half*

John Bishop son of Robert and his associates as written below hold one tenement, formerly of Walter at The Stair, lately called Bowlere and now called **WELLS** tenement and they then owe the lord 5s.10d. in rent at the (4) terms and 21d. in aid at the feast of St Andrew the apostle and in Autumn 3 boon works with men price 6d.,

thus **John Bishop**, Robert's son holds a [un-named] **PARCEL OF LAND and MEADOW** lying near Henry Hexstall's meadow towards the east, near Thomas Cardon's land towards the west, land formerly of William Coiffe towards the south and land lately of Richard Fisher towards the north and it contains (f.14) *1 half acre and 2 dayworks* (Margin: right hand: *he holds there 2 acres and 1 rod thence 6 and a half pence each year*)

Folio 14

and **he holds** of the same tenement in **a meadow called JOPISMEADE**, lying near Thomas Crudd's land towards the east, Henry Hexstall's land towards west, land of John A Barton and the said Henry's land towards the north and near the water there called Jopislake towards the south and it contains *a half acre and 8 dayworks*

Margin: right hand: 1) *John Callys holds of the same tenement 1 acre 3 rods, 1 daywork* 2) *he holds there 2 acres, 3 rods and 3 dayworks, themce 8d. each year.*

John Fechet and **Thomas [Fechet]** hold of the said tenement **a parcel of land in a meadow called WESTHEY**, lying near Henry Hexstall's land towards the west, near the lady of the manor's land towards the south, Richard Fisher's land east, the said John Bishop's land north and it contains *1 acre and a half and 9 dayworks*

and **they hold** [written above: *now of Thomas Fisher*] in the said **meadow called WESTEY** lying near Henry Hexstall's land towards the east, the said John Bishop's land west, the lady of the manor's land towards the south, Thomas Barton's land towards the north and it contains *3 rods and 9 dayworks* [written above: *now Fisher*]

and **they hold** in a **meadow called WARELAKE** lying near the said John Bishop's land towards the east, west and north and Henry Hexstall's land south and it contains **5** *dayworks*

Margin: right hand: *they hold then 5 acres, 9 and a half dayworks, thus 15d. and a half pence each year* left hand: *now J.F., John Fische*

Reginald Herst and **John A Barton** feoffees to the use of John Bishop the son and heir of Richard Bishop son of William, hold **a parcel of land and meadow in a meadow called WARELAKE** lying near Henry Hexstall's land towards the east, land of the said John Bishop son of Robert towards the west and south and Thomas Bishop's land towards the north and it contains *3 rods* [written above: *now J. Bishop*]

and **they hold** one **piece of land called BOWLERIS** lying near John A Stable's land towards the west, land formerly of William Andrewe and formerly of William Honewold towards the east and south, near the lane leading to a meadow called Jopismeade and the said John A Stable's land towards the north and it contains *3 acres, 3 rods and 2 dayworks*

and **they hold** in a **piece of land called the BROOK AT ANDREWY** lying at the highway leading from John A Stable's dwelling house to the meadow called Jopismeade north and east, near Richard Fisher's land south, land lately of William Andrew west and it contains *half an acre, 7 and a half dayworks*

Margin: right hand: *he holds then 3 rods, 2 and a half dayworks, thus 2d. each year*

Thomas Crudd [written above: *now J Fisher*] holds of the said tenement **a parcel of land and meadow in a meadow called JOPISMEADE** three yards, lying near the lady of the manor's geld-land towards the east and near Henry Hexstall's land and land of the said John Bishop son of Robert towards the west, Thomas Fisher's land north, the running water there called Jopislake south and it contains *3 rods, 2 and a half dayworks*

Folio 15 Margin: right hand: *he holds there 3 and a half acres, 3 and a half dayworks thus 14d. and a half pence each year*

William Andrewe's heirs hold of the same tenement one **MESSUAGE with a GARDEN AND A SMALL PIECE OF LAND** lying near the highway there leading from the cross called Johns at Stable's cross as far as Jopis mead towards the north, near Richard Fisher's land towards the east and south, land of the same men's heirs towards the west and it contains *1 acre, 6 and a half dayworks*

and **they hold one piece of land called BOWLEYS**, near Richard Fisher's land and near the aforesaid messuage lately of the said Richard Andrewe towards the west, Richard Fisher's land towards the south, the aforesaid messuage and the highway leading from the cross called John at Stable's cross as far as Jopismeade towards the north and it contains *3 acres, 1 rod and 7 dayworks*

Margin: right hand: *he holds there half an acre, 9 and a half dayworks, thus 2d. each year*

Henry Hexstall [written above: *now Bishop*] holds then in the **meadow called WARELAKE** one parcel of land and meadow lying near Thomas Carden's land towards the east, land of John Bishop son of Robert in le Westeye south, near land formerly of William Bishop west and Thomas Bishop's land called le Sere north and it contains *9 and a half dayworks*

and **he holds** another parcel of land and meadow **in a meadow called WESTEY**, lying near land lately of William Coiffe east, west and north, near the water there called Lodeweir pool south and it contains *half an acre*

Margin: right hand: *he holds there 8 and a half acres and 1 daywork, he thus owes 2s.1d. and a half each year.*

Richard Fishere holds [written above: *John by right of his wife now J Fisher*] of the same tenement **one piece of land called the MEDFIELD**, lying near the lane leading as far as the meadow called Jopismeade towards the east, the same Richard's land and land lately of William Fisher towards the west, meadow called Warelake towards the south, the same Richard's house, in which he lives towards the north and it contains *3 acres, 1 rod except a quarter of one parrock*

and **he holds one piece of land called ROLANDS with a MESSUAGE and GARDEN and small water meadow adjoining called COCKYSBROOK**, near the aforesaid lane leading to Jopismeade towards the east, the same man's land called Eastfield and land lately of William Andrewe west, near the aforesaid piece of land called Eastfield and Medfield south and near land formerly of William Bishop and of William Andrewe north and it contains *3 and a half acres, 3 perches*

and **he holds in a meadow called THE HOPE** [written above: *now John Fisher*] lying near John Bealde's land south, the lady of the manor's land west and the same Richard's land north and it contains *1 acre, 3 rods and 2 dayworks*

Folio 16 Margin: right hand: *he holds there 1 rod, 7 dayworks, 6 feet, thus 1d. each year*

Thomas Carden holds of the same tenement **one parcel of meadow in a meadow called WARELAKE** lying near land of John Bishop son of Robert towards the east, Henry Hexstall's land towards the west, Richard Fisher's land towards the north, near the water there called Warelake towards the south and it contains *1 rod, 7 dayworks and 6 feet* [written above: *now Thomas Somer*]

Margin: right hand: *he holds there 2 acres, 1 rod and 6 dayworks, thus 6d. and a half each year*

John At Stable [written above: *now J Fisher*] holds of the same tenement **one piece of land called CLARKSCROFT**, lying near land lately of William Bishop towards the east and south, near the same John at Stable's piece of land called Culverhouse field towards the west, near the common way leading from Revecocks cross as far as Fisthell towards the north and it contains *2 acres, 1 rod and 6 dayworks*

Margin: right hand: *he holds there 2 acres and 7 dayworks, thus 6d. farthing each year* left hand: *now JF*

John Beald holds [written above: *now JF*] in the **UTTERLERYS called LETWETENE one parcel of meadow** lying near the Brickweir pool towards the east, land of Henry Hexstall and of Richard Fisher towards the west, land lately of William Coiffe towards the south and near the said Henry's land towards the north and it contains *3 rods, 1 daywork and a half*

and **he holds** in **a meadow called LE HERBERYS** in a parcel lying near land of John Bishop son of Robert son towards the east, the lady of the manor's land west and Henry Hexstall's land south and north and it contains *1 rod, 7 dayworks*

and **he holds** of a **meadow called HERBERYS** lying near land lately of William Coiffe east, the lady of the manor's land and Richard Fisher's land west and Henry's land north and south and it contains *1 acre except 3 perches and 1 quarter*

Total of acres is: *30 acres, 3 rods and 9 dayworks and 6 feet*

thus 3d. for each acre and 3d. less in all and they owe half a penny for each acre in reliefs

---

JOPES TENEMENT

Folio 17

Margin: left hand: *Jopes tenement 5s. 8d. and 15 pigs*

John Bishop son of Robert and his associates as written below hold one tenement formerly of John King now called **JOPES** tenement and they then owe 10s. 2d. in rent to the lord each year and in Autumn 3 boon works with two men price 6d. etc.

They then owe the lord yearly at the feast of St Martin for 3 sows, 15 pigs and all (f.17) (Margin: right hand: *he then holds 2 acres 1 rod 1 and a half dayworks, thus each year 10d. and a half pence and 1 pig and 1 quarter*) the tenants of the manor there who are called joint tenants of the aforesaid manor hold 11 sows in the forest of Northfrithe through the whole year, unless in a prohibited month and each year for every sow they must render 5 pigs at the aforesaid feast of St Martin or the value of these, that is to say: that if the pannage should be plentiful, then they shall render 2s. for each pig and 18d. if the pannage should be sparse and 12d. if there should have been no pannage and in Winter they shall receive 1 quarter of barley for each sow and they owe each year for each of the pigs of the allocation 12d. of their registered rent for each sow.

Then the aforesaid **John Bishop** holds in a **parcel of land called SOMYSFIELD** lying near land lately of William Andrewe and land of the same John towards the south, land lately of the said John Bishop called Aldrett towards the north, near Thomas Fisher's barn and garden formerly of John Jelott of Fishell hill towards the east and the same John Bishop's land to the west and it contains [written above: *now J Fisher*] *2 acres, 1 rod, 1 daywork and a half*

Margin: right hand: *he holds 2 acres, 3 rods, 8 and a half dayworks, thence 12 and a half pence each year and he owes a pig and a half.*

Thomas Fisher [written above: *now J Fisher*] holds there one **piece of land lying at FISHERHILL**, that is before the gate lately of Richard Jelott of Fisher hill, near the highway there leading from the Borne cross as far as the dwelling house lately of Thomas Fromonde at Water towards the east, the lane called Hevelane south, John Bishop's land called Somerfield and land of the said Thomas towards the north and land lately of Thomas Fromond at Water west and it contains *3 rods, 6 and a half dayworks*

and **he holds** in **his own MESSUAGE** in which he lives, lately of John Jelott of Fishhill, lying near the common way leading from Borne cross as far as the dwelling house lately of Thomas Fromond east and south, John Bishop's land west and John at Stable's land north and it contains *3 rods*

and **he then holds** a [un-named] **PARCEL OF LAND** near the common way leading from the Borne as far as the aforesaid dwelling house lately of the said Thomas Fromonde east, near the lane there called Hevygate lane towards the south, land lately of the said

133

Thomas Fromond towards the west, towards the north moreover the same Thomas Fisher's land and it contains *half an acre except half a perch*

and **he holds** in the same [parcel of land] **THOMAS FISHER'S BARN** and in a [un-named] **SMALL PARCEL OF LAND** adjoining lately purchased of the said John Bishop, as its metes and bounds there are marked and shown, *2 dayworks*

Folio 18 and [written above: *Robert Fisher*] **he holds** (f.18) **one parcel of land in a meadow called JOPISMEADE** lying near John A Barton's land towards the west, the lady of the manor's dwelling house there towards the east, land of Henry Hexstall and Thomas Crudd's land towards the south and near land lately of William Honewold and the land of Richard Fisher towards the north and it contains *3 rods*

Margin: right hand: *he holds 11 acres, 3 rods and 1 daywork, thus 4s.2d. and a half pence each year and he owes 5 pigs, a half, one quarter and 1 leg of pork*

Richard Fisher holds in **a meadow called LE HOPE** and named **THE ACRE** lying near Henry Hexstall's land towards the east, near the aforesaid meadow called le Hope towards the south and the water there towards the north and near the same Richard's land towards the west and it contains *one half acre and a half daywork*

and **he holds** in **a piece of land called WESTEYS**, lying near the lady of the manor's land towards the south, land lately of William Coiffe towards the west, Henry Hexstall's land towards the north and near the same Richard's land towards the east and it contains *3 and a half rods and half a daywork*

and **he holds** in **a meadow called JOPISMEADE** lying near John A Barton's land west, Thomas Fisher's land towards the south, the same Richard's land and land lately of Thomas Fromonde at Walter [Water] towards the north and land formerly of William Honewold towards the east and it contains *1 rod and 6 dayworks*

and **he holds** in **a piece of land called LITTLEHAM** lying near the aforesaid Thomas Fromond's land east, land called Jopismeade now of John Salmon west and the same Richard's land south and north and it contains *1 acre, 3 rods, 3 dayworks*

and **he holds** there **four** [un-named] **PIECES OF LAND** lying side by side situated at the lane called Stonylane north, the lane there leading to the dwelling house lately of the said Thomas Fromonde called Jolfisshagh south and the lane leading to the meadow called Jopismeade west, thence *1 acre, 3 rods and 2 dayworks* in **a piece of land called FISHALL,** in **HARDING FIELD** *1 half acre, 7 dayworks,* in **STONYFIELD** *3 acres, 3 rods, 1 and a half dayworks* and it contains in all *7 acres, 1 rod and a half daywork*

Margin: right hand: *he holds there 3 acres, 8 and a half dayworks, thus 14d. and a half pence each year and he owes one pig a half and 1 leg of pork*

Henry Hexstall holds in **a meadow called the ERBERIS** lying at the Wareditch and near Joan Frictar's [sic - recte Frutar] meadow towards the east, the meadow of John Bealde carpenter and of Richard Fisher towards the south, near the said Richard Fisher's meadow called Northmesteye towards the west, the running water there called Jopislake north and it contains *1 acre and a half, 4 dayworks and a half*

and **he holds one parcel of land and meadow in a meadow called JOPISMEADE** lying near Thomas Crudd's meadow east, meadow of John Bishop son of Robert south, John A Barton's meadow towards the west, Thomas Fisher's meadow north and it contains *9 dayworks*

Foilo 19 and **he holds** then in the said **meadow called JOPISMEADE** (f.19) lying near land of the said John Bishop and John A Barton's land towards the east, the water there called Jopislake south, the said John Bishop's land called Bearlake towards the west, John Salmon's land called Jopisfield north and it contains *1 acre, 1 rod and 5 dayworks* [written above: *now J Fishar*]

Margin: right hand: *he holds 4 acres 1 rod and 7 dayworks, thus 18d. three farthings each year and he owes 2 pigs, 1 leg of pork and a half*

John Salmon of Helden [written above: *now J Fishere*] then holds **one piece of land called JOPISFIELD** lately of John Jelott of Fishill, lying before the gate of Richard Fisher's dwelling house and near Jopismeade towards the west, near the said Richard's land towards the east and north, near the aforesaid meadow called Jopismeade south and it contains *8 acres, 1 rod and 7 dayworks etc.*

Margin: right hand: *she holds 1 acre, 3 dayworks, thus 6d. three farthings each year and she owes 3 quarters of a pig.*

Joan Fromond at Water holds then for the term of her life **one piece of land called THE CROFT** in the lane lying near Thomas Fisher's land east, the lane there called Hevilane towards the south, near land lately of William Andrew towards the west, land of John Bishop son of Robert towards the north and it contains *1 acre and 1 daywork*

and **she then holds** in a **GARDEN with a HOUSE built upon it called HENTLOVE**, lying at the common way there leading from the Hevigate as far as Lawrence Farman's meadow called Watbaldsmeade towards the east, land of the said Richard Fisher towards the west and north, to the meadow called Jopismeade towards the south and it contains a *half acre and 2 dayworks*

Margin: right hand: *he holds 3 acres except 1 and a half dayworks, thus 12d. three farthings and they owe 1 pig and a half*

William Andrew's heirs [written above: *now JF*] now hold **one piece of land called the MUGGEFIELD** lying near a piece of land lately of Thomas Fromond at Water towards the east, the lane there called Heveilane towards the south, the land of Thomas Fisher, of John at Stable and of the said John Bishop towards the west and moreover towards the north the said John Bishop's land and it contains *3 acres except 1 daywork and a half*

Margin: right hand: *he then holds 3 rods of land except 1 daywork 1 quarter and 1 perch, thus 3d. and a half pence each year and a quarter of a pig and a half*

John A Barton holds in **a meadow called JOPISMEADE** lying near Henry Hexstall's land towards the west, land of John Bishop son of Robert towards the south, to land of Thomas Fisher, of Henry Hexstall and of Richard Fisher east and to land called Jopisfield north and it contains 3 rods of land except *1 daywork, 1 quarter and 1 perch.*

Margin: right hand: *she holds 6 dayworks, thus half a penny each year and she owes a half of a leg of pork.*

Alice now **Thomas Fisher's wife** [written above: *now J Fishere*] and lately William Honewold's wife, holds **one parcel of land there in a meadow called JOPISMEADE**, near the geld-land of the lady of the manor towards the east and land lately of John Jelott of Fishill towards the south and Richard Fisher's land west and it contains *6 dayworks*

Folio 20 **Total of acres is:** *30 acres and 3 dayworks*, thus 3d. farthing for an acre and half a penny more in all and for each acre 1d and more in relief, 2d. in all, that is to say, for 7 and a half acres half a penny and for two acres, 1 perch, less 3 perches 1 pig in all

---

FISHLAND TENEMENT

Margin: left hand: *Fishland 2s.6d.* right hand: t*hey hold 3 acres, 1 rod and 6 dayworks 1 perch, thus 3d. farthing and a half each year*

Thomas Fisher and his associates as written below hold the whole of one tenement formerly of Gilbert Fisher now named **FISHLAND** and they then owe the lady 21d. each year in aid at the feast of St Andrew the apostle and in Autumn they shall do 3 boon works with 3 men, price 9d. and they shall fish with the lady's nets where and when the lady should wish and to provide food for the lady.

Then the aforesaid **Thomas [Fisher]** holds in **a parcel of land called MORESFIELD**, lying near the same man's land in the same piece of land towards the east, garden of the same Thomas and formerly of Richard Jelott towards the west, land lately of John Pulter tanner towards the north, and to the south moreover land lately of Thomas Fromond at Water and it contains *1 half acre except 2 perches and a half*.

And then **he holds** then in **a piece of land called STONEYHUTTOCKS** lying near land lately of the said Thomas Fromond north, south and west and near land of the same Thomas Fisher and lately of John Jelott of Fishill east and it contains *3 rods, 3 dayworks*

and **he holds in a GARDEN** lately of Richard Jelott lying before the same Thomas Fisher's gate and the same man's land to the east, the highway there leading from the Borne Cross as far as the dwelling house lately of the said Thomas Fromond west, near the little common of Fish hill there north and near land lately of the said Thomas Fromond south and it contains *1 acre and 3 dayworks*

Joan Fromond formerly the wife of Thomas Fromond At Water holds for the term of her life **two pieces of land** lying together at the Borne **called the CROSSES AT BORNE** situated near land lately of William Pally towards the east, near the common way there leading from the Borne cross there as far as Thomas Fisher's land west, Joan Frutar's land towards the south and near the highway there leading from Goldhill towards Tonbridge towards the north and it contains *3 acres and 2 rods*.

and **she holds 1 piece of land at HEVYGATE** lying near the said Thomas Fisher's land towards the east and north, the same Joan Fromond's land south and the common way leading from the Borne cross as far as the dwelling house lately of Thomas Fromond (f.21) west and it contains *3 rods, 8 and a half dayworks*

(margin: right hand: *she holds 5 and a half acres, 8 and a half dayworks, thence 5d. three farthings each year*)

and **she then holds one piece of land called THREE YARDS** lying near land [blank] towards the east, the said Thomas Fisher's land towards the north, Lawrence Farman's land towards the south and the same Joan's land towards the west and it contains *1 acre* of land

Margin: right hand: *he then holds 1 acre, 3 rods, 5 dayworks and a half, thus 1d. three farthings each year.*

Richard Pally then holds [written above: *now Cinge*] in **a piece of land called CUTTISBRAYNE** lying near the same William's land in the same piece of land towards the east, land lately of Thomas Fromond at Water at the Borne cross west, near the aforesaid highway leading from Goldhill as far as Tonbridge towards the north and towards the south moreover Agnes Gambon's land and it contains *1 acre, 3 rods,   5 dayworks and a half*

Margin: right hand: *she holds 1 acre and a half and 2 dayworks, thus 1d. and a half pence each year*

Agnes Gambon [written above: *now John Fisher*] holds in **a piece of land called CATTISBRAYNE**, lately of John Gambon lying near the land of the same Agnes towards the east, land lately of the said Thomas Fromond west, William Pally's land north, Joan Frutar's land towards the south and it contains *1 acre and a half and 2 dayworks*

Margin: right hand: *she holds 5 acres, 6 dayworks and 1 perch, thus 5d. each year*

Joan Frutar then holds **two pieces of land lying together called KINGSBROME AT FISHILL** near the highway there leading from the Borne cross as far as Fishill towards the west, land formerly of the said Thomas Fromond towards the north, near Julia Watte's land, near land lately of John Gambon east and near Agnes Pulter's land towards the south and the lands contain *4 acres, 3 rods, 8 dayworks and a half*

and **she holds** there **one small PARCEL OF LAND** [written above: *now John a Stable holds*] **and a meadow called OUTER HERBERYS** lying near the Warediteh there towards the east, near the water there called Jopisweir towards the north and Henry Hexstall's land towards the south and west and it contains *7 dayworks and a half and 1 perch*.

Margin: right hand: *she holds 3 and a half dayworks, thus 4d. each year*

Agnes Pulter [written above: *now J Fisher*] formerly the wife of John Pulter tanner, holds **one MESSUAGE in which she lives at Fishill** with a **GARDEN** and **THREE PIECES OF LAND** adjoining to Thomas Fisher's land and land lately of Robert Watte towards the east, to the highway there leading from the Borne cross as far as the said Thomas Fisher's dwelling house towards the west, to John [? recte Joan] Frutar's land towards the north and to a little common there and to the said Thomas Fisher's land south and it contains *4 acres, 3 rods and a half*

Folio 22

Margin: right hand: *they hold 1 acre a half and 4 dayworks, thus 1d. and a half pence each year.*

John Fichet and **Thomas Fichet** (written above: *now John Wells*) then hold **land in the OUTER HERBERYS**, lying near land of Henry Hexstall and John Beald, carpenter towards the west, the ditch called Ware ditch there towards the east, John Bishop's land south and the said John Beald's land north and it contains *one acre, a half and 4 dayworks*

Margin: right hand: *he holds 4 acres, 1 rod and 5 dayworks, thus 4d. farthing each year.*

John Bishop holds a **parcel of land and meadow called the OUTER HERBERYS** lying near the lady of the manor's geld-land towards the east, William Coiffe's land north, land of the said Henry Hexstall and John Beald towards the west, the said John Beald's land towards the south and it contains *1 acre, 3 rods, two and a half dayworks* (written above: *now John Bishop*)

and **he then holds** in another **piece of land called CLEMENTS HILL** another named Herberys lying near the aforesaid lady of the manor's geld-land towards the east, near the same woman's land called the Outer Herberys and Henry Hexstall's land towards the north, near land of the Posterne called the Lodweir and Wartbakerede towards the west and the water there pertaining to the Posterne towards the south and it contains (written above: *now John Bishop*) *2 acres, a half, 2 and a half dayworks.*

Margin: right hand: *he holds 3 acres, 3and a half dayworks, thus 3d. each year.*

Henry Hexstall then holds (written above: *now John Fisher*) **3 pieces of land and meadow called the INNER HERBERY** lying near the meadow formerly of John Bishop, Robert's son called the Herberys towards the east and south, near water called the Lodeweir and the meadow called the Posterne gate towards the west and the same Henry's land towards the north and it contains *1 acre, 1 rod and 8 dayworks*

and **he holds** in another **parcel of land and meadow called THE HERBERY** lying near the said John Bishop's meadow east, the same Henry's land towards the south, land called the Lodeweir of the Postern west, the meadow of John Beald carpenter north and it contains *half an acre, 3 and a half dayworks*

and **he holds** in the said **piece of land called LE ARBER** lying near the meadow lately of William Coiffe east, the said John Beald's meadow towards the south and north and the aforesaid [land - omitted] called the Lodeweir west and it contains *3 rods and 2 dayworks*

and **he holds in the said meadow [LE ARBER]**, lying near the said John Beald's meadow east, west and south, Richard Fisher's meadow towards the north and it contains *1 rod, less 2 feet.*

Total of acres is: *30 acres, 3 rods, 4 and a half dayworks and 1 and a half perches,*
thus 1d. for each acre and three farthings less in all and he owes no relief because he does not owe rent, as it is shown above.

Folio 23
ODAMYS TENEMENT

Margin: left hand: *Odamys tenement 2s.9d.* right hand: *Joan Fromond At Water then holds 5 acres, 3 dayworks and 3 feet, thus 10d. and a half pence each year*

Joan, lately the wife of Thomas Fromond At Water and her associates as written below hold the whole of one tenement formerly of Nicholas Odam, now called **ODAMYS** tenement and they then owe 2s. in rent each year to the lady of the manor and 6d. in aid at the feast of St Andrew the apostle and they owe three boon-works with 1 man price 3d.

Then the aforesaid **Joan [Fromond]** holds for the term of her life, one [un-named] **PIECE OF LAND with the NEW BARN built thereon**, lying next to the said Joan's boundary called the croft under the barn, lying near the same Joan's land and near Fisher's land towards the east, near the common way there leading from Borne cross as far as the same Joan's dwelling house towards the west, the said Joan's messuage towards the south, the lane at Hevygate towards the north and it contains *2 acres, a half and 7 and a half dayworks* [written above: *now J Fisher*]

and **she holds** in **her MESSUAGE in which she lives with a GARDEN** and **SMALL PIECE OF LAND** adjoining, that is to say, near Lawrence Farman's land south, the same man's land north and east and near a certain lane there leading from Hevygate as far as the said Lawrence's meadow there towards the west and it contains *1 acre, 3 rods, 1 and a half dayworks*

and **she then holds one parcel of land and in a meadow called JONETEYE** lying near Henry Hexstall's land east, Peter Fisher's land towards the south, Richard Pynchon's land towards the west, Thomas Fisher's land towards the north and it contains *half an acre* [written above: *John A Barton*], *1 and a half dayworks*
and **she holds** [land – omitted?] **in a certain lane called Hentelove lane** leading to the meadow lately of Walter Beald, now of Lawrence Farman and it contains *3 dayworks and 1 perch*

Margin: right hand: *he holds 2 acres, 8 dayworks, thus 4d. and a half each year.*
Lawrence Farman then holds **one meadow called WATTE BEALDS MEAD** lying near John de Jerlim's land and John At Stable's land towards the east, the lady of the manor's geld-land towards the west, John A. Barton's meadow towards the south, land of Joan Fromond At Water towards the north and it contains *2 acres and 8 dayworks.*

Folio 24

Margin: right hand: *he holds 4 and a half acres and 1 daywork, thus 1d. farthing each year*
John A Barton then holds in **a meadow called JONEYE** lying near James Gosse's land towards the east, the lady of the manor's geld-land west, Thomas Fisher's land towards the south and it contains *1 rod*

and **he holds one parcel of land in the said meadow [JONEYE]**, adjoining the same John A Barton's land towards the south and north, the said James Gosse's land towards the east and the lady of the manor's geld-land west and it contains *half an acre, 7 and a half dayworks*

and **he then holds a piece of land and meadow called LE CAMERE**, near the said James's land east, the lady of the manor's geld-land west, the same John A Barton's land north and south and it contains *1 acre, 3 and a half dayworks*

and **he then holds 1 piece of land called LICIDMEADE** lying near John At Stable's land east, the lady of the manor's geld-land west and the running water towards the south and Lawrence Farman's land north and it contains *2 and a half acres.*

Margin: right hand: *he holds 1 acre, a half, except 1 daywork, thus 3d. each year*
Thomas Fisher holds in **a meadow called JONETEYE** lying near the said John A Barton's land north, the lady of the manor's geld-land towards the west, near land of Joan Fromond At Water towards the south, near James Gosse's land towards the east and it contains *3 rods except 1 daywork*

and **he then holds** in a **piece of land and meadow called POPEYE** lying near John A Stable's land east, the weir called Sarotoweir pool south, the lady of the manor's geld-land west and Peter Fisher's land north and it contains *3 acres.*

Margin: right hand: *he holds 1 acre, 3 dayworks, thus 2d. farthing each year*

Peter Fisher then holds in **a piece of land and meadow called JONETEYE** lying near Henry Hexstall's land east, the lady of the manor's geld-land west, Richard Pynchon's land and land lately of Thomas Fromond at water north and Thomas Fisher's land towards the south and it contains *1 acre, 3 and a half dayworks*

Folio 25 Margin: left hand: *now Solmon* right hand: *he holds 1 acre, thus 2d. each year*

John At Stable then holds in **a piece of land and meadow called POPEY** lying near the lady of the manor's geld-land towards the west, Thomas Fisher's land north and south, the same John At Stable's land called Great Hope towards the east and it contains *1 rod* of land

and **he then holds** in **a piece of land and meadow called GREAT HOPE** lying near the same John's land towards the east, the land of the same said Thomas and the lady of the manor's geld-land west and land of the said John and Thomas north, water called the Gateweir pool towards the south and it contains *3 rods* of land

Margin: right hand: *he holds half an acre, 3 dayworks and 1 perch, thus 1d. farthing each year*

Richard Pynchon [written above: *now Cardnell*] holds in **a piece of land called JONETEYE** lying near Peter Fisher's land towards the south, the lady of the manor's geld-land towards the west, land lately of Thomas Fromond at water towards the east and land lately of John Jelott of Fishill, now of Thomas Fisher north and it contains *half an acre, 3 dayworks, 1 perch*

Total of acres is: *15 acres, 3 rods, 7 dayworks,*
thus 2d. for each acre and 1d. more in all and they owe 1d. and a half pence in relief for 4 acres

---

KNETT THE HOGGS TENEMENT

Margin: left hand: *he holds KnecheHoggs tenement 13s.10d.* right hand: t*hey hold 7 acres, 3 rods and 4 dayworks, thus 3s.7d. three farthings each year*

John Bishop son of Robert and his associates as written below hold one tenement formerly of Richard Knechehoggs now called **KNECHEHOGGS** tenement and they then shall owe the lady of the manor 15d. rent and 21d. in aid at the feast of St Andrew the apostle and three boon works with two men in Autumn price 6d., deduction having been made for food and twenty small works, price half a penny for each work and 24 great works, price 2d. for each work and carrying service price 4d. and they must plough one acre in Winter and one acre during Lent and they shall harrow and for each acre they shall receive four loaves price 2d. and eight herrings price 1d. and the work of two acres is worth 12d., deduction having been made for food, in addition heriot and relief.

Then the aforesaid **John Bishop** then holds **3 pieces of land lying side by side called FISHILL FIELD, SOUTHFIELD** and **LORLAYES** near John Astobed's land south, the land lately of William Honewold and Henry [Hexstall's] land west, land of the said Henry and Peter Fisher's land north, the same John Bishop's land called Somerfield and land lately of William Andrew east and it contains *7 acres, 3 rods, 4 dayworks*

Folio 26 Margin: right hand: *he holds 2 acres, a half and 6 dayworks, thus 14d. three farthings each year*

Thomas Bishop [written above: *Roger Goodmond holds, now Colyns*] then holds **one piece of land called THE FIELD AT BREDETT** otherwise called **WESINGLAND** lying at the common there called the Bredett towards the east, near a certain lane there to Henry Hexstall's land called the Petys towards the west, the said Henry's land and John at Stable's land towards the north and near the highway there leading to the aforesaid common called the Bredett as far as the gate called Coiffe's gate towards the south and it contains *2 and a half acres and 6 dayworks*

Margin: right hand: *he holds 2 and a half acres and 6 dayworks, thus 14d. three farthings each year*

John At Stable then holds **one piece of land called LORLAYES** lying before the messuage lately of William Andrew, lying near land lately of the said William towards the east, land formerly of William Honewold towards the west, the said John Bishop's land north, the common way leading from Stable's cross as far as Fishill towards the south and it contains *3 acres, 3 rods, 1 and a half dayworks*

and **he holds one piece of land called THE CROFT AT BORNE**, lying near the highway there leading from Borne cross as far as Fishill towards the east, to Peter Fisher's garden towards the west, near the highway there leading from Goldhill as far as Tonbridge towards the north, the said Peter Fisher's land south and it contains *1 acre, 6 and a half dayworks*

and **he then holds one piece of land** lately purchased from John Bishop **called JELOTTISTALDRET**, lying near land called Payneterist croft towards the east, Henry Hexstall's land north, the said John Bishop's land towards the west, the said John Bishop's land and Thomas Fisher's garden, lately of John Jelot of Fishill towards the south and it contains *2 acres and 1 daywork*

Margin: right hand: *he holds 4 acres, 6 and a half dayworks, thus 2d. farthing each year*
Thomas Fisher then holds **two pieces of land side by side called THE CLERTIS**, situated near the lane leading from the Borne cross as far as Fishill towards the east, Peter Fisher's land towards the west and south and John at Stable's land north and it contains *3 acres, 1 rod, 5 and a half dayworks*

and **he holds** *1 rod and 6 dayworks* in **a garden called TURKSHAGH**

and of the same man *1 and a half rods* in **his own GARDEN where he lives**

Folio 27 Margin: right hand: *Peter Fisher then holds 5 acres, 3 rods and 7 dayworks, thus 2s. 9d. each year*

Peter Fisher then holds in **his MESSUAGE in which he lives, with the GARDEN** lying near John at Stable's land and the same Peter Fisher's land east, the common way there and the land leading to the spring called Knechehogg's well towards the west, near the highway there leading from Goldhill as far as Tonbridge towards the north and near a piece of land of the same man called Berefield south and it contains *1 acre, 3 dayworks*

and **he then holds** in **one garden called the WELLHAGH**, lying near the aforesaid lane leading to the aforesaid spring towards the east, near Henry Hexstall's land west and it contains *3 dayworks*

and **he then holds one piece of land called BERECROFT** lying near the aforesaid messuage and John at Stable's land north and Thomas Fisher's land, lately of John Jelott of Fishill east and it contains *2 acres, except 2 dayworks*

and **he then holds one piece of land called the RYSTHET** lying near the same Peter's land towards the east, south and north and Henry Hexstall's land west and it contains *1 acre, 4 and a half dayworks*

and **he then holds one piece of land called POPECROFT** lying near the said Henry's land and the same Peter's land east, the said Henry's land towards the west, the said John Bishop's land towards the south and the same Peter's land towards the north and it contains *3 rods except 2 dayworks*

and **he then holds in a piece of land called the MARLEPIT**, lately purchased of Gilbert Schelove, lying near Thomas Fisher's land called the Clerte towards the north and it contains *1 acre of land*

Margin: right hand: *she holds two acres and half a daywork, thus 11d. each year.*
Joan Frutar holds of the said tenement **one MESSUAGE in which she lives, with a GARDEN and a PIECE OF LAND adjoining**, lying near the highway there leading from Goldhill as far as Tonbridge and to Hameletun called Totehill towards the east, the aforesaid highway towards the north, the highway leading from Hadlow Street as far as Tonbridge towards the west and moreover Henry Hexstall's land towards the south and it contains *2 acres and half a daywork.*

Margin: right hand: *he holds half an acre and 1 daywork, thus 2d. and a half pence each year*
Richard Fisher then holds in **one garden called WELLHAGH** situated near Thomas Fisher's garden called Turkshagh towards the east, the common way there called Stony lane, leading from John at Stable's dwelling house towards Fishill towards the south, the said John at Stable's land called Lorleyes west and north and it contains *half an acre and 1 daywork*
Margin: left hand: *now John Fisher holds the whole tenement:*

Total of acres is: *30 acres and 4 dayworks*,

thus 5d. and a half pence for each acre and 1d. more in all and for 10 acres they then owe 1d. farthing in relief

---

Folio 28
TANNER'S TENEMENT

Margin: right hand: *Henry Hexstall holds 18 acres, 3 rods and 1 daywork, thus 8s.11d. three farthings each year* left hand: *Tannerys tenement 7s.1d. from the total of the whole tenement as is shown in the ancient rental 12s.6d. and the 8ᵀᴴ part then in the lord's hands, thus it ought to be assessed at 18d. and a half pence for the 8ᵀᴴ part*
Henry Hexstall with his associates holds the whole of one tenement lately of John at **TANNERS** formerly of Nicholas Tanner, that is of Ferlingate land and three parts of Ferlingate and they thus owe 14d. a farthing and a half each year to the lord in rent and 18d. farthing and half a farthing to the lord in aid at the feast of St Andrew the apostle and they owe 105 small works, price of each work half a penny and they owe 21 great works, price of each work 2d. and they must plough 1 acre and 1 rod, price 10d. and a half and they owe seven parts of a carrying service, price 3d. and a half pence and they must provide five men for three boon-works price 5d.

Thus the aforesaid **Henry** holds **one MESSUAGE with a garden and 2 pieces of land adjoining called TANNERS** lying near the land of John Bishop son of Robert called Fissthelhelfield and Peter Fisher's land towards the east, John at Stable's land called Wateris and the garden of John Beald carpenter towards the south, the highway leading from Hadlow Street towards Tonbridge west and the same Henry's land called Upfield towards the north and it contains *11 and a half acres and 4 dayworks*

and **he then holds two pieces of land lying together near the common called UPPER TANNERS' FIELD and in SHROPSFIELD** lying together at the common there called Tothehill and Peter Fisher's land east, the same Henry's land south, the highway there leading from Hadlow Street as far as Tonbridge west, Joan Frutar's garden, formerly of John King towards the north and it contains *6 acres, 1 rod, 2 and a half dayworks*

and **he holds** [written above: *now Thomas Fichet*] **one piece of land called THE HAMME** of the same tenement, lying near John at Stable's land called Paynters croft and le Aleret, formerly of John Bishop son of Robert towards the east and south and towards Peter Fisher's land and the land of the said John Bishop west and the said Peter Fisher's land towards the north and it contains *3 rods, 4 and a half dayworks*

Margin: right hand: *he holds 2 and a half acres, 8 dayworks, thus 15d. three farthings each year*
John At Stable then holds **one piece of land with a GARDEN adjoining called WALTERS**, lying near [Henry - omitted] Hexstall's land and the said John Bishop's land east, the highway there leading from Hadlow Street towards Tonbridge towards the west and the said Henry's land and the garden of the said John Beald carpenter towards the north and the land lately of the said William Honewold towards the south and it contains *2 and a half acres, 8 dayworks*

Folio 28

Margin: right hand: *he then holds 1 acre except 2 and a quarter perches, 2d. three farthings each year*
John Beald carpenter then holds **one garden called WALTERISHAGH** lying near the said Henry's land towards the north and east, the said John at Stable's land towards

the south, the highway there leading from Hadlow Street to Tonbridge towards the west and it contains *1 acre except 2 and a quarter perches*

Margin: right hand: *he holds 3 acres 7 dayworks, 1 perch. 18d. three farthings each year*

Thomas Fisher as by right of Alice his wife formerly William Honewold's wife, holds for the term of the said Alice's life, **one piece of land called REDLAND** in front of John At Stable's gate, lying near John Bishop's and John Stable's land towards the east, the highway there leading from Hadlow Street as far as Tonbridge towards the west, near the common way leading from the said John Stable's dwelling house as far as Jopis meade towards the south, the said John at Stable's land towards the north and it contains *3 acres, 1 rod, 7 dayworks and 1 perch*

Margin: left hand: *now John Fisher holds the whole tenement.*

Total is: *25 acres, 1 rod, 6 dayworks and 1 perch*,
thus 5d. three farthings for each acre, in all three farthings less and then for ten acres 1d. farthing in relief

Margin: left hand: *to make inquiry concerning Tanners tenement* However the tenants of the said tenement ought to have 12d. as their assessment as here follows in the writings

Memorandum that the tenants of Tanners tenement ought to have as their assessment for that tenement, from small works for 13 works and an eighth part of half a penny and for 21 great works and an eighth part of 5d. farthing and they must plough 1 acre, a half and 1 rod and for the eighth part of the same, 1 farthing and the eighth part of half a penny

---

PEACOCK'S TENEMENT

Margin: left hand: *Peacocks tenement 11s. 10d.*

John Bishop son of Robert Bishop and his associates as written below hold one tenement formerly of Gervase Bishop called **PEACOCKS** tenement and for this they ought to owe the lord 15d. each year in rent and 21d. in aid at the feast of St Andrew the apostle and they shall plough and harrow half an acre in Winter and half an acre during Lent price 6d., as above and they shall have, as above and they owe a hundred small works, price of each work half a penny and twenty great works, price of each work 2d. and 3 boon-works with two men, price 6d. (f. 30) (Margin: right hand: *John Bishop holds 21 acres except three and three quarter perches, thus 7s. and three farthings each year*) and one carrying service price 3d.

Folio 30

Thus the aforesaid **John** then holds **one piece of land called the BROADFIELD** lying near John A Barton's land towards the south, land of the said John A Barton, of Lawrence Farman's, of Henry Hexstall and of the said John Bishop towards the west, near the same John Bishop's and John A Barton's land towards the east, the said Henry Hexstall's land towards the north and it contains *16 acres, 3 rods except 3 and three quarter perches*

and **he holds in a piece of land called the LONGFIELD** lying near John A Barton's land towards the south, near the same John Bishop's land in the same piece towards the east, the same John Bishop's land called the Broadfield towards the west and near the said Henry's land towards the north and it contains *1 acre* of land

and **he then holds one piece of land called the RISSHETT** lately of John Wyke, lying near the said Henry's land towards the south, the same John Bishop's land and the said Henry's land towards the east and Lawrence Farman's land towards the west and north and it contains *3 acres and 1 rod*

Margin: right hand: *he then holds 10 acres, 3 rods, 3 and a half dayworks, thus 3s. 7d. farthing each year*

Lawrence Farman [written above: *now Wells*] then holds at **FRAPELANES one small piece of land and meadow** lying near the said John Bishop's land towards the south, the said Henry's land towards the east, a piece of land of the same Lawrence called Frapelanes towards the west, land lately of William Bishop towards the north and it contains *1 acre, 4 and a half dayworks*

and **he then holds one MESSUAGE with a small piece of land adjoining called FRAPELANES** together with **one piece of land adjoining called STONYBYLLS** lying near the said John Bishop's land, near land lately of the said William Bishop and near the above mentioned meadow towards the east, near the highway there leading from the gate called Coiffe's gate as far as Penbridge towards the west, land lately of the said William Bishop towards the north and near a certain lane there called Bemitslane towards the south and it contains *6 acres and 2 dayworks*

and **he then holds one piece of land called BEMITTIS**, lying near Henry Hexstall's land east, the highway there leading from the aforesaid gate called Coiffe's gate as far as Tonbridge towards the west, the aforesaid lane there towards the south and it contains *2 acres, a half, 7 dayworks*

Folio 31 Margin: right hand: *he holds 3 acres except 1 daywork, 1 perch, 1 quarter thus 12d. each year*
Henry Hexstall [written above: *now John Bishop*] then holds **one piece of land called the RYSSHETT** lying near the said John Bishop's land called the Broadfield towards the east, Laurence Farman's land called the Metis towards the south and west and the said John Bishop's land towards the north and it contains *3 acres except 1 daywork, 1 perch and 1 quarter*

Margin: right hand: *he holds half an acre and half a daywork thus 2d. each year*
Richard Pynchon then holds **one piece of land called HOLMANS** lying near land lately of William Bishop towards the east and south, the land moreover of same Richard towards the north and west and it contains *half an acre and half a daywork*

Total of acres is : *35 acres, 1 rod, 2 dayworks, 1 quarter, 1 perch*,
thus 4d. for each acre and more for 1d. in the whole tenement and the relief for 11 acres 3 rods is 1d. farthing

---

POCOCKS TENEMENT Margin: left hand: *Peacocks tenement 11s.10d.*
Henry Hexstall and his associates hold one tenement formerly of Walter Holman now called **POCOCKS** (sic) tenement and for this they owe the lord 20d. in rent and 21d. in aid at the feast of St Andrew the apostle and they shall plough and harrow half an acre of land in Winter and half an acre during Lent, as above and they shall receive, as above and they owe a hundred small works, price half a penny for each work and twenty great works, price 2d. for each work and 3 boon-works with two men, price 6d. and one carrying service price 4d.

Thence the aforesaid **Henry** holds **2 pieces of land lying side by side called SNOD**, situated near the same Henry's land called Quindscroft and Sketelands towards the east, John Bishop's land towards the south, the same Henry's land called Pococks towards the west and land lately of William Bishop called Malynred towards the north and these contain *4 acres, 1 rod except a half daywork*

and **he then holds two pieces of land lying side by side called POCOCKSCROFT and NEWBARN**, lately acquired of John Beald carpenter, lying near a piece of land of Robert Bishop son of William towards the east, John Bishop's land called the Broadfield towards the south, the said John Bishop's land called Rysshett and Lawrence Farman's land called Frapelanes and land lately of William Bishop called Holmans towards the west, near the same Henry's wood and land, and near land lately of the said William Bishop towards the north and it contains *3 acres, a half, 2 and a half dayworks*

and **he holds one piece of land called POCOCKS** lying near the aforesaid piece of land called the Newland towards the west, the said John Bishop's land towards the south

and the same Henry's land towards the east and north and it contains *3 acres, 1 rod,*   6
and a half dayworks

Folio 32   and **he holds** in **one grove called POCOCKS GROVE** lying near land (f. 32) (Margin: right hand: *now John Fisher Henry Hexstall then hold 16 acres 3 rods 2 dayworks, thence 5s. 8d. each year* left hand: *now Thomas Barton*) lately of Stephen Frutar towards the east, the same Henry's land towards the south and land lately of William Bishop towards the west and north and it contains *2 acres and a half daywork*

and **he then holds one** [un-named] **PIECE OF LAND** lately acquired of Stephen Frutar lying near the same Henry's land called Pocockslane towards the west and it contains   *1 acre, a half and 3 dayworks* [written above: *he holds 3 rods*]

and **he then holds one piece of land called POCOCKSCROFT** lying near John at Stable's land called the Broadfield towards the east, the land of the said Robert Bishop son of William towards the south, the same Henry's land, formerly of Stephen Frutar towards the lane there called Pococks lane towards the north and it contains *2 acres of land,*   1
and a half dayworks

Margin: right hand: *they hold 3 acres, 1 rod thus 13d. each year*

John Fychett and **Thomas Fichet** [written above: *now John Wellis*] then hold **one piece of land** lately of William Coiffe **called BRODETISFIELD** lying near land lately of William Bishop called Malinrede towards the south, the highway there leading from Hadlow Street as far as Tonbridge towards the east [sic recte: *towards the west*], John at Stable's land towards the west and near the common there called Brodetisphayne towards the north and it contains *3 acres and 1 rod*

Margin: right hand: 1) *They hold 13 and a half acres except a half daywork, thus 3s. 7d. each year.* 2) *Now John Greentree 7 acres*

Reginald Herst and **John A Barton** [written above: *now John Fisher*], feoffees to the use of John Fisher and of the heirs of Richard Bishop son of William then hold **one piece of land called MALYNRED** lying near the highway there leading from Hadlow Street as far as Tonbridge, near land lately of Stephen Frutar and Henry Hexstall's land towards the east, the said Henry's land and John At Stable's land towards the west, land of John At Stable and land lately of William Coiffe towards the north and the said Henry's land towards the south and it contains *6 acres of land, a half and a half daywork* [written above: *now Bishop*]

and **they then hold 8 parcels of land lying side by side called HOLMAYNYS** situated near the said Henry's land and Lawrence Farman's land towards the south and the said Henry's land towards the east, near the highway there leading from the gate called Coiffesgate as far as Tonbridge and Richard Pynchon's land towards the west and land of the said Richard and Henry towards the north and it contains *7 acres, except 1 daywork and a quarter, 1 perch*

Folio 33   Margin: right hand: *he holds 1 and a half acres, thus 6d. each year*

John At Stable (written above: *now Jo Fisher*) then holds in **a piece of land called BRODETISFIELD** lying near land lately of William Bishop called Malynlede towards the south, the same John A Stable's land towards the north and Henry Hexstall's land towards the west and it contains *1 and a half acres*

Then the total is: *35 acres, 1 daywork except 1 quarter of 1 perch,*
thus 4d. for each acre and 2d. more in all and then for 11 and a half acres 7 dayworks [they owe] 1d. farthing in relief

PYNCHON'S TENEMENT   Margin: right hand: *they hold 2 acres and 6 dayworks, thus 3d. three farthings each year*:   left hand: *Ivo Longfrithe 6d.*

Richard PYNCHON (written above: *now Barton*) **and his associates** as written below hold the tenements formerly of Ivo Longfrithe and lately of William Goldfinch lying next to the gate called Coiffesgate and thus they owe the lord 6d. each year in rent.

Then the aforesaid **Richard** holds **one MESSUAGE with a GARDEN and a PIECE OF LAND adjoining** to the highway there leading from the gate called Coiffesgate as far as Tonbridge towards the east and to the two lanes of land of the same Richard called Ivotslanes towards the west and south and to land lately of William Coiffe towards the north and it contains *3 acres, 6 dayworks*

Margin: right hand: *they hold 1 acre, 1 rod, 6 and a half dayworks, thus 2d. farthing each year*
John Fychett and **Thomas Fichet** then hold **one piece of land called the REYD** lying near the park [called - omitted] the Northfrith towards the north, the said Richard Pynchon's land towards the south and the lane there called Ivotslane towards the west and near the highway leading from the aforesaid gate as far as Tonbridge towards the east and it contains *1 acre, 1 rod, 6 and a half dayworks*
Margin: left hand: *it is assessed.*

The total then is: *3 acres, a half, 2 and a half dayworks,*
thence 1d. three farthings for each acre and for the whole they owe 1d. and a half in relief

---

FICHET'S TENEMENT

Margin: right hand: *they hold 13 acres, 1 rod, 3 dayworks, thus 16d. and a half pence each year:* left hand: *William Longfrithe 3s.6d.*
John FICHET and **Thomas Fichet** (written above: *now John Wells*) **and their associates** hold one tenement formerly of William Longfrithe and thus they pay 3s.6d. to the lord each year in rent,

Then the aforesaid **John** and **Thomas** hold **one MESSUAGE with a GARDEN and 4 PIECES OF LAND adjoining** and with another land adjoining there **called WYKHAMES**, formerly of William Coiffe, lying near Richard Pynchen's land towards the east, near Northfrithe plain towards the west, the highway there leading from Brodisplain as far as Coiffesgate towards the south and near Robert Watt's land towards the north and it contains *7 acres, 3 rods and 2 dayworks*

and **they then hold in three pieces of land** within the aforesaid metes and bounds as is written above east, that is to say in the **RODE, BODYFIELD and JOLYNES** and they then contain *5 acres, a half and 1 daywork*

Folio 34

Margin: right hand: *he holds 17cres, a half and 9 dayworks, thus 22d. each year*
John Crocher (written above: *now Richard Colyn*) then holds as by right of Juliana his wife, formely the wife of Robert Watt **one MESSUAGE with a GARDEN and 5 PIECES OF LAND** lying side by side, near land of Robert Bishop son of William and land of Richard Fisher junior son of John towards the east, the park called the Northfrith towards the west, near the lane there called Birchwoods lane towards the north and the land lately of William Coiffe and the aforesaid park towards the south and it contains *16 and a half acres and 9 dayworks*

Margin: right hand: *he holds 2 and a half acres and 3 dayworks thus 3d. each year*
Robert Bishop son of William (written above: *now John Guge smith, now Thomas Somer*) then holds **one piece of land called CALVESLEASE** lying near Thomas Cardon's land towards the north, Martin Gogger's land called the Birgelswoods towards the west, land lately of William Bishop and formerly of Walter Bealde towards the east and land of Richard Fisher junior son of John towards the south and it contains *2 and a half acres and 3 dayworks*

Total is : *33 acres, a half and 10 dayworks,*
thus 1d. farthing for each acre and more, half a farthing in all and they owe 1d. farthing in relief for 4 acres

145

HOLMANS TENEMENT

Margin: right hand: *they hold 7 acres and 5 dayworks, thus 7d. farthing each year and they owe three fourths of a pig, 1 leg of pork and a fourth part of a half leg of pork* left hand: *Holemanys tenement 20d. and 2 pigs and a half*

Richard Pynchon (written above: now Richard Wells) *and his associates* hold one tenement formerly of Walter Holman, now called **HOLMANS** tenement and for this they shall owe the lord 20d. each year in rent and then at the feast of St Martin they owe the lord 2 and a half pigs for half of a sow.

Thus the aforesaid **Richard** holds **one piece of land called the LONG CROFT** lying near land lately of William Coiffe towards the east and west, near the highway there leading from Brodetis plain as far as the gate called Coiffesgate towards the south and the said Richard's land towards the north and it contains *1 acre, a half, 1 daywork*

and **he then holds one piece of land called THE REYE** lying near the same Richard's land east and the said William Coiffe's land towards the west, south and north and it contains *1 acre, 1 rod and 7 dayworks*

and **he then holds one small piece of land called THE PITTS** lying near land lately of the said William Coiffe and the same Richard's land towards the west, south and north and it contains *4 and a half acres*

and **he then holds** another **piece of land called THE PITTS** lying near land of Richard Fisher junior son of John towards the east, land (f.35) of the same Richard Pynchon and land lately of the said William Coiffe towards the south and west and the same Richard Pynchon's land towards the north and it contains *1 acre, 3 and a half dayworks*

Folio 35

and **he then holds** another **piece of land called THE PITTS** lying near the said William Coiffe's land towards the west, land lately of Robert Watt north, land of Richard Fisher son of John east, the same Richard Pynchon's land south and it contains *3 acres and a half daywork*

Margin: right hand: *he holds 5 acres, 5 dayworks thus 5d. and half a farthing each year and he owes half of a pig, 1 leg of pork and 4 parts of 1 leg of pork* left hand: *Richard Pynchon holds*

John Fychet (written above: now John Wells) and Thomas Fichet then hold **four pieces of land lying side by side called HASCOCKS** situated near the highway there leading from Brodetslane as far as the gate called Coiffesgate towards the south, Henry Hexstall's land and land of Richard Fisher son of John towards the north, Richard Pynchon's land towards the west, the said Henry's land and a certain lane there towards the east and it contains *5 acres and 5 dayworks*

Margin: right hand: *he holds 4 acres, a half and 6 dayworks, thus 4d. and a half pence and half a farthing each year and he owes a half of a pig, a half of a leg of pork and 4 parts of a half leg of pork* left hand: *Richard Pynchon holds*

Henry Hexstall (written above: now Richard Wellis) holds thus certain **pieces of land called the KNIGHTS PITS** lying near the said Henry's land towards the east, land lately of William Coiffe towards the south, the land of the said Richard Fisher junior son of John called Sandhersts pits towards the west, the lady of the manor's land and John At Stable's land called Bromfield towards the north and it contains *3 acres, 3 rods, 6 and a half dayworks*

and **he then holds A CERTAIN LANE** there leading to the same Henry's aforesaid land and it contains *3 rods except half a daywork*

Margin: right hand: *he holds 2 acres, 1 and a half dayworks, thus 2d. and 1 quarter of a pig each year*

Richard Fisher junior, John's son (written above: now Richard Colyn) then holds **two pieces of land lying side by side, called SANDHERST PITS,** situated near the said Henry Hexstall's land towards the east, Richard Pychon's land towards the west, William Coiffe's land towards the south and land lately of Robert Watt towards the north and it contains *2 acres, 1 and a half dayworks*

Margin: right hand: *she holds 1 acres, 5 and a half dayworks, thus 1d. and half a farthing each year and she owes a leg of pork and 1 pig and 4 parts of a half leg of pork*
The lady of the manor then holds (written above: *now Richard Crude, now J Welles*) in **lands called THE PITS,** lately of John Brodell the bastard, as the metes and bounds thus appoint and show, containing *1 acre, 5 and a half dayworks*

Total is: *20 acres, 3 dayworks*,
thus each year 1d. and in relief they owe 1d. farthing for each acre, for 8 acres 1 daywork, 1 pig and half a daywork more

---

Folio 36
KNIGHTS TENEMENT

Margin: right hand: *he then holds 8 acres, 7 dayworks, thus 8d. farthing each year*
left hand: *Knightstones tenement 12d.*
Henry Hexstall (written above: *now Richard CruddWWells*) **and his associates** hold the whole tenement formerly of Nicholas Tanner called Knightsland, now called **KNIGHTS** tenement and thus they owe the lord 7d. each year in rent.

Thence the abovesaid man [**Henry Hexstall**] holds **one piece of land called the KNIGHTS FIELD** lying next to the Pits, near land of John Beald carpenter called Davisfield and John At Stable's land at Broadhill towards the east, the said John At Stable's land called Broomfield towards the north, near land lately of William Bishop towards the south and the land of the lady of the manor and the same Henry's land towards the west and it contains *8 acres and 7 dayworks*

Margin: right hand: *he then hold 2 acres, 1 rod, 3 and a half dayworks, thus 2d. farthing each year*

John At Stable (written above: *now Richard Colyns*) holds one [un-named] **PIECE OF LAND** lying next to Broadsplain, situated near the said Henry's land towards the north and west, near John Bealde's land towards the east and land moreover lately of William Bishop and the common there called Broads plain towards the south and it contains *2 acres, 1 rod, 3 and a half dayworks*

Margin: right hand: *he then holds one and a half acres of land, thus 1d. and a half pence each year*

John Bealde carpenter (written above: *now J Bishop*) then holds in a **piece of land called DAVISFIELD** one parcel of land of the said tenement lying near the said Henry's land towards the west, the same Henry's land towards the east and south and land lately of William Bishop and John At Stable towards the north and it contains *one acre* of land *and a half*

Total then is: *12 acres and a half daywork*
thus for each acre 1d. and in relief [they owe] a farthing for each acre

---

BROOMFIELDS TENEMENT

Margin: right hand: *they hold 4 acres and 3 dayworks, thus 19d. three farthings each year*
left hand: *Broomfields tenement 4s. each year*
John At Stable (written above: *now J Fisher wright*) **and his associates** hold one tenement formerly of Walter Bishop now called **BROOMFIELDS** tenement and for this they owe the lord 4s. each year in rent at 4 terms of the year.
Thence the aforesaid **John** holds **one piece of land called the FOUR ACRES**, lying near land lately of William Bishop towards the east and north, Henry Hexstall's land towards the south, the lady of the manor's land called the Broad pits towards the west and it contains *4 acres and 3 dayworks*

Folio 37
Margin: right hand: *he then holds 6 acres except 4 dayworks, thus 2s.4d. farthing each year*
Thomas Bishop son of William then holds **two [un-named] PIECES OF LAND** lying side by side near the same Thomas's land of the tenement called Stydings tenement towards the east, near a piece of land of Robert Bishop son of the said William called

Calbyske towards the west, the aforesaid Thomas Cardon's land towards the north and near the aforesaid piece of land of the said John At Stable south and it contains *6 acres* of land *except 4 dayworks*

Total is: *10 acres and 1 daywork*,
thus 4d. three farthings for an acre and in all half a penny more and he owes 1d. and a half pence in relief for 1 acre and 1 rod

---

STIDYNGS TENEMENT

Margin: right hand: *he holds 6 and a half acres except 1 daywork thus 22d. each year:* left hand: *Stidings tenement 22d.*
The above said **Thomas Bishop** (written above: *now John Fisher wright*) holds the whole of one tenement formerly of Amicia **STIDYNGS** and for this he owes the lord 16d. each year in rent and 6d. in aid at the feast of St Andrew the apostle and the whole aforesaid tenement lies in two pieces of land situated that is towards the highway there leading from Hadlow Street towards Tonbridge towards the east [sic: recte *towards the west*], the same Thomas's land and John A Stable's land towards the west, Thomas Cardon's land towards the north and land of John A Beald carpenter towards the south and it contains *6 and a half acres, except 1 daywork*

Total is: *6 and a half acres of land except 1 daywork*,
thus 3d. and a half for an acre and in all three farthings more and he owes 4d. in relief in the whole tenement as for a fourth part of the rent according the constitutions of the manor

---

BERWYS TENEMENT

Margin: right hand: *they hold 4 and a half acres, 1 and a half dayworks, thus 20d. three farthings each year* left hand: *Brewis tenement 15s. 3d.*
John Bishop son of Robert (written above: *now John Bishop*) **and his associates** as written below hold one tenement formerly of William of Bedyll lately of Walter Hamenet, now called **BERWYS** tenement and for this they owe 2s. 8d. each year in rent and 21d. in aid at the feast of St Andrew the apostle and 3 boon-works with two men, price 6d., deduction having been made for food and 120 small works, price of each work half a penny and 24 great works, price of each work 2d. and they owe 1 carrying service price 4d. and they must plough one acre in Winter and one acre during Lent and they shall harrow and for each acre they shall receive four loaves price 2d. and 8 herrings price 1d. and the work of two acres is worth 12d., deduction having been made for food.

Thence the aforesaid **John Bishop** holds **one piece of land called the GRETBERGH** lying near the lady of the manor's land and the land lately of Richard Mayne towards the east, the lane called Bergwis lane towards the south (f. 38), near land of Stephen Frutar and land of John Pulter tanner now deceased west and land lately of Richard Mayne called Petland north and it contains *4 acres, a half, 1 and a half dayworks*

Folio 38

The lady of the manor then holds in the aforesaid **land called GRETBERGH** lying near the land lately of Gilbert Shereve (written above: *now William Pulter*) towards the east, land formerly of Richard Mayn (written above: *the heirs of William Shecreve*) and the same John Bishop's land towards the south, the said John Bishop's land towards the west and the said Richard Mayn's land called Petland towards the north and it then contains *1 acre* of land

Margin: right hand: *he holds 4 and a half acres and 7 dayworks, thus 4d. and a half pence and a half farthing each year*
John Bishop (written above: *now Jo Bishop*) also holds one piece of land calls **BUNTANYSBREGH** lying near land lately of Stephen Frutar and Gilbert Shereve's land towards the east, the lane there called Berghwis lane towards the north, land lately of William Honewold, now of Thomas Fisher called Honewolds burgh towards the west

and near land lately of Gilbert Shereve (written above: *William Pulter*) and the lady of the manor's land called Kemeland towards the south and it contains *4 acres, a half and 4 dayworks*

Margin: right hand: *he holds 4 acres 4 dayworks, thus 18d. and a half pence each year*
Lawrence Farman then holds one piece of land called **LAWRENCE'S BURGH** lying near land lately of Stephen Frutar towards the east, near Thomas Fisher's land towards the west, Agnes Pulter's land towards the north and near the lane there called Berghwis lane towards the south and it contains *4 acres and 4 dayworks*

Margin: right hand: *he holds 5 acres, 3 rods and 3 perches, thus 2s.2d. and a half pence each year*
Thomas Fisher (written above: *now Jo Fisher*) then holds **one piece of land called HONEWOLDS BURGH** lying near the aforesaid John Bishop's land towards the east, John At Stable's land and Stephen Frutar's land towards the west, land lately of Gilbert Shereve towards the north, the lady of the manor's land called Great Kemeland towards the south and it contains *1 and a half acres of land, 6 and a half dayworks*

and **he then holds one piece of land called THE BURGH** lately acquired of John Pulter tanner, lying near Lawrence Farman's land and the said John Pulter's land towards the east, near the highway there leading from Hadlow Street as far as Tonbridge towards the west, the said Lawrence's land and a certain lane there called Berghwis lane towards the south and the aforesaid highway towards the north and it contains *4 acres, 4 dayworks and 1 perch*

Folio 39   Margin: right hand: *he holds 1 acre, 3 rods, 2 and a half dayworks, thus 8d. farthing each year*
Martin Cogger (written above: *now Robert Miller of Kemsing*) then holds **one** [un-named] **PIECE OF LAND** lying towards a piece of land and the highway there called Little Petland towards the north, John Bishop's land towards the south, land lately of Stephen Frutar and of Lawrence Farman (written above: *of John Bishope*) towards the south, land lately of John Pulter towards the west and it contains *1 acre, 3 rods, 2 and a half dayworks*

Margin: right hand: *he then holds 4 acres, 3 rods, 6 and a half dayworks, thus 22d. and a half pence each year.*
Gilbert Shereve (written above: *now of John Bishop*) then holds **one** [un-named] **PIECE OF LAND** lying near the aforesaid John Bishop's land and the same Gilbert's land towards the east and the said John Bishop's land towards the west and north, the lady of the manor's land called Kemeland towards the south and it contains *2 acres, 4 dayworks*

and **he then holds** another [un-named] **PIECE OF LAND** of the said John Bishop towards the east, near land lately of William Honewold, now of Thomas Fisher towards the south, Joan Frutar's land towards the west and the lane called Berghwis lane towards the north and it contains *2 acres 3 rods, 2 and a half dayworks* (written above: *now John Fisher*)

Margin: right hand: *they hold 1 acre, 4 and a half dayworks, thus 5d. a half farthing each year*
William Shereve's heirs (written above: *now the heirs of Fane Colyer*) then hold **one** [un-named] **PIECE OF LAND** lately acquired of John Simond senior of Palmer Street lying near the said Gilbert Shereve's land towards the east, John Bishop's land towards the west, the land of the lady of the manor towards the north and near the lane there called Berghwis lane towards the south and it contains *1 acre, 4 and a half dayworks*

Margin: right hand: *she holds 4 acres, 3 rods, thus 22d. each year*
Agnes Pulter (written above: *now Robert Miller of Kemsing*) then holds **one piece of land called BERGHWIS** lying near Martin Cogger's land and John Bishop's land towards the east, Thomas Fisher's land towards the west, the highway leading from Hadlow Street as far as Tonbridge towards the north, land of Lawrence Farman and Joan Frutar's land towards the south and it contains *4 acres, 3 rods, except half a daywork*

Joan Frutar (written above: *now John Fisher*) then holds **one piece of land called**

Folio 40

MOREBERGH lying near the lane there called Berghwise lane towards the north, John a Stable's land and land of John Fisher senior towards the south, Gilbert Shereve's land towards the east, John A Barton's land towards the west (f.40) (Margin: right hand: *she holds 7 acres 4 dayworks, thence 2s. 8d. and a half pence each year*) and it contains *4 acres,* *3* *rods and 2 dayworks*

and **she then holds** another **piece of land called the EIRGHI ACRE**, near the aforesaid lane there towards the south, Agnes Pulter's land towards the north, John Bishop's land towards the east and Lawrence Farman's land towards the west (written above: *now Farman*) and it contains *2 acres, 1 rod and 1 daywork*

Total then of the whole is: *39 acres a half, 9 dayworks and 1 perch*, 4d. and a half pence and a half farthing for each acre, in all less by one penny farthing and the relief for 5 acres is 1d.

CARDON'S TENEMENT

Margin: right hand: *he holds 1 half acre except half a daywork, thus 2d. and a half pence each year* left hand: *headland 2 and a half pence*

Thomas CARDON (written above: *modo Thomas Somer*) holds **one piece of land called the HEADLAND** formerly of Walter At Stare lying near the land of the same Thomas towards the east, land called Birchwood towards the west and north, land of Robert Bishop son of William called Calves lease towards the south and he thus owes 2d. each year in rent and half a penny in aid at the feast of St Andrew the apostle and it contains *1 and a half acres of land, except half a daywork*

BIRCHWOOD TENEMENT

Margin: right hand: *he holds 30 acres, a half, 5 and a half dayworks, thus 4s. 7d. each year:* left hand: Birchwoods 4s. 7d.

Martin Cogger (written above: *now John Enge Roverds 10 acres Welles*) holds divers parcels of land at **BIRCHWOOD** formerly of William Robond and John Goman and once of Barowyn and he then owes 21d. to the lord each year in rent and he holds there all the tenement formerly of Nicholas Clark in hand: and lately of Thomas At Croch which is called **TEN ACRES**, thus he owes 2s. 4d. to the lady [of the manor] each year in rent and 6d. in aid at the feast of St Andrew the apostle and all the above said things pertaining from the two aforesaid tenements of the said Martin's land lie next to the small common called the Slethe at the highway there leading from Palmer Street cross as far as Northfrith and to the park called Northfrith west and north, Thomas Cardon's land and land of Robert son of William Bishop called Calves lease east, and the said Robert's land and land of Robert Watt south and it then contains *30 acres, a half and 5 and a half dayworks*

Total is : *30 and a half acres, 5 and a half dayworks* and he then owes 12d. farthing in relief

---

folio 41
WELSHES TENEMENT

Margin: right hand: *they then hold each year of the lord 3 acres 5 dayworks, thus 3d. and a half farthing each year and they owe 1 quarter of a pig and a half* left hand: Welshe tenement 3s. 6d. *another total of the whole tenement is 5s. 3d. and 7 pigs*

Henry Hexstall and his associates as written below (written above: *now John Roberd*) hold one tenement formerly of Richard Palmer, now called **WELSHE** tenement and thus they owe the lord 20d. each year in rent (written above: *2s. 6d.*) and 14d. in aid at the feast of St Andrew the apostle (written above: *21d.*) and they shall plough and harrow their own part of 1 acre of land, price according to the amount as above 4d. and 2 boon-works with two men price 4d. and the third part is then in the lord's hand: and they owe 5 pigs for one sow each year, as is above in the assessment.

Then the aforesaid **Henry** holds **1 piece of land called THE CROFT AND SLEDE** lying near land lately of William Bishop towards the east, land formerly of Robert Watt towards the west and north, near the highway there leading from Palmer Street cross as far as Northfrith towards the south and it then contains *3 acres and 5 dayworks* formerly of Nicholas Penyale's wife

Margin: right hand: *he holds 7 acres and 3 rods, thence 7d. three farthings each year and half, three quarters of a pig and half, and a half and 1 quarter of a leg of pork*

John Crocher (written above: *John Roberde*) then holds as by right of Juliana his wife **two pieces of land lying side by side called THE BROOKS**, formerly of Robert Watte, lying near the demesne land of Phaines towards the east, land lately of John Brewer carpenter and the highway there at Ashwood towards the north, land lately of William Bishop towards the south and the aforesaid highway at Ashwood towards the west and it contains *3 acres 3 rods except 1 and a half perches*

and **he then holds two pieces of land lying side by side called THE BROOM CROFTS**, situated near the said Juliana's aforesaid two pieces of land towards the north, the said Henry Hexstall's land towards the east, the highway there leading from Ashwood as far as Hoggetts gate towards the west and the highway there leading from Palmers Street cross as far as Northfrith towards the south and it contains *4 acres of land and a half daywork*

Margin: right hand: *they hold 8 acres thus 8d. each year and they owe 1 pig*

Reginald Herst and **John A Barton** (written above: *Robert Pawley*) feoffees for the use of John Fisher, [and - omitted] Richard Bishop son of William, hold **3 pieces of land lying side by side** next to le Sleade aforesaid **called WOSINGSLAND** lying near the said Elizabeth Colepeper's land for the term of her life called Walshgrove and Denise Grubbe's land towards the east, land lately of John Brewer carpenter towards the north, land lately of Robert Watt towards the west and the land of John Simond senior and the said Denise's land towards the south and it contains *8 acres*

Folio42 Margin: right hand: *he holds 1 acre 8 dayworks thus 1d. farthing each year and he owes 1 leg of pork* left hand: *now John Roberts*

Robert Bishop (written above: *now Richard Howtre or William Were's heirs hold*) then holds as by right of Agnes his wife **one piece of land called THE SNOD** lying near Denise Grubbe's land towards the east, the same Agnes's land towards the west, Martin Cogger's land towards the south and land lately of William Bishop towards the north and he holds *1 acre, 8 dayworks*

Margin: right hand: *he holds 16 acres, 9 dayworks, thence 16d. three farthings each year and he owes 2 pigs and three quarters*

William Grubb (written above: *now Robert Miller of Kemsing*) then holds by right of Denise his wife **one piece of land called UPCROFT**, lying near land lately of William Rowe towards the east, the same Denise's land towards the west and south and near the lady Elizabeth Colepeper's land called Walshbroom towards the north and it contains   *2 acres, 1 and a half dayworks*

and **he then holds two pieces of land** lying side by side **called THE UPCROFTS**, lying near land lately of John Simond senior called the Westcrofts and land lately of Thomas Towe towards the south, near the grove and a piece of land of the same Denise called Broomfield towards the north, near the aforesaid piece of land called the Upcroft towards the east and near the aforesaid grove towards the west and it contains *6 acres, 3 rods and a half daywork*

and **he then holds** in **a piece of land called BROMFIELD** lying near the aforesaid piece of land called the Upcrofts towards the south, the said lady Elizabeth Colepeper's land and the grove called the Welshgrove towards the north, east and west and it contains *4 acres, 1 rod and 7 dayworks*

and **he then holds one** [un-named] **GROVE** adjoining the said lady Elizabeth's aforesaid grove called the Welshgrove and the same Denise's land towards the east, land lately of

William Bishop west, the said lady Elizabeth's land towards the north, the same Denise's land and land lately of William Bishop towards the south and it contains *8 acres*

Total of acres is: *41 acres, 1 rod, 2 dayworks* in the tenants' hand,
thus 1d. for each acre, 1d. more in all and they owe half a penny and a farthing in relief, 5 pigs, in all 7 pigs and a half and for 8 acres, 1 rod, a half daywork, except half daywork to 1 pig from the whole tenement

---

Folio 43
PALMER'S TENEMENT

Margin: right hand: *they hold 1 acre, 3 rods and 6 dayworks, thus 7d. and a half each year:* left hand: *Palmers tenement 11s.10d.*

James Foster and his associates as are written below hold (written above: W*alter Trice holds*) one tenement formerly of Simon Palmer now called **PALMERS** tenement and for this they owe 15d. each year in rent and 21d. in aid at the feast of St Andrew the apostle and 3 boon-works with two men in Autumn price 6d. and they owe a hundred small works, price of each half a penny and they owe 20 great works, price of each work is 2d. and one carrying service price 4d. and they must plough half an acre in Winter and half an acre during Lent price 6d. as above, deduction been made for food.

Thence the aforesaid **James** holds **one MESSUAGE with a GARDEN and with two PIECES OF LAND adjoining**, lately of Robert Burdon next to Palmers Street cross, situated adjoining the highway there leading from the said cross as far as Northfrith towards the east, the highway there leading from Hadlow Street as far as Tunbridge towards the south, Henry Johnson's land towards the west and north and it contains *1 acre, 3 rods and 6 dayworks*

Margin: right hand: *he holds 11 acres, 1 rod and half a daywork, thus 3s.8d. and a half pence each year*

Henry Johnson [written above: *now S Somer*] then holds **one MESSUAGE with a GARDEN and a small PIECE OF LAND** adjoining **called PALMERS PLACE** in which he lives, situated near the highway there leading from Palmers Street as far as Northfrith towards the north, the same Henry's land called Crouchefield towards the east, Henry's piece of land called Develand towards the south, Henry Hexstall's land towards the west and it contains *1 acre, 1 rod, 6 and a half dayworks*

and **he then holds one piece of land called CROUCHFIELD** lying near the highway there leading from the aforesaid cross called Palmer Street cross as far as the park called Northfrith north, near James Foster's land and the said Henry's land towards the east, south and west and it contains *6 acres, 1 and a half dayworks*

and **he then holds ONE PIECE OF LAND with a GARDEN adjoining called BEWEBAMER** situated at the highway there leading from Hadlow Street as far as Tonbridge towards the south, Thomas Cardon's and Henry Hexstall's land towards the west, the said Henry Johnson's messuage and land of the said Henry and James Foster's land towards the east and it contains *8 acres, 3 rods, 2 and a half dayworks*

Margin: right hand: they hold 3 acres, 3 rods, 1 and a half dayworks, thus 15d. each year
Henry Hexstall and John Symond of Palmer Street senior (*written above: now S Somer*) then hold **one** [un-named] **PIECE OF LAND** lying near Henry Johnson's land towards the east and south, the said John Symond's land towards the west, the highway there leading from Palmer Street as far as Northfrith towards the north and it contains *3 acres, 3 rods, 1 and a half dayworks*

Folio 44

Margin: right hand: *she holds 8 acres, 1 rod ,6 and a half dayworks, thus 2s.9d. each year*
Denise Grubb then holds [written above: *now Robert Meller of Kemsing thence Edward Gibson holds 2 acres 8d.*] **2 MESSUAGES with a GARDEN and TWO PIECES OF LAND**, adjoining to the messuage formerly of William Rowe towards the east, the messuage of John Simonds senior west, the same Denise's land north, to the highway

leading from Palmer Street cross as far as Northfrith towards the south and these contain *2 acres, a half and 5 dayworks*

and **she holds one PIECE OF LAND there with a GARDEN adjoining called WALTHEHAGH** otherwise called the **FIELD AT NAYSSTHE** and it lies near land lately of Thomas Rowe east, the same Denise's land and land lately of the said John Symond called the South towards the west, the same Denise's land called the Upcrofts towards the north, near the aforesaid highway there towards the south and it contains   *3 and a half acres, 6 dayworks*

and then **she holds one** [un-named] **SMALL PIECE OF LAND**, adjoining the same person's aforesaid garden towards the east, to land formerly of William Bishop towards the west, the same Denise's land and the said John Symonde's land towards the south and near the said Denise's grove towards the north and it contains *2 acres, 5 and a half dayworks*

Margin: right hand: *he holds 9 dayworks, thus 1d. each year.*

John Symond senior of Palmer Street [written above: *now W Reve*] then holds **one MESSUAGE with a GARDEN in which he dwells**, adjoining to the said Denise Grubb's land east, Martin Cogger's land towards the west, the said Martin's and the said Denise's land towards the north and to the highway there leading from Palmer Street cross towards Northfrith south and it contains *9 dayworks*

Margin: right hand: *he holds 4 acres, 1 rod, 4 and a half dayworks, thus 17d. each year*

Martin Cogger then holds **one piece of land called THE WESTCROFT** with one barn built upon it, adjoining Denise Grubb's land and to the said John Symond's messuage towards the east, to land lately of Thomas Rowe towards the west, to the said Denise's land towards the north and the aforesaid highway there leading towards Northfrith towards the south and it contains *2 acres, except 1 and a half dayworks*

and **he holds one piece of land there called THE SOUTH,** adjoining to the said Denise's land and to land lately of William Rowe towards the north, to land lately of Thomas Rowe towards the west and the abovesaid highway towards the south and it contains *2 acres, 1 rod and 5 dayworks* [written above: *now Roberds*]

Folio 45   Margin: right hand: *she holds 4 acres, 1 rod and 6 dayworks, thus 17d. each year*

Margery Rowe [written above: *now of Stephen Somer*] holds **one MESSUAGE with a GARDEN and TWO PIECES OF LAND** formerly of Thomas Rowe, for the term of her life, adjoining Martin Cogger's land towards the east, the abovesaid Denise's land towards the west and north and to the aforesaid highway leading as far as Northfrith to the south and they contain *4 acres, 1 rod and 6 dayworks*

Margin: right hand: *he holds 3 acres, 4 and a half dayworks 8d. and a half pence*

Robert Bishop holds [written above: *now J Robards*] then as by right of his wife Agnes **one piece of land called THE SOUTH** lying near Martin Cogger's land towards the east, near the aforesaid highway leading as far as Northfrith towards the west and south, the land lately of William Bishop north and it contains *7 acres, 4 and a half dayworks*

Total is: *36 acres, 1 rod, 7 and a half dayworks*, thus 4d. for each acre and 2d. less in all and for 4 and a half acres half a penny in relief

---

WEKERLYD'S TENEMENT

Margin: right hand: *he holds 7 acres, 3 and a half dayworks, thus 2s. 5d. three farthings each year*
left hand: *Wekerylds tenement 13s. 8d.*

Robert Bishop son of William as by right of Agnes his wife and his associates as written below, hold one tenement, formerly of Richard Wekerylds now called **WEKERYLD'S** tenement and for this they owe the lord 4s. in rent and 21d. in aid at the feast of St Andrew the apostle and 80 small works, price of each work half a penny and 16 great works, price of each work 2d. and they must plough one acre in Winter and one acre during Lent and they shall harrow and they shall receive as above price 12d. and in Autumn they shall owe 3 boon works with two men, price 6d and one carrying service price 4d.

Thence the abovesaid **Robert** holds, as by right of the said Agnes for the term of her life, **one MESSUAGE with a GARDEN** adjoining, lately of William Rowe, adjoining land of the same Agnes and Joan Frutor's garden towards the east, Denise Grubb's land towards the west, land of the same Agnes (and) the said Denise's land towards the west, the highway leading from the cross called Palmer Street cross towards Northfrith on the south and it contains *3 rods, 9 dayworks*

and **he holds** there the [un-named] **REMAINING PARCELS OF LAND** lying together adjoining the aforesaid messuage of the said Agnes, Joan Frutar's garden, John Tailoure's land, Martin Cogger's land south, land of Nicholas Borne east, land of the lady Elizabeth Colepeper called Stonyfield and Welshbrome towards the north, Denise Grubb's land north (sic) and it contains *6 acres, 4 and a half dayworks*

Folio 46   Margin: right hand: *1) The same Walter holds 1 acre and a half acre thus 6d each year*   *2) He holds 9 acres, 5 and a half dayworks, thus 3s. 1d. three farthings each year*   *3) And John Wright's heirs hold 7 and a half acres, 5 dayworks, a half 2s. 2d. three farthings each year*

Joan formerly Stephen Frutar's wife [written above: *now Walter Trice*] then holds **one MESSUAGE** there **called AYLARDSHAGH** adjoining to land of John Taillour of Mereworth towards the east, to land lately of William Rowe towards the east and north, to the aforesaid highway leading as far as Northfrith towards the south and it contains *3 rods, 6 and a half dayworks*

and then **she holds** another **GARDEN** next to Palmer Street cross lying near a messuage and a piece of ground called Bacryscross, lately of William Burden now of Nicholas Borne towards the west and north, near the highway there leading from Hadlow Street as far as Tonbridge towards the east and near the aforesaid highway leading as far as Northfrith towards the south [written above: *Walter Trice*] and it contains *3 and half acres, 3 and a half dayworks*

and then **she holds** one **piece of land called THE ROWE** lying near the same Joan's land called Stonyfield and land lately of Robert Burdon called the Rowe towards the north, the lane there leading to land called Stonyfield west, the same Joan's land east and it contains *1 acre, a half and 8 and a half dayworks*

and **she holds** there **[land]** called **LEYLAND** lying near the common way there called the New way towards the east, land lately of William Burden towards the west, the same Joan's land called Monks field towards the north and the same Joan's land and land of James Gosse towards the south and it contains *2 acres, a half and 1 daywork* of the said tenement

and **she holds** there **one piece of land called MONKS FIELD** adjoining the aforesaid common way called the New way towards the east, land formerly of William Burden called the Rowe towards the west, the highway there leading from Hadlow Street as far as Tunbridge towards the north and to land of the same Joan called Leyland south and it contains *3 acres, 1 rod and 6 dayworks*

Margin: right hand: *he holds 3 rods, 3 dayworks, thus 3d. farthing each year*

John Taylour [written above: *modo Jo Borne now Johnson*] **of Mereworth** then holds **one GARDEN with a small piece of ground adjoining called WOKERYLDISHAGH** adjoining to Joan Frutar's garden towards the west, to Martin Cogger's land towards the east, land lately of William Rowe towards the north, to the highway there leading towards Northfrith towards the south and it contains *3 rods,   3 dayworks*

Folio 47   Margin: right hand: *he holds 6 and a half acres, 5 and a half dayworks, thus 2s. 3d. three farthings each year*   left hand: *now John Umfrey*

Martin Cogger [written above: *now J.B now Johnson*] then holds **one piece of land called EVECROFT**, lying near the piece called Hachfield towards the east, near the said

John Taylor's land towards the west, land of the said Martin towards the north, near the aforesaid highway leading as far as Northfrith towards the south and it contains *3 rods and 5 dayworks*

and then **he holds one** [un-named] **PIECE OF LAND** lying from the west part of 1 piece of land called Hachfield to the said John Taylor's land towards the west, land lately of William Rowe towards the north, near the same Martin's aforesaid piece of land called Overcross towards the south and it contains *1 acre*

and then **he holds one piece of land called HACHFIELD** lying near the said Nicholas Borne's land and (land) lately of William Burdon east, near the said Nicholas's land north, near the aforesaid land of the same Martin west and near the aforesaid highway leading towards Northfrith south and it contains *4 acres, 3 rods and half a daywork*

Margin: right hand: *he holds 12 acres, 1 rod and 2 dayworks, thus 4s. 3d .three farthings each year*

Nicholas Borne holds **one MESSUAGE with a GARDEN and 8 pieces of land** adjoining, formerly of William Burdon called **BARRIS CROFT, UPPERFIELD** and **THE CORNMEARE** lying near the highway there leading from Hadlow Street as far as Tonbridge and the garden of Joan Frutar towards the south, near the highway leading from the cross called Palmer street cross as far as Northfrith towards the west, near Martin Cogger's land towards the north, near land of the lady Elizabeth Colepeper called Sedgebrook and John Bishop's land towards the east and it contains *10 and a half acres*

and **he holds one piece of land there called BOGCROFT** lying near the aforesaid land called Somingsbrook towards the east, the said lady Elizabeth's land called Stony field north, land of Martin Cogger south and near land lately of William Rowe west and it contains *1 acre, 3 rods and 2 dayworks*

Margin: right hand: *he holds 1 and a half acres and 9 and a half dayworks thus 7d. farthing each year*

John Carter's heirs [written above: *now John Wright's heirs*] then hold **one piece of land called THE ROW** lately of William Burdon, lying near John Frutar's land towards the east and south, near the highway there leading from Hadlow Street as far as Tonbridge towards the north, near Nicholas Becher's land towards the west and it contains *1 acre, a half, 9 and a half dayworks*

Margin: right hand: *he holds 1 rod and 4 dayworks thus 1d. farthing each year*

John Bishop [written above: *now J Borne now Johnson*] then holds **one** [un-named] **PARCEL OF LAND** lying below Sedgebrook, lying near Nicholas Borne's land called the Cornmeare towards the west and north, near the same John Bishop's land in the same piece towards the east, near the highway there leading from Hadlow Street towards Tonbridge south and it contains *1 rod and 4 dayworks*

Folio 48

Margin: right hand: *she holds 1 acre and 2 dayworks, thus 4d. farthing each year*

The lady of the manor [written above: *now Richard Colepeper's heirs*] then holds **one piece of land and pasture called SENYNGESBROOK**, lying near the lady Elizabeth Colepeper's land called Sedgebrook towards the east, Nicholas Borne's land towards the west and south, the said lady Elizabeth's land called Stonyfield towards the north and it contains *1 acre of land and 2 dayworks*

Total is: *39 acres, 5 dayworks*
4d. for each acre and 7d. more in all, that is 1d. for 5 and a half acres and 3 dayworks and 1d. and a half pence in relief for 3 acres and 3 rods

---

SOMERS TENEMENT

Margin: right hand: *they hold 3 acres, 1 rod and 2 dayworks, thus 20d. three farthings each year and for this they owe half and a quarter of a pig* left hand: *Somers tenement 11s. 5d.*

John Bishop son of Robert and his associates as written below hold one tenement formerly of William at Longfrith, now called **SOMERS** tenement and they then owe the lord 2s.4d. in rent and they shall plough half an acre of land in Winter and half an acre during Lent, price 6d. as above and they shall owe 80 small works price of each half a penny and 16 great works, price of each work 3d. and 21d. in aid at the feast of St Andrew the apostle and in Autumn they shall make 3 boon-works with two men price 6d. and one carrying service price 4d.

Thence the abovesaid **John** holds **one piece of land there called THE HAME** lying near a certain lane called Seylleys lane towards the east, land lately of John Mayne called the Pit lane towards the west, the highway there leading from Hadlow Street towards Tonbridge north and near the lady of the manor's piece called Solefield south and it contains *3 acres, 1 rod and 2 dayworks*

Margin: right hand: *1 half acre except 2 and a half perches, 9 and a half pence each year and 1 quarter of a pig and 1 leg of pork*

John Symond senior [written above: *now Robert Meller*] holds **one piece of land called PETLAND** lying near the said John Bishop's land towards the north, Martin Cogger's land towards the west and south, land of the lady of the manor towards the east and he holds *1 acre, a half except 2 and a half perches*

Margin: right hand: *he holds 1 acre thus 7d. three farthings each year and 1 quarter of a pig and 3 parts of a leg of pork*

Martin Cogger then holds [written above: *now Robert Meller*] **one piece of land called LITTLE PETLAND** lying near a piece of land called More Petland towards the east, land of Agnes Pulter towards the west, the highway there leading from Hadlow Street to Tonbridge towards the north and a piece of land of the same Martin south and it contains *1 acre of land and 1 rod*

Folio 49 Margin: right hand: *she holds 15 acres, 3 rods and 1 daywork, thus 8s.3d. each year and she owes 3 pigs, a half leg of pork and she owes 1 quarter of 1 leg of pork*

The Honourable lady Anne duchess of Buckingham and lady of the manor [written above: *Henry Walter, now in Thomas Renald's hand:*] holds **one piece of land called THE MANIFIELD** of the said tenement, formerly in the tenure of John Bishop son of Robert, lying near land lately of Gilbert Shereve and John Goding's land called Cathmores towards the east, land lately of the said Gilbert and Lawrence Forman's land towards the west, land lately of William Bealde called Blackmans brook and John Fantor's land called the Maylis brook towards the north and John Goding's land towards the south and it contains *12 acres and 7 dayworks* of the aforesaid tenement and not more which are in the same piece of land are 2 acres of land [written above: *now in John Bishop's hand:*] of the tenement called Moylis tenement

and the aforesaid **lady of the manor** then holds another **piece of land called SOLEFIELD** lying near the lane there called Seyleys lane east, the same lady's land and the said John Bishop's land north and near Gilbert Shereve's land south and it contains *4 acres, a half and 4 dayworks*

Total is: *16 acres, 3 rods and 3 dayworks,*
thus 6d. farthing for an acre and 1d. more in all and 1d. three farthings for 5 acres, 1 rod, 7 dayworks in relief and then they owe the lord 5 pigs each year and 3 acres, 1 and a half rods except 2 dayworks, to one pig

---

HAMENETT'S TENEMENT

Margin: right hand: *they then hold 4 acres, 3 rods, 4 and a half dayworks, thus 2s.6d. each year and 1 pig and a fourth part of 1 leg of pork* left hand: *Hamenet's tenement 12s.1d.*

Gilbert Shereve and his associates as written below hold one tenement formerly of Walter Hamenett, now called **HAMENETT'S** tenement and thence they owe the lord 2s.6d. each year in rent and 21d. at the feast of St Andrew the apostle in aid and 80 small works, price of each work half a penny and 16 great works, price of each work 2d. and they must plough one acre during Winter and one acre during Lent price 12d. as above and they owe one carrying service price 4d. and in Autumn 3 boon works with two men price 6d.

Then the abovesaid **Gilbert** holds **one MESSUAGE in which he dwells with a GARDEN and 2 PIECES OF LAND** lying side by side near the lane there called Seyleys lane and Berghwys lane towards the east and south, the lady of the manor's land and land lately of Thomas May [and of] John Symond senior towards the west and the said lady of the manor's land called the Solefield towards the north and it contains *3 acres, a half and 2 dayworks*

and then **he holds** one [un-named] **PIECE OF LAND** adjoining John Carslake's land called Hamenetts towards the east, John Bishop's land and the same Gilbert's land towards the west, Joan Frutor's land towards the north and the said John Bishop's land towards the south [written above: *now Som'*] and it contains *1 acre, 1 rod, 2 and a half dayworks*

Folio 50 Margin: right hand: *she holds 1 acre a half and 1 daywork thence 9d. farthing each year 1 quarter of a pig and a half leg of pork*

Joan Frutor then holds [written above: *now Henry Kane now Ste Somer*] **one piece of land called THE CROFT AT HAMMETTS** and it lies near John Carslake's land called Hammetts towards the east, Gilbert Shereve's land towards the south, John Bishop's land towards the west and near the lane there called Berghwis lane towards the north and it contains *one acre, a half and 1 daywork*

Margin: right hand: *he holds 4 acres, a half 6 and a half dayworks thus 2s.5d. each year and 1 pig*

John Carslake then holds [written above: *now the heirs of John Reynold*] **3 pieces of land lying side by side called HAMENETTS with one small water meadow** adjoining to John Goding's land at Mayny street and Peter Fromond's land towards the east, Gilbert Shereve's land and the said Joan Frutor's land towards the west, John Goding's land and the common way there called Maynystreet towards the north and the same John Carslake's land called the Broadfield and John Bishop's land towards the south and it contains *4 acres, a half, 6 and a half dayworks*

Margin: right hand: *she holds 5 acres, 1 rod, 4 and a half dayworks thus 2s.9d. each year and 1 pig, 1 leg of pork and a fourth part of 1 leg of pork*

Alice formerly Peter Fromond's wife then holds **one piece of land called SHORSACRE** lying near John Goding's land called Cochmoris towards the east, John Carslake's land towards the west, the lady Margaret Fromond's land, the same Alice's land and the aforesaid John Carslake's land towards the south, and the land of the aforesaid John Carslake, aforesaid Alice's land and land of John Goding called Maynys meade towards the north and it contains *4 acres, 1 rod, except 1 and a quarter perches*

and then **she holds one piece of land and pasture called THE BROOK** lying near the said John Goding's land towards the east and north, the same Alice's land called the Hellys towards the south and land of the said John Carslake called Hamenetts towards the west and it contains *one acre, 4 and a half dayworks*

John Goding holds there [written above: *now Thomas Reynolds*] **one piece of land called MANYSFIELD** at Maynystreet lying near the aforesaid John's land towards the east, John Carslake's land and the lane there towards the west, near land lately of Peter Fromond and of the said John Carslake towards the south and a certain lane there leading to land formerly of John Bishop called Blackmanys and the same John Goding's land **Folio 51** towards the north and it contains *3 acres* (f.51), *3 rods*

(Margin: right hand: *he holds 7 acres and a half daywork there, thus 3s.7d. three farthings and 1 pig and half each year*)

and **he holds one meadow called MAYNYS MEADE** there lying near the said John Goding's land towards the east, the same John Goding's land and land lately of Peter Fromond towards the west, land lately of John Bishop called Blackmaynes towards the

157

north and land lately of the aforesaid Peter Fromond towards the south and it contains *2 acres and 8 dayworks*

and **he holds 2 pieces of land** there lying side by side, **called THE BROOKS** adjoining Peter Fisher's land and lately of Thomas Fromond of Goldhill, Watte Hamenettes towards the east and the same John Goding's land and land lately of Peter Fromond towards the west and land of the same John Goding called Cochmoris towards the north and the said Thomas Fromond's land south and it contains *1 acre and 2 and a half dayworks*

Total is: *24 acres, 1 rod and 7 dayworks,*
thus 6d. farthing for an acre and 1d. less in all and they owe 5 pigs each year and in relief 1d. farthing for four acres and for 4 acres, a half, 7 and a half dayworks and less half a daywork in all

---

MOYLES TENEMENT

Margin: right hand: t*hey holds 4 and a half acres and 7 dayworks, thus 3s.4d. each year*
left hand: *Moylys tenement 12s.7d.*

Lawrence Farman [written above: *now Reynolds*] **and his associates** as written below hold one tenement formerly of William Nowell, now called **MOYLES** tenement and thence they shall owe 3s. to the lord of the manor in rent and 21d. in aid at the feast of St Andrew the apostle and 80 small works, price of each work half a penny and 16 great works, price 2d. for a work and they must plough 1 acre of land in Winter and 1 acre during Lent, price 12d. as above and in Autumn they shall owe 3 boon works with two men price 6d. and they shall owe one carrying service price 4d.

Thence the abovesaid **Lawrence** holds **one piece of land called BLACKMANS** lying near the land lately of John Bishop called Great Blackmans tenement towards the east, near the tenement lately of Gilbert Shereve, now of John Symond junior towards the north, towards a lane there called Seyleys lane on the west and towards another lane there leading from John Goding's land called Maynys meade and another [lane] towards the south and it contains *4 acres and 7 dayworks.*

Folio 52

Margin: right hand: 1) *John Symond senior then holds 2 and a half acres and 6 dayworks, thus 22d. each year* 2) *John Symond junior holds 4 acres of land, thus he owes 2s.9d. and a half pence each year* left hand: *now John Bland*

John Symond senior of Palmer street then holds [written above: *now Walter Trice*] **one MESSUAGE with a GARDEN and TWO PIECES OF LAND adjoining, called SEYLYS,** lying near Henry Hexstall's land towards the east, near the highway there leading from Hadlow street as far as Tonbridge towards the north, near the small water meadow there formerly of Gilbert Shereve south, towards the lane there called Seylys lane towards the west and it contains *2 and a half acres and 5 dayworks* [written above: *John Fromond junior holds, now Somer*]

and then **he holds 2** [un-named] **PIECES OF LAND** adjoining in the same way with one small water meadow, adjoining lately of Gilbert Shereve called the Valtys, adjoining land lately of John Bishop called Blackmans and Henry Hexstall's land east, to the lane there called Seylys lane towards the west, land of John Symond senior called Seyleys towards the north, Lawrence Farman's land towards the south and it contains *4 acres* of land

Margin: right hand: s*he holds 1 acre, 1 and a half dayworks, thus 8d. and a half each year*

Joan Frutor then holds [written above: *now Walter Trice*] **one piece of land and pasture called MOYLIS BROOK** lying near Matilda Broker's land called Blackmans brook towards the east, Henry Hexstall's land towards the west, the land of the aforesaid Henry and Nicholas Beacher's land towards the north and land lately of John called the Blackmans field towards the south and it contains *1 acre and 1 daywork.*

Margin: right hand: 1) *he holds 3acres, a half and 5 and a half dayworks, thus 2s.7d. farthing each year* 2) *6d.*

Henry Hexstall then holds [written above: *now Thomas Somer*] in **one piece of land called CROCHLAND** lying next to the cross called Palmer street cross, land lately of William Burdon, now of Nicholas Beacher towards the east, land of John Symond senior called Seylyes towards the west, the highway there leading from Hadlow street as far as Tonbridge towards the north, land of the same Henry and Joan Frutor's land towards the south and it contains *3 acres except 1 and a half dayworks*

and then **he holds** one [un-named] **SMALL WATER MEADOW** adjoining on the south part of the said piece of land called Crouchland [written above: *now John Roberde*] and it contains *a half acre and 8 dayworks*

Folio 53   Margin: right hand: *she holds 2 acres of land, thus 16d. three farthings each year*

The lady of the manor then holds [written above: *now Thomas Reynald*] in a **piece of land** lately of John Bishop **called GREAT BLAKMANSFIELD** of the aforesaid tenement, lying on the west part of the same piece that is of the small water meadow of the aforesaid Lawrence Farman and of the said John Symond junior called les Valtis and she holds *2 acres* of land

Total is: *18 acres and 1 daywork*

thus 8d. farthing for each an acre and more in all 2 and a half pence and a half penny in relief for 1 acre

---

CROCHLAND TENEMENT   Margin: right hand: *he holds 2 acres and 1 rod and 8 dayworks, thus 10d. each year*

left hand: *Crouchland 2s. each year*

Henry Hexstall [written above: *now R Somer*] and Nicholas Beacher hold the whole tenement formerly of John Attcrouch called **CROCHLAND** and they then owe the lord 2s. each year in rent.

Thence the aforesaid **Henry** holds in a [un-named] **PIECE OF LAND** there lying next to the cross called Palmer street cross lying in length near land formerly of William Burden, now of the aforesaid Nicholas towards the east, the same Henry's land in the same piece of land towards the west, the highway there north and it contains *2 acres, 1 rod and   8 dayworks*

Margin: right hand: *he holds 3 and a half acres, 2 dayworks, thus 14d. each year*

Nicholas Becher then holds [written above: *now Walter Trice*] **one piece of land called CROUCHLAND** formerly of Walter Burden adjoining to land formerly of the said William called the Rowe, now of John Carter's heirs, to Joan Frutor's land, Robert Burden's land called Stonyfield towards the east, the said Henry's land of the same tenement towards the west, to the highway there towards the north, to land of Matilda Broker and to Joan Frutor's land south and it contains *3 and a half acres, 2 dayworks*

Total then is: *6 acres*

thus 4d. for an acre each year and then in relief a half penny for each acre

---

BLACKMANS TENEMENT   Margin: left hand: *Blackmans tenement 13s. 8d.*

John Goding [written above: *now Reinaldes*] **and his associates** hold one tenement formerly of Ivo at Longfrith, now called **BLACKMANS** tenement and for this they shall owe the lord 3s. each year in rent and 21d. at the feast of St Andrew the apostle in

Folio 54   aid and they shall plough and harrow half an acre in (f.54) Winter and half an acre during Lent, price 6d as above and a hundred small works price of each work a half penny and twenty great works, price of each work 2d. and 3 boon works with two men price 6d. and one carrying service 3d.

Thence the abovesaid **John Goding** holds **one piece of land** formerly of John Symond senior **called COCHMORIS** lying near Peter Fisher's land towards the east, the same John Goding's land called Mansmeade towards the west, near land lately of Agnes Pulter and land lately of John Bishop called Blackmans land towards the north and near the same John Goding's land called the Brooks and the said Peter Fisher's land towards the south and it contains *2 and a half acres, 4 dayworks*

Margin: right hand: 1) *he then holds 2 acres, 2 dayworks, thus each year* [blank] 2) *and thence he owes 1 quarter of a pig and a half*

Peter Fisher then holds **2** [un-named] **PARCELS OF LAND** lying side by side with a certain lane pertaining to the same, leading from a way there called the New way towards the east, lying near John Goding's land towards the west, the piece of land and pasture of the same Peter towards the south, the same Peter's land from the lord of Peckham in Hadlow and the aforesaid way called the New way towards the east, Peter Fromond's land and land of Matilda Broker, lately of William Beald north and it contains *2 acres and 2 dayworks*

Margin: right hand: *he holds 6 acres, 5 and a half dayworks, thus 3s.4d. each year and he owes 1 pig and 1 quarter*

John Umfrey [written above: *now Reinaldes*] then holds **one** [un-named] **PIECE OF LAND,** formerly of Agnes Pulter lying near Matilda Broker's land towards the east and north, land lately of John Bishop called Blackmans field towards the west, the said John Goding's land called Cochmoris towards the south and it contains *6 acres, 5 dayworks*

Margin: right hand: *she holds 8 acres, 1 and a half rods, thus 4s.6d. and a half each year and she thus owes 1 half pig and 1 leg of pork and a half*

Matilda Broker [written above: *now Reynolds*] then holds **one piece of arable land called THE BLACKMANSFIELD** lying near land lately of Peter Fromond towards the east, land lately of Agnes Pulter, now of John Humphrey towards the west (f.55) and to the same Matilda's land towards the north, land lately of Peter Fisher towards the south and it contains *3 acres, a half, 1 and a half dayworks*

Folio 55

and **she then holds a piece of land called LITTLE BLACKMANYS FIELD** lying near the abovesaid piece of land of the same Matilda towards the south, land lately of Agnes Pulter on the west and the same Matilda's land on the east and north and it contains *1 acre* of land *except 3 and a quarter perches*

and **she then holds** certain **parcels of land there called BLACKMANS BROOK** lying near James Gosse's land towards the east, Joan Frutor's land called Moylesbrook west, land of the said Joan Frutor, of Richard the son and heir of John Carter and Nicholas Becher north, land formerly of the said John Bishop called Blackmans land south and they contain *3 acres, 3 rods, 4 and a half dayworks*

Margin: right hand: *she holds 3 acres except half a daywork, thus 19d. and a half pence each year and she then owes 1 half pig and 1 leg of pork and a half*

Joan Frutor [written above: *now John Usmor's heirs now J Wright's heirs*] then holds **one piece of land called STONYFIELD** adjoining James Gosse's land towards the east, the same Richard Carter's land and lately of Robert Burdon towards the west, to the same Joan Frutor's land on the north and land of Matilda Broker towards the south and it contains *3 acres except half a daywork*

Margin: right hand: *he holds 2 acres, 2 rods and 4 dayworks, thus 17d. and a half pence each year and half a pig and half of a leg of pork*

Richard the son and heir of John Carter [written above: *now the heirs of J Osmor now the heirs of J Wright*] then holds **one piece of land called STONYFIELD** lately of Richard Burdon, lying near Joan Frutor's land towards the east, Nicholas Beacher's land called Church Acres towards the west, the said John (sic - recte Joan) Frutour's land and the said Nicholas's land towards the north and the land of the said Matilda Broker towards the south and it contains *2 acres, 3 rods and 4 dayworks*

Total is: *25 acres* thus 6d. and a half pence for an acre and more, half a penny in all and they shall owe 5 pigs and then 1d. in relief for 4 acres, 6 and a half dayworks except 1 daywork and they shall owe 1 pig for 5 acres

ALEYNSLOVE TENEMENT

Margin: right hand: *they hold 9 acres, 1 rod, 8 dayworks, thus 9d. and a half each year*
left hand: *Aleynslove tenement 2s.1d.*

Nicholas Bourne and his associates hold the whole of one tenement formerly of Alice Parmenter, now called **ALEYNSLOVE** tenement and thence they shall owe 12d. in rent to the lord each year, 10d. and a half pence in aid at the feast of St Andrew the apostle and 3 boon works with one man price 3d.

Folio 56

Thence the aforesaid **Nicholas** then holds 3 [un-named] **PIECES OF LAND** lying side by side at Aleynslove (f.56) Aleyenslove next to the New way, adjoining the acre of land called lords acre and the piece of land called Mannemeade of the same Nicholas towards the east, the aforesaid common way called the New way towards the west, to two pieces of land of the same John called le Strake Thoumedeys meade towards the north, Peter Fromond's land as by right of Alice his wife and Peter Fisher's land towards the south and these lands contain **7 *acres, 6 and a half dayworks***

and **he then holds 1 piece of land called THE MAYNE MEAD** as named before lying near the same man's aforesaid piece of meadow called Thomenedeys meade towards the north, near the aforesaid acre of land called lord's acre towards the south, the running water there called the Bourne towards the east and the same John's land towards the west and it contains *1 acre, 1 rod, 1 daywork*

and **he then holds** another **piece of land called THE STRAKE** lying near the aforesaid piece of meadow called Thomenedeys meade west, the aforesaid common way there called the New way towards the west (sic), land lately of Gilbert Newman towards the north, the aforesaid lands of the same Nicholas south and it contains *one acre and a half daywork*

Margin: right hand: *he holds 2 acres and 2 dayworks, thus 2d. each year*
Peter Fisher [written above: *now John A Barton*] then holds one [un-named] **PIECE OF LAND** lying near the aforesaid common way called the New way towards the west, the said John Carslake's land towards the east and north, land lately of the said Peter Fromond as by right of Alice his wife towards the south and it contains *2 acres and 2 dayworks*

Margin: right hand: *she holds 3 acres, 1 and a half rods, thus 8d. farthing each year*
Alice lately the wife of Peter Fromond [written above: *now Tho Reynold*] then holds **one piece of land called THE REID** lying near the aforesaid [and] the common way towards the east, Matilda Broker's land called Blackmans towards the west and the lane of same Matilda there towards the north and the said Peter Fisher's lane there towards the south and it contains *3 acres, 1 and a half rods*

Margin: right hand: *she holds 1 acre, 3 rods and 1 daywork thus 1d. three farthings each year*
Matilda Broker then holds one [un-named] **PARCEL OF LAND** with a certain lane adjoining to the same, near James Gosse's land towards the east and north, near the land of the same Matilda towards the west and near the land of the said Alice Fromond, lately Peter's wife towards the south and it contains *1 acre, 3 rods and 1 daywork*

Folio 57

Margin: right hand: *he holds 7 acres, 1 rod and 5 dayworks thence 7d. farthing each year*
James Gosse [written above: *now Thomas Reinald*] holds **one piece of land called KINGS FIELD** near the abovesaid common way towards the east, the said Matilda's land towards the west and near a certain lane of the said Matilda towards the south and the same James's land on the north and it contains *3 acres, 1 rod, 1 and a half dayworks*

and **he holds 3 pieces of land lying side by side called ALEYN LOVE**, lying near the abovesaid common way called the New way towards the east, Joan Frutor's land and the said Matilda's land towards the west, the said Joan Frutor's land and the aforesaid common way towards the north, the same James's land called Davysefield and the said Matilda's land called Blackmans brook towards the south and they contain *5 acres, 7 dayworks (and) a half*

Margin: right hand: s*he holds 2 acres thence 2d. each year*
Joan Frutor then holds [written above: *now JohnWright's heirs*] in **a piece of land called**

LEYLAND lying near the common way towards the east, the same Joan's land towards west and north and near the said James Gosse's land south and it contains *2 acres*

Margin: right hand: *she holds 1 acre, thus 1d. each year*
the lady of the manor then holds [written above: *now Henry Fane*] **one acre of land called LORDS ACRE** lying near the water called the Borne towards the east, John Carslake's land and land lately of Peter Fromond towards the west, Thomas Salman's garden [versus north and south - omitted] thence 1d. each year

Total then is: *27 acres and 5 dayworks*,
thus 1d. for an acre and a half penny more in all and in relief a half penny for 4 and a half acres

---

SYMONDS TENEMENT

Margin: right hand: *John Simond then owes 8d. each year* left hand: *8d. each year*
John **SYMOND** of Palmer street senior holds one [un-named] **PARCEL OF LAND** formerly of Nicholas Akerman lying next to Sedgebrooksgate, near the highway there next to Hadlow bourne towards the east, near land of the lady Elizabeth Colepeper for the term of her life called Eastfield, of the manor of Peckham in Hadlow towards the west, near land lately of William Rodle called the Brooks at Hadlow bourne towards the north, near the forstall leading from Hadlow bourne as far as the manor of Peckham aforesaid towards the south and it contains *1 acre, a half except 1 daywork, 2 and a quarter perches*
and he thus owes 8d. each year and he then owes 2d. in relief

Folio 58

Margin: right hand: *he owes 2 hens each year price 2d.* left hand: *for the geld land 2 hens price 2d.*
John Symond of Palmer street senior holds [written above: *now John Edmede*] **one geld land lying in a mill lately situated there called THE MALT MILL** and the geld-land lies in length from the aforesaid mill as far as the piece of land of the lady Elizabeth Colepeper for the term of her life called Hylt meade and to the water there which lately flowed to the aforesaid mill towards the north, to land formerly of William Rodle there called the Brooks towards the south and it contains *half an acre*
and he thus owed 2 hens each year price 2d. and then nothing in relief

---

PAYNES TENEMENT

Margin: right hand: *they hold 9 and a half acres and 8 dayworks, thus they owe 3s.2d. each year* left hand: *Paynes tenement 13s.10d.*
John Newman maltster and his associates as written below hold the whole tenement formerly of Simon Payne, now called **PAYNES** tenement and for this they shall owe the lord 15d. each year in rent and 21d. in aid at the feast of St Andrew the apostle and 3 boon works with two men in Autumn price 6d., deduction having been made for food and twenty small works, price of each work a half penny and 24 great works, price of each work 2d. and they shall owe one carrying service price 4d. and they must plough one acre during Lent and they shall harrow and they shall receive 4 loaves price 2d. and 8 herrings price 1d for each acre and 8 herrings price 1d. and the value of the work of 2 acres is 12d., deduction having been made for food as above.

Then the abovesaid **John** holds **one piece of land called TEYNTESFIELD** adjoining the lady of the manor's land of the same tenement towards the east, James Gosse's land towards the west, land lately of John Ninge in the Borne and the same John's land called Bramblefield on the north, the highway there leading from Hadlow bourne as far as Little loamwood towards the south and it contains *2 acres and 3 rods*

and **he then holds** an aforesaid **parcel of land called BRAMBLE FIELD**, near the aforesaid land, formerly of the said John Ninge called Hobbeilottes west, the same John Newman's land called the Ketehammie towards the north, James's land and the same John

Newman's land called Tentefield south and it contains *6 acres, 3 rods and 8 dayworks*

Margin: right hand: *he holds 1 and a half acres, 8 and a half dayworks, thence 6d. each year*

John Nynge son of John then holds [written above: *now Walter Trice*] in **a piece of land called THE BORNE**, lying near the lady of the manor's land of the same tenement in the said piece of land on the east, land of the said John Newman maltster called Bramblefield towards the west, land of the same John Newman called Teyntefield towards the south, land of Hadlow rectory the north and it contains *1 and a half acres, 8 and a half dayworks*

Folio 59 Margin: right hand: *he holds 4 acres, 1 rod, 1 and a half dayworks, thus 17d. each year*

James Gosse holds [written above: *now John Kegon, now Keble*] in **two pieces of land lying side by side called WESTMANLAND and the THREE HERNYN CROFTS**, adjoining to land of the said John Newman maltster called Teyntfield towards the east, the same John Newman's land called Bramblefield, to land lately of John Nynge called Hobbeilotts towards the north, to the highway there leading from Hadlow borne towards Little loamwood towards the south and west and it contains *4 acres, 1 rod, 1 and a half dayworks*

Margin: right hand: *he then holds twenty acres of land, 8 and a half dayworks thus 6s. 8d. each year*

Hugh Nynge then holds [written above: *now the heirs of Richard Keble*] **4 pieces of land lying side by side called TUBBYNGS FIELD** and **HOBBEIELOTTS, KETEHAM** and **CROYDONSFIELD** adjoining the said John Newman's lands, James Gosse's land and to the highway there leading from Hadlow bourne as far as Little loamwood towards the south and to the said highway and to the messuage of John Newman labourer and to Alice Palmer's land towards the west. Thence he holds *5 acres except 1 daywork* in a piece of land called **KETEHAMME**; in a piece of land in **HOBBEILOTTS** [written above: *now John Kigon*] *3 acres, 1 and a half rods*; in **TUBBINGSFIELD** *5 acres a half and 6 dayworks*; in **CROYDONS FIELD** *6 acres, 8 and a half dayworks*

Margin: right hand: *he holds half an acre and 2 dayworks thence 2d. each year*

John Newman labourer holds there [written above: *now Richard Keble's heirs*] **one MESSUAGE with a garden and a small piece of land adjoining to a piece of land called CROYDONSFIELD** as abovesaid towards the east, to the highway there leading from Hadlow bourne as far as Little loamwood towards the west, land lately of Gilbert Newman called Gilbertsfield towards the north and to Alice Palmer's land towards the south and it contains *half an acre and 2 dayworks*

Margin: right hand: *she holds half an acre and 8 dayworks, thus 3d. each year*

Alice Palmer holds [written above: *now the heirs of Richard Keble*] **one** [un-named] **SMALL PARCEL OF LAND** lying near land called Croydons field towards the east and south, the abovesaid highway leading from Little loamwood towards the west and the land of the said John Newman labourer towards the north and it contains *half an acre and 8 dayworks*

Folio 60 Margin: right hand: *she then holds 5 acres and 3 dayworks, thus 20d. each year*

The lady of the manor then holds [written above: *now Walter Trice*] in **a piece of land called THE BORNE** adjoining to the rectory's land there towards the east and north, land of John Nynge son of John, in the same piece towards the west and the said lady's land towards the south and it contains *2 and a half acres*

and **she then holds one** [un-named] **PIECE OF LAND** lying near the said John Nynge's land called Mill land towards the east, land of John Newman maltster called Teyntefield towards the west, the said lady's land called the Borne towards the north, the highway leading from Hadlow bourne as far as Little loamwood towards the south and it contains *2 acres, a half, 4 dayworks*

Total is: *42 acres, 9 and a half dayworks,* thus 4d. for an acres and in all 2d. more

**FLETCHERS
TENEMENT**

Margin: right hand: *they hold 24 and a half acres, 2 dayworks, 1 and a half perches*, thus 3s.5d. *each year* left hand: *Fletchers tenement 7s.3d.*

Richard Colepeper esquire and his associates as written below hold their whole tenement formerly of Richard Fletcher called **FLETCHERS** tenement and they shall then owe the lord 4s. each year in rent and 21d. in aid at the feast of St Andrew the apostle and they shall plough and shall harrow 2 acres of land price 7d. as above and they shall receive as above and they shall owe three boon works with two men price 6d.

Thence the above named **Richard Colepeper** then holds **one garden, one piece of land called MEDFIELD with the FORSTALL** adjoining the same next to Little loamwood, called William Fromonds, **one meadow called FROMONDS MEADE and one piece of land and meadow called LORCOCKS MEADE**, adjoining to the common way called Little loamwood, to land lately of Gilbert Newman called the field afore Newmans gate, to the said Elizabeth Colepeper's land for the term of her life called the Mill bourne and the old Mill pond towards the east, to a certain lane leading to the meadow called Christs meades and to a meadow called Fechetts meade, now of John Wybarne esquire towards the west, to the land of the demesne of West Peckham pertaining to the manor of Mereworth towards the north and to the running water there called the Bourne towards the south and it contains *24 and a half acres, 2 dayworks, 1 and a half perches,*

thus in the aforesaid **GARDEN** *2 acres, 1 rod and 1 daywork, 1 quarter, 1 perch* and in the **MEDFIELD** with the FORSTALL *8 acres, a half except 1 daywork, a half perch and half a quarter*, in **LORCOCKS MEADE** *3 acres, a half and 4 dayworks* and in **FROMONDS MEADE** *10 acres and 8 dayworks*

Folio 61

Margin: right hand: *she holds 4 acres, a half, 3 perches, a half and 1 quarter of land thus 7d. and a half pence each year*

The lady Elizabeth Colepeper then holds [written above: *now Cottons*] for the term of her life **one piece of land called THE MILL BOURNE** adjoining to land lately of Gilbert Newman and land lately of John More senior called Croydon towards the west, to Richard Colepeper's land called Fromonde towards the north and land lately of John More senior towards the south and a certain bridge now leading to the same piece of land from the highway there, *4 and a half acres, 3 and three perches, a half and 1 quarter.*

Margin: right hand: *he holds 4 acres, a half, 7 dayworks, a half and half a perch, thus 8d. each year*

Richard the son and heir of John Carter of Sele holds **one MESSUAGE with a piece of land adjoining**, formerly of the said John More **called CROYDONS**, lying near the highway there leading from Hadlow bourne as far as Little loamwood towards the east, the pond of the mill called the corn mill towards the west, the said lady Elizabeth Colepeper's land called the mill bourne and the lane leading to the aforesaid mill bourne towards the north to the lane leading to the abovesaid mill called the corn mill towards the south and it contains *3 and a half acres, half a daywork and half a perch*

and **he then holds** one [un-named] **PIECE OF LAND** lying near the aforesaid highway towards the east, near the said lady Elizabeth's land called the mill bourne towards the west and near the land lately of Gilbert Newman called the field afore Newmans gate towards the north and near the aforesaid lane leading to the aforesaid piece of land called the mill bourne towards the south and it contains *1 acre, a half and 8 dayworks*

Margin: right hand: *he holds 8 acres, a half and 7 dayworks, thus 14d. and a half pence each year* left hand: *John Kigon holds the Waterships, thus 5d. and a half pence each year*

John Newman maltster (written above: *now John Richard Somer holds 5 and a half acres and 9d. each year*) then holds **one piece of land called THE FIELD AFORE NEWMANS GATE** lying near the aforesaid highway towards the east, land of Richard Colepeper esquire and the aforesaid lady Elizabeth's land called the mill bourne towards the west, the common called Little loamwood towards the north, land of Richard Carter son and heir of John Carter south and it contains *5 acres and 9 dayworks*

and **he then holds** a **piece of land called THE WATERSHIPS** lying near William Parrocke's messuage north, near the water there, which lately flowed from the cornmill as far as the maltmill south and west and the highway leading from Hadlow lane as far as Little loamwood east and it contains *3 acres, 1 rod and 8 dayworks*

Folio 62 Margin: right hand: *he holds 9 and a half acres and half a daywork, thus 16d. each year*
John At Stable then holds [written above: *now John Kigen, now Keble*] **one MESSUAGE with lands adjoining** lately of William Parrocke **formerly called BROMPTONYS** lying near the aforesaid way leading towards Little loamwood towards the east, near the running water there from the aforesaid cornmill towards the west, near a certain lane there leading to the aforesaid mill called the cornmill towards the north, to land of the said John Newman maltster called Watership towards the south and it contains *9 acres, a half and half a daywork*

Total of acres is then: *51 acres, 3 rods, 3 dayworks,*
a half, thus 1d. and a half pence and a half farthing and in all 2d. and a half more and in relief three farthings for 3 acres, 1 rod

---

GIBBONS TENEMENT

Margin: right hand: *Nicholas Stopersfield then holds 33 acres, 7 and a half dayworks and 1 perch, thus 21d. each year* left hand: *Gibbons tenement 2s.6d. and a half*
The tenants of a tenement formerly of John son of Hamo Fromond [written above: *now William Whetenhall now Dorbell*] called **GIBBONS** tenement hold half a ferling of land and they then owe 18d. to the lord each year in rent and 10d. and a half pence in aid at the feast of St Andrew the apostle and they owe 3 boon works with one man price 3d.

Thence Nicholas Stopersfield holds **one MESSUAGE in which he lives with a garden and 8 pieces of land adjoining, together with two pieces of land adjoining** lately of John Martin, **called GIBBONS**, lying near the highway there leading from Tonbridge as far as West Malling east, land lately of Gilbert Newman called the Broadfield, land lately of John Salman and land lately of the said Gilbert called the fullersfield, the rectory's land there and the house of the vicarage towards the south and it contains *33 acres, 7 dayworks, a half and 1 perch in all.*

Thus there are *6 acres, 1 rod, 6 and a half dayworks* in the aforesaid 2 pieces of land lately of John Martyn, and **William Hogett** still holds there *1 acre* on which **A BARN** has been built next to the vicarage

Margin: right hand: *they hold 16 acres, 1 rod and 8 dayworks, thus 10d. and a half each year* below: *now John*
Gilbert Newman's heirs then hold (written above: *now Richard Newman's heirs 7 acres, 4d. and a half pence each year*) **one piece of land called KETHAM with one grove**, adjoining to the rectory's land there towards the east, land lately of the said Gilbert and Hugh Nynge's land west, land lately of the said Gilbert called the fullersfield north and land lately of the said Gilbert called Bramblesfield south and it contains *8 acres and 9 dayworks*

Folio 63 and **they then hold** (f.63) (Margin: right hand: *Richard Somer holds 9 acres, 1 rod,   8 dayworks 6d. each year*) **one piece of land called FULLERSFIELD** lying near Nicholas Stopersfield's land towards the east, land lately of the said Gilbert towards the west, the said Nicholas's land and land lately of John Salman towards the north, land lately of the said Gilbert called Kethamme towards the south and it contains *8 acres, 9 dayworks*

Total of acres is: *48 and a half acres, 5 dayworks and 1 perch,*
thus half a penny, half a farthing each year and in all 1d. and half a farthing more

---

PECKHAM'S TENEMENT

Margin: right hand: 1) *14d.* 2) *2s.8d.*
Richard Colepeper esquire [written above: *Cotton*] holds the whole of one tenement

formerly of Thomas **PECKHAM** lying in an ancient park, thence each year he owes 14d. for two ploughshares

and the said **Richard Colepeper holds with Joan Brewer** the whole of one tenement in the new park, formerly of William Gifferey and lately of Richard son of John Palmer, as is shown in an ancient rental. Thence he then owes the lord 20d. in rent each year and 6d. in aid and 3 boon works with 1 man price 3d. and 8d. for one ploughshare

---

SEWAYNE TENEMENT

Margin: left hand: *Sewayne, Richard Nepaker 2s.*

Richard Nepaker [written above: *sometime Richard Broke now George Moulton*] holds the whole land called **SEWAYNE**, formerly of John, son of Hamo Fromond lying next to the **LAWDAY PLACE OF HADLOW**, near land lately of John Mounssy, now of John Eliott towards the east, the common called loamwood and the same Richard's garden towards the west, the said place called Lawday place and the aforesaid common towards the north and the same Richard's garden south and it contains *3 acres, 3 rods,* 2 *dayworks*

and he then owes 8d. each year in rent and 2d. in aid at the feast of St Andrew the apostle and for 2 ploughshares price 14d.

Total of acres is: *3 acres, 3 rods and 2 dayworks*, thus 6d. and a half pence for an acre and in all a farthing and a half more and he then owes 2d. in relief for an acre, 3 rods and 6 dayworks 1d.

Folio 64
HONEWOLD'S TENEMENT

Margin: right hand: *hey hold 1 acre thus 1d. and a half pence and a half farthing each year*   left hand: *Honewold 4s. 3d. and a half pence*

The tenants of the tenement formerly Akerman [written above: *Richard Broke now George Moulton*] now called **HONEWOLDS** tenement, thence they owe the lord 3s. each year in rent and 10d. and a half pence at the feast of St Andrew the apostle and 3 boon works with two men price 2s.6d.

Thence the aforesaid **Richard Nepaker of loamwood** then holds **one MESSUAGE in which he dwells**, formerly of Nicholas Edward, adjoining to John Pelsounte's lands towards the east and south, to the common called loamwood and to the same Richard's piece of land called Swaynesland towards the north, to the aforesaid common towards the west and it contains *1 acre*

Margin: right hand: 1) *he holds 8 and a half acres except 1 daywork and 2 perches*   2) *the full total of the said John Pelsount is 13 acres, 1 rod, 3 and a half dayworks 21d. and a half pence each year*

John Pelsounte then holds [written above: *the aforesaid RB now George Moulton*] **2 pieces of land lying side by side called BRAMBLESFIELD and THE LONGFIELD** lying near the same John Pelsounte's land towards the east, the highway leading from Hadlow street as far as West Malling towards the west, near Richard Nepaker's messuage towards the north and the same John Pelsounte's land and the messuage lately of Robert Crakebenne towards the south and it contains *8 and a half acres, except 1 daywork and 2 feet*.

Item **he holds** another **piece of land lying there called TUBBINGES** lately of John Osbarne lying near the same John Pelsounte's piece of land towards the west and north, near the highway leading from Dorants cross as far as Goldhill towards the south and it contains *2 and a half acres except one perch*.

Item **he holds** another [un-named] **PIECE OF LAND** of the same tenement and it lies near the aforesaid piece of land lately of the said John Osbarne towards the east, near land lately of the said Robert Crakebenne west, the said John Pelsounte's land north and near the highway there leading from Dorants cross as far as Goldhill south and it contains

2 acres, 1 rod, 3 and a half dayworks

Margin: right hand: *he holds 2 acres except 2 and a half half perches thus 3d. each year*

John Martyn holds [written above: *R Walter now John Burton*] of the same tenement in **his MESSUAGE in which he lives, with a parcel of GARDEN and a piece of land adjoining** in Hadlow street, adjoining to James Gosse's garden, from the garden now of Thomas Watson, to John A Barton's garden, to the same John Martyn's garden and to the highway east and south, to the garden lately of Roger Newman and land lately of John Nynge towards the west and to Hadlow rectory towards the north and it contains *2 acres, except 2 and a half perches*

Folio 65

Margin: right hand: *he holds 2 acres except a half perch and 1 quarter thus 3d. and half a farthing each year*

John Nynge holds [written above: *John Nyng smith now Walter Trisse*] of the same tenement [a piece of land] **called MILL LAND**, lying near the said John Martyn's land towards the east, the lord's land there towards the west, the land of the said rectory towards the north, near the highway there leading from Hadlow as far as Little loamwood towards the south and it contains *2 acres except a half perch and 1quarter*

Margin: right hand: *he holds half an acre and half a daywork, [he owes] three farthings*

John Osbarne holds [written above: *J. Pery's heirs, now William Solman*] of the same tenement in **a parcel of a MESSUAGE with a garden adjoining**, formerly of Deye, lying near the demesne called Cotmans field towards the east, near the highway there leading from Tonbridge as far as West Malling towards the west, near John Partrich's land towards the north and near Edward More's messuage and the garden of the demesne called the Lord's garden towards the south and it contains *half an acre and a half daywork*

Margin: right hand: *the lady of the manor holds 1 rod in the lady's hand, a farthing*

The lady of the manor holds [written above: *now William Salman's heirs*] of the same tenement **one garden called THE LORD'S GARDEN**, lying near the demesne land called Cotmans field towards the east, near Edward More's messuage towards the west, near John Osbarne's garden towards the north, near the garden formerly of John Akerman, now of J[oan] the wife of John Penyval wife towards the south and it contains *1 rod*

Margin: right hand: *Edward More 2 dayworks, a half (he owes) a farthing*

Edward More holds [written above: *now William Salman*] in **his own MESSUAGE with two houses built upon it**, lying near the aforesaid garden called the Lord's garden towards the east, near the highway there leading from Tonbridge as far as Malling towards the west, near the said John Osbarne's garden towards the north and the garden lately of John Akerman towards the south and it contains *2 dayworks*

Margin: right hand: *Joan Peniale half an acre 5 and a half dayworks, a half penny, a farthing and a half*

Joan the daughter and heir of Thomas Nepaker, now John Peniale's wife, holds (written above: *now of John Lovynden's heirs*) of the same tenement **one MESSUAGE with a garden** adjoining formerly of John Akerman, lying near the demesne land there called Cotmans field towards the east, near the highway there leading from Tonbridge as far as Malling towards the west, near the said garden called the Lord's garden and near the said Edward More's messuage towards the north and near the highway leading from Hadlow street as far as Yalding towards the south and it contains *half an acre, 5 and a half dayworks*

Folio 66

Margin: right hand: *8 acres, 1 rod, 1 and a half dayworks and 13d. and a half pence*

Item **Matilda Broker** holds [written above: *formerly Thomas Lack now Walter Trice*] in **a piece of land called GREAT MAGGINHAM** lying near the meadow of the lady (of the manor) called the Cornmead towards the east and north, near the said Matilda's land in the same piece of land called Cotland towards the south, near lands of Richard

Colepeper esquire and John Bishop's land west and it contains *8 acres, 1 rod, 1 daywork, a half and 1 perch*

Margin: right hand: *and it contains in Blackberrys half an acre, 1 rod and 3 dayworks and in Walleys 2d. farthing or 1d. farthing*

Roger Newman's heirs hold [written above: *formerly J Nynge smith, now W Trice*] of the said tenement **one MESSUAGE with a GARDEN adjoining called BLACKBERRYS** and **one MESSUAGE adjoining, lately of Roger Walley**, adjoining to John Martyn's messuage towards the east, to John Nynge's land and the highway there leading from Hadlow street as far as the mill called the corn mill towards the west and land of the said John Nynge and John Martyn towards the north [omitted – and it contains *half an acre, 1 rod, 3 dayworks*]

Margin: right hand: *3 acres, 3 and a half rods 6d.*

Item **Robert Crakbenne** holds [written above: *once Richard Broke now Moulton*] **one MESSUAGE with a garden and a piece of land** adjoining John Pelsunte's [land - omitted] towards the east and north, near Loamwood common towards the west, near the highway leading from Dorants cross as far as Goldhill towards the south and it contains *3 acres, 3 rods and 5 dayworks except half a perch*

The full total of that tenement is: *32 acres, 1 rod, 6 and a half dayworks*, thus 1d. and a half pence and half a farthing for each acre and in relief 1d. and half a farthing for 3 acres

---

COIFFE'S TENEMENT

Margin: right hand: *they hold 1 acre, thus 8d. each year* left hand: *John Coiffe's tenement 16d. each year*

The tenants of the tenement formerly of **John COIFFE** owe the lord 8d. each year in rent and a plough share price 8d. [written above: *Once Nicholas sometime J Borne*]

Thence **Nicholas Stoperfield** holds *1 acre* of land lying in a piece of land called **THE ELSTEMS**, near the land of the same Nicholas towards the east and north, near John Partriche's land towards the west, near the demesne land there called Cotmans field towards the south

Margin: right hand: *he holds 1 acre thus 8d. each year*

John Partriche then holds [written above: *lately J Pery's heirs, now W Salmon*] **one acre** in a [un-named] **PIECE OF LAND** of the same John lying near the said Nicholas's lands toward the east and north near the same John Partriche's land towards the south and near the highway leading from Hadlow Street towards West Malling [west - omitted] and it contains as above

Total of acres is : *2* [acres]
thence 8d. each year for each acre and in relief they owe 1d. for 1 acre [note at left hand: side: *they do not owe relief*]

It is not clear to which tenement the following six pieces belong

Margin: right hand: *he holds 1 rod of meadow 3 hens price 3d.* left hand: *3 hens price 3d.*

Nicholas Stoperfield holds [written above: Farmare: *in the lord's hand*] *1 rod* of land and meadow in the demesne meadow called the **COURTMEADE** once of Richard Beale as it shown in the ancient rental, lying near the demesne meadow there called More Courtmeade towards the east and north, near the running water there called the bourne towards the west and south and he then owes 3 hens each year, price 3d., as is shown etc.

Margin: right hand: *he holds 3 acres, 3 rods except 1 daywork, a half and a 4ᵀᴴ part of 1 perch thus 1d. and a half pence each year* left hand: *John Newman 1d. and a half pence*

John Newman maltster holds [written above: *now Richard Newman's heirs*] **one MESSUAGE with a piece of land and meadow adjoining called SMITH'S LAND** in the ancient rental and he owes 1d. and a half pence in aid at the feast of St

Andrew the apostle and at his own cost he shall make the iron work for 1 plough using thelord's iron and he must enclose Morton close which belongs to the lord and it contains *3 acres, 3 rods except 1 daywork, a half and a fourth part of 1 perch*

Margin: right hand: *and she owes then 1d. each year in rent*

Matilda Broker holds [written above: *sometime T Somer now Walter Trice*] **one MESSUAGE in which she lives**, once of Gilbert Kempe and formerly of Richard White as is shown in an ancient rental, which lies near the demesne land called Napilton towards the east, near John Somer's messuage and John Herbarde's shop towards the south, near the highway there leading from Tonbridge as far as West Malling towards the west and near the highway leading from Hadlow street towards Yalding towards the north and it contains [blank]

Margin: right hand: *3d. each year*   left hand: *John Somer, Henry Hexstall, John Herbarde 3d. each year*

John Somer and **John Herbarde** and **Henry Hexstall** hold [written above: *now Nicholas Somer*] one tenement formerly of John son of Hamo Fromond, that is, **one MESSUAGE** formerly of Adam Saunder and they shall then owe 3d. in rent each year and it lies near the common way leading to Hadlow church towards the west, near the demesne land called Napilton towards the east, near Matilda Broker's land towards the north, Henry Hexstall's messuage called the lord's place towards the south and it contains [blank].

Thence **John** holds [written above: *now Walter Trice*] **one SHOP with a small garden** adjoining on the north part of the said John Somer's messuage and it contains [blank].

Now **John Somer** and **Henry Hexstall** then hold **one SHOP** and it contains [blank]

Total is: [blank]
and they shall then owe 1d. and a half pence in relief

Folio 68
COSWYNS TENEMENT

Margin: right hand: *Nicholas Borne then holds 3 acres except 3 perches, thus 15d. each year*   left hand: *Coswyns tenement 13s.6d.*

The tenants of the tenement formerly of John Crouche now called **COSWYNS** tenement and they shall owe 16d. each year to the lord in rent for this and 21d. in aid at the feast of St Andrew the apostle and 3 boon works with two men in Autumn, price 6d., deduction having been made for food and 120 small works, price of each work half a penny and 24 great works, price of each work 2d. and they shall owe one carrying service, price 4d. and they must plough one acre in Winter and one acre during Lent and they shall harrow and they shall have 4 loaves, price 2d. for each acre and 8 herrings, price 1d. and the work of two acres, deduction having been made for food, is worth 12d.

Nicholas Borne then holds in **a piece of land called BOUNDSFIELD** lately purchased of the lady Margaret Fromond, **otherwise called MORE BRECKLESHAM** lying near the land lately of Richard Nepaker towards the east, the lane there called Bounds lane towards the north and west, near the same Nicholas's land in the same piece of land towards the south and it contains *3 acres except 3 perches*

Margin: right hand: *2 acres and 8 dayworks*

William Nepaker then holds [written above: *sometime J Hale now Walter Trice*] **one MESSUAGE in which he dwells with a garden and piece of land adjoining called THE LEE**, lying near the same William's lands towards the east and west, near the same William's lands called Wibornland towards the south, near the same William's land and the lane leading from Dorants cross as far as Goldhill and to the garden called Hamonds garden towards the north and it contains *2 acres and 8 dayworks*

Margin: right hand: *2 acres, 1 rod, 6 and a half dayworks*

The same **William** then holds **one** [un-named] **PIECE OF LAND** lying near Agnes Nepaker's land towards the [east - omitted] and north, near the same William's land south and west and it contains *2 acres, 1 rod, 6 and a half dayworks*

Margin: right hand: *3 acres, 3 rods, 1 and a half dayworks*
Item he then holds **one** [un-named] **PIECE OF LAND** lying near the same William's messuage and near his lands towards the east, near lands called Dorants and Elstens towards the west, near the aforesaid land called Dorants and the same William's land towards the north and the aforesaid land called Elstens towards the south and it contains *3 acres, 3 rods, 1 and a half dayworks*

Margin: right hand: *he holds 3 and a half acres and 4 dayworks*
Item **he holds** then **two** [un-named] **PIECES OF LAND** there lying together at the lane there leading to the same William's dwelling house towards the east, near the aforesaid land called Dorants towards the west, the same William's lands towards the south, the highway there leading from Dorants cross as far as Goldhill towards the north and it contains *3 acres, a half and 4 dayworks*

Margin: right hand: *he holds 3 rods, 8 dayworks 5.d*
And he holds [written above: *formerly J Borne now T Borne*] **one** [un-named] **PIECE OF LAND** next to Robards plain, lying near the lane called Bowdys lane towards the north and it contains *3 rods and 8 dayworks* of land

Margin: right hand: *and the 3 rods & 8 dayworks to John Aborne as is belowe written*
Folio 69   **Total of the acres of the said William Nepaker is:** *12 acres, 3 rods, 8 dayworks* in all, thus 5s.1d. each year for these

Margin: right hand: *John Goding then holds 2 acres, 1 and a half dayworks, thus 10d. each year*
John Goding then holds [written above: *once J now Thomas Borne*] **one piece of land** lately purchased of Richard Nepaker **called BRECKLESHAM** lying near the lane there leading to the same John's land called Harry Fromonds towards the east and north, near two pieces of land called the crofts at Borns stile towards the south, near Nicholas Borne's land towards the west and it contains *2 acres, 1 and a half dayworks*

Margin: right hand: *he holds 8 acres, 3 rods, 4 and a half dayworks, thus 3s.10d. each year*
William Hogett holds [written above: *formerly Nicholaus B now T Borne holds*] **one MESSUAGE and 3 pieces of land adjoining called DORANTS** adjoining to William Nepaker's land towards the east, to the highway there leading from Hadlow street as far as West Malling towards the west and near the highway leading from Dorants cross as far as Goldhill towards the north and near land called the Elstonyls towards the south and it contains *8 acres, 3 rods, 4 and a half dayworks*

Margin: right hand: *he holds 6 acres, 1 daywork, a half and 1 perch, 2s.6d. three farthings and he holds in the same 1 acre of Scharland*
Nicholas Stoperfield then holds [written above: *formerly J B now T Borne*] one piece of land called **ELSTONS** lying near William Nepaker's land towards the east, the same Nicholas's land in the same piece called Scharland and the highway there leading from Hadlow street as far as West Malling towards the west, the said William Nepaker's land and the lands called Dorants north and the demesne land there called Cotmans field and John Partriche's land south and it contains *6 acres, 1 daywork, a half and 1 perch*

Total is: *32 acres, 3 rods and 5 dayworks*,
thus 5d. and half a farthing for each acre and in all three farthings less and they owe half a penny in relief for 4 acres, 8 and a half dayworks

---

HAYMOND'S TENEMENT   Margin: right hand: *they hold 2 acres, a half and 8 dayworks, thus 12d. each year*
left hand: *the tenants of Hamonds 18d.*
The tenants of the tenement of Halpound, formerly of Nicholas Akerman, now called **HAYMONDS** [written above: *formerly Richard Broke now G Moulton*] and thence they shall owe the lord 12d. each year in rent and 3d. in aid at the feast of St Andrew the apostle and 3 boon works with 1 man price 3d.

Thus **John Pelsounte** then holds **one piece of land called the CHURCH'S**

CROFT lying near the same John's land towards the east, west and north and near the highway there leading from Dorants cross as far as Goldhill towards the south and it contains *2 acres and 7 dayworks*

Folio 70

Margin: right hand: *he holds 1 acre, 8 dayworks thus 6d. each year*

Item **William Nepaker** then holds [written above: *John Hale now Walter Trice*] **a parcel of land at HAYMONS WELL** near the lane leading as far as the same William's dwelling house towards the west, near the highway there leading from Dorants cross as far as Goldhill and near the lane called Wilkens lane towards the north and near the same William's land towards the east and south and it contains *1 acre and 8 dayworks*

Margin: right hand: *8 and a half dayworks*

Item he holds then **one** [un-named] **small GARDEN** lying near the same William's land towards the north, south and east and near the aforesaid lane leading to the said William's dwelling house towards the west and it contains *8 and a half dayworks*

Total is: *4 acres, 3 and a half dayworks*
and thus 4d. and a half pence for each acre and then in relief three farthings for an acre

---

RODBARD'S TENEMENT

Margin: right hand: *he holds the whole tenement 21 acres and 2 dayworks called Rodbards tenement, thus he owes 2s. 3d. and a half pence each year* left hand: *Rodbards tenement 2s. 3d. and a half pence. Now John Pelsount holds it*

John Pelsounte holds [written above: *formerly William Richards now G Moulton*] a tenement of the said ferling of land, formerly of Rodbarde now called **RODBARDS** tenement and therefore he owes 8d. each year in rent and 11d. and a half pence in aid at the feast of St Andrew the apostle and 1 ploughshare price 8d.

and the aforesaid tenement lies in **a MESSUAGE with a garden and 8 pieces of land** adjoining, lately of William Nepaker, lying near Nicholas Borne's land called Bownds and land of Richard Nepaker land towards the east, the same Pelsounte's land towards the west, near Richards Nepaker's land and near land lately of John Mounssy towards the north and near the highway there leading from the cross called Dorants cross as far as the lane called Wilkens lane and to Goldhill towards the south and it contains *21 acres, 3 rods and 2 dayworks*

Total is: *21 acres, 3 rods and 2 dayworks*,
thus 1d. farthing for an acre, in all 1d. farthing more and in relief he owes 2d. for the whole

---

Folio 71
HECOTT'S TENEMENT

Margin: right hand: *he holds 3 acres, 1 rod, 5 and a half dayworks, thus he owes 2s. 8d. each year* left hand: *Hecotts tenement 2s. 8d.*

Richard Steyle [holds - omitted] [written above: *J Hale now T Walter*] **certain lands called PARTRICK CLOSE** formerly of Nicholas Akerman and John Hecott now called **HECOTTS** formerly of Andrew Nepaker and he then owes the lord 2s. 8d. in rent each year, lying near lands lately of Richard Wastan towards the east, the said Richard's land towards the west, land of Thomas Wastan's heirs towards the south and the highway there at Rodbards plain towards the north and it contains *3 acres of land, 1 rod, 5 and a half dayworks*

Total of acres is: *3 acres, 1 rod, 5 and a half dayworks*,
thus 9d. and a half pence for an acre and more in all and he owes 8d. in relief for the whole

---

PENDER'S TENEMENT

Margin: right hand: *he holds 4 and a half acres, 2 and a half dayworks, thus 9d. each year* left hand: *Richard Steyle pender 9d. each year*

Item the said **Richard Steyle** holds [written above: *J Hale now the aforesaid T Walter*]

171

certain lands formerly of Renkyn called **PENDER** and he thus owes the lord 9d. each year in rent, lying near the aforesaid land called Hecotts and near the highway there towards the north and east and near the same Richard's land towards the west and south and it contains *4 acres* of land, *a half, 2 and a half dayworks*

Total is: *4 and a half acres, 2 and a half dayworks*, thus 2d. for each acre and then 2d. farthing in relief for the whole

Margin: right hand: *he holds thus 2d. each year* left hand: *Richard Steyle*

The same **Richard Steyle** holds [written above: *J Hale now T Walter*] there *a half acre* of land formerly of John Hecott and he thus owes 2d. each year for a half acre

---

FOSTER'S TENEMENT

Margin: right hand: *they hold 5 acres, 3 rods, 3 dayworks and 3 perches, thus 17d. and a half pence each year* left hand: *Fosters tenement 4s.1d. and a half pence*

The tenants of the tenement formerly of Robert Tubbings [written above: W. *Crysere's heirs now G Moulton*] hold a half ferling of land of Cowpere now called **FOSTERS** tenement and they shall then owe 4s. each year to the lord in rent and 10d. and a half pence in aid at the feast of St Andrew the apostle and 2 hens price 2d. at Christmas as is shown in an ancient rental.

Thence **John Goding** holds in **a piece of land at HARRY FROMONDS** lying near the same John's land in the same piece towards the east, near land there called Fosters field lately of William Simonds carpenter towards the west, near a certain lane there leading to the tenement called Harry Fromonds towards the north and near the demesne land there called Little Groveland towards the south and it contains *5 acres, 3 rods,   3 dayworks and 3 perches*

Folio 72

Margin: right hand: 1) *John Goding 1 and a half acres and 8 dayworks, total 7 acres, 1 daywork and 3 perches in all, thus 22d. each year* 2) *thus 5d. each year* left hand: *John Goding*

Item the same **John Goding** then holds [written above: *formerly J B now T Borne*] **2 pieces of land lying side by side, called THE CROFTS AT BORNE STILE** lately purchased of Richard Nepaker, lying near land lately of the said William Symonds carpenter called Fosters field towards the east, near Nicholas Borne's land lately purchased of the lady Margaret Fromond towards the west and near the same John's land there in the aforesaid piece and the lane leading to the land called Harry Fromonds towards the north and to the demesne land called Great Groveland [written above: *now Borne*] towards the south and it contains *1 acre, a half and 8 dayworks*

Margin: right hand: *he holds 2 acres, 1 rod, 3 and a half dayworks, thus 6d. and a half pence each year* left hand: *Nicholas Borne*

Item **Nicholas Borne** then holds [written above: *sometime John Borne, now T Borne*] in **a piece of land called BOUNDS FIELD, formerly named MORE PRECKLESHAM**, lately purchased of the lady Margaret Fromond, lying near the said John Goding's land towards the east, land of William Nepaker formerly of John Mounssy towards the west, the same Nicholas's land in the same piece towards the north, near the demesne land there called Great Groveland south and it contains *2 acres, 1 rod, 3 and a half dayworks*

Margin: right hand: *he holds 2 acres, thus 6d. each year*

William Nepaker holds [written above: *sometime J now T Borne*] **1** [un-named] **PARCEL OF LAND** of the said tenement in a piece of land lying next to Grovelands mere towards the south, near the lane there called Bounds lane towards the north and near the highway there leading from Robards plain as far as Goldhill west and it contains *2 acres*

Margin: right hand: t*hey hold 5 acres, 1 rod, 3 and a half dayworks, thus 16d. each year* left hand: *the heirs of William Symonds carpenter and John Godyng*

The heirs of William Symonds carpenter [written above: *formerly the heirs of W Caiser, now G Moulton*] hold **one piece of land** of the said tenement, **called FORSTERS**

FIELD lying towards John Goding's land of the same tenement towards the east, lands of Hadlow manor towards the south, near lands of the said manor called Groveland and land lately of Richard Nepaker towards the west, near the lane there leading to land lately of Henry Fromond towards the north [size-omitted]   (est. *5 acres, 1 rod, 3 dayworks*)

Total of acres is: *17 acres, 8 dayworks and 3 perches*,
thus 3d. for an acre and half a penny less in all and they owe 2d. farthing in relief for 4 acres and 1 rod

---

Folio 73
SPALDING'S TENEMENT

Margin: left hand: 1) *Spaldinges 3s.* 2) 8 acres
The tenants of John Lyn's tenement [written above: *Whetenhall*] now called **SPALDINGS** and for this they shall owe the lord 3s. each year in rent.
Thus **William Whetenhall esquire** then holds *13 acres of land* **in one piece of land called the WESTFIELD** and for this he shall owe 2s. each year
And **John Goding** holds *4 acres* in **one piece of land there called THE BROME**, 12d. each year

Total is: *12 acres*
and in relief for an acre [blank]

LOCKBRIDGE'S TENEMENT

Margin: right hand: *they hold 2 acres, 2 dayworks, 3 and a quarter perches*
left hand: *Lockbridge 2s.1d.*
The tenants of the tenement of half a ferling of land formerly of Robert **LOCKBRIDGE** [written above: *sometime J B now T Borne*] thus owe the lord 16d. each year in rent and 6d. in aid at the feast of St Andrew the apostle and 3 boon works with one man price 3d.

Thus **Walter Burgeys** then holds **one piece of land called THE POPLARS BROOK** lying near land lately of Robert Watton towards the east and south, near land of John Bealde of Wrotham towards the west, near John Ashdowne's land and the land of the same Walter towards the north and it then contains *2 acres, 2 dayworks, 3 and a quarter perches*

Margin: right hand: *he holds 1 acre, a half, 1 and a half rods, 3 perches, a half and 1 quarter, thus each year 10d. for 3 acres, 3 rods, 8 dayworks and 3 perches*
And the aforesaid **Walter** holds [written above: *J B now T Borne*] **one piece of land called HOBBS FIELD** of the same tenement, lying near John Ashdowne's land towards the east, John Martyn's land towards the west, Alice Stretende's land towards the north, land of John Bealde of Wrotham and the same Walter's land towards the south and it contains *1 acre, a half, 1 and a half rods, 3 perches, a half, a quarter*

Margin: right hand: *he holds 1 acre, a half, 1 rod, 5 dayworks, 2 perches, a half, 1 quarter and a half, thus 4d. and a half pence each year*
John Bealde of Wrotham then holds [written above: *once John Bovenden's heirs, now Henry Fane*] **one piece of land called GOOSELAND** lying near Walter Burgey's land towards the east and north, near John Martyn's land towards the west, the same John Bealde's land towards the south and it contains *1 acre, a half, 1 rod, 5 dayworks,   2 perches, a half, 1 quarter and a half*

Margin: right hand: *2 acres, 1 rod except 1 daywork and 1 perch, thus 5d. and a half pence each year*
Alice Stretende holds in the same tenement [written above: *sometime J Bovenden's heirs, now Henry Fane*] **one piece of land called THE OXBROOKS CROFT** lying near John Ashdowne's land towards the east, John Martyn's lands towards the west, Walter Burgey's land towards the south, near the highway there leading from Hadlow street as far as Yalding towards the north, that is lying at Reydgate from the east part and it contains *2 acres, 1 rod, except 1 daywork and 1 perch*

Folio 74

Margin: right hand: *1 acre, 1 rod, 3 perches, a half and 1 quarter, thus 3d. each year*

John Ashdowne then holds [written above: *sometime T Somer now Walter Trice*] **one piece of land called THE BROOK**, near land of Robert Wotton and Nicholas Borne's land towards the east, near land of Alice Stretende and Walter Burgeys's land towards the west, near the said Walter's land towards the south, moreover near the highway there leading from Hadlow street as far as Yalding towards the north and it contains *1 acre, 1 rod, 3 perches, a half and 1 quarter*

Margin: right hand: *he holds 3 rods, 3 dayworks and 1 quarter, 1 perch, thus 2d. each year*

Item **Henry Ashdowne** holds of the said tenement lying on another part of the highway there in **a small** [un-named] **PIECE OF LAND** with the lane leading to the said John's dwelling house and with the largest part of the same **JOHN'S BARN built upon it** on the north part of the said piece, thus that the whole great entrance of the aforesaid barn stands upon the said tenement and the said piece of land, lying near the same John Ashdowne's land east and north, the demesne land there towards the west and the highway there leading from Hadlow street as far as Yalding towards the south and it contains *3 rods, 3 dayworks and 1 quarter of a perch*

Total of acres of the said tenement is : *10 acres 8 dayworks and 3 quarters, 1 perch and a half*,

thus 2d. and a half pence for each acre and 1d. in relief for 2 and a half acres of land

---

ASHDOWNE'S TENEMENT

Margin: right hand: *he then owes 12d. each year as is shown in an ancient rental*   left hand: *Agnes At Weald's tenement 12d. each year in rent*

Henry **ASHDOWNE** holds the whole of one tenement formerly of Agnes At Weald as is shown in an ancient rental, that is, **one MESSUAGE in which he lives with a garden and 2 pieces of land adjoining, with a small parcel of a barn** of the same, from the north part of the same barn, lying near the demesne land there and Nicholas Borne's land towards the east, near the said demesne land north and west and a parcel of land of the abovesaid tenement, formerly of Robert Lockbridge and near the highway there leading from Hadlow street as far as Yalding towards the south and it contains *6 acres, 6 dayworks* in all

Total of acres is: *6 acres and 6 dayworks*,
thus 2d. each year and he owes 3d. in relief

Folio 75
GROVE TENEMENT

Margin: right hand: *they hold 3 acres, 3 rods and 1 daywork thus they owe 18d. each year*   left hand: *Grove tenement 3s. 2d. farthing each year*

The tenants of the tenement formerly of Agnes At Weald [written above: *now J Lowson now Tyrrye*] of the land of the Grove, now called **GROVE** tenement lying next to Grove street and they shall then owe 10d. farthing each year in aid at the feast of St Andrew the apostle and 22 small works, price half a penny for each work and 6 great works, price of each work 2d. and 1 boon work with one man price 1d. and a fourth part of one carrying service, price 1d. and they shall plough and harrow half an acre, price 3d. as above.

Thence **John Martyn** then holds **one piece of land called THE GROVE FIELD** lying near land of John Bealde of Wrotham towards the east and the highway there leading from Goldhill as far as West Malling towards the west, near the demesne land there called the South Reeds north, Robert Wotton's land called Caustone south and it contains *3 acres, 3 rods and 1 daywork*

Margin: right hand: *he holds 6 acres except 1 perch and a quarter, thus he owes 2s. each year*

Item **John Bealde of Wrotham** then holds [written above: *William Martyn holds and formerly J Bovenden's heirs, now Henry Fane*] **one piece of land called LAWRENCE**

LAND otherwise called GOOSELAND lying near Robert Wotton's land called Caustone and Walter Burgey's land towards the east, near the said Robert Wotton's land towards the south, near the demesne land there called the Reeds, the said John Martyn's land and the same John Bealde's land towards the north and it contains *6 acres except 1 perch and a quarter*

Total of acres is: *9 acres, 3 rods, 2 perches, a half and 1 quarter*
thus 4d. for an acre and 1d. less in all and he does not owe relief because he does not pay rent

---

STOPERFIELD'S TENEMENT

Margin: left hand: *Stoperfields tenement 15s. 9d.*
The tenants of the tenement formerly of Hugh Caustone and William Stoperfield, now called **STOPERFIELDS** tenement hold four acres of land which they acquired of William Usserey and three acres which they acquired of Nicholas Tanner and six acres of land which were formerly of Geoffrey at Grove and one messuage and 2 acres of land which were formerly of Robert Pudding and a fourth part of half a ferling of land which was lately of Nicholas Tanner through a charter of the lord earl of Stafford as is shown in an ancient rental, for 15s. 9d. rent each year

Folio 76

Margin: right hand: *she holds 4 acres, 4 dayworks, thus 22d. each year*
Thence **Alice lately Peter Fromond's wife** then holds [written above: *sometime T Somer now T Borne*] **one piece of land called BROOMFIELD** lying near the demesne land called the lord's acre towards the east, near the common way there called the New way towards the west, land lately of John Carslake at Alayneslove and Peter Fisher's land towards the north and near the common way called the New way and Thomas Knight's land towards the south and it contains *4 acres and 4 dayworks*

Margin: *they hold 5 and a half acres except 3 quarters of one perch, thus they owe 2s. 5d. and a half pence each year*
Item **the heirs of Richard Pawleye** then hold [written above: *now Pauleye*] **one piece of land called THE PARKFIELD** lying near William Martyn's land towards the east, near the meadow and land of the demesne there towards the west and north and near the common way there leading to Thomas Salman's dwelling house called Robardswent towards the south and it contains *5 and a half acres, except three quarters of one perch*

Margin: right hand: *he holds 3 acres and 7 dayworks*
Item **William Martyn** then holds [written above: *sometime T Levesode now W King*] **one piece of land called THE PARKFIELD** lying near the highway there leading from Goldhill towards West Malling towards the east, the land of William Palley's heirs towards the west, the demesne land there called Fishers Acres towards the north, near the common way there called Robardswent towards the south and it contains *3 acres and 7 dayworks*

Margin: right hand: *he holds 9 acres, 1 rod and a half daywork, thus he owes 4s. 1d. and a half pence each year*
Item the same **William Martyn** then holds [written above: *now T Levesode*] **one piece of land called THE BARN FIELD on which parcel a barn and a house has been built**, lying near land lately of John Robards and the highway leading from Goldhill as far as West Malling towards the east, land of William Perott's heirs called the Skeyffe and the same William Martyn's land towards the west, the said John Robard's messuage and land towards the north and the same William Martyn's messuage towards the south and it contains *3 acres, 3 rods, 3 and a half dayworks*

Folio 77

Item the same **William holds one piece of land called THE BROADFIELD** of the same tenement lying near a certain lane there called Skeyffe lane towards the east, near the same William Martyn's land towards the west and south and the land moreover of

William Perott's heirs called the Skeyffe towards the north and it contains *2 acres and 9 dayworks*

Margin: right hand: *he holds 3 rods, thus 4d. each year*
Henry Plogg then holds [written above: *now William Solleman's heirs*] **one piece of land called THE KINGSCROFT** lying near land of Alice the wife of Gilbert Fromond towards the north and south and land of the lady's demesne called Cotland being in William Martyn's hands called the Westfield towards the east, land lately of William Piper called Pipers towards the west and it contains *3 rods*

Margin: right hand: *she holds 3 and a half acres and 3 dayworks, thus she owes 18d. and a half pence each year*
Item **Alice the wife of Gilbert Fromond** then holds [written above: *now William Solman's heirs*] **one MESSUAGE with a garden and a small piece of land adjoining called ROBARDS** lying near William Martyn's land towards the south, near the highway there leading from Goldhill as far as Malling towards the east, near a certain lane there called Skeyffes lane and the said William Martyn's land towards the west and near the common way there leading from Thomas Salman's dwelling house as far as the highway leading from Goldhill to [West] Malling north and it contains *1 acre and 1 rod*

Item the said **Alice** then holds [written above: *William Salman's heirs*] **one** [un-named] **PIECE OF LAND** lying near the land of same Alice, lately acquired of Richard Herbarde towards the east, near the aforesaid land called Pipers towards the west, near the aforesaid common way there towards the north, the said Henry Plogg's land towards the south and it contains *1 acre and a half daywork*

Item the said **Alice** holds **one** [un-named] **PIECE OF LAND** lately acquired of Richard Herbard lying near Thomas Salman's land towards the east, the same Alice's land in the same piece towards the west, the land of the said Henry Plogg and of the said William Martyn land towards the south and near the abovesaid common way leading below Hadlow meadow towards the north and it contains *1 acre, 1 rod and 2 dayworks*

Folio 78 Margin: right hand: *he then holds 1 acre, 1 rod and 7 dayworks, thus 7d. each year*
Thomas Salman then holds **one piece of land called THE PARK CROFT** lying near land of William Perot's heirs towards the east, the land of the said Alice Fromond wife of Gilbert towards the west, the lands called Cotlands being in William Martyn's hands towards the south and near the aforesaid common way leading below Hadlow meadow on the south part towards the north and it contains *1 acre, 1 rod and*   7 *dayworks*

Margin: right hand: *they hold 2 acres, 1 rod and a half daywork, thus 11d. and a half pence each year*
Item **the heirs of William Perot** then hold [written above: *now William Salmon's heirs*] **one** [un-named] **PIECE OF LAND** at the Skeyffe lying near the aforesaid common way below the aforesaid Hadlow meadow towards the north, near the land of aforesaid heirs towards the south and near the aforesaid lane there called Skeyffe lane towards the east and Thomas Solman's land towards the west and it contains *2 acres, 1 rod and half a daywork*

Margin: right hand: *he holds 8 acres, 3 rods, 3 and a half dayworks, thus 3s. 11d. each year*
Robert Wotton then holds [written above: *sometime Reginald Peckham, now Henry Fane*] **one piece of land called THE FIELD AT CAUSTONES CROSS** lying near the same Robert's land towards the east, the highway leading from Goldhill as far as West Malling towards the west, near John Martyn's land called the Grosfield towards the north, near a certain lane there leading to the land at Buntanhall towards the south and it contains *8 acres, 3 rods, 3 dayworks, a half*

Total of acres is: *35 acres, a half, 7 dayworks, a half and 1 perch*,
thus 5d. farthing for each acre and in all 1d and a half pence more and no relief as I believe that the tenants (hold) as they state, through a charter in an ancient rental etc.

PUDDINGS TENEMENT

Margin: right hand: *they hold 8 acre, a half, 3 and a half dayworks, thus 5s. 3d. farthing each year* left hand: *the tenants of Puddings 6s. 10d.*

The tenants of the tenement formerly of Hugh of Caustone now called **PUDDINGS** tenement of land formerly of Alan Pudding [written above: *sometime Reginald Peckham now Henry Fane*] and they therefore owe the lord 4s. 3d. farthing each year in rent and 15d. three farthings in aid at the feast of St Andrew the apostle and they shall plough a half acre 1 rod during Winter and a half acre and 1 rod during [Lent -omitted] price as above and 3 boon works with two men price 6d.

Thence **Robert Wotton** then holds **1 piece of land called CROUCHLAND** lying near the same man's lands at Caustone towards the east, William Martyn's land and near the highway (f.79) leading from Goldhill as far as West Malling towards the west, near a certain lane there leading from the said highway as far as the lands at Butanhall towards the north and near the said William Martyn's lands towards the south and it contains *8 acres, a half, 3 and a half dayworks*

Folio 79

Margin: right hand: *he then holds 2 acres and 2 dayworks thus 18d. three farthings each year*

William Martyn then holds [written above: *now Thomas Levesode*] **one** [un-named] **PIECE OF LAND** lying at the gate of the same William's dwelling house near the highway there leading from Goldhill as far as West Malling towards the west, near Robert Watton's land towards the east and north and near the said William Martyn's land called Eastwosys towards the south and it contains *2 acres, a half and 2 dayworks*

Total of acres is: *11 acres and half a rod and a half daywork,* thus 7d. for each acre and in all half a penny less and in relief he then owes 1d. farthing for each acre

EASTWOSYS TENEMENT

Margin: right hand: *he holds 4 acres and 3 dayworks, thus 23d. three farthings each year* left hand: *the tenement of the Eastwosys 2s. 11d. and a half pence*

William Martyn holds [written above: *now Thomas Levesode*] **two pieces of land lying side by side**, now called **EASTWOSYS** formerly of William Stoperfield as is shown in an ancient rental and he therefore owes the lord 11d. each year in rent and 14d. in aid at the feast of St Andrew the apostle and the aforesaid two pieces of land lie near the lands lately of Robert Watton and near land of Thomas Fromond of Goldhill called the meade at Bourne next to Rodfords bridge towards the east, near the highway there leading from Goldhill as far as West Malling towards the west, the same William Martyn's land north and the aforesaid highway and the said Thomas Fromond's land as was written before towards the south and it contains *4 acres and 3 dayworks*

Margin: right hand: *she holds 2 acres of land, thus 11d. three farthings each year*

The lady Margaret Fromond then holds [written above: *now Thomas Fromond*] **2 acres of land in a meadow called THE DORNEMEADE** at Rotfords bridge lying near the same Margaret's land in the same meadow, of the tenure of Caustone towards the east, near the highway there and near William Martyn's land towards the west, land of Caustone towards the north and the running water there called the Bourne towards the south and it contains as above, that is, *2 acres* of land

Total of acres is: *5 acres and 3 dayworks,* thus 5d. three farthings and a half for each acre and more by 1 farthing in total and they then owe 2d. three farthings in relief, that is 1d. farthing and a half for three acres of land

Folio 80
BUNTANYS TENEMENT

Margin: right hand: *they hold 16 acres 1 rod, 2 and a half dayworks, thus 6s. 3d. each year* left hand: *Butans tenement 13s. 10d.*

The tenants of the tenement formerly of John Buntan now called **BUNTANYS** tenement [written above: *at Caustone now Reginald Peckham now Henry Fane*] shall thus owe the lord 15d. each year in rent and 16d. in aid at the feast of St Andrew the apostle and 3 boon works with two men in Autumn, price 6d., deduction having been made for food and 120 small works, price of each work half a penny and 24 great works, price of each work 2d. and they shall owe one carrying service price 4d. and they must plough one acre in Winter and one acre during Lent and they shall harrow and for each acre they shall have 4 loaves price 2d. and 8 herrings price 1d. and the work of two acres is price 12d., deduction having been made for food.

Thence the aforesaid **Robert Watton** holds **2 pieces of land lying side by side at Caustone called CAUSTONES FIELD**, lying near William Nepaker's land at Buntansalle towards the east, the same Robert's land towards the west and near the lane there leading to the land at Buntanshale towards the north and near the lands and meadow there lately of Thomas Fromond of Goldhill and Alice Stretende's meadow towards the south and it contains *16 acres, 1 rod, 2 and a half dayworks*

Margin: right hand: *he holds 4 acres, 3 rods, 6 dayworks each year*

Item **Walter Burgeys** then holds [written above: *now J Levesothe junior now J Levesode and now Walter Trice*] **one** [un-named] **PIECE OF LAND with a garden and wells adjoining** at Buntanhall near William Nepaker's land towards the east and north, land lately of Robert Watton at Caustone towards the west, near the lane there leading to John Bishop's field called the Vicar's field towards the south and it contains *4 acres, 3 rods and 6 dayworks*

Margin: right hand: *he then holds 1 7 acres, 3 rods, 9 dayworks in all thus 3s. and half a pence*

Item the same **Walter** holds of the same tenement [written above: *now Walter Style now the heirs of George Roydon gent. and now Henry Fane*] **certain** [un-named] **PIECES OF LAND** lying side by side at Buntanhall aforesaid, near John Bishop's land called the Vicar's field towards the east, near William Nepaker's land towards the west, the lane there leading to the land called the Vicar's field towards the north and Alice Stretende's meadow towards the south and these pieces contain *3 acres and 3 dayworks*

Folio 81   Margin: right hand: *he then holds 5 acres, thus 22d. three farthings each year*

John Bishop then holds of the said tenement in **a field called the VICAR'S FIELD** lying near the same John's land in the same field and near a piece of land there of the said John Bishop towards the east and south, near land of Walter Burgeys and William Nepaker's land towards the west and the said William Nepaker's land towards the north and it contains *5 acres of land*

Margin: right hand: *he then holds 6 acres, 3 rods, 8 and a half dayworks, thus 2s.7d. three farthings each year*

William Nepaker then holds at Buntanhall [written above: *sometime Walter Steyle now Henry Fane*] **1 piece of land called ROBARDS CROFT** lying at Walter Burgeys's land towardsthe east and south, land formerly of Robert Watton towards the west and north and it contains *1 acre, 1 rod and 1 daywork.*

Item the same **William** [holds - omitted] another **parcel of land** [written above: *now of George Roydon's heirs*] **called LITTLE LIMPETON** lying near Alice Stretend's land towards the east, land of Robert Watton towards the north and west and near land of Walter Burgeys and the same William's land towards the south and it contains *2 acres [and] a half and 4 dayworks*

and **he holds one small** [un-named] **PIECE OF LAND** lying near the said John Bishop's land called the Vicar's field towards the east, near lands of the said Walter Burgeys towards the west and north and near the aforesaid lane leading to the aforesaid piece of land called the Vicar's field towards the south and it contains *half an acre and   5 dayworks* [written above: *now George Roydon's heirs*]

and the same **William Nepaker** holds **one piece of land with a garden adjoining, called PAGES CROFT** lying near the said Robert Watton's land towards the west, Alice Stretende's meadow called the Dornmeade south and the aforesaid lane leading to the aforesaid piece of land called the Vicar's field north and it contains *2 acres, 1 rod, 8 and a half dayworks*

Total of acres is: *36 and 1 rod,*
thus 4d. and a half pence and a half farthing for an acre and less in total in all by half a penny and therefore they owe 1d. farthing in relief for 12 acres

---

Folio 82
LAKE(1)
TENEMENT

Margin: right hand: *he holds 6 acres, 1 rod, 3 and a half dayworks, thus 4s. 4d. farthing each year*
left hand: *the tenement of William Lake 11s. 9d.*
The tenants of the tenement formerly of William at **LAKE** [written above: *now of William Whetnall Dorrells*] owe 10s. in rent each year and 20d. in aid,
thus **William Fader** holds **one piece of land called THE MILLFIELD** lying near the land of the heirs of Thomas Fromond of Goldhill towards the east, near the lane there leading as far as the mill called Pery's mill towards the west, near the land lately of Thomas Baker of Sussex towards the north and near the same William Fader's messuage towards the south and it contains *6 acres, 1 rod, 3 and a half dayworks*

Margin: right hand: *they hold 3 acres, 3 rods, 6 dayworks 2d. farthing each year*

Item **the heirs of Thomas Baker of Sussex** then hold [written above: *now Patenden now Dorrells*] **a piece of land called BAKERSFIELD** lying near land of Richard Baker of East Peckham towards the east and north, near the aforesaid lane there leading as far as Pery's mill towards the west and land of Thomas Fromond of Goldhill and William Fader's land towards the south and it contains *3 acres, 3 rods and 6 dayworks*

Margin: right hand: *he holds 6 acres, 1 rod and 3 dayworks, 4s. 4d. farthing each year*
Item **Richard Baker of East Peckham** then holds [written above: *now J Patynden*] in **a piece of land called THE 8 ACRES** lying near the same Richard's land towards the east, Katherine Bishop's land towards the west, the said Katherine's land and land lately of William Hexstall esquire towards the north, land of the heirs of Thomas Baker of Sussex towards the south and it contains *6 acres, 1 rod and 3 dayworks*

Margin: right hand: *she then holds 1 and a half acres, except a half daywork, 12d. farthing and a half each year*
The lady Margaret Fromond then holds for the term of her life [written above: *now Thomas Fromond*] in **a piece of land called YOUNG'S FIELD** lying near the said Richard Baker's land towards the east, near William Fader's land towards the west, land of the heirs of Thomas Baker of Sussex towards the north, the highway there leading from Pery's mill as far as Seffrayins plain towards the south and it then contains *1 and a half acres, except a half daywork*

Total of acres is: *17 acres, 2 dayworks,*
thus 8d. farthing there for an acre and in all three farthings more and 1d. three farthings in relief for each acre except 1 quarter

---

PAGINHERST
TENEMENT

Margin: left hand: *Paginherst 12d.*
The tenants of the tenement formerly of Thomas Weald, now called **PAGINHERST** then owe 12d. each year in rent, as is shown in an ancient rental,
thence **John Keyser of East Peckham** then holds [blank]

Folio 83
BROOKE
TENEMENT

Margin: left hand: *Brooke tenement 7s. 3d.*
The tenants of the tenement lately of Peter Atte Brook now called **BROOKE** tenement [written above: *the whole tenement in the tenure of Henry Fane*] through half a ferling of land then owe the lord 11d. and a half pence in rent each year and 10d. and a half pence in aid at the feast of St Andrew the apostle and they shall make 3 boon works

price 3d. and they shall owe 60 small works price of each work half a penny and 12 great works, price of each work 2d. and they shall owe a half part of one carrying service price 2d. and they must plough a half acre in Winter and a half acre during Lent price 6d. as above.

Thus **John Fromond of Goldhill** then holds **one piece of land called LONGREIDE** lying near the same John's land towards the east, the lane there called Twetynlane towards the west and north and land of John Fromond of Kempynhale Whedcrofts and land of the same John Fromond of Goldhill towards the south and it contains *2 acres, 1 rod, 2 and a half dayworks*.

Item **John Fromond** holds **2 pieces of land lying side by side called THE BROOKS AT LONGREIDIS**, then lying near land of the same John Fromond of Goldhill towards the east, west and south and near a certain lane there called Twetynlane towards the north and it contains *2 acres, 1 rod, 6 and a half dayworks*

The same **John Fromond** holds **2 [un-named] PIECES OF LAND** lying equally next to Brookgate near the same John Fromond's land and land lately of William Honewold towards the east, the same John's land towards the west, near the lane there called the Brooklane and the same John's land called the Winterys towards the south and near the aforesaid lane called Twetynlane towards the north and it contains *3 acres, 1 rod, 8 and a half dayworks*

The same **John Fromond** holds **2 pieces of land lying side by side called WINTERYS and the EASTFIELD** lying near the lane there called the Brooklane leading to Jordanslake towards the east, the same John's land towards the west and north and the same John's land and the aforesaid lane towards the south and it contains *four acres, 3 rods and 8 dayworks*

The same **John** holds **one piece of land** formerly of Thomas Walter **called THE EASTFIELD** lying near the lane there leading to Jordans lake towards the east, to land lately of John Honewold, now of John Andrew towards the south, land of the same John Fromond of Goldhill towards the west and north and it contains *2 acres, a half, 8 and a half dayworks*

The same **John** holds **one piece of land called CALCHISCROFT** lying near the same John Fromond's land towards the east, the land lately of William Honewold towards the south, near the lane called the Brooklane towards the west and it contains *2 acres of land except 1 daywork*

Folio 84 The same **John** holds **4 pieces of land lying side by side called MIDREDYS** lying near lands lately of John Bowring called the Hellys towards the east, near the same John Fromond's land and land lately of William Honewold [written above: *Thomas Fisher*] towards the west, near the same John's meadow called Wilkens meade towards the south and the aforesaid lane called the Brooklane towards the north and it contains *7 acres and 1 rod*

The same **John** holds **one piece of land and meadow called WILKENSMEADE** lying near the lane there called the Medlane towards the east, the common there, that is at Jordanslake towards the west, near land lately of William Honewold [written above: *now Thomas Fisher*] and the same John's land towards the north and the running water there towards the south and it contains *3 acres, a half and 1 daywork*

The same **John Fromond** then holds **one piece of land called the CROFT AT WAREND** lying near the same John Fromond's land towards the east and south, land lately of William Honewold now of Thomas Fisher towards the north, the lane there leading to Jordans lake towards the west and it contains *1 acre, a half, 1 and a half dayworks*

The same **John Fromond** then holds **one piece of meadow called ANOYTELAND** lying near land lately of William Honewold, now of Thomas Fisher towards the east, near the water there called Jordans lake and John Carslake's land, now of Nicholas A Borne towards the west, the running water there towards the north and the running water there called Vicar's water towards the south and it contains *3 acres, 6 and a half dayworks*

The same **John Fromond** then holds **one piece of meadow called THE LITTLE ANOYTELAND** lying near land lately of William Honewold now of Thomas Fisher towards the east and north, land of John Andrew senior towards the west and near the water flowing there from Winterys weir towards the south and it contains *a half acre and 8 dayworks*

The same **John Fromond** then holds **2 pieces of land and meadow called FULGRYSHOPES** lying near the same John Fromond's land called The Hope between the bridges there towards the east, land lately of William Honewold now of Thomas Fisher towards the west, the running water there from Jordans lake towards the north and the water there flowing from Winterys weir south and it thus contains *1 and a half acres, 5 and a half dayworks*

Folio 85 Margin: right hand: *he then holds 37 acres, 2 dayworks thus 3s.4d. farthing each year*

The same **John Fromond** then holds **one piece of meadow called THE HOPE** lying between the bridges near the water flowing there from Winterys weir towards the east and south, the water flowing there from Jordans lake towards the north and west and it there contains *1 acre, 1 rod, 6 and a half dayworks*

Alice, formerly the wife of William Honewold, now Thomas Fisher's wife holds **one PIECE OF LAND** of the aforesaid tenement **called [BLANK]**, lying near land of John Fromond of Goldhill towards the east and south, land of the said John Fromond and of John Andrew's towards the north, near the lane there leading to Jordans lake and the said John Andrew's land towards the west and it contains *2 acres, 1 rod, except 2 feet*

And the said **Alice**, now Thomas Fisher then holds **2 pieces of land and meadow called ANOTEYLANDS** lying near land of the said John Fromond of Goldhill towards the east and west, the water flowing there from Jordans lake towards the north and near the water flowing there from Winterys weir south and it contains *2 acres, 2 and a half dayworks*

And the said **Alice** now Thomas Fisher then holds **one parcel of meadow called ANOTEYLAND** lying near John Andrew's land towards the east, land of John Fromond of Goldhill towards the west and north, the running water there from Winterys weir towards the south and it then contains *a half acre, 6 and a half dayworks*

Margin: right hand: *she then holds 8 acres, thus 8d. and a half pence each year*

And the said **Alice** now Thomas Fisher then holds **one [un-named] PIECE OF LAND** at the Brookgate lying near Gilbert Fromond's land towards the east, the lane there called the Brooklane towards the south and west, land of the heir of Thomas Fromond of Goldhill towards the north and it then contains *1 acre, 1 rod, 3 and a half dayworks*

The same said **Alice** now Thomas Fisher then holds **one piece of land called THE THREE CORNERED PIGHTEL** lying near the lane there called the Brooklane towards the east and south, land of John Fromond of Goldhill towards the west and the lane called Twetyn lane towards the north and it then contains *1 acre, 2 and a half dayworks*

Folio 86 Margin: right hand: *he holds 1 acre, 3 rods, 7 and a half dayworks, thus each year [blank]*

John Carslake holds of the said tenement in a **piece of land called WHEREHILL** lying near the water flowing there from Peckham wood as far as the common called Jordans common towards the east, the water there flowing from Carslake weir as far as John A Barton's sluice lately called the Winterys weir towards the west, the water flowing there, that is from the said John A Barton's sluice to the aforesaid common called Jordans towards the north, near the sluice and water called Winterys weir pools towards the south and it then contains *3 rods and a half* part is for the said John Carslake and not more because 3 rods in the same piece of land pertain to William Carslake son of the said John by right of Agnes his wife

The same **John Carslake** then holds **one piece of land and meadow called**

CARSLAKES ANOTE ISLAND lying near land of John Fromond of Goldhill towards the east, the water flowing there from Peckhams wood to the common called Jordans common towards the west, to the water and the common called Jordans towards the north and near the water flowing there from Winterys weir as far as the sluice of John Fromond of Goldhill towards the south and it contains *1 acre, 2 and a half dayworks*

Margin: right hand: *he then holds 3 rods, thus three farthings each year*
William Carslake [written above: n*ow Henry Fane*] then holds, as is stated above, in **a piece of land called WHEREHILL**, just as the measurements and bounds are written above and it contains *3 rods* of land

Margin: right hand: *he then holds 3 rods, each year [blank] The said John's whole total is 2 acres, a half, 7 and a half dayworks, thus 3d. each year*
The same **John Carslake** then holds [written above: *now Henry Fane*] **one piece of land called THE THREE YARDS** lying near the common called Jordans common towards the east and south and near the land called Wismans Acre and John A Stable's land towards the west and near John Andrew's land towards the north and it contains *3 rods*

Margin: right hand: *he holds 13 and a half acres and 2 dayworks, thus 14d. farthing each year*
John Raynalde then holds [written above: *now Henry Fane*] **8 parcels of land lying side by side called THE HILLS, THE LONGMEAD and PENDERYS HOPES** lying near land of Richard Colepeper esquire called John Fromonds and named Pery's brook and Pery's town towards the east, near land of John Fromond of Goldhill towards the west, land of the lady Margaret Fromond, Robert Hall and Richard Colepeper towards the north, near the water and the land of the said John Fromond of Goldhill and the water called Buntanwater towards the south and these lands contain *13 and a half acres, 2 dayworks,* thus in **PENDERS HOPES** *2 acres, 1 rod, 4 and a half dayworks* and in **THE HILLMEADE** *2 and a half acres and 2 dayworks*

Folio 87
Margin: right hand: *she holds 8 acres, 1 rod and 8 dayworks, thus 10d. each year*
The lady Margaret Fromond then holds **two parcels of land and meadow called CHALONERS MEADES** lying near Robert Hall's lands towards the east, the lane there called the Brooklane towards the west, land lately of Nicholas Fromond towards the north, land lately of Gilbert Harding, now of Gilbert Fromond and near Robert Hall's land and land lately of William Honewold towards the south and these parcels then contain *3 acres, less 1 and a half perches*

and **she then holds one piece of land called STOCKLEASE** lying near the aforesaid meadow called Chaloners meade towards the north, land of Robert Hall and Gilbert Fromond's land towards the east, the said Gilbert's land and the lane called Hollyslake towards the south and the said Gilbert Fromond's land west and it contains *2 acres [and] a half, 3 and a half dayworks*

And **she then holds one piece of land called DEEPMEADE** lying near the said Robert Hall's meadow towards the east, land of Richard Colepeper esquire called John Fromonds and land lately of Thomas Knight towards the north, land lately of William Podde's heir and the said Thomas Knight's land towards the west, John Raynalde's land called Hellys towards the south and it contains *2 acres, 3 rods and 5 dayworks*

Margin: right hand: *he holds 1 acre, 3 rods and 12 dayworks thus 2d. farthing each year*
Gilbert Fromond then holds [written above: *now Henry Fane*] **one piece of land called HOGETTSHAW HOPE**, lying near John Andrew's land towards the east, near the lady Margaret Fromond's land towards the west, near Robert Hall's land towards the north, near the lane there leading as far as the land called the Hills and the Deepmead towards the south and it contains *half an acre and 1 daywork*

The same **Gilbert** holds **one** [un-named] **PIECE OF LAND** lately of Gilbert Harding in which lies the common way leading to Margaret Fromond's land called Stocklease towards the east and north, near land lately of William Honewold, now of Thomas Fisher towards the west, near the aforesaid lane there leading as far as the aforesaid land called the Hellys towards the south and it then contains *1 acre, 1 rod and 6 dayworks*

Folio 88 Margin: right hand: *he holds 4 acres, 1 rod, 8 and a half dayworks, thus 4d. three farthings each year*

John Andrew then holds **one parcel of meadow in a meadow called ANOTELAND** lying near land of John Fromond of Goldhill towards the east, land lately of William Honewold in the same piece of meadow [written above: *now of Thomas Fisher*] towards the west and north, near the water flowing there from Winterys weir towards the south and it then contains *half an acre and 6 dayworks*

The same **John Andrew** holds **one** [un-named] **PIGHTELL at Hillsgate** lying near land lately of William Podd [written above: *Peter Fisher*] and the lane called the Deeplane towards the east, near Gilbert Fromond's land [written above: *William Fenn*] towards the west, Robert Halls's land towards the north and near the lane there called Hellys lane towards the south and it contains *a half acre and half a daywork*

The same **John Andrew** holds in **a piece of land called THE BARNFIELD** one parcel of land with a garden adjoining lately of John Honewold, lying near the lane there called the Brook lane and leading to the water called Jordanys lake towards the east, the said John Andrewe's land towards the west, land of John Fromond of Goldhill towards the north, John Carslake's and John A Stable's land towards the south and it contains *3 acres, 7 and a half dayworks*

The same **John Andrew** then holds **one garden called MAYNARDS HAGH** lying near land lately of William Honewold [written above: *Fisher*] towards the east and south, near the lane there leading as far as Jordans lake towards the north and west and it then contains *3 and a half dayworks*

Robert Hall then holds **one piece of land and meadow called HALLS HALF ACRE** lying near the water flowing there from Jordans lake and Winters weir towards the east, west and south, the land of John Fromond of Goldhill towards the north and it contains *half an acre, less 2 perches*

Margin: right hand: *the same man holds*

The same man holds **piece of land and meadow in the DEEPMEADS** lying near Thomas Knight's land and land formerly of William Podde towards the east, land of the heir of Thomas Fromond of Goldhill towards the west, Gilbert Fromond's land north, the said Gilbert's land and John Andrew's land towards the south and it contains *1 and a half acres*

Folio 89 Margin: right hand: *he then holds 3 acres and 1 daywork, thus 3d. each year*

The same man holds **one piece of land and meadow called HALLS DEEPMEADE** lying near John Raynald's land towards the east and south, near land of Thomas Fromond of Goldhill's heirs called the Deep meade towards the west, the said Richard Colepeper's land called John Fromondes towards the south [sic - recte north] and it then contains *1 acre, 1 and a half dayworks*

Margin: right hand: *he holds 2 acres of land and 5 dayworks, thus 2d. farthing each year*

Thomas Knight then holds **one piece of land and meadow called COPPINGS MEAD** lying near the lady Margaret Fromond's land towards the east, near Robert Hall's land towards the west, the land lately of William Podd towards the south and Gilbert Fromond's land towards the north and it contains *1 acre, 1 rod and 5 dayworks*

The same **Thomas** holds **in the same piece of meadow** [**COPPINGS MEAD**], lying near land of Thomas Fromond of Goldhill towards the east, the lane there called the Deep meade towards the south, Robert Hall's and John Andrew's land towards the west and near the meadow there called Coppings meade towards the north and it contains *3 rods* of land

Total of the full acreage is: *82 acres of land and 1 daywork,*
thus 1d. and a fourth part of one farthing for each acre and half a farthing less in all and 1d. farthing and a half for 41 acres in relief of the same

Folio 90
LAKE (2)
TENEMENT

The tenants of the tenement formerly of William at Grove [written above: *now Henry Fane*] now called the **LAKE** tenement shall owe the lord 6s. each year in rent and 21d. in aid and 80 small works, price of a work half a penny and 16 great works, price of a work 2d. and 3 boon works with 2 men in Autumn price 6d.

Thence **John Fromond of Kempinhale** [written above: *now Henry Fane*] holds there **one piece of land with a certain lane** there and the aforesaid piece of land **called KEMPINFIELD** lying near John Andrew's land towards the east and south, near the land lately of Richard Knight towards the west, near the aforesaid lane towards the north and it contains *4 and a half acres and 5 dayworks* [written above: *now Henry Fane*]

The same **John** then holds [written above: *now Henry Fane*] **2 pieces of land and lying side by side called THE WHEATCROFTS with a lane there**, adjoining to land of John Fromond of Goldhill towards the east and north, to a lane there and Richard Knight's land towards the west and to John Andrew's land and to the aforesaid lane towards the south and it then contains *3 acres, 1 rod, 4 and a half dayworks*

The same man then holds [written above: *now Thomas Martyn*] **one piece of land called BELE SANDHERSTS CROFT** lying near land of the heirs of Thomas Fromond of Goldhill towards the east, near the lane there leading as far as the water called Gibbons lake towards the west, Richard Knight's land and land of the said Thomas Fromond of Goldhill's heirs towards the north and the aforesaid water called Gibbons lake towards the south and it contains *1 acre, 4 and a half dayworks*

The same man holds [written above: *now Thomas Martyn*] **one piece of land and meadow called LAKE MEADE with a pit there called THE UPTEYE** situated within it, lying near John Andrew's land towards the west, near the common situated there at the aforesaid water called Gibbons lake towards the east, the same John Fromond's land and Walter Martyn's land north and Richard Knight's land and meadow towards the south and it contains *1 acre, 3 rods* of land

Folio 91

The same man then holds [written above: *now Thomas Martyn*] **one MESSUAGE in which he dwells with a barn and a piece of land,** together with **a small parcel of land, situated in a small piece of land called the CLOBCROFT adjoining the same messuage with the garden**, near a certain lane there leading to the aforesaid water called Gibbons lake towards the east, Walter Martyn's land towards the west, the same John Fromond's land called Clobcroft and the said Walter's land towards the north and the same John Fromond's land towards the south and it contains *4 acres, 8 dayworks*

The same man then holds [written above: *now Thomas Martyn*] **one** [un-named] **PIECE OF LAND** lying near the water there flowing to Winters weir towards the east, near the aforesaid water called Gibbons lake towards the west, the lane there leading as far as Tanners brooks towards the north and near land of Richard Colepeper esquire towards the south and it contains *a half acre, 6 and a half dayworks*

The same man then holds [written above: *now Thomas Martyn*] in **one parcel of land with the house built upon it, called THOMAS AT GROVE** lately acquired of Richard Knight, lying near land of the heirs of Thomas Fromond of Goldhill towards the east, near the lane there leading to the aforesaid water called Gibbons lake towards the west, the same John Fromond's land towards the south and the said Richard Knight's land towards the north and it contains *half an acre, 5 and a half dayworks*

Margin: right hand: *he then holds 3 acres, 3 rods, 2 and a half dayworks and thus each year he owes 1 pig, a half and 1 quarter*

Item **Walter Martyn** then holds [written above: *now Thomas Martyn*] **one piece of land called THE SOUTHFIELD** lying near land of John Fromond of Kempinhall towards the east, the said John Fromond's and John Andrew's land towards the south, the highway there leading from Goldhill as far as Hartlake towards the west and near the same Walter's land towards the north and it contains *3 acres, 3 rods, 2 and a half dayworks*

John Andrew junior then holds [written above: *now T Martyn*] **one small piece of land and pasture called THE HALF ACRE AT STRODE,** lying near land of John Fromond of Kempinhall towards the east, the highway there leading from Goldhill as far as Hartlake towards the west, near Walter Martyn's land towards the north and Richard Knight's land towards the south and it contains *half an acre, 3 and a half rods*

Folio 92 Margin: right hand: *he then holds 7 acres, 2 dayworks, thus 2s. 3d. each year and he owes 3 pigs and 1 leg of pork*

The same **John Andrew** senior then holds [written above: *now Henry Fane*] **two parcels of land lying side by side called THOMAS SIMONS BROOKS,** lying near land of the heirs of Thomas Fromond of Goldhill towards the west, the same John Andrew's land and land of John Fromond of Kempinhall towards the north and the common way leading as far as Tannerys brooks towards the south and these parcels contain *1 and a half acres and 5 dayworks*

The same man holds **two parcels of land lying side by side called HONEWOLD'S FIELDS,** near the same John Andrew's and John at Stable's lands [written above: *now Henry Fane*] towards the east, land of John Fromond of Goldhill towards the north and lands of William and John Reynolds and land of the same John Andrew towards the south and it contains *4 acres, 6 and a half dayworks*

The same **John Andrew** then holds [written above: *now Henry Fane*] **one parcel of land in a piece of land called THE BARNFIELD,** lying near the same John Andrew's land in the same piece of land towards the east, the same John Andrew's land towards the west, near John At Stable's land called the Broomcroft towards the south and it contains *half an acre and 7 dayworks*

Margin: right hand: *he holds 1 acre, 4d. each year and 1 quarter of 1 leg of pork and a half*

John A Stable then holds [written above: *Henry Fane*] **one piece of land called THE BROWNCROFT** lying near Nicholas Borne's and John Reinald's lands towards the south and east and near John Andrew's land towards the north and west and it then contains *1 acre* of land

Margin: right hand: *he holds 2 acres, 4 and a half dayworks, each year 8d. farthing, and 1 leg of pork and half a pig*

John Fromond of Goldhill then holds **one piece of land called HELLERSLAND or HELLERSCROFT** lying near the same John's land towards the east and north, John Andrew's land towards the south, land of John Fromond of Kempinhale towards the west and it then contains *2 acres, 4 and a half dayworks*

Folio 93 **The lady Margaret Fromond** then holds for the term of her life **one piece of land called [BLANK]** lying near Richard Knight's land towards the east, west and north and near land of John Fromond of Kempinhale towards the south and it contains *1 acre, half a daywork*

Margin: right hand: *she holds 1 and a half acres and 4 dayworks, thus 6d. each year and three quarters of 1 pig*

Item **the said lady Margaret** then holds [written above: *now Henry Fane*] **one parcel of land in a piece of land called THOMAS SYMONDS BROOK,** lying near John Andrew's land towards the east, land of John Fromond of Kempinhale towards the west, near Richard Knight's land towards the north, near the common way there leading to the lands called Tanners brooks towards the south and it contains *half an acre, 3 and a half rods*

Margin: right hand: *he holds 3 acres, 2 and a half dayworks, thus 12d. each year and he then owes 1 pig, 1 quarter and 1 half*

William Carslake then holds [written above: *now Henry Fane*] through Agnes his wife **one piece of land and pasture called TANNERS BROOKS,** lately of Thomas Walter, lying near the running water there called Winters water towards the east and south, near John Andrew senior's land and the lane there leading from Gibbonslake as far as the aforesaid lands called Tanners brooks towards the north and west and it contains *2 acres and 1 daywork*

The same man then holds **one piece of land called WISEMANS ACRE** lying near the same William's land towards the east, John Andrew's land towards the west, land of John At Stable and the said John Andrew's land towards the north, the same William's land and the abovesaid water called Winters water towards the south and it contains *1 acre, 1 daywork*

Item **Richard Knight** then holds [written above: *now Broke Moulton*] **one piece of land and meadow called LAKE MEADE** lying near the lady of the manor's land towards the east, Thomas Knight's land and the said lady of the manor's land towards the south, John Andrew's land and land of John Fromond of Kempinhale towards the north, near the highway there at Strode and leading from Goldhill as far as Hartlake towards the west and it contains *2 acres and 5 dayworks*

Folio 94

Margin: right hand: *he holds 9 acres, 9 dayworks and half a perch, thus 2s.11d. and a half pence each year, 4 pigs, 1leg of pork and a half*

The same **Richard Knight** then holds [written above: *now John Penehall now Thomas Martyn*] **one piece of land called KEMPINFIELD** lying near land of John Fromond of Kempinhale towards the east, land lately of Thomas Fromond of Goldhill towards the west, the same Richard Knight's land towards the north, land of the said John Fromond of Kempinhale, John Andrew's land and land lately of the said Thomas Fromond towards the south and it contains *3 acres, except half a daywork*

The same man then holds [written above:*now Thomas Martyn*] **one MESSUAGE with a garden and a piece of land adjoining called KNIGHTSFIELD** lying near a certain lane there leading to John Andrew's land towards the east, near a certain lane there leading to the running water called Gibbons lake towards the west, near another lane there called Twetyn lane towards the north, the lands of John Fromond of Kempinhale, land lately of Thomas Fromonde of Goldhill and the same Richard Knight's land towards the south and it contains *4 acres and 5 dayworks except 1 perch and a half*

Margin: right hand: *she holds 5 dayworks, thus half a penny each year and she then owes a half leg of pork*

Item **the lady of the manor** then holds [written above: *T Martyn holds*] **one parcel of land lying in a piece of land called KNIGHTFIELD**, near the said Richard Knight's land towards the east, west and south and the aforesaid lane there called Twetyn lane towards the north and it contains *5 dayworks*

Total of acres is in all: *44 acres, 1 rod and 3 and a half dayworks and half a perch*,
thus 4d. for an acre and always 1d. less in 7 and a half acres and 18d. for relief in the whole tenement, that is for 5 and a half acres 2d. farthing, 1 and a half dayworks and 1 perch and 1 pig for 2 acres, 8 and a half dayworks and the aforesaid tenants owe 20 pigs each year

Folio 95
LOTEWOOD
TENEMENT

f.95 Margin: right hand: *they hold 6 acres 1and a half rods, 12d. each year*   left hand: *Holdenne now called Lotewood 20d. each year*
The tenants of the tenement formerly of John Holdenne, now called **LOTEWOOD** [written above: *now Thomas Raynolde*] shall owe the lord 20d. each year in relief.
Thence **John Raynold** then holds **one piece of land and meadow called MORELOTE WOOD** lying near the meadow called Foremeade towards the west, John Towne's meadow towards the east, the lands lately of Thomas Fromond of Goldhill, of John Fromond of Kempinhale, of Henry Wiseman, of the said John Towne, of Joan Frutar, of Nicholas Denys and land of the same John Raynold towards the north and near the water there which flows to the sluice called Finches weir towards the south and it contains *6 acres, 1 and a half rods*

Margin: right hand: *he holds half an acre, 4 and a half dayworks, thus 1d. each year*

John Fromond of Kempinhale then [written above: *now John Towne*] holds **one piece of land called AYLARDS ACRE**, lying near John Raynold's land towards the south, near the meadow called Great Roundhale towards the east, near the land of Thomas Fromond of Goldhill towards the west and north and it contains *a half acre, 4 and a half dayworks*

Margin: right hand: *he holds 3 and a half acres and 3 dayworks, thus 7d. each year*

William Towne and **John Watte of Capele** then hold [written above: *now J Towne now Walter Ripping's heirs*] **one parcel of land and meadow called LOTE WOOD** lying near the meadow called Great Roundhale towards the north and east, near John Raynold's land called Lote wood towards the west and the water flowing there as far as Vinters weir towards the south and it then contains *3 acres, a half and 3 dayworks*

Total of acres is: *then 10 acres, a half, 2 and a half dayworks*
in all, thus 2d. for an acre and in all 1d. less and they shall owe half a penny in relief for each acre

---

Folio 96
JORDANS TENEMENT

Margin: right hand: *total each year 10s. 3d. and thus 3s. 8d. as the reeve's allocation*
left hand: *Jordans tenement 13s. 11d.*

The lady of the manor holds the whole tenement called **JORDANS** tenement lying together in two pieces of land called Kemelands and she therefore owes 16d. each year in relief as is shown in an ancient rental and 21d. in aid at the feast of St Andrew the apostle and for 3 boon works with two men price 6d. and 5s. for 120 small works price of each work half a penny and 4s. for 24 great works each work price 2d., and for the plough for 2 acres price 12d. and for one carrying service price 4d.

Thus **John Bishop** then holds **2 pieces of land lying side by side called LITTLE KEMELANDS** containing *10 acres of land* and he therefore owes in fee farm each year as is declared in a certain charter made there by the lord of Tonbridge castle in the third year of king Edward III [Jan. 1329 - Jan. 1330] that is, to hold by him and his heirs paying 5s. 3d. each year as is shown in his charter sealed by the lord
Margin: left hand: *note carefully: 6 Ed. 4 [4TH March 1466-1467]*

And **Richard Pynchon** holds **one piece of land called GREAT KEMELAND** containing *10 acres* through copy of the court held in 6TH year of king Edward IV [March 1466-March 1467] paying 5s. each year

Total of acres: [blank]

LAWERK TENEMENT

Margin: left hand: *Larke tenement 12s. 4d.*

The lady of the manor holds the whole tenement called **LAWERK** formerly of John at Grove lying at Larkhale, lying near the meadow called the Northfrith towards the south and west and she owes 15d. in rent each year and 21d. in aid at the feast of St Andrew the apostle and 4s. 2d. for a hundred small works, price of each work half a penny and 3s. 4d. for twenty great works, price of each work 2d. and for 3 boon works with 2 men price 6d. and for 2 acres of land for the plough at the time as above, price 12d. and then for one carrying service, price 4d.

Margin: left hand: *note carefully*

Thus **Thomas Fader** holds [written above: *now Richard Horne*] through copy of the court as is shown in the reeve's account there, by paying 6s. 8d. each year and so 5s. 8d. in the reeve's allowance each year

Total of acres: [blank]
In much later hand: *Here one or more leaves are wanting*

APPENDIX

Folio 99
The last pages of the manuscript relating to neighbouring parishes [and manors] are included here for the sake of completeness.

and by pontifical authority we grant and concede that it should be converted to their own particular uses and we have appointed it with all things which pertain to the same to be held as a possession in perpetuity, saving a suitable vicarage in the same church, the presentation to which shall pertain to the same men in the religious life. We establish this particular vicarage and wish it to be endowed with all the small tithes, oblations, offerings, pannages and all other things pertaining to the altarage, except the tithe of hay in all parts of that parish, saving those tithes of twenty acres of meadow which the lord the earl of Gloucester now holds in the same parish, on the east part of the parish mentioned. The vicars of the said church shall in future receive the tithes of these twenty acres in perpetuity, whosoever shall have held them and those vicars shall have a hall with chambers attached to it and gardens together with four acres of land with the tithes issuing from the same and from two acres of wood of the demesne of the said church just as is marked by certain bounds and also the two shillings of annual rent, which John, called the king, of the said Peckham and his heirs shall pay to the vicars in perpetuity for whatever lands which the same John holds of the aforesaid churches' fee, together with the tithe issuing from the same lands and the vicars shall receive all the tithes of the gardens of the whole parish which are dug by foot. In addition the said prior and convent shall pay all ordinary charges relating to that church and also extraordinary expenses which pertain to them as their portion according to the right, honour and custom of our church of Rochester, also saving in all things and keeping intact the rights and customs of any other church whatever and so that these matters may obtain the force of permanent validity we have enforced the present writing by the protection of our seal. Given at Bromley 19TH October in the year of the lord 1387 and the fifth year of our consecration.

Written below in later hand: *1387 14TH November*:
Here follows a recital of the instrument above part of which is lost but remedied by this which follows.

Confirmation of the chapter of Rochester of the same settlement.
The prior[1] of the monastery of St Andrew the apostle Rochester and the convent of the same place send greeting in Christ Jesu the saviour of all mankind to all sons of holy mother church to whom the present letters shall have come. You will have known that at the request of our most dear friends the prior and convent of the monastery of Leeds in Canterbury diocese, we have inspected and have diligently examined word for word, the charter of our venerable father the lord Thomas by the grace of God bishop of Rochester [2] about the appropriation made in this form to them of the church of Little Peckham, Rochester diocese and we have neither cancelled nor revoked nor obliterated any part of it under this form: Thomas by the grace of God bishop of Rochester sends greeting in God who is the true salvation of all to all sons of holy mother church to whom the present letters shall have come. Among the other works of piety which are known to be of concern to the pastoral office, we believe that it is of the utmost importance that a merciful eye should be bestowed upon the poor and oppressed and so that those who show this concern may receive perpetual blessing with every favour and that since their charity has begun in a praiseworthy manner (f.100) their state of life may be improved and their possessions and their goods may be augmented. Therefore, we, observing the good conduct and the generous hospitality of the prior and convent of the monastery of Leeds, of the Order of St Augustine, within Canterbury diocese, which they mercifully bestow

Folio 100

1. John de Sheppey OSB 1380 -1419

2. Thomas Brinton OSB 1373 -1389

upon poor people and pilgrims and as we desire that the works of charity so begun may increase in a praiseworthy manner in the future, by the invocation the name of Christ, by the guidance of divine love, so influenced by considerations of necessity and expedience and persuaded by the prayers and mediation at the demesne of the king and queen of England, have appropriated the church of Little Peckham within our diocese, which is now vacant, the right of patronage and presentation which is known to pertain to the same prior and convent, to the same prior and convent and their aforesaid monastery and by pontifical authority concede and grant that the church may be transferred to their own uses and we assign it with all its assets pertaining to it, to be held by them in perpetuity, saving a competent vicarage in the same church, the presentation of which shall be held by the same men in the religious life. We institute this particular vicarage and wish it to be endowed with all the small tithes, oblations, offerings, pannages and all other things pertaining to the altarage, except a tithe of the hay throughout the same parish, apart from that of twenty acres of meadow which the lord the earl of Gloucester now holds there on the east part of the memorable parish. The vicars of the said church shall receive in perpetuity the tithes of these particular twenty acres whoever shall have held them in the future. The vicars shall have a hall with chambers attached to it and a garden together with fourteen acres of land with the tithe issuing from them and from two acres of wood of the demesne of the said church just as is shown in certain bounds and also two shillings of annual rent which John, called *the King* of the said Peckham and his heirs shall pay to the said vicars in perpetuity from those particular lands which the same John holds of the fee of the aforesaid church, together with the tithe of land issuing from the same and the said vicars shall receive all the tithes of the gardens of the whole parish which are dug by foot. Moreover the prior and convent shall pay all ordinary charges relating to that church and also the extraordinary charges which pertain to them as their portion by the right, honour and custom of our church of Rochester, also saving in all things and preserving completely the rights and customs of any other church whatsoever and so that these matters may obtain the force of permanent validity we enforce the present writing by the protection of our seal. Given at Bromley 19th October in the year of the Lord 1387 and the fifth year of our consecration. Therefore that while awaiting the sons' agreement to the paternal donation, it is essential that we give enforcement and validity to that appropriation which we are granting and also that we confirm it to those men in the religious life at Leeds and their monastery in perpetuity by our authority and that of our chapter, as we know with certainty that this grant has been made by unanimous assent. In testimony of which matter we have considered it appropriate to place the common seal of our chapter upon these present letters. Given in our chapter 21ST October in the above said year of the Lord. From comparison with the register of Thomas Wardegar' Register T.

Written below in later hand: *12TH November, 1387*

Folio 101
The Manor of Mereworth

Kent 15 June 1579
The survey of certain manors there of the right honorable the lord of Abergavenny taken in June 1579 20th year of our sovereign queen Elizabeth

Margin: right hand: The manor of Mereworth: Building. **The place meted about with a fair entrance into the said place a bakehouse covered with tile, the old brewhouse covered with tile, the storehouse covered with tile, the great stable, the long stable covered with tile, the old garnarde [granary?], the gatehouse with a pigeon house over it covered with tile, the great barn covered with tile, the hay barn covered with thatch, the fodder house and the stall covered with thatch and the slaughter house uncovered**

Margin: right hand: *demesnes in the lord's hands.*

1) **The park of Mereworth** contains by measure after 16 feet and a half to the perch 106 acres, 1 rod worth by the year: *106 acres, 1 rod*

2) **Town mead** measured containing *6½ acres* et a half rod, worth by the year: *6 and*

a half acres and half a rod

3) **Long mead** contains by measure 12 acres one rod and half a rod worth by the year: *12 acres, 1 rod, half a rod*

4) **Potford mead** contains by measure 11 acres 3 rods worth by the year: *11 acres, 3 rods*

5) **Ladyfeld pasture** contains by measure 67 acres 5 perches worth by the year: *67 acres, 5 perches*

6) The **Bakehouse mead** contains by measure 2 acres 1 rod worth by the year: *2 acres, 1 rod*

Total of acres: *211 acres, 1 rod, 5 perches*

Margin: left hand: *parcel of the demesnes let out by the year at the will of the lord*
right hand: 1) *19 acres*   2) *12 quarters of wheat*   3) *rent 12d.*

Thomas Hunte holds a **WATER MILL with the pound and water courses with one parcel of land lying to the mill** containing 3 rods and one other parcel of land lying to the highway leading to Malling containing *half an acre* with the mill shot containing *17 and a half acres* and rented per annum

Folio 102 Margin: left hand: *86 acres, 3 rods, 20 perches*

John Tuttesham and **Hugh Wood** holds at the lords will **THE GREAT NORTH FIELD** containing *66 acres, 3rods, 20 perches*, **LITTLE NORTH FIELD** containing *12 acres, 3 rods*, the **meadow called THE FORSTAL** behind the great barn containing *3 acres, one rod* and rented by the year 30 quarters of wheat

Margin: right hand: *46 acres, 1 rod, 17 perches* left hand: *12 quarters of wheat*

John Bulfinche holds of the lord **THE SMITHFELD** containing 8 acres, the south *courtreds* containing *3 acres, 1 rod*, the meddle *courtreds* containing *6 acres less ten perches*, the north *courtreds* containing *7 acres, 20 perches*, **THE BROKE FIELD** containing *9 acres, 24 perches*, **MARTENS CROFT** containing *2 acres, 23 perches*, **THE LAY LANDS** containing *10 acres, 3 rods* and rented by the year

Margin: right hand: 1) *13 acres, 1 rod.* 2) *rent:* [blank]

Mrs Weldon holds at the will of the lord these parcels of the demesnes of Mereworth and rent for the same with other lands in West Peckham as there it shall be set down: viz. **BRODFELD** containing *8 acres, 2 rods*, **SHEPCOTEFELD** *4 acres, 1 rod*, with one rod of land lying between the lands of the heirs of John Wright to the south, to the highway and to the lands of Sir Thomas Walsingham and the water course north and west lying in East Peckham

Total: 165 acres, 1 rod, 37 perches
Total of the demesnes with the park of Mereworth: *376 acres, 4 rods, 2 perches*
The rent: *54 quarters of wheat*
Rent: *12d*

Folio 103 Of meadow or hay belonging to the manor
Any wood unmeasured containing by estimation [blank]
The wood called the Lords wood containing by estimation [blank]
The old hay, sometime wood, and now pasture in the tenure of Sir Thomas Fane knight and rented by the year
Margin: left hand: *Advowsons*: The gift of the rectory pertaining to the lord of this manor and Edward Stybe is now incumbent there which rectory with the profits is worth by the year, glebe annexed to the same rectory *26 and a half acres*
Margin: left hand: *Fairs*: There has been, in times past, on the feast day of St Lawrence [10TH August] a fair kept in the forstal adjoining to the church and that the toll and profit appertaining to the Lord of this manor worth by the year

Custom due to the Lord by the tenants

Here follows the tenants, what rent they pay yearly and what customs and services are due by them to the Lord of this manor particularly set down, viz:

Item every tenant ought to till for every 2 acres of arable land, pasture or meadow ground lying with in the manor of Mereworth holding of this manor one daywork of land for the Lord year in and when the demesnes are to be sowed and to reap so much wheat yearly

Folio 104

Item the tenants of this manor for every *xvto acres* of arable land, pasture or meadow that lies in Mereworth ought to find one cart with 2 horses, beasts and a driver to carry out the Lords stall's and stable dung, and the Lord to find 2 carts during the whole carriage of it, with fillers for all the carts, the lord to find for the drivers of the tenants carts, for every one of them, 4 herrings with enough bread and drink every day during the whole carriage

Item the Lord ought to keep a bull and a boar within the manor as well, for the use of the tenants as for the use of the Lord, and likewise a pound

Margin: left hand: *Woods or oaks*: Touching certain oaks at Herne pound, the tenants at this court of survey cannot find who is the very owner of them but they say that they are standing within the parish of Mereworth

Margin: left hand: *Lands detained from the lord:* Memorandum: that Sir Thomas Walsingham knight withholds from the Lord *one acre* of land lying in NUTBEAM, parcel of the demesnes of Mereworth and that the said acre by the tenants is perfectly known to be of the said demesnes and that the said Sir Thomas hath heretofore yielded rent to the lord of this manor for it

The tenants of this manor dying seized of his lands and tenements must pay the best beast and the first part of his rent for relief; seek the lords records for that

---

Tenants of Merewoth Manor

Margin: left hand: *Mereworth:*

John Woodgate holds freely by deed dated the 3rd day of October in the 18th year of the reign of our sovereign lady queen Elizabeth etc [1576] **one MESSUAGE or tenement, one orchard and 4 pieces of land containing** *9 acres*, more or less, lying in Mereworth aforesaid to have and to hold the premises to him and to his heirs forever by the rent of 12d. by the year besides heriot: the best beast after the death of the tenant, relief the [blank] part of the years rent and suit of court from 3 weeks to 3 weeks

Margin: left hand: *John Bulfinch and others*

John Bulfinch and **William his son** hold freely by deed dated the 12th day of January in the 10th year of the reign of our sovereign lady queen Elizabeth [1573/74] **one wood called COLPANNES** and **one piece of land called BUNTINGES** to the same wood adjoining containing *8 acres and 1 rod* lying in Mereworth to have and to hold to the said John and William and to their heirs for ever for the rent of 2s. by the year besides heriots and reliefs and suite of court and services as is aforesaid

John Waston holds by deed freely dated the 27th day of March in the 9th year of the reign of our sovereign lady queen Elizabeth [1567] **one piece of land** containing *6 acres* in Mereworth to hold to him and to his heirs for ever doing suit of court and the service above specified and rent by the year 12d.

Folio 105

The same **John Waston** holds freely by deed as it is said **2 parcels of land** whereof the **one is called EDWARDS** the other **GILBERTS** containing by estimation *6 acres* in Mereworth to hold to him and to his heirs for ever doing suit of court and the services aforesaid and rent by the year 16d.

The said **John Waston** with **Thomas Crowhurst** and **Robert Crowhurst** hold freely by deed as it is said, **a MESSUAGE or tenement and 5 parcels of land** containing about *17 acres* in Mereworth to hold to them and to their heirs for ever doing suit of court and the services aforesaid and rent by the year 3s.

Thomas Cotton knight holds freely as it is said **one acre of land** lying in Mereworth **in a parcel of land called SWANTON QUARRY** to hold to him and his heirs for ever doing suit of court and the service above specified and rent by the year 1d. **Thomas Fane** knight holds by free deed as it is said certain lands to hold to him and to his heirs by the yearly rent of 7s.

Thomas Walsingham knight holds by free dead as it is said **YOKEPLACE** and certain lands thereunto belong lying in Mereworth to hold to him and to his heirs for ever doing suit of court and the services aforesaid and rent by the year 9s.2½d.

Memorandum: that the said **Sir Thomas Walsingham** withholds *one acre* from the lord of this manor lying in the **NUTBEAM** being parcel of the Lords lands

Richard Lane esquire holds by free deed as it is said **one principal MESSUAGE with divers other tenements, cottages, barns, outhouses, dovehouse, gardens or orchards, closes and certain lands** to hold to him and to his heirs for ever doing suit of court and the services aforesaid and rent by the year 30s.10½d.

The same **Richard** holds by free deed as it is said **TWO PARCELS OF LAND** in Mereworth late John Brokes and contains *6 acres* to hold to him and to his heirs for ever doing suit of court and the services aforesaid and rent by the year 17d.

John Roberts gent. holds by free deed as it is said certain lands to hold to him and to his heirs for ever by what suit or service the homage knows not but rent by the year 6d.

Folio 106 **John Bridger** holds by free deed as it is said **one MESSUAGE, a barn, a close, a garden, an orchard, 4 parcels of land** containing by estimation *20 acres* to hold to him and to his heirs for ever doing suit of court and the yearly services aforesaid and rent by the year 4s.4d.

The same **John Bridger** holds as it is said by the last will and testament of Nicholas Collin for certain years yet not ended **one MESSUAGE, one barn, one close, one garden and 3 pieces of land** containing *10 acres* to hold to him for certain years and then to Nicholas Collin the son of Richard Collin and his heirs for ever doing suit of court and the services aforesaid and rent by the year 2s.2d.

Thomas Tuttisham holds by free deed as it is said **7 PARCELS OF LAND** lying in Mereworth containing *24 acres* to hold to him and to his heirs for ever doing suit of court and the services aforesaid and rent by the year 5s.10d.

George Turke holds by free deed as it is said **one MESSUAGE with 2 outhouses, one close, one garden, one orchard and divers parcels of land** containing by estimation *6 acres* to hold to him and to his heirs for ever doing suit of court and the services aforesaid and rent by year 19½d.

John Turke holds by free deed as it is said **one MESSUAGE, one barn, one outhouse, one close one garden, one orchard and 2 parcels of land** in Mereworth containing *6 acres* to hold to him and to his heirs for ever by court suit and services aforesaid and rented by the year 19½d.

John Bettes by free deed as it is said **one MESSUAGE, one barn, one outhouse, one close, a garden, one orchard and 7 pieces of land** in Mereworth containing by estimation *20 acres* to hold to him and to his heirs for ever by suit of court and the services aforesaid and rented by the year 4s.2½d.

John Pattenden holds by free deed as it is said **one cottage and 3 parcels of land** lying in Mereworth containing by estimation *9 acres* to hold to him and to his heirs by suit of court and the yearly services aforesaid and rented by the year 22d.

Thomas Turke holds by free deed as it is said **a kitchen, an outhouse, a close, a garden, a hemplat, an orchard and one parcel of land** lying in Mereworth containing by estimation *6 acres* to hold to him and to his heirs by suit of court and the yearly services aforesaid and rented by the year 19d.

Jeffrey Morgan and **William Huggin** hold by free deed as it is said **one MESSUAGE, one close and 5 pieces of land** lying in Mereworth containing by estimation *10 acres* to hold to them and to their heirs by suit of court and the services

APPENDIX

aforesaid and rented by the year 3s.4d.

Folio 107 **Nevell Delahope** holds by free deed as it is said **2 MESSUAGES, 2 barns, 2 outhouses, 2 closes, 2 gardens, 2 orchards and 9 parcels** of land in Mereworth containing by estimation *37 acres* to hold to him and to his heirs by suit of court and the yearly services aforesaid and rented by the year 8s.2d.

The heirs of John Monn hold by free deed as it is said **a PARCEL OF LAND** lying in Mereworth containing by estimation *9 acres* whereof **2 woodlands and the rest arable** to hold to them and to their heirs by suit of court and rented yearly 3s.4d.

John Monn together with the heirs of Hampton holds by free deed as it is said **a cottage and 3 parcels of land** in Mereworth containing by estimation *30 acres* whereof **one parcel of** *3 acres* lie in the park in consideration whereof they have **one parcel of land** lying amongst the lands above said parcel of the lords demesnes by exchange containing *5 acres* to hold to them and to their heirs by suit of court and the yearly services aforesaid and rented by the year 9s.1d.½d.

Edward Batchler and **William Bytchler** hold by free deed as it is said **2 cottages, one barn, 2 gardens and one parcel of land** containing by estimation *4 acres* lying in Mereworth late Thomas Tuttisham: to hold to them and to their heirs by suit of court and the yearly services aforesaid and rented yearly 12d.

The heirs of John Morgyn hold by free deed as it is said **one MESSUAGE, one kitchen, one close, one garden and one parcel of land** in Mereworth containing by estimation *2 acres* to hold to them and to their heirs by suit of court and the yearly services aforesaid and rented by the year 8d.

Robert Batchler and **the heirs of Edward Gyles** so hold by free deed as it is said **one cottage, one garden and a parcel of land** containing by estimation *2 acres* in Mereworth to hold by and to them and to their heirs by suit of court and the yearly services aforesaid and rented by the year 5d.

Folio 108 **Robert Moncastell** holds by free deed as it is said **one MESSUAGE, one kitchen, one close, one garden and one orchard containing** *half an acre* in Mereworth to hold to him and to his heirs by suit of court and the yearly services aforesaid and rented yearly 1d.

Thomas Halle holds by free deed as it is said **one MESSUAGE, one barn, one outhouse, one close, one garden and 3 parcels of land** containing *7 acres* in Mereworth to hold to him and his heirs by suit of court and other services as is aforesaid and rented yearly 20d.

The heirs of Thomas Stridle do hold freely as it is said 2 parcels of land containing *6 acres* lying in Mereworth to hold to them and to their heirs by suit of court and other services as aforesaid and rented by the year 3d.

William Roffe holds in the right of Joan his wife **2 parcels of arable land** containing *5 acres* in Mereworth to hold to the said Joan and her heirs by suit of court and other services as is aforesaid and rented by the year 6d.

The churchwardens of Mereworth do hold of this manor to the use of the poor of the parish **3 parcels of woodland and pasture** in Mereworth containing by estimation *6 acres* and rented by the year 6d.

John Man of Frante holds by free deed as it is said certain lands to hold to him and to his heirs by the yearly rent of 3s.7d.

One annual rent of 40s. have been yearly paid for **certain marsh lands lying at Cliffe** now detained by my lord Cobham now Lord Warden 40s.

Richard Coleper gent holds by deed freely as it is said **one parcel of woodland called SNYTTES** to hold to him and to his heirs by suit of court and other services as is aforesaid and rented by the year 5d.

Total of the rents of the freeholders: *£7.14s.½d*

Folio 109

The demesnes at West Peckham

f.109 Margin: left hand *Kent, West Peckham: demesnes*

Mrs Weldon holds at the will of the lord those parcels of the lords demesnes following viz: **THE HASELWOOD** containing by measure at 16 feet and a half to the perch   *84 and a half acres*,

THE LORDS GARDEN containing of like measure *8 acres, 20 perches*,

CROCKERS containing *6 acres*, the lord's demesnes *3 acres, one and a half rods*,

THE LORD'S CROFT on the south side of the church of Peckham containing *half an acre, 8 perches*,

HORING BROKES, full of elders containing *9 acres, 20 perches*.

The said **Mrs Weldon** hath **THE BRODEFELD** and **SHEPECOTEFELD** with *one acre* of arable land lying in the **field called NUTBEAM** being parcel of the lords demesnes of Mereworth as it is set down in the survey of Mereworth

for all which parcels above said she rents to the lord yearly *111 and a half acres,   28 perches, 10 quarters of wheat*

2 Crofts lying in **Hadlow,** parcel of the lord's demesnes in Peckham containing *3 and a half acres, 30 perches* and lies to Sir Thomas Cotton pale north and now in the occupation of Robert Pawley and rent by the year 3s.4d.

Margin: left hand: *Alomepitte commons and wood*

Item **one little toft** lying north-west to the lord's garden being **ALOMEPITT The common called THE HURST** contains by estimation *100 acres*, the woods on the same belong to the lord of this manor, the pannage and herbage to the tenants for which the said tenants are to inclose the Lords garden from the church wall to the [blank] but containing 18 perches

The common called LITTLE LOMEWOOD containing *30 acres* lying in Hadlow the which the tenants say that they have heard it should belong to the Lord of this manor

---

Services and duties due to the Lord by the freeholders of West Peckham

Margin: left hand: *heriots, reliefs*

First at this survey the said freeholders tenants of this manor yielded in verdict that the lord after the death of every tenant dying seized of his lands and tenements must pay to the lord for an heriot, the best live beast that he or they have had or have and for relief the 4th part of his whole years rent of his lands for the proof of which relief the tenants pray favour to see some records of the Lord for that they are at this time uncertain thereof

---

Tenant Freeholders

Sir Thomas Cotton knight holds by free deed as it is said certain lands late his fathers and before Richard Colepepers esquire and other lands late Tuttishams lying at Lomewood and land late purchased of Welbecks and rents yearly 36s.

Folio 110

The same **Sir Thomas Cotton** holds by free deed as it is said certain lands late purchased of George Whittenhall esquire lying at Lomewood containing *13 acres* sometime John Brokes to hold to him and to his heirs for the yearly rent of 2s.1d.

The same **Sir Thomas Cotton** holds by free deed as it is said **one meadow,** late Richard Mounks, to hold to him and to his heirs for the yearly rent of 3d.

The said **Sir Thomas Cotton** holds by free deed as it is said **one MESSUAGE, 2 gardens and 3 pieces of land** late George Whittenhalls in Hadlow containing *5 acres* and **one MESSUAGE and** *half one acre* **of land** late Gammounes to hold to him and to his heirs for the yearly rent of 6d.

The same **Sir Thomas Cotton** holds by free deed as it is said **certain lands late John Stace** to hold to him and to his heirs for the yearly rent of 6s.2d.

The said **Sir Thomas Cotton** holds by free deed as it is said **certain lands late John Sutors** to hold to him and to his heirs for the yearly rent of 13d.

The said **Sir Thomas Cotton** holds by free deed as it is said **certain lands late John Osmers called WOULSIES** to hold to him and to his heirs for the yearly rent of 20d.

The same **Sir Thomas Cotton** holds by free deed as it is said **2 gardens** lying in West Peckham and **one croft of land late Smithes** to hold to him and to his heirs for the yearly rent of 4½d.

The same **Sir Thomas Cotton** holds by free deed as it is said **certain lands sometime Rainolde** to hold to him and to his heirs for the yearly rent of 4d.

The same **Sir Thomas Cotton** holds by free deed as it is said **certain lands late Croweterst and sometime Mounkes called WYGMERDAINE** to hold to him and to [his] heirs for the yearly rent of 14½d.

The same **Sir Thomas Cotton** holds by free deed as it is said **certain lands called HURSTGATE sometime Collens** to hold to him and to his heirs for the yearly rent of 4d. yielding unto the Lord of this manor after the death of the tenant for an heriot his best beast dying seized of the aforesaid lands in fee simple or in fee taile and relief that is the 4th part of the years rent and court suit from 3 weeks to 3 weeks

Folio 111   **John Ryvers knight** holds by free deed as it is said *one acre and one yard* of **meadow in Hadlow in a meadow there called FOREMEDE** to the mead of Thomas Barton called Colton mede west, to the river there south, to the residue of the meadow called foremede east, to the land called Cronburie, late Henrie Fishers north,

one other meadow called TWISTLAKE lying in Hadlow aforesaid between foremede and Cowlease, to the river there north and south and it contains *two acres and three yards*

one other meadow called COWLEASE containing *5 acres* lying in Hadlow to the river there north, to the meadow of the Lords of St Johans east, and to the common river there east and south, to the mede called Castells south and to the meadow of the said John Rivers west

and *three acres and a half* of meadow in **PRETTISHOPS**

six acres in **SOWTH WOODS**

one acre [un-named] between south woods and Jenkins Iland

and *one acre and a half* in **JYNKINS ILAND**

and **also one other meadow called LADISHOPE** containing *2 acres and one yard* to hold to him and to his heirs for ever doing court suit and other services as is aforesaid and rented by the year 10s.½d.

Henry Fane esquire holds by free deed as it is said **9 pieces of land called GAMMONS LAND** lying in Hadlow together to the lands called Cronbury late Henrie Fishers south, to a lane there leading into a meadow called foremede west, to the lands late Henrie Fishers and to the lands of the said Henrie Fane called litlestone roade east to hold to him and to his heirs doing court suit and other services as is aforesaid and rent by the year: 16s.4d.

William Darrell gent holds by free deed as it is said **3 pieces of land** containing *10 acres* in Hadlow together to the common there called little Lomewood north and west, to the land of Robert Fareman west, to the land called Millerds and fullerfeld south, to the lands of the said William Darrell east to hold to him and to his heirs by suit of court and other services as is aforesaid and rent by the year: 20d.

Folio 112   **Thomas Tuttisham** gent holds by free deed as it is said **one CAPITAL MESSUAGE with divers buildings, closes, one garden, 3 orchards and one meadow called SMITHES MEDE together lying to the same messuage** containing in the whole *6 acres* in West Peckham to the Queen's highway there leading from West Peckham to East Peckham east and north, to the parsonage lands there north west and south, and to the lands of the foresaid Thomas Tuttisham called Smithes croft east and rented yearly 2s.

and one other building and one other hamlet of land and one meadow called **COLVERHOWSE MEDE** containing *3 acres* together lying to the lands of Thomas Walsingham knight called Estlands south and east, to the Queen's highway leading from Mereworth to West Peckham north and to the Queens highway leading from West Peckham to East Peckham west, for the yearly rent of 12d.

and **also 2 barns with divers buildings, closes and 3 pieces of land together lying over against the capital messuage** containing *30 acres* whereof **one is called THOMALAND, the second ESTBYN and the third LONG GARDEN** and lie to the lands of the aforesaid Thomas Walsingham north, to the Queen's highway leading from the Hurst to the church of West Peckham west, to the Queen's highway leading from West Peckham to Mereworth south, to the demesne lands of Mereworth east and rent yearly 4s.

and **also one other piece of land called ORDLE PITTES** containing *3 acres and a half* lying to the Queen's highway leading from West Peckham to East Peckham, and to the orchard of the said Thomas Tuttisham called Ordlepitt garden north, to the lands of Nevell Delahey called Cockes land west, to the parsonage of West Peckham south, and to the lands of John Wright east, and rent yearly 8d.

and **also four pieces of land and wood** containing *14 acres* whereof **one is called TUTTISHAMS DANE, the second JAMES HILL, the third ESTDOWNE** together lying to the demesnes and to the common called le Herst west, to the lands of Sir Thomas Cotton knight called Bexe and Quarrey Swanton north, and to the lands of Thomas Cotton called Hellifeld east, to the vicarage wood of West Peckham and to the common there called the Hurst south, **the 4th piece of wood called WESTDOWNE** and lies to the demesne lands of West Peckham called the Lords dane and to the lands of Sir Thomas Cotton knight called Wigmore dane north, and to the common the west, south and east, and to the lands of the said Thomas Tuttisham called Estdowne east, by the yearly rent of 2s.1d.

and **also one other piece of woodland** containing *one acre* lying to the lands of the said Sir Thomas Cotton called Tunbridge dane east, and to another piece of woodland of the said Sir Thomas Cotton north, and to the common there west and south, by the yearly rent of 2d. and **also one other piece of woodland called SWERDDICH** containing **one acre** and lies at the Hurst, to the common there east, north and west and to the lands of the said Thomas Cotton and George Baker south, by the yearly rent of 2d.

Folio 113 There is no folio 113

Folio 114 The same **George [Baker]** holds **one tenement, one barn, one shop, one garden and 2 orchards** containing *one acre and a half* lying in West Peckham to the Queen's highway leading from West Peckham to Gov(er)hill north, to the lands and orchard of Sir Thomas Cotton west and south and to the lands of the said George Baker east by the yearly rent of 10d.

and **also one cottage and one piece of land and wood next to the Herstgate** containing *3 acres* in West Peckham, to the common there north, to the lands of the said Sir Thomas Walsingham east and south and to the lands of the said Thomas Tuttisham west **and one parcel of land called PERVELL CROFT** by the yearly rent of 8d.

and **also one other piece of land** containing *one acre* **lying at the Hurst,** to the lands of the said Sir Thomas Cotton west, to the lands of Sir Thomas Walsingham south, to the lands of Thomas Tuttisham east and north and to the common there called the Herst east, by the yearly rent of 2d. which is in the whole 14s.2d. to hold to him and to his heirs for ever by the foresaid rents, suit of court and other the services as is aforesaid

Robert Pawley holds by free deed as it is said **one messuage or cottage, one garden, one piece of land called BRUERS and 2 other pieces of land, 2 orchards, one barn called BASSIANS** together lying in Hadlow containing *7 acres*, to the common there called lomewood east, to the land of the said Sir Thomas Cotton called Scottispittes south, to the lands sometime Walter Carpinters north, by the yearly rent 12d.

and **also one other piece of land called LICHFELD** lying in Hadlow, to the common there called lomewood south, to the lands of the said Sir Thomas Cotton called Scottispittes east, and to the lands of Thomas Tuttisham north and west, and contains *one acre and a half* and rent by the year 3d., in the whole 17d. to hold to him and his heirs for ever by the rent aforesaid, suit of court and other services as is aforesaid

The heirs of John Carpinter holds by free deed as it is said **2 gardens and one piece of land called BUCKFELD** containing *3 acres and a half* together being in Hadlow to the common there called lomewood east, to the lands of the said Sir Thomas Cotton north and west, to the lands of Robert Pawley called Bassians south, by the yearly rent of 7d.

and **also 3 pieces of land** containing *5 acres* in Hadlow, to the lands of Thomas Tuttisham south, to the lands of Sir Thomas Cotton called longlands west, to the demesne lands there north, to the lands of the said Sit Thomas Cotton called blacklands east, by the yearly rent of 10d. in all 17d. to hold to them and to there heirs for the rent aforesaid, suit of court and other services as is aforesaid

Folio 115   There is no folio 115

Folio 116   **The heirs of John Kennye** holds **2 pieces of land** lying in West Peckham **at Gov(er)hill**, to the lands of Thomas Cotton east, south and west and to the Queen's highway there leading from Roughey to West Peckham against the north by the yearly rent of 18d.

John Betts holds **one piece of land called COCKESLAND** lying in West Peckham to the highway leading from East Peckham to West Peckham against the north, to the lands of Thomas Tuttisham gent called Smithscroft against the west, and to the parsons land there against the south, and to the lands of the said Thomas Tuttisham called Orlepittes on the east, containing *4 acres* and rent per annum 16d.

Richard Sommer holds **a cottage** with *half an acre* **of land** parcel sometime of **SCOTTISPITTES** lying in Hadlow to the common there called lomewood south and east to the lands of the said Thomas Cotton called Scottispittes north and west and a yearly rent of 1d.

Thomas Polhills the younger holds in the right of his wife **3 pieces of land called GILBERTS** containing *10 acres* lying in Hadlow, to the lands of William Darrell and Robert Fareman and to the common there called Lytle lomewood against the north, to a lane there leading from lomewood to Hadlow mill west, to lands of Harrie Keble south, and to a piece of land of Richard Somers called fullersfeld east, and rent per annum 20d.

Thomas Bourne holds freely *2 acres* of [un-named] **meadow** lying in Hadlow to the lane called Crongberye sometime Harrye Fisher's against the north, to the river there south, to a mead called foremede west, and to the residue of the mead of the said Thomas Bornes against the west and north, yearly [rent] 10½d.

Total of the rents of the freeholders: £6 9s. 6½d. £1 of [cautyn]
Total of the rents of the demesnes: *3s.4d.*
Total of the grain: *10 quarters of wheat*

The writing hereof ended the 10th of July, 1583, the 25th year of Elizabeth
Per me Ro **Thomas Fey**
Finish

INDEX

Reference numbers in *italics* indicate pictures and references in **bold** indicate maps and plans on those pages

A

Abergavenny, Lord, 4, 190
accidents, 51, 63
Acre, The, Jopes tenement, 135
advowsons, Mereworth church, 191
Agnes at Weald, 175
agriculture, 44, 46, 47-51, 106, 107, 116
 controls by manor courts, 30-1, *39*
 farm sizes, 47, **47**, 103-4
Akerman, John, **24**
Akerman, Nicholas, 163, 167, 171, 172
Aland, Thomas, 36
Aldington, Court of dens, <u>100</u>
aletasters, 32, 34-5
Aleynslove tenement, **9**, 18, **22**, 79
 1581 survey, 162-3
Alomepitt, West Peckham, 195
Alorne, Nicholas, 121
amercements, 31, 32-3, 35, 39-41
Andrew, John, 121, 186
 Brooke tenement, 184
Andrewe, William, *3*, 133, 136
Anne, Dowager Duchess of Buckingham 5,
 23, 52, 114
 amercements, 36, 41
 estate administration, 44
 fishing, 13, *13*, 48
 pig dues, 28
 Aleynslove tenement, 163
 Berwys tenement, **16**, 149
 Cotmansfield, 19-20, 24, **24**
 Holmans tenement, 15, 148
 Honewolds tenement, 19, **24**, 168
 Jordans tenement, **16**, 23, 188
 Kenes tenement, 11, **12**, 125
 Lawerk tenement, 188
 Moyles tenement, 160
 Paynes tenement, 164
 Somers tenement, 157
 Wekerylds tenement, **17**, 156
Anote Island (Anoyteland), 23
 Brooke tenement, 181-2, 184
Appletons (Napiltons), 20, **20**, 24
arable farming, *39*, 47-8, 50-1, 103-4, 106,
 107
 Wekerylds tenement, 17
Arber, Le, Fishland tenement, 13, 138
Ashdowne, Henry, 21, 175
Ashdowne, John, Lockbridges tenement,
 175
Ashdownes tenement, **9**, 21, 26, 175
Ashes Lane (was Palmer Street), 14, 16-17,
 17, 51, **57**, 62
Ashwood highway, **17**, 58, 62
assaults, 34, 36, 41

assembly places, 100
Ateyrfield (Jankmyr), 128-9
Atwood, Thomas, 115
Audeley, Hugh de, 78
Austen, Stephen, 110
Awland, Thomas (1517), 68
Aylards Acre, Lotewood tenement, 188
Aylardshagh, Wekerylds tenement, 155
Aylesford (royal vill), 105
Ayshdown, William, 37
Aysschedown, Richard, 34

B

Bacon, Thomas, 38
Bacris (Barris Croft) Cross, 99
Badsell manor, Five Oak Green, 71, 72,
 72, 93
bailiffs, 31
Bakehouse mead, Mereworth park, 191
Baker, George, West Peckham, 197
Baker, Richard, East Peckham, 121, 180
Baker, Thomas, of Sussex, 180
Bakersfield, Lake tenement, 180
baking, regulations, 31
Barne (Berne) family, 107
Barnes Place, **57**, **61**, 62, *62*, 82, 108
Barnes Street, 23
Barnfield, Brooke tenement, 184
Barnfield, Lake (2) tenement, 186
Barnfield, Stoperfields tenement, 176
Barris Croft, Wekerylds tenement, 99, 156
Barton, John, 68, 70, 121
 Pynchon's tenement, 145-6
 Welshes tenement, 152
Barton, John A., 68, 130, 139, 162
 Jopes tenement, *3*, 136
 Kenes tenement, 124-5, 126
 Pococks tenement, 145
 Wells tenement, 132
 Wodmanys tenement, 126-7
Barton, Thomas, 44, 97
Basset, John, 116
Basset, Marion, 85-6
Bassians barn, Hadlow, 197
Batchler, Edward, Mereworth manor, 194
Batchler, Robert, Mereworth manor, 194
Battle Abbey, 22, 111
Baynes, Sir James, 68
Beald (Bealde, Beal, Bele) family, 88-92
Beald, John, 88, 90, 121, 134
Beald, Margaret, 90, 92
Bealde family, 88-92, **90**, **91**
 wills, 45, 81-92
Bealde, Agnes, widow of William, 89
Bealde, Johanne, 90, **90**

Bealde, John (carpenter), 15, 89, **90**, 121,
 144
 Fishland tenement, **52**
 Knights tenement, 148
 Tanners tenement, 142-3
 will, 45, 90
Bealde, John of Wrotham, 89, 174, 175-6
Bealde, Lawrence, 90, **90**
 will, 45, 91-2
Bealde, Margaret, 90, **90**, 92
Bealde, Richard will, 45, 89-90
Bealde, Richard (1), 69, 88, 89, **90**
Bealde, Richard (2), 90-1
Bealde, Thomas, 91, 92
Bealde, William, 82, 89
Beale, Richard, 169
Becher, Nicholas, 160
Bedyndenn, John (1512), 68
Bele, Johan (Johanna), 91
Bele Sandhersts Croft, Lake (2) tenement,
 185
Bele, William, 91, 92
Bembuin, John (1509), 68
Bemittis, Peacocks tenement, 144
Benson, Thomas (1496), 68
bequests, 45, 68-70
 Sir John and Lady Rivers, 76
 John Bishop (2), 85
 William Bele, 91
 William Bishop, 83
Berde, John, 85, 87
Berecroft (Bear Croft), Cowling tenement,
 11, 122
Berecroft, Freferding tenement, 128
Berecroft, Knett the Hoggs tenement, 141
Berefield, Cowling tenement, 123
Berghwis, Berwys tenement, **16**, 150
Berne (Barne), John, 108
Berne (Barne), Richard, 107, 108
Berton, John, 90
Berwys tenement, **9**, **16**, 26
 1581 survey, 149-51
 see also Brewis tenement
Best, John (1546), 68
Bethersden parish, farm sizes, 47, **47**
Betson, John (1540), 68
Bettes, John, Mereworth manor, 193
Betts, John, West Peckham, 198
Beult river, 21
Bewebamer, Palmers tenement, 153
Bidborough (Bitberea), 84, 86
Birchwood tenement, **9**, 151
Birchwoods Lane, **17**, 62
Bishop family, 11, 70. 83-8, **84**
 1581 survey, 42, 43, 44
 Cowling tenement, 10-11, **10**, **11**

Kenes tenement, 11, **12**
wills, 5, 83-7, 98-9
Bishop, Agnes, wife of Robert, 83
Bishop, Alice, 84
Bishop, Gervase, 11, 83, 126, 127, 143
Bishop, Joan, 84, 85, 86
Bishop, John, 34, 39, 68-9, 131, 138
    Buntanys tenement, 179
    Jordans tenement, 23, 188
    Knights tenement, 148
    Peacocks tenement, 144
    Wekerlyds tenement, 156
Bishop, John, son of John, **84**, 85-6, 87, 121, 149
Bishop, John, son of Richard, 10-11, *10*, **11**, 83, 87, 122-3, 132
Bishop, John, son of Robert, 10-11, *10*, **11**, 83, 84, **84**, 85, 87-8
    Berwys tenement, **16**, 149-50
    Cowling tenement, 25, 122
    Freferding tenement, 83, 127-8
    Jopes tenement, 134
    Kenes tenement, 11, 122-3
    Knett the Hoggs tenement, 13, 140
    Peacock's tenement, 83, 143-4
    Somers tenement, 156-7
    Walter at Stair tenement, 129-30
    Wells tenement, 132
    Wodemany's tenement, 83, 126
Bishop, Richard, son of Robert, 86-7
Bishop, Richard, son of William, **11**, 83, 84, 123
    will, 86, 126-7, 132
Bishop, Robert, d.1535, son of John Bishop (2), **84**, 86-7, 121
Bishop, Robert, son of William, **12**, 83, 84, **84**, 125
    Palmers tenement, 154
    Wekerylds tenement, 154-5
    Welshes tenement, 152
    Fichet's tenement, 146
Bishop, Thomas, 11, 25, 87-8, 123, 125, 131
    bad behaviour, 34, 41, 87
    Freferding tenement, 128
    Knett the Hoggs tenement, 140
Bishop, Thomas, son of Robert, **84**, 86
Bishop, Thomas, son of William, 83, 84, **84**, 148-9
Bishop, Walter, 83
Bishop, William (senior), 5, 11, **11**, 83-4, **84**, 124
Bitberea (Bidborough), 84, 86
Black Death, 19, 24, 27, 42, 50, 111
Blackberrys, Honewolds tenement, **24**, 169
Blackmans brook, 161
Blackmans field, 161
Blackman's Lane, 17, 18, 51, **57**, **61**
Blackmans, Moyles tenement, 159
Blackmans tenement, **9**, **22**
    1581 survey, 160-1
    pig dues, 28, 29

Blake, N. F., 108-9
Blakehouse, John (1471), 68
Bodyfields, Fichet's tenement, 146
Bogcroft, Wekerylds tenement, **17**, 156
Boleyn, Sir Thomas, 115
boonwork, 27, 123, 151
Born, John, 69, 91, 131
Borne Cross, 99
Borne, John, 131, 156, 173
    Coiffes tenement, 169
Borne, Nicholas, 156, 170, 173, 175
Borne, Thomas, 171, 173, 174, 176
Borne, The, Paynes tenement, 164
Botany stream, Tonbridge, 55, **57**
Bothegate, 78
Boucher, Thomas, 115
boundary crosses, 98-9
Bounds, 21, 79
Boundsfield, Coswyns tenement, 170
Boundsfield (formerly More Precklesham), Fosters tenement, 21, 173
Bourne Grange (later part of Hadlow College), 19
Bourne Mill, *18*, *22*, 50, **57**, 58
Bourne family, 70
Bourne, Nicholas, 34
    Alleynslove tenement, 162
Bourne, Thomas, 198
Bourne river, 18, **22**, 49-50, 56, **57**, 58-9, **61**
Bourne Stile, 21
Bourneside Farm, 18, **22**, **57**, 59, *59*
Bowlere (later Wells) tenement, **9**, 26
    see also Wells tenement
Bowleris, Wells tenement, 132
Bowleys, Wells tenement, 133
Bradley, Prof. Richard, 105
Bramble field, Paynes tenement, 163
Bramblesfield, Honewolds tenement, 167
Branbridge (Slades Bridge), 56, *56*, **60**, 105, *106*
Brandon, Peter, 105
Brecklesham, Coswyns tenement, 171
Bredett field, 140
Brenchley, 45
Brewer, Joan, 19, 167
Brewer, Richard, 19
brewing, 50, 114
    regulations, 31, 34-5, *35*, 40
Brewis Lane (later Sherriff's Lane), 15-16
Brewis tenement, **9**, 16, *16*
    see also Berwys tenement
Brick making, **14**, 15, *15*
Bridger, John, Mereworth manor, 193
bridges, 63
    river Bourne, 58-9, 62
    river Medway, 55-7, *55*, *56*, *57*
Broadfield, Peacock's tenement, 143
Broadfield, Stoperfields tenement, 176-7
Broads Plain (Brodetisphayne, Bredett) common, 62, 65, 140
Brodefeld, Mereworth manor, 191

Brodefeld, West Peckham, 195
Brodell, John, 148
Brodetisfield, Pococks tenement, 145
Broke, Richard, 167, 169, 171
Brokefield, Mereworth manor, 191
Broker, Matilda, 20, 161, 170
    Aleynslove tenement, 162
    Coiffes tenement, **20**, **24**
    Honewolds tenement, 168-9
Brome, The, Spaldings tenement, 174
Bromfield, Welshes tenement, 152
Bromptonys, Fletchers tenement, 166
Brook at Andrewy, Wells tenement, 132
Brook, The, Hamenetts tenement, 158
Brook, The, Lockbridges tenement, 175
Brooke, John, 68
Brooke tenement, **9**, 23, 26, *54*, 65, 79, 81
    1581 survey, 180-4
Brooks at Longreidis, Brooke tenement, 181
Brooks, The, Hamenetts tenement, 159
Brooks, The, Welshes tenement, 152
Broom Crofts, Welshes tenement, 152
Broomfield, Stoperfields tenement, 176
Broomfield tenement, **9**, 15, 26, 83
    1581 survey, 148-9
Browncroft, Lake (2) tenement, 186
Bruers, Hadlow, 197
Brydges, Elizabeth, wife of Ralph Fane, 45, **71**, 74, 94
Buckfeld, Hadlow, 198
Buckingam, Edward Stafford, Duke of, 44, *44*, 101-2
Buckingham, Duchess of *see*, Anne, Dowager Duchess of Buckingham
Buckingham, Henry Stafford (1454-1483), 5, 78
Buckingham, Humphrey Stafford, Duke of, 5, 78
Bulfinch, John and William, Mereworth manor, 191, 192
Bulfinch, Thomas, 131
Buntan, John, 178
Buntanhale (Buntinghale), 84
Buntanys tenement, **9**
    1581 survey, 178-80
Buntanysbregh, Berwys tenement, **16**, 149-50
Buntinges, Mereworth manor, 192
Bunyards, 91
Burdon, William, 156, 160
Burgeys, Margaret, 34
Burgeys, Walter, 121, 174, 179
Burgh, The, Berwys tenement, **16**, 150
burial instructions, 68-9
Burton family, 70
Burton, John, 168
butchers, *35*
    regulations, 35, 40
Byshop, John, 68-9
Bytchler, William, Mereworth manor, 194

C

Cage Green, 65, 101
Cage Park, 44, 73, 106, 115
Calchiscroft, Brooke tenement, 181
Calveslease, Fichet's tenement, 146
Capel parish, **6**, **8**, 71, 72, 85, 86
Carden, Thomas, 133
Cardensmeade, **12**, 124, 125
Cardnell, 140
Cardon, Thomas, 151
Cardons tenement, **9**, 16-17, 26
    1581 survey, 151
Carey, Sir George, 43, 82
    1587 settlement, 114
Carey, Sir Henry, 103
carpenters, 35
Carpenters Lane, 18, 50, 66
Carpinter, John, 198
carrying services, 27
Carslake, John, 158, 182-3
Carslake, William, 183, 186-7
Carslakes, Anote Island, 183
Carter, Richard, 161, 165
cattle, 33, 51, 53, 110, 115, 116
    fatttening, 9, 13, 48, 58
    river crossings, 55, 57, 60
Cattysbrayn land, 90
causeways, 63
Causton (Caxton) family, 107-9
Causton, Hugh de, 7, 22, 93, 107, 109, 178
    Stoperfield tenement, 22, 92, 176
Caustones Cross, Stoperfields tenement,
    177
Caustones field, Buntanys tenement, 179
Caustons cross, **22**, 99, 177
Caustons manor, 6, **6**, 21, **61**, 83, 93, 99,
    107-9
    Beald family, 88
    court rolls, 32, 83
Caxton, William, 107-9, *107*, *108*
    alleged birthplace, *108*
Cayser, William, 84
Cemetery Lane (later Durrants Cross), 20,
    22, **61**, 62
cereals, 49-50, 52
Chafford Place, Penshurst, 75, 76
Chalklin, C. W., 64, 103-4
Chaloners Meades, Brooke tenement, 183
Champens brook, 128, 129
Chapelyn, Thomas, 125
Chaplam, Thomas (tithingman), 32
charcoal, 43
Chiddingstone parish, farm sizes, 47, **47**
Chidley Cross, East Peckham, 95
Chipstead, Chevening, 94
Chown, George, 84
Chown, John, 85, 87
Christmeade, 124, 128, 131
Church Place (formerly Lords Place), 67
    see also Lords Place
church registers, 70, 82
Church Street, *14*, 20, **24**, 67
    1901, *30*

Church's croft, Haymonds tenement, 171-2
churchwardens, Mereworth manor, 194
Cinge, 137
Clanricarde, Earl of, 46
Clare family, *5*, 7-8, 16, 21, 107
    North Frith park, 101
Clare, Gilbert, 16, 78, 107
Clare, Richard (Richard of Tonbridge), 67,
    106-7, 121
Clarkscrofte, Wells tenement, 133
Clements Hill, Fishland tenement, **52**, 138
Clertis, The, 141
Cliffe, Mereworth manor, 194
Clobcroft, 23, 79
Clobcroft, Lake (2) tenement, 185
clothmaking, 18, 19
Cob, Richard, 81-2
Cobham, Lord, Mereworth manor, 194
Cochmoris, Blackmans tenement, 160-1
Cockesland, West Peckham, 198
Cockysbrook watermeadow, 133
Coffin path, 70
Cogger, Martin, 34, 150, 151, 154
    Somers tenement, 157
    Wekerylds tenement, 155-6
Coiffe, John, 169
Coiffe, William, 62, 83, 133, 146
Coiffes tenement, **9**, **20** 20, **24**, 93
    1581 survey, 169
Cokkes, John, 86
Cokks, Margaret, 85
Colcoff, Sir Ralph, 68, 69
Colleyne, George, 65
Colpannes, Mereworth manor, 192
Colpeper, Richard, 194
    Fletchers tenement, 165
Colverhowse Mede, West Peckham, 196
Colyn family, 70, 140
Colyn, Richard, 146, 147, 148
common land, 18, 53, 64-6, **64**, 106, 110
    enclosure, 37, 65, 66
    West Peckham demesne, 195
Compton, Sir William, 37
constables, election, 32, 33
coppicing, 15, 44, *44*, 104
Coppings Mead, Brooke tenement, 184
corn mills, 50, 58
Cornmeare, The, Wekerylds tenement, 156
Correnden, **14**, **17**
Coswyns tenement, **9**, 20, 93, 99
    1581 tenement, 170-1
Cotlands, **22**, 93
Cotmansfield, 19-20, 24, **24**
cotmen, 24
Cott in the Payne of Eyland, **12**, 128
Cotton family, 74-5, 113, 166-7
Cotton, Sir Robert, 113
Cotton, Sir Thomas, 109-110
    Mereworth manor, 192-3
    West Peckham, 195-6
Cotton, William, 109
Coulton Mead, 97

Court Lane, 20, **22**, **24**, **57**, 61
court leet, 31, 40
    see also view of frankpledge.
Court Lodge, 23, 67, 95, 110
court of dens, Aldington, 100
court rolls, *see* manor courts
Courtmead, 23, 169
courts baron, 30-1, 32, 33-4, 38-9
    see also manor courts
Cowlease, 196
Cowling mead, **11**, 122
Cowling tenement, **9**, 10-11, *10*, **11**,
    122-3
    tenants' payments, 25-6
Cowlingfield, **11**, 122
Crakbenn, Robert, 169
Cranborrows Weir, 97
crimes, 34, 36-7, 39, 41
Crocher, John, 14
    Fichet's tenement, 15, **17**, 146
    Welshes tenement, 152
Crochers, Wodemany's tenement, 127
Crochland, Moyles tenement, 160
Crochland tenement, **9**, 18, 26
    1581 survey, 160
Crockers manor, West Peckham, 195
Croft and Sled, Welshes tenement, 151-2
Croft at Borne, 141
Croft at Hammetts, The, 158
Croft at Warend, Brooke tenement, 181
Croft, The, Jopes tenement, 136
Croft, The, Wodeman's tenement, 126
Croft under the House, Cowling tenement,
    11, 123
Crofts at Borne Stile, Fosters tenement,
    173
Crombury manor, **6**, **9**, 21, 32, **61**, 97, 107
Cromwell, Thomas, 114, 115
Crosse, John (1528), 68
Crosses at Borne, Fishland tenement, 137
crosses, roadside, **6**, 70, 98-9, *98*
Crouche, John, 170
Croucher, John, 34
Crouchfield, Palmers tenement, 153
Crouchland, Puddings tenement, 99, 178
Crouchland tenement, *see* Crochland
    tenement
Croweterst, 196
Crowhurst, Thomas and Robert,
    Mereworth manor, 192
Crowley, Robert, 74
Croydons, Fletchers tenement, 165
Croydonsfield, Paynes tenement, 164
Crudd family, 43, 70, 97
Crudd, Richard, 148
Crudd, Thomas, 131
    Freferding tenement, **12**, 97, 129
    Kenes tenement, **12**, 125, 126
    Wells tenement, 132-3
Cuckoo Lane, 57, 62, 65
Culpeper family, 19, 44, 74-5, 113
    North Frith, 102-3

Culpeper, Alexander, 103
Culpeper, Lady Elizabeth, *18*, 34, 121
    Fletchers tenement, 18, 58, 165
    knight's fee, 34, 78
    Peckham manor, **17**, 18
Culpeper, John, 19
Culpeper, Richard, 18, 19, 78, 121
    Bourne mill, **57**, 58
    Fletchers tenement, 165
    Peckhams tenement, 166-7
Culpeper, Thomas, 102, 103
customary book, 110
custumals *see* surveys
Cutthorne Cross, Huddersfield, 100
Cuttisbrayne land, Fishland tenement, 137

D

Darrell, William, 196
Davisfield, Knights tenement, 148
Dean's Plank, 56, **57**
death taxes *see* heriots
Deepmeade, Brooke tenement, 183, 184
Deering bridge, 59
Delahope, Nevell, Mereworth manor, 194
demesnes, 5-6, **22**, 23-4
    Mereworth park, 191
    West Peckham, 195
Dene, The, Freferding tenement, 128, 129
Denman, William, 115
dens, 100, 106
Dering, Dorothy and Elizabeth, **71**, 72
disputes, 30, 31, 34
ditches, maintenance, *36*, 37, 41, 63, 92
Dog Kennel path (Skeyffe Lane), **22**, 59,
    61, *62*, *63*
Domewright, John, 116
Dorants, Coswyns tenement, 99, 171
Dorants Cross *see* Durrants Cross
    (Cemetery Lane)
Dornemeade, Eastwosys tenement, 178
Dorrell (Darrell) family, 113, 180
Dorrells, William Whetnell, 180
Down, Thomas, 36
drove roads, 51, 105
Duck's bridge, 56
Dudley, John (later duke of
    Northumberland), 102
dues in kind, 28-9
Dukes Place, 19
Dumbreck, W.D, v, **14**, 51, 97
Dunbar, Thomas, 35
Durrants Cross (Cemetery Lane), 20, 59,
    61, *62*, 99
Dyer, Christopher, 42

E

East Barming, 89
East Peckham, **6**, **8**, 43, 66, 78, 95
    church, 89
    old track, *62*
Eastfield, Brooke tenement, 181
Eastfield, Freferding tenement, 128

Eastfield, Walter at Stair tenement, 131
Eastwosys tenement, **9**, **22**, 178
Edwards, Mereworth manor, 192
eels, 48-9, 55, 58
    selling, *48*
Eight acres, Lake tenement, 180
Eirghi acre, Berwys tenement, **16**, 151
Elstems, The, Coiffes tenement, 169
Elstons, Coswyns tenement, 171
Elton, C.I., 65
Erberis, Jopes tenement, 135
    see also Herberys
estate management, 30-1, 109-10, 111-14
Estbyn, West Peckham, 197
Estdowne, West Peckham, 197

F

Fader, Thomas, 23, 188
Fader, William, 180
Fane, Colyer, 74
Fane family, 45, 70, 71-5, 108, 113
    see also Vane family
Fane, Elizabeth (neé Brydges), 45, **71**, 74,
    94
Fane, Francis, Earl of Westmorland, 75, *75*
Fane, George, *72*, *73*, 75
Fane, Henry, 36, 65, 73, 74, 121, 163
    Brooke tenement, 180-1, 183
    Buntanys tenement, 178-9
    Lake (2) tenement, 185, 186-7
    Lockbridges tenement, 174-5
    Stoperfield tenement, 177
    West Peckham, 196
Fane, Henry, brother of William, 1456 will,
    94
Fane, Henry of Hadlow (1469-1533) m.
    Alice Fisher, 71, 72, 93-4
Fane, John of Hadlow d. 1542, **71**, 72
Fane, Ralph (1510-52), 45, **71**, 72-3, 74,
    94, 102
Fane, Richard son of John, **71**, 72
Fane, Richard of Badsell, 71, 72
Fane, Thomas, 113
    1532 will, 94-5
Fane, Thomas and Helen Somerset,
    monument, *74*, 75
Fane, Thomas, Mereworth manor, 193
Fane, Thomas of London, **71**
Fareman, Lawrence, 124
farm sizes, 47, **47**
    North and South Frith, 103-4
Farman, John, 35, 123
Farman (later Ferman), Lawrence, *10*, **11**,
    12, 121
    Berwys tenement, 150
    Cowling tenement, **10**, 123
    Freferding tenement, 128, 129
    Moyles tenement, 159
    Odamys tenement, 139
    Peacock's tenement, 143-4
    Walter at Stair tenement, 13, 130
    Wodemany's tenement, 126, 127
farms/ sizes/ chart, **47**

Faulkner's Oast, 15, **17**
feoffment, 33, 88, 89, 90-1
Ferlingate, Tanners tenement, 142
Fey (Fet), Thomas, 198
Fichet (Fychett), John and Thomas, 14, 127,
    130, 132
    Fishland tenement, **52**, 138
    Holmans tenement, 147
        Pococks tenement, 145
Fichet's tenement, **9**, 15, **17**, 146
Fichett, Richard, 33
Fish Hall (Fishill), **52**, **57**, 136, 138
    "manor", **6**, 13-14, 73, 75, 77, *99*, 107
Fisher family, 13, 48, 70, 113
    1581 survey, 42, 43
Fisher, Alice, 71, 72
Fisher, Alice, wife of Thomas, *3*, 136, 143
    Brooke tenement, 182
Fisher, John, 33, 85, 124, 130, 133
    Berwys tenement, 150-1
    Broomfields tenement, 148
    Fishland tenement, 137, 138
    Hoggs tenement, 142
    Jopes tenement, 134, 136
    Pococks tenement, 145
Fisher, Peter, 39, 90, 121
    Aleynslove tenement, 162
    Blackmans tenement, 161
    Knett the Hoggs tenement, 13, 140,
        141
Fisher, Richard, 33, **52**, 102, 115, 121, 131
    Freferding tenement, 129
    Jopes tenement, 135
    Knett the Hoggs tenement, 142
    Wells tenement, 133
Fisher, Richard, jun., 147
Fisher, Thomas, 34, 39, 87, 98, 99, 121
    Berwys tenement, 150
    Fishland tenement, 13-14, 136-8
    Freferding tenement, 128-9
    Jopes tenement, 134-5
    Kenes tenement, 125, 126
    Knett the Hoggs tenement, 13, 141
    Odamys tenement, 139
    Tanner's tenement, 143
    Walter at Stair tenement, 13, 130-1
    Wells tenement, 132
Fisherhill, Jopes tenement, 134-5
Fisher's lease, 97
Fishill common, 65
Fishill field, Knett the Hoggs tenement, 140
Fishill (Fish Hall) *see* Fish Hall (Fishill)
fishing, 13, *13*, 58
    eels, 48-9, 58
    trade, 94
Fishland tenement, **9**, 13-14, 48, **52**
    1581 tenement, 136-8
    little common, 65
    rent, 26
Fitzherbert, John and Anthony, 112
FitzRalph, Simon, 122
Fletcher, William, 82

Fletchers tenement, **9**, 18, 50, 99
    1581 survey, 165-6
food shortages, 45
footpaths, *56*, 60, *62*, *63*, 99
    maps, **6**, **17**, **57**
Foremede, Hadlow, 196
Forest Row, Ashdown Forest, *108*
Forstal, The, Mereworth manor, 191
Forstall, Fletchers tenement, 165
Forsters field, 173-4
Foster, James, 153
Fosters tenement, **9**, 21, 22
    1581 survey, 173-4
Frankish people, 105
Frapelanes, Peacock's tenement, 143-4
freemen, 106
Freferding tenement, **9**, 11, **12**, 83
    1581 survey, 127-9
Fromond family, 7, 21, 44, 70, 74-5,
    77-83, 113
    Brooke tenement, 23
    family trees, **79-81**
    wills, 79-82
Fromond, Alice, wife of Gilbert, 79, **80**,
    81, 177
Fromond atte Water
    Alice, widow of Peter, 79, 80, **80**, 158,
      162
    Alice, widow of Peter Stoperfields
      tenement, 176
    Joan, 79, **80**, 81, 99, 137
    Joan, Jopes tenement, *3*, 79, 136
    Joan, Odamys tenement, 138--9
    Peter, 80, 81
Fromond, Bartholomew, 82, 83
Fromond, Gilbert, 78, 79, 81
    Brooke tenement, 183-4
Fromond, Johane, 78
Fromond, John
    Gibbons tenement, 166
    Sewayne tenement, 167

Fromond, John (receiver), 78, 121
Fromond, Nicholas, 34-5, 77, 78
Fromond of Fishall, Thomas, 77
Fromond of Goldhill, **61**, 79, **79**
    John, 78, 79, **79**, 82, 122
    John, Brooke tenement, 23, 181-2
    John, Lake (2) tenement, 186
    John, son of Lady Margaret, 79, **79**, 80
    Lady Margaret, 78, 79-80, **79**, 81-2,
      122
      Brooke tenement, 23, 183
      Coswyns tenement, 170
      Eastwosys tenement, 178
      Fosters tenement, 173
      Lake (2) tenement, 186
      Lake tenement, 180
    Richard, 80, 81, 82, 178, 180
    Thomas, 21, 69, 77, 78, 79-81, **79**,
      82, 180
    Thomas, Eastwosys tenement, 178
Fromond of Kempinghale
    John, 79, 80, **81**, 82, 121
    John, Lake (2) tenement, 185
    John, Lotewood tenement, 188
    Margaret (d.1482), 80, **81**, 82
    Richard, 81, **81**
Fromond, Roger, 80
Fromond, William, 35, 79-80, 82-3
Fromonds manor, **6**, 21, **61**, 77, 82, 88, 107
    Cotton family, 109-10, 113
Fromonds mead, Fletchers tenement, 165
Frutar, Joan, 98, 141, 150-1, 158
    Aleynslove tenement, 162-3
    Blackmans tenement, 161
    Fishlands tenement, **52**, 137
    Moyles tenement, 159
    Wekerylds tenement, 155
Fulgryshopes, Brooke tenement, 182
Fullersfield, Gibbons tenement, 19, 166
fulling, 18, 58
    mill, 59

furzefields, **14**, 15
Fychett (Fichet), John and Thomas, 14, 15,
    127, 145
Fychett (Fichet), Richard, 33
Fychett, *see also* Fichet (Fychett), John and
    Thomas

G

Galton, John, 34, 36, 87
Gambon, Agnes, 98, 137
Gammons land, Hadlow, 196
gavelkind, 5-6, 9, 74, 88, 89, 113
    tenants, dues, 29
Geldland, **22**
Gentlemen Pensioners, 45, 73, 102
Geoffrey at Grove, 92, 176
Gerthe, Thomas, 91
Gervases land, Kenes tenement, **12**, 124
Gibbons tenement, 18-19, 21, 93
    1581 survey, **9**, **24**, 166
Gifferey, William, 19, 167
Gilbert, Count of Eu, Normandy, 106
Gilberts, Hadlow, 198
Gilberts, Mereworth manor, 192
Gloucester, Earl of, Gilbert de Clare, 7,
    107, 189, 190
Goblands farm, 21
Godfrey, Thomas, 115
Goding (Godinge), John, 21, 78, 121,
    158-9
    Blackmans tenement, 160-1
    Coswyns tenement, 171
    Fosters tenement, 21, 173
    Spaldings tenement, 174
Goding (Godinge), William, 34, 88
Godings (later Hadlow Place), **61**, 62
Godyng (Goding, later Golding), John, 7,
    21, 84
Godyng (Gooding) family, Fromonds
    manor, 70, 77
Goldfinch, William, 145
Goldhill (Golden Green), 20, 21, **61**
Goldhill manor, 6, 32, **61**, 88, 107
Goldhill mill, **57**, 59
Goldsmyth, Elizabeth, 85
Goldsmyth, Simon, 86
Goman, John, 151
Gomme, G.L., 100
Gonner, E. C. K., 64
Goodman, Roger, 140
Gooseland (Lawrence land), Grove
    tenement, 175-6
Gooseland, Lockbridges tenement, 174
Gosse, James, 69, 90, 121, 162, 164
Gosse, Thomas (1443-7), 68
Goudhurst, 94
Grand Inquisition (later Grand Jury), 32-3,
    37, 38, 78
    jurors, 38-9

Skeyffe Lane (aka Dog Kennel Path) at Robards, Stoperfield tenement.

grazing, 47, 51, 53, 58, 102, 115
    common land, 64, 66
    see also cattle; pannage; pigs
Great Blackmansfield, Moyles tenement, 160
Great Hope land, Odamys tenement, 140
Great Kemeland, Jordans tenement, **16**, 188
Great Magginham, Honewolds tenement, 168-9
Great North field, Mereworth manor, 191
Grenetre, Margaret, 67
Gretbergh, Berwys tenement, **16**, 149
Grosse, James, 34, 36, 58-9
Grove field, 175
Grove tenement, **9**, 21, 89
    1581 survey, 175-6
Grove, Welshes tenement, 152-3
Grubb, Denise, Palmers tenement, 153-4
Grubb, William, 152
Guge, John, 146
Guildford, Sir Henry, 102
Gyles, Edward, Mereworth manor, 194

H

Hachfield, Wekerylds tenement, 156
Hadecher, Reginald (1516), 68, 70, 98
Hadloe, Nicholas de, and son, 67
Hadlow, **6**, **24**, 47-50, **60**, *61*
Hadlow bridge cross, 59, 70
Hadlow Castle, 23, 24, 95
Hadlow church, 67-69, *67*, 70
    Rivers family monument, 51, *75*, 76
Hadlow College, 19
Hadlow Common, **22**, 64-6, **64**
Hadlow manor, 4, 5-6, 18, 75, 77, 95, 101-2
    1581 rental, 43, 112, 121
    1587 rental, 29, 65, 103, 114
    administration, 109-10, 111-12, 113-14
    courts *see* manor courts
    sub-manors, 6, **6**, **9**, 21, 100, 107, 109
    tenements, 8, **9**
Hadlow parish, 6, **6**, **8**, 47-50
    1720 survey, 114
    1835 survey, 66
    1858 map, 66
    register, 95
    sub manors, 6, **6**, **9**, 21, 107, 109
    tenements, 8, **9**
Hadlow Place, 6, **6**, 17, **57**, 94, 107
    Fane family, 45, 72, 74, 94
    manor courts, 32, 34
Hadlow Stair, 49, *55*, 58, 61, 97
    manor courts, 32, 35, 87
    maps, **6**, **9**, **52**, **57**
Hadlow vicarage, 19
Hale brothers, 33
Hale, J., 170, 172
Hale street, 95
Half Acre at Strode, The, Lake (2) tenement, 186

Hall, Robert, 47, 184
Halle, Thomas, 127, 194
Halls Deepmeade, Brooke tenement, 184
Halls Half Acre, Brooke tenement, 184
Hallysland, 127
Halpound tenement (Haymonds), **9**, 171-2
Hame, The, Somers tenement, 157
Hamenett tenement, **9**, 26, 28, 29
    1581 survey, 157-9
Hamenetts, 158
Hamme, The, Tanner's tenement, 142
Hampton, Robert, 86
Hampton's mill, 58
Harding field, Jopes tenement, 135
Harding, Gilbert, 183
Harmon, Richard (tanner), 69
Harper, Sir George, 102-3
Harry Fromonds, Fosters tenement, 173
Hart, Edward, 116
Hartlake bridge, 23, **54**, 55-6, *55*, **57**
Hartlake Farmhouse, 23
harvests, 45, *48*
Hascocks land, Holmans tenement, 147
Haselwood, West Peckham, 195
Hawkynnys land, 82
Haycher, Richard, 92
Haymonds tenement, **9**, 20, 171-2
Haymons well, Haymonds tenement, 172
Headcorn parish, farm sizes, 47, **47**
Headland, Cardons tenement, 151
Heatis, William, 122
Hebard, John, 70
Hebard, Richard, 70
Hecott, John, 172, 173
Hecotts tenement, **9**, 21, 172
Hellersland (Hellerscroft), Lake (2) tenement, 186
Hellis, Thomas, 70
Henley, Joanna, 81
Henry VIII, 44, 51, 114
Hentlove, Jopes tenement, 79, 136
herb gardens, *52*, 79
    see also Herberys
Herberd (Herbarde) John, 20, **20**, 70, 170
Herberd (Herbarde), Richard, 45, 70, 177
Herberys, 13-14, 52, **52**, 138
    Herberys lane, *53*
    Wells tenement, 134
    see also Erberis
heriots, 28, 30-1, 32, 40, 84, 123
    West Peckham, 195, 196
Herne pound, Mereworth, 192
Herst, Reginald, 126, 132
    Kenes tenement, 124-5
    Pocockes tenement, 145
    Welshes tenement, 152
Hevygate, 137
Hewe, David (1475), 68
Hexstall, Henry, 15, **24**, 43, 133, 170
    Coiffes tenement, 20, **20**
    Crochland tenement, 160
    Fishland tenement, **52**, 138

    Holmans tenement, 15, 147
    Jopes tenement, 135
    Knights tenement, 15, 148
    Moyles tenement, 160
    Palmers tenement, 153
    Peacocks tenement, 144
    Pococks tenement, 144-5
    Tanners tenement, 14, 142
    Welshes tenement, 151
Hexstall, William, 43
Heyward, Richard, 122
High House Lane, **9**, 58, 62, 65
High Street, stream, 58, 59, *59*
Higham Broom, Cowlings tenement, **11**
highways, 60-3
    repairs, 36, 63
Hilden manor, Hildenborough, 71
Hildenborough parish, **8**, 101
Hillmeade, Brooke tenement, 183
Hills, The, Brooke tenement, 23, 183
Hobbeielotts, Paynes tenement, 164
Hobbs field, Lockbridges tenement, 174
Hogett, William, 99, 166
    Coswyns tenement, 20, 171
Hogettshaw Hope, Brooke tenement, 183
Hoggs tenement, **9**, 65, 98-9
    see also Knett the Hoggs tenement
Hogswell, 65
Hogyn, John, 38
Holdenne, John, 187
Holman, Walter, 144, 147
Holmans, Peacock tenement, 144
Holmans tenement, 15, 147-8
    pig dues, 28-9
    woodland, *88*
Holmanys, Pococks tenement, 145
Holworthy, Richard, 108
Holybone, John, bequests, 69
Honewold, William, *3*, 70, 182
Honewolds burgh, Berwys tenement, **16**, 150
Honewold's Fields, Lake (2) tenement, 186
Honewolds tenement, **9**, 19, **24**, 167-9
Hoo, 89
Hope, The, 135
Hope, The, Brooke tenement, 182
Hope, The, Wells tenement, 133
Horing Brokes, West Peckham, 195
Horne, Richard, 188
horse breeding, 73, 102
Horsmonden parish, farm sizes, 47, **47**
Houghton, Ralph (1504), 36, 68, 69
Howell, David (1465), 68
Huggin, William, Mereworth manor, 193-4
hundreds, 100, 106
Hunebere, 98
Hunte, Thomas, 191
hunting, 43, 47, 106, 113, 114-15
    North Frith, *103*, 106, 107
Hunton, **8**, 82, 100, 109
Hunton church, 81
    Fane family monuments, *74*, 75, *75*

Hurst common, West Peckham manor, 66, 195

Hurstgate, West Peckham manor, 196

I

Ightham, 58, 113

inheritance *see* gavelkind

'inmen', 106

Inner Herbery, Fishland tenement, 13, **52**, 138

Inquisitions Post Mortems, 78, 107

Ippenbury, Dionysia (Denise), 69, *69*, 99

iron industry, 43-4, *43*, 45-6, 49, 113-14
    1580 survey, 76, 103
    1587 survey, 114

Isley, Sir Henry, 103

Ivo Longfrith 145, 160

J

James Hill, West Peckham, 197

James House (formerly Durrants), 20, *59*, 99

Jankens field, Walter at Stair tenement, 130-1

Jankmyr (Ateyrfield) field, Freferding tenement, 128-9

Jelott, John, 140, 141
    Jopes tenement, 136, 137

Jelottistaldret, Knett the Hoggs tenement, 141

John a (at) Stable, 83, 90, 98, 127
    Broomfields tenement, 148
    Fishland tenement, 137
    Fletchers tenement, 166
    Knett the Hoggs tenement, 140-1
    Knights tenement, 15, 148
    Lake (2) tenement, 186
    Pococks tenement, 145
    Tanners tenement, 142
    Wells tenement, 133

John at Grove, 188

John at Stable's cross, 98

John atte Berne, 107, 108

John's barn, Lockbridges tenement, 175

Johnson, Henry, 17, 70, 153
    Wekerylds tenement, 155-6

Jolynes land, Fichet's tenement, 146

Joneteye (Joneye), Odamys tenement, 139

Joneye meadow, Odamys tenement, 139

Jopes tenement, *3*, **9**, 13, 28
    1581 survey, 134-6

Jopis Mead *see* Jopismeade (Jopis Mead)

Jopis Sere, 128, 131

Jopisfield, 136

Jopislake, 13

Jopismeade in Warelake, 130

Jopismeade (Jopis Mead), **52**, 129

Jopismeade (Jopis Mead), Jopes tenement, 135, 136

Jopismeade (Jopis Mead), Wells tenement, 132-3

Jordans common, 23, 65

Jordan's lake, 23

Jordans tenement, **9**, 23
    1581 survey, 188
    labour services, 16

Judd, Sir Andrew, 95-6

Jynkins Iland, West Peckham, 196

K

Kagebodyll demesne, *10*, **12**

Kebbyll (Keble), Richard, 34, 36, 82, 164, 166

Kegon, John, 164, 165, 166

Kelchers Lane, 56, *56*, **57**

Kemelands, Jordans tenement, 188

Kempe, Gilbert, **20**, **24**, 170

Kempe, Richard, 20

Kempinfield, Lake (2) tenement, 185, 187

Kempinghale, **54**

Kene, John, 83, 125

Kene, Ralph, 11, 123

Kenes tenement, **9**, *10*, 11, **12**, 97
    1581 survey, 123-6
    money rents, 26

Kennye, John, West Peckham, 198

Kete croft land, Wodemanys tenement, 127

Keteham, Paynes tenement, 164

Ketham, Gibbons tenement, 166

Keyfield, Wodemany's tenement, 127

Keyser (Cayser) family, East Peckham, 113

Keyser (Cayser), John, 180

Keysers bridge, 56, **57**

Kigon (Kegon), John, 164, 165, 166

kilnfield, **14**

Kilwardby, Robert, Archbishop of Canterbury (d.1279), 31

King, John, of Peckham, 189, 190

King, Richard, 121

King, William, 68, 176

Kings field, Aleynslove tenement, 162

King's Head inn, *14*, 20, 67

King's highway, 56-7, 98-9

Kings land, 122

king's peace *see* view of frankpledge

Kingsbrome at Fishill, 137

Kingscroft, Stoperfields tenement, 177

Kirtlington manor, Oxfordshire, 37, 38-41

Knechehoggs, Richard, 140

Knett the Hoggs tenement, **9**, 13, 26, 51
    1581 survey, 140-2
    see also Hoggs tenement

Knight, Richard, Lake (2) tenement, 23, 187

Knight, Thomas, 121, 184

knights' fees, 5, 7, 21, 78

Knights field, 148, 187

Knights pits, Holmans tenement, 147

Knights tenement, **9**, 15, 65, 148

Knightsfield, Lake (2) tenement, 185-7

Knole park, 115

Knyght, John (1471-76), 68

L

labour services, 16, 18, 24, 26-8, 30, 111
    Brooke tenement, 180-1
    Kenes tenement, 123
    Weald, 48
    Wekerylds tenement, 17, 154-5

Lack, Thomas, 168

Ladishope, West Peckham, 196

Ladyfield pasture, Mereworth, 191

Lake (1) tenement, 59
    1581 survey, **9**, 180

Lake (2) tenement, 1581 survey, **9**, 29, 185-7

Lake Mead, Lake (2) tenement, 187

Lake tenement, **9**, 23, 26, 28, **54**, 79

Lake, William, 180

Lambarde, William, 65, 113, 115

Lamparde, Thomas, 65

Lancaster, Roger, 3, *4*

land measurement, 21-2

land transactions, 30-1, 33-4, 40
    Causton family, 107

Lane, Joan, 85

Lane, Richard, Mereworth manor, 193

Large, Robert, 108-9

Larkhale (Lawerk), 23, 58, 84, 188

Latter, Robert, 122

Lawday Place, 19, **22**, 100, 109

lawdays, 100

Lawerk tenement, **9**, 23, 188

Lawrence, John, 88

Lawrence land (Gooseland), Grove tenement, 175-6

Lawrence's Burgh, Berwys tenement, **16**, 150

Le Camere, 139

Leder, William (1587), 68

Lee, The, Coswyns tenement, 170

Leeds monastery, appropriation of Peckham church, 4, 189-90

Leigh, **8**, 73, 75, 115

Levesode, J., 179

Levesode, Thomas, 176, 178

Levesothe, J. jun., 179

Leyland, Aleynslove tenement, 162-3

Leyland, Wekerylds tenement, 155

Lichfeld, Hadlow, 198

Licidmeade, Odamys tenement, 139

listed buildings, map, **6**

Little Anoyteland, Brooke tenement, 182

Little Blackmans field, 161

Little Bridge, Tonbridge, 55, **57**

Little Kemelands, Jordans tenement, **16**, 188

Little Limpeton, Buntanys tenement, 179

Little Lomewood, 195

Little mill, **57**, 59

Little Peckham *see* West Peckham.

Little Petland, Somers tenement, **16**, 157

Littleham, Jopes tenement, 135

livestock, 51
    see also cattle; pigs

Lockbridge, Robert, 174
Lockbridge tenement, 21, 22, 26, 89
    1581 survey, 174-5
Lodeweir, 13, **52**
Lollardy, 45, 70
Lomewood (later, Hadlow) common, 19,
    53, 65-6, 100
    1769 map, **64**, 66
Lomewood manor, 6, **6**, 107
    court rolls, 31-4, 35, 87
London, 75, 76
Lonewood (Loamwood) Common (later
    Hadlow Common), 18, 19, 53,
    65-6, 100
    1769 map, **64**, 66
Long Croft, Holmans tenement, 147
Long Garden, West Peckham, 197
Longcroft, Cowley tenement, **11**, 122
Longfield, Honewolds tenement, 167
Longfield, Peacock's tenement, 143
Longfrithe, Ivo, 145, 160
Longfrithe, William, 146, 156
Longmead, Brooke tenement, 183
Longreide, Brooke tenement, 181
Longshots cross, *10*, 98
Longshott (Longshot) land, **12**, **52**, 128
    Walter at Stair tenement, 129, 130,
    131
Lorcocks Meade, Fletchers tenement, 165
Lord Acre, Aleynslove tenement, 163
Lords Croft, West Peckham, 195
Lord's garden, Honewolds tenement, **24**,
    168
Lord's garden, West Peckham, 195
Lord's Land (demesne), **22**, 23-4
Lords Place (now called Church Place), 14,
    14, 20, **20**, **24**, *30*, 67
Lorlayes, Knett the Hoggs tenement, 140
Lotewood tenement, **9**, 26, 79
    1581 survey, 187-8
Lovyndon, John, 168
Lower Lake bridge, 56, **57**
Lowlings, 75
Lowson, J., 175
Lyn, John, 174

M

Maidstone, 20, 58, 78
Maitland, F. W., 112
maltmill, 18, 50, 58, 163
maltster (polenter), 121
    see also Newman, John
Malynred, Pococks tenement, 98, 145
Man, John of Frant, Mereworth manor, 194
Manifield, The, Somers tenement, 157
manor courts, 2, 30-41, 100, 107
    administration, 29, 109-14
    amercements, 31, 32-3, 35, 39-41
    court rolls, 31-2, 38, 39, 40, 41, 107
    customary book, 110
    manuals, 31, 37, 38
    procedures, 37-41, 109-10

Manor of Wrotham, The (Jane Semple), 89
manorial estates, 5-6, 7, **9**, 23-4
    Mereworth Park, 191
    West Peckham, 195
manors, 22, 37-41, 109-10
    administration, 29, 109-14
    customary book, 110
    estate management, 30-1, 109-10,
    111-14
    sub manors, 6, **9**, 21, 107, 109
Manysfield, Hamenetts tenement, 158
Mardebery, John, 68
Markham, Gervase, 51, 103
marl pits, 15, **17**, 26, 51
Marlepit, Knett the Hoggs tenement, 141
Marny, William, 91
Marten, John, 65
Marten's Croft, Mereworth manor, 191
Martin, John, senior, 121, 166
Martin, Walter, 121
Martin, William, 121
Martyn, John, **24**
    Grove tenement, 175
    Honewolds tenement, 168
Martyn, Thomas, Lake (2) tenement, 185-
    6, 187
Martyn, Walter, 79, 185
Martyn, William, 23, 176-7, 178
Matthews Lane, 66
Maynards Hagh, Brooke tenement, 184
Mayne mead, Aleynslove tenement, 162
Mayns meade, Hamenetts tenement, 158-9
Mead atte Walteris, 123
Medfield, Fletchers tenement, 133, 165
Medow, Henry (1536), 68
Medway, river, 8-9, 11-13, 21, 54-8, **54**,
    105
    1627-9 survey, 49, 54-5
    bridges, 55-7, *55*, *56*, **57**
    crossings, 55-7, **57**, 105
    flood plain tenements, 13, 23, 48-9
    grazing for cattle, 51
    old course, *10*, 11, 13, *13*, **52**, 55, *55*,
    57, 97
    resources, 48, 49
    see also Hadlow Stair
Meer, John (1554), 68
meeting places, 100
Meller, Robert of Kemsing, 153
Mercers' Company records, 108
Mereworth, **8**, 61, 75, 113
    1720, 114
    woods, 106, 191, 192
Mereworth Castle, 61, 75, 115
Mereworth church, **60**
Mereworth manor, 4, 66, 190-3
    tenants, 192-4
Meyrick, Thomas, 115
Midredys, Brooke tenement, 181
Mildmay, Walter, 91
milking, *85*
Mill Bourne, Fletchers tenement, 58, 165

Mill ditch, 11, *11*
Mill House, *10*, 11, **12**, 50, 83, 124
Mill land, Honewolds tenement, 168
Miller, Nicholas, 65
Miller, Richard, 34, 37
Miller, Robert of Kemsing, 150, 152
Millfield, Lake tenement, 180
mills, 18, *18*, 49-50
    milling regulations, 35
    use of river Bourne, **57**, 58-9
Mistress Marsh, Freferding tenement, **12**
Moncastell, Robert, Mereworth manor, 194
money rents, 25-6
Monks field, Wekerylds tenement, 155
Monn, John, Mereworth manor, 194
More Brecklesham, Coswyns tenement,
    170
More, Edward, **24**, 168
More Precklesham (later Bounds field), 173
Morebath, Devon, 100
Morebergh, Berwys tenement, 151
Morelote wood, Lotewood tenement, 187
Moresfield, 136-7
Morgan, Jeffrey, Mereworth manor, 193-4
Morgyn, John, Mereworth manor, 194
mortality, 51
    1597 rates, 45
    Black Death, 19, 24, 27, 42, 50, 111
Motelands, 121
Mottis land, Wodmaneys tenement, 126
Mottist Croft, Wodemany's tenement,
    126-7
Moulton, Broke, 187
Moulton, George, 167, 171-2
    Fosters tenement, 173
Mounks, Richard, 195, 196
Moyles tenement, **9**, 26
    1581 survey, 159-160
Moylis brook, Moyles tenement, 159
Mrs. White's weir, 56
Muggefield, Jopes tenement, 136
Multon, Jane, 113

N

Napiltons (Appletons), **20**, **24**
Nepicar (Nepaker) family, 20, 70
Nepicar (Nepaker), Joan, 168
Nepicar (Nepaker), Richard, 100, 121,
    125, 167
    Honewolds tenement, 19, 167
Nepicar (Nepaker), William, 179-80
    Coswyns tenement, 170-1
    Fosters tenement, 173
    Haymonds tenement, 172
Neville, Sir Edward, 102, 103, 115
Neville, Sir George, 4
Neville, Sir Thomas, 115
New Barn, Odamys tenement, 139
Newbarn, Pococks tenement, 144
Newman family, 70, 169
    Gibbons tenement, 70, 166

Newman, John (poulter), 35
Newman, John (labourer), 36, 164
Newman, John (maltster), 18, 20, 28, 92, 121, 169-70
    Fletchers tenement, 165-6
    Paynes tenement, 163-4
Newman, Richard, 35, 169-70
Nielson, Nellie, 110-111
North Frith meadows, 102
North Frith Park, **9**, *43*, **60**, 101-4, *103*
    bank and ditch boundary, *102*
    hunting, 17, 43, 47, *103*, 106-7
    livestock, 51, 53, 62, 73
    pigs, 13, 28, 53
    poaching, 115-16
    Speed's 1611 map,, **104**
    wild life, 52-3
    woodland, 43, 44, *44*, 46
Northmesteye pasture, 52, 81
Norton, William, 35
Nuemede, 78
Nutbeam, Mereworth manor, 192, 193
Nutbeam, West Peckham manor, 195
Nynge, Hugh, Paynes tenement, 164
Nynge, John
    Honewolds tenement, 169
    Paynes tenement, 164

O

Oak Weir (Knokewere), 56, 78
Odamys tenement, **9**, 26, 79, 138-40
offences, 36-7
Old barn, Fish Hill common, *65*
Old Barn, High Street, *19*
Old Trench farm, 44, 104
open air meeting sites, 100
Ordle Pittes, West Peckham, 197
Osbarne, John, 167, 168
Osmers, John, 196
Otford park, 115
Outer Herberys, Fishland tenement, 13, **52**, 137, 138
Oxbrooks Croft, Lockbridges tenement, 174
Oxenhoath, **6**, 19, **22**, 58, 64, 66
Oxenhoath woods, West Peckham, 106

P

Pages Croft, Buntanys tenement, 179-80
Paginherst tenement, **9**, 180
Paines Island, Fishers Lease, **12**, **52**, 97, 129
Palmer family, 17
Palmer, Alice, 17, 164
Palmer, Richard, 17
Palmer, Richard, son of John, 19, 167
Palmer, Simon, 153
Palmer Street (now Ashes Lane), 14, 16-17, **17**, 51, **57**, 62
    cross, 70, 98, 99
Palmer's Place, 17, **17**, 153
Palmers tenement, **9**, **17**, 26
    1581 survey, 153-4

pannage, 28, 53, 106, 107
    Jopes tenement, 134
    North Frith, 13, 102
    West Peckham, 189, 190, 195
Pantos, Aliki, 100
paper mills, 58
Park Croft, Stoperfields tenement, 23, 177
Parkfield, Stoperfields tenement, 22-3, **22**, 176
Parrocke, William, 166
Parrockes, Fletchers tenement, 99
Partriche, John, **24**, 169
Partrick Close (now called Hecotts), 172
Patenden (Patynden), J., 180
Pattenden, John, Mereworth manor, 193
Pattenson, William (1545), 68
Pawley (Palle) family, 70
Pawley (Palle), Richard, 137
    Stoperfields tenement, 176
Pawley (Palle), Robert, 152, 195
    Hadlow, 197-8
Pawley (Palle), William, 65, 67, 68, 137
Pawley (Palle), Wyatt, 95
Payn, Christopher, 70
Payne of Eyland, Freferdings tenement, **12**, 97, 129
Paynes (Fishers Lease) Island, **12**, **52**, 97, 129
Paynes tenement, **9**, 18
    1581 survey, 163-4
Peacocks tenement, **9**, 14, 26, 83
    1581 survey, 143-4
Peck, Samuel, 3-4
Peckham manor, 4, 17, 18
Peckham Place, Thomas Rivers, 77
Peckham, Reginald, 177, 178
Peckham, Thomas, 19, 121, 167
Peckhams manor, 6, **9**, 17, **17**, 18, 19, **22**, 107
Peckhams tenement, 19, 166-7
Pelsount, John, 20, 167
    Haymonds tenement, 171-2
    Rodbards tenement, 172
Penders tenement, 172-3
Penderys Hopes, Brooke tenement, 183
Penehall, John, 187
Penhurst, George, 115
Pennenden Heath, Maidstone, 100
Penshurst, 49, 51, 75, 76
Penshurst park, 76, 115
Perot, William, 177
Pervell Croft, West Peckham, 197
Peryn, Alice, **80**, 81
Peryn, John, **80**, 81
Perys (Pierce) mill, 50, **57**, 59
Perystown, 23
Peter atte Brook, 180
Petland, Somers tenement, **16**, 157
Philipott, Thomas, 88
Philpott, Widow, 65
Pierce (Perys) mill, 50, **57**, 59
Pightell at Hillsgate, Brooke tenement, 184
pigs, *27*, *28*, 29, 53
    dues in kind, 28-9

see also pannage
pits for marl, 15, *15*, **17**, 51, 62
Pitts, The, Holman tenement, 62, 147, 148
Pitts Wood, 15, 62
Plane, John, 96
Plane, Thomas, 115
Playne family, 94-6
Playne, Mary, 96
Playne, Michael, 44, 95
Playne, William, 95-6
Playne, Wyatt, 44, 95
Plogg, Henry, 177
ploughing, 27, *50*
Pluckley parish, farm sizes, 47, **47**
Plumpton, John (1460), 68
poaching, 43, 102, 114-16
Pococks Grove, 145
Pococks tenement, **9**, 14, 26, 65
    1581 survey, 144-5
Pocockscroft, 144, 145
Polhills, Thomas, 198
Popecroft, Knett the Hoggs tenement, 141
Popeye (Popey) land, Odamys tenement, 139-40
Poplars Brook, The Lockbridges tenement, 174
populations 1608, 48
Postern bridge, **10**, 55, **57**
Postern forge, **10**, 55, **57**
Postern Park, 44, 73, 106
    poaching, 114-15
Potford mead, Mereworth, 191
Pottekyn, Henry, 35, 36
Potter, Richard, 115
Poult House, **14**, 15, **17**, **57**, 62
poulter, 35, <u>121</u>
Pretellis garden, Kenes tenement, **12**, 125
Prettishops, West Peckham, 196
Price, Thomas, 116
Procter, Elizabeth, 94
Procter, John, 94
Protestantism in the Weald, 45, 46, 69-70, 96
    Elizabeth Fane, 74, 94
Pudding, Alan, 178
Pudding, Robert, 92, 176
Puddings tenement, **9**, 22, **22**, 26, 99
    1581 survey, 178
Pulter, Agnes, 138, 150, 161
Pulter, John (tanner), **16**, 150
Pygtell field, 123
Pympe, John, 84
Pynchon family, 70
Pynchon, Richard, 121, 140, 144
    Holmans tenement, 15, 147
    Jordans tenement, **16**, 188
Pynchon's tenement, **9**, 14, 145-6

R

Rainolde, West Peckham, 196
Raynalde (Raynold), John, 183, 187

Reade, Thomas, married Joan Vane, 71
rectory land, 19, **24**
Redland, Tanner's tenement, 143
Reeve family, 70
Reid, The, Aleynslove tenement, 162
Reinalde (Reynald, Reinald), Thomas, 159, 160, 162
relief payments, 15, 26, 28, 33-4, 40
    "heriots", 30-1, 33
rentals (custumals)
    Beald family, 88-9
    Bishop family, 88
    see also surveys
rents, 15, 25-6
Reve, W., Palmers tenement, 154
Revecocks cross, 99
Reyd land, Pynchon's tenement, 146
Reye, The, Holmans tenement, 147
Reynald (Reynold, Reinald), John, 158
Reynald (Reynold, Reinald), Thomas, 158, 159, 160, 162
Richard at Hill (Helle), **12**, 47, 125
Richard atte Berne, 107, 108
Richards, William, 172
Rigon, Robert, **81**, 82
rippiers, 94
Rippings, Walter, 188
Risshett (Rysshett), Peacocks tenement, 143, 144
river boat, *54*
Rivers family, 45, 75-7, 103, 108
Rivers, Clement, 75
Rivers, Edward, 76-7
Rivers, George (d. 1632), 76, 77
Rivers, Lady Joan, 45, *75*, 76, 77
Rivers, Sir John, 75-6
Rivers, Sir John and Lady Joan, 67, 74, 75-6, 77
    memorials, 51, *75*, 76
Rivers, Richard, 75
Rivers, Thomas (d. 1657), 77
    see also Ryvers

roads, 60-3, *99*
    repairs, 36, 37, 41, 63, 69, 92
roadside crosses, **6**, 70, 98-9, *98*
Robarde (Robards, Roberde), John, 99, 154
    Welshes tenement, 151, 152
Robarde (Robards, Roberde), Walter, 121
Robards Croft, Buntanys tenement, 179
Robards, Stoperfields tenement, 177
Roberts, John, Mereworth manor, 193
Robond, William, 151
Rochester Register, *c*. 975, 67
Rodbards tenement, **9**, 20, 172
Rode land, Fichet's tenement, 146
Rodgers, Michael, 43, 101
Roffe, William, Mereworth manor, 194
Rolands land, Wells tenement, 133
Rose Cottage, Three Elm Lane, 99, *99*
Rose Revived, The, 17, **17**
Rowe, Margery, 154
Rowe, Thomas, 154
Rowe, William, 155
Rowe, The, Wekerylds tenement, 155, 156
Rysthet, Knett the Hoggs tenement, 141
Rysthet (Rysshett), Peacocks tenement, 143, 144
Ryvers, John, Foremede, Hadlow, 196

S

St. Lawrence fair, Mereworth, 191
St. Andrew's Feast, 25, 26
St. Lawrence fair, Mereworth, 191
St. Mary's Church, Hadlow, 67-9, *67*, 70
    Rivers family monument, 51, *75*, 76
St. Olaves church, Southwark, 85
Salams, John, 90
Sallman, John, Jopes tenement, 3
Salman, Thomas, 177
Salmon, Alexander and Lawrence, 44, 70
Salmon, John, 136
Salmon, William, 168, 169, 177
Sandherst pits, Holmans tenement, 15, 147
Saunder, Adam, **24**

Schelove, Gilbert, 141
schooling, *85*
Scottispittes, Hadlow, 198
Seal, 73
Searle, Eleanor, 111
Seatons, 83
Sedgebrook (Somings brook), **17**, 58, *58*
Sedgebrookgate, 58
    flooding, 62
Sedgehill, Kenes tenement, **12**, 124, 125
Sedgehill meade, Kenes tenement, **12**, 125
Segars, George, 112
Selys (Seyles), Moyles tenement, **17**, 159
Semple, Jane, 89
Senyngesbrook, Wekerylds tenement, **17**, 156
Sere, The, Freferding tenement, 128
Setons land, Kenes tenement, 124
Setrenys land, Kenes tenement, **12**, 124-5
Sevenoaks, 89
Sewayne tenement, 167
Sewer Commission survey, 48-9, 55, 97
Sharynden (Sherenden) farm, 85, 86
Shaw, William, 35-6
Shepcotefeld, Mereworth manor, 191
Shepecotefeld, West Peckham, 195
Shereve, Gilbert, 150, 157-8
Shereve, Gilbert and William Brewis tenement, 16, **16**
Shereve, William, 150
Shipbourne, **6**, **8**, 73, 89, 100, 101, 114
    population in 1608, 48
Shoemaker, Richard, 36
Shorsacre, Hamenetts tenement, 158
Shropsfield, Tanner's tenement, 98, 142
Sibseye, Thomas, 78
Simond family, 70
Simond, John, sen., 121, 150
Skeyffe Lane (Dog Kennel path), 59, **61**, 62, *63*
Skinners' Company, 95-6
Skoclyns (Scokklis) holding, 88, 89, 90, 91
Slethe common, 65
Smeltes Meede, 78
Smithes Mede, West Peckham, 196-7
Smithfield, Mereworth manor, 191
Smith's land, 169-70
Snell, Johanna, 81
Snell, John, 81-2
Snod, Pococks tenement, 144
Snod, The, Welshes tenement, 152
Snowe, Thomas (1560), 68
soil improvement, 50-1
Sole Street *see* Three Elm Lane
Solefield, Moyle tenement, **16**
Solefield, Somers tenement, 157
Solleman (Solman, Salman), William, 140, 168, 177
Somefield afore Newmans gate, Fletchers tenement, 165-6

Skeyffe Lane (aka Dog Kennel Path) at Robards, Stoperfield tenement.

Somer family, 43, 70, 115
Somer, Henry, 115
Somer, Isabelle, 34, 35
Somer, John, 20, **20**, 34, 68, 91, 121, 170
Somer, Nicholas, 70, 170
Somer, Richard, 70, 166, 198
  Fletchers tenement, 165
Somer, Stephen, 153, 154, 158
Somer, Thomas, 44, 146, 160, 170, 175
Somerhill, 46
Somers tenement, **9**, 26, 28, 29
  1581 survey, 156-7
Somings brook (Sedgebrook), **17**, 58, *58*
Somysfield land, Jopes tenement, 134
Sore, Le, Kenes tenement, **12**, 124
South Frith manor, farm sizes, 47, 104
South Frith Park, 43, 46-7, 106
  poaching, 115-16
South, The, Palmers tenement, 154
Southborough, 72
Southfield, Knett the Hoggs tenement, 140
Southfield, Lake (2) tenement, 185
Southwark, 94
Sowth woods, West Peckham, 196
Spaldings tenement, **9**, 21, 174
Speldhurst, 89
Stabbykobit, Agnes, 33
Stable, John, 121
Stace, John, 195
Stace, William (1572), 68
Stafford, Anne *see* Anne, Dowager Duchess of Buckingham
Stafford, Edward, Duke of Buckingham, (d. 1521), 44, *44*, 75, 101-2
Stafford, Henry, second Duke of Buckingham (1454-83), 5, *5*
Stafford, Humphrey, first Duke of Buckingham (d. 1460), 5, 78
Stafford, Ralph (later first Earl of Stafford), 16
Stair court rolls, 32, 87
Stair barn, 128
Stair House, 85, 98
Stair *see* Hadlow Stair
Stairbridge, Kenes tenement, **11**, **12**, 83, 97
Stallions Green, 23
standing surety, 34
Starkey, John (1595), 68
Steers Place, 66
Steggehills, Kenes tenement, **12**, 124
Steyle (later Style), Richard, 21, 42, 172-3
Steysbarn, Wodemany's tenement, 126
Stidings, Amicia, 15
Stidings tenement, **9**, 15, 26, 149
Stidulph, Agnes, 71, **71**
Stidulph, Thomas and Alice, Tudeley church, *73*
Stocklease, Brooke tenement, 183
Stoneland land, Kenes tenement, 126
Stoney field, Peckhams manor, **17**
Stoneyhuttocks, Fishland tenement, 137
Stony Hawe, Kenes tenement, **12**, 126

Stony Lane, **52**, *63*
Stonybylls, Peacocks tenement, 144
Stonyfield, Blackmans tenement, 161
Stonyfield, Jopes tenement, 135
Stoperfield (Stubberfield) family, 70, 92-4, **92**
Stoperfield (Stubberfield), Henry, 44, 92, 93-4
Stoperfield (Stubberfield), Nicholas, 19, 23, 28, 81-2, 93
  Coiffes tenement, 169
  Coswyns tenement, 171
  Gibbons tenement, **24**, 166
Stoperfield (Stubberfield), Nicholas, son of Thomas, 93-4
Stoperfield (Stubberfield), Thomas, 36, 82, 93, 96
Stoperfield (Stubberfield), William, 92, 178
  Stoperfield tenement, 176
Stoperfield tenement, 22, **22**, 26, 92-3
  1581 survey, 176-7
  labour services, 25
Strake, The, Aleynslove tenement, 162
Stretende, Alice, 121, 122, 174
Stridle, Thomas, Mereworth manor, 194
Stubberfield family, 70, 92, 96
  see also Stoperfield (Stubberfield) family
Stubberfield, Henry, 93-4
Stybe, Edward, 191
Style Place, 43, 109
Style, Walter, 42, 179
Styles, Richard, 34
suit of court, 31
surveys (custumal, rental), 1, 22, 23-4, 112-13, 176
  1460, 2, 3-4, *3*, *4*, 5, 112
  1495 for Wrotham, 111
  1538 for Wrotham, 112
  1541 for North Frith park, 51, 102
  1579 for Mereworth, 190-4
  1581, 42-3, 112, 121-88
  1583 West Peckham, 195-8
  1587, 43, 103, 114
Sutors, John, 195
Swanton Quarry, Mereworth manor, 192-3
Swaynes (Swaines) house, **9**, **57**, 100
Swerddich woods, West Peckham, 197
Swift, Richard, 121
Syden, Hugh, 86
Sydney family, 43-4, 49
Symonds, Alice, 37
Symonds, John, 18, 34, 82, 87
  Moyles tenement, 159
  Palmers tenement, 153, 154
  Somers tenement, 157
  Symonds tenement, 163
  will for cross repairs, 98
Symonds tenement, **9**, 50, 58
  1581 survey, 163
Symonds, Thomas, 37, 115
Symonds, William, 173-4
Symonson's 1596 map, **60**, 61

T
Tanner, John, 88
Tanner, Nicholas, 15, 92, 142, 176
Tanner, William, 92
Tanners Brook, Lake (2) tenement, 186-7
Tannerys (Tanner's) tenement, **9**, 14, 26
  1581 survey, 142-3
  labour services, 25
tanning, 35
  regulations, 40
Taylor, Nicholas, 87
Taylour, John (of Mereworth), 155
Teise, river, 21
tenancies, 5, 7-8, 25-6
  changes, 30-1, 33-4
  dues in kind, 28-9
  tenant status, 19-20
tenements, 1, 7-10, 10-21, 13, 14, 22-3, 111
  aid and relief payments, 26
  map, **9**, **10**
  with pits, 15, 26, *26*, 147-8
  see also named tenements, e.g. Somers tenement
tenterfield, 18
Teston bridge, **60**, 61
Teyntesfield, Paynes tenement, 163
theft, 37
Thomaland, West Peckham, 197
Thomas at Grove, 23, 79
  Lake (2) tenement, 185
Thomas Fisher's barn, Jopes tenement, 135
Thomas Symonds Brook, Lake (2) tenement, 186
Three Cornered Pightel, The, Brooke tenement, 182
Three Elm Lane, 13, 14, 51, **57**, **61**, 62, 94
  marl pits, 51
  water erosion, 63
Three Hernyn crofts, Paynes tenement, 164
Three Yards land, Fishland tenement, 137
Three Yards, The, Brooke tenement, 183
tile making, *15*
timber, 43, 107, 114
  North Frith, 51, 103
Tithe map of 1842, 102
tithingmen elections, 32, 33
Tonbridge, 5, **8**, 21, 60, 106
  1587 rental, 65
  Causton family, 107
  church, 89
  iron industry, 45-6
  Lowy, **104**, 106
  Playne family, 94-6
  Robert Bishop and son Richard, 86
  Stoperfield family, 92, 94
Tonbridge Castle, 5, 16, 20, 21, 47, 78
  gateway, *114*
Tonbridge rectory, 94
Tonbridge School, 95-6
Torkesey, Robert, **84**, 87
Tothe Hill common, 65

Tottenham, Middlesex, court rolls, 37, 38, 39, 40, 41
Towne, John, 188
Towne, William, 188
Trench Farm, 44, 104
Treyardyn land, 126
Trice family, 70
Trice, Walter, 44, 110, 155, 170
 Buntanys tenement, 179
 Crochlands tenement, 160
 Haymonds tenement, 172
 Honewolds tenement, 168-9
 Moyle's tenement, 159
 Palmer's tenement, 153
 Paynes tenement, 164
Tubbings, Honewolds tenement, 167
Tubbings, Robert, Foster tenement, 173
Tubbingsfield, Paynes tenement, 164
Tudeley, 78, 85, 115
 church, *72*, *73*, 75, 89
Tunbridge Wells, 1720, 114
Turke, George, Mereworth manor, 193
Turke, John, Mereworth manor, 193
Turke, Thomas, Mereworth manor, 193
Turkshagh, Knett the Hoggs tenement, 141
Turner, John (1513), 68
Tutesham, Richard, 84
Tuttisham family, 195
Tuttisham, John, 191
Tuttisham, Thomas, 194, 195
 Mereworth manor, 193
 West Peckham, 196-7
Tuttishams Dane, West Peckham, 197
Twistlake, Hadlow, 196
Twyford bridge, Yalding, 57, **60**, 61, 105, *105*
Twysden, Sir Roger, 104
 court of dens, 100
Tyrrye, 175

U

Umfrey, John, 161
Upcroft, Welshes tenement, 152
Upper Hagh, The, Kenes tenement, **12**, 125
Upper Tanners' field, 142
Upperfield, Wekerylds tenement, 156
Upteye, The, Lake (2) tenement, 185
Usmor (Osmor), John, 161
Usserey, William, 92, 176
Utterlery's, Le Twetene, 134

V

Vane family *see also* Fane family
Vane, Henry of Tonbridge, 71
Vane, Joan married Thomas Reade, 71
Vane, John d. 1488, 71
Vane, Richard of Hollanden, 71
vegetables, 52
Vicar's field, Buntanys tenement, 84, 179
Victoria Road, 22, **22**, 59, 62, *63*, 93
view of frankpledge, 31-3, 34-7, 38, 92
 court leet., 31, 40

lawdays, 100

W

Waderstist croft, Freferding tenement, 129
Wakefield, Yorkshire, court rolls, 32, 37, 38, 39, 40, 41
Walker, John, 115
Walley, Roger, 169
Walmsley's weir, *10*, 55
Walsham le Willows, Suffolk court rolls, 37, 38, 39, 40, 41
Walsingham, Sir Thomas, 192-3
Walter at Stair (Steyre), 97, 151
Walter at Stair (Steyre) tenement, **9**, 11, 13, 129-32
 rent, 26
Walter, Henry, 87, 157
Walter, John, 35, 68
Walter, Thomas, 97, 98, 126, 172-3, 181
Walterishagh, Tanners tenement, 142-3
Walters at the Stair, Wodemanys tenement, 127
Walters Haugh, Hadlow street, 89, 90
Walters, Tanner's tenement, 142
Walthehagh, Palmers tenement, 154
wapentake meeting places, 100
Warde, 78
Warelake meadow, 13, 130, 132, 133
Warnicke, Retha, 113
Waston, John, Mereworth manor, 192
water birds, 49
Water mill, Mereworth manor, 191
Wateringbury, 66, 100
Waterships (Waterslippe), 18, 166
waterways, obstruction, 31, 36, *36*
Watte Bealds mead, Odamys tenement, 139
Watte, John of Capele, 188
Watton, Robert, 179
Watton, William, 7, 34, 121
Watts garden, Wodemany's tenement, 126
waywardens, 63
Weald, 48, 105-114
 agriculture, 29, 50, 103-4
 commons, 64, 65
 creation and maintenance of manors, 21, 22
 farm sizes, 47, **47**, 104
 poaching, 114-6
 Protestantism, 45, 70
 roads, 60-3
Weald, Thomas, 180
Weir meadow, **52**, 97
weirs, 23, **52**, 54, 55, 56
 for fishing, 48, 49, 59, 60
Wekerylds, Richard, 154
Wekerylds tenement, **9**, 17, **17**, 99
 1581 survey, 154-6
Wekes, George, 115
Welard, John, 84
Weldon, Mrs, West Peckham, 195
Wellar, John (1556), 70
Weller, William, 44

Welles, J., 145, 148, 151
Wellhagh, Knett the Hoggs tenement, 141
Wells family, 70, 143
Wells, John, 138, 146, 147, 148
Wells, Richard, 147
Wells, W., 148
Wells tenement, **9**, 26, **52**, 98, 99
 1581 survey, 132
Welshes tenement, 17, 26, 28
 1581 survey, 151-3
 maps, **9**, **17**
 pig dues, 28, 29
Werelake meadow, Walter at Stair tenement, 130
Wesingland, Knett the Hoggs tenement, 140
West Malling, 20, 45, 60, 61
West Peckham church, 4, 189-90
 Elizabeth Culpeper tomb, *18*
 grant to Leeds monastery, 4, 189-90
West Peckham manor, 4, 66, 195-8
West Peckham parish, **6**, **8**, 22, 101, 107
 Oxenhoath woods, 106
West Peckham vicarage, altarage and tithes, 189, 190
West Wickham, 108
Westcroft, Palmers tenement, 154
Westdowne, West Peckham, 197
Westey (Westhey) meadow, 131, 132, 135
Westeye land, **52**, 131, 133
Westfield, Spaldings tenement, 174
Westmanland, Paynes tenement, 164
Wheatcroft, 128, 131
Wheatcrofts, Lake (2) tenement, 185
Wherehill, Brooke tenement, 182, 183
Whettenstall family, 46, 113
Whettenstall, John, 91
Whettenstall, William, 21, 166, 174
White, Richard, 20, **20**, **24**, 170
Whittenhall, George of Hadlow, 195
Wibarne (Wybarne) family, 112-13
Wibarne (Wybarne), Anthony, 112-13
Wibarne (Wybarne), John, 12, 112, 124, 165
Wichenden bridge, 55, **57**
Widerstiscroft land, 128
Wilkensmeade, Brooke tenement, 181
Willard, David, 46, 76, 97
 iron industry, 44, 46, 49
 rent rises, 43, 103, 114
 stream diversion, 43, 49, 55, 57
William at Grove, 23, 185
William at Helle, 123, 125-6, 129
William at Hill, *10*, **11**, **12**
William at Lake, 50, 79, 180
William Longfrith, 146, 156
Winterys, Brooke tenement, 181
Wisemans Acre, Lake (2) tenement, 187
Witney, Kenneth, 21, 105, 106, 107
Wodemanys tenement, **9**, 11, 83, 126-7
 aid payments, 26
Wokeryldishagh, 155

Wood, Hugh, 191
Woodgate, John, Mereworth manor, 192
woodland, 43-4, 52-3, 106, 107
    Holmans tenement, *88*
    in Hadlow, 1799, **101**
    North Frith, 43, 52-3, 103, 104
    place names, 16-17
    Sir John Rivers's will, 76
    timber industry, 43-4, *44*, 46
Woodmaneys tenement, **9**, 11, 26, 83, 126-7
Wosingsland, Welshes tenement, 152
Wotton, Robert, 99, 177, 178

Woulsies, West Peckham, 196
Wrights, J, 161, 162
Wrotham, **8**, 42
    surveys, 112, 113
Wrotham park, 115
Wyatt, Sir Thomas, 95
Wybarne family *see* Wibarne (Wybarne)
    family
Wygmerdaine, West Peckham, 196
Wyke, John, 92, 143
Wykhames, Fichet's tenement, 146
Wyks, John, 35

Wyks, Richard, 35, 82
Wyxe, Thomas (1556), 68

Y

Yalding, **8**, 45, 58, 81
    road, 61-2, **61**
Yerlishells, Kenes tenement, **12**, 125
Yokeplace, Mereworth manor, 193
Young's field, Lake (1) tenement, 180

Z

Zell, Michael, farm sizes, 47, **47**